HISTORY AND

CW01032899

HISTORY AND FREEDOM

Lectures 1964–1965

Theodor W. Adorno

Edited by Rolf Tiedemann

Translated by Rodney Livingstone

polity

First published in German as *Zur Lehre von der Geschichte und von der Freiheit (1964/65)* by Theodor W. Adorno © Suhrkamp Verlag, Frankfurt am Main, 2001.

This English edition first published in 2006 © Polity Press
Reprinted in 2008

Polity Press
65 Bridge Street
Cambridge CB2 1UR, UK

Polity Press
350 Main Street
Malden, MA 02148, USA

All rights reserved. Except for the quotation of short passages for the purpose of criticism and review, no part of this publication may be reproduced, stored in a retrieval system, or transmitted, in any form or by any means, electronic, mechanical, photocopying, recording or otherwise, without the prior permission of the publisher.

ISBN-13: 978-07456-3012-0
ISBN-13: 978-07456-3013-7 (pb)

A catalogue record for this book is available from the British Library.

Typeset in 10.5 on 12 pt Sabon
by SNP Best-set Typesetter Ltd, Hong Kong
Printed and bound in the United States by Odyssey Press Inc., Gonic, New Hampshire

For further information on Polity, visit our website: www.polity.co.uk

The publication of this work was supported by a grant from the Goethe-Institut.

CONTENTS

world and individual conscience; *methesis* [participation] of
the spirit • Theodicy of rupture and concrete possibility

The concept of the character mask • Individuation and
socialization • Identity and the semblance of
reconciliation • 'Sowing one's wild oats' • Intellectual
forms of self-preservation and human breakdown;
identification with the aggressor • Acquiescing in self-
destruction; concretism; psychology as cement

The course of the argument • The concept of universal
history (I) • The concept of universal history (II) • False
mastery and vindication of induction; Hegel's theory of
history • Freedom and the individual in Hegel • The
individuality in antiquity and the early modern
age • History from the standpoint of the victor

Benjamin's XVIIth thesis • Temporal core and
non-identity • Continuity and discontinuity • History as a
gigantic exchange relationship • The total state and the rule
of competing cliques • Dialectic of the particular • The
concept of chance; the utopia of knowledge • Hegel's
critique of the totality; course of the argument

Notes: Spirit of the people and universal spirit; universal
history as universal tribunal; pseudo-concreteness; repressive
archaisms; anti-Cartesian elements in Vico, Montesquieu,
Herder and Hegel; cult of the nation

The nation: a bourgeois form of organization; departure
from natural forms of association • The path to delusions
of race • Progressive aspects of the nation • The principle
of nationality and natural history • The equality of the
organization of life today • Hegel's theory of national spirit

obsolete; decentralization through technology • Germany
'the belated nation' • Predominance of the universal over
the individual; objective reason split off from subjective
reason • 'Infernal machine'; natural history in Hegel

The concept of second nature • Nature and history
mediated • Critique of 'historicity'; meaning and
chance • Philosophy as interpretation (I); transience and
allegory; philosophy's transition to the concrete; history as
secularized metaphysics • Philosophy as interpretation (II);
hermeneutics • Practice thwarted; critique of the
metaphysics of time

The history of nature, allegory, criticism • Secularized
melancholy; theory of interpretation; Hölderlin's *The Shelter
at Hardt* • Immediacy as the product of history; Hegel and
Marx; art • The pleasures of interpretation • The concept
of progress as a link between philosophy of history and the
theory of freedom • Critique of nominalism • 'Whether
progress exists'

Towards conceptual synthesis • Progress as a way of
averting catastrophe; the global social subject • Kant's idea
of humanity • Benjamin's critique of progress • Progress
and redemption in St Augustine • Escaping the trammels of
the past • Progress mediated by society • Reconciliation
and conflict in Kant; progress as absolutely mythical and
anti-mythical

PART III *Freedom*

The concepts of freedom and the spell; concentration on free will; freedom as the epitome of resistance to the spell

EDITOR'S FOREWORD

Towards the end of the nineteenth century Nietzsche produced his 'observations out of season' in order to register his abandonment of history in favour of 'life'. It may appear to be similarly 'unseasonal' now to publish a course of lectures of Adorno's in which he insists on the importance of history and its philosophy, as if for the sake of survival in the future. Once it became obvious that the communist project of mapping out the future path of history had collapsed, books began to pile up whose authors took it more or less for granted that history was now at an end and that the human race had now arrived at an ominous-sounding *post-histoire*. Not infrequently it was assumed that Adorno's name would be found among those who shared this conservative contempt for history. In fact he was not to be discovered there, as can be seen from the course of lectures he gave in the middle of the 1960s on *History and Freedom*. Admittedly, like Adorno's philosophy as a whole, these lectures convey the message that hitherto the concept of history as progress had been a failure and that consequently the historical process represented a continuation of the same thing, a stasis that was still the stasis of myth. However, to Adorno's mind this insight did not imply an apologia for the immutability of the mythic state: post-history cannot exist where there has not even been any history because prehistory still persists.

The end of history had already been announced once before, in Hegel's theory of universal history, although with a slightly different emphasis. In the last part of his *Lectures on the Philosophy of*

History, Hegel had said that 'the Christian world was the world of completion; the grand principle of being is realized, consequently the end of days is fully come. The Idea' (by which he means philosophy) 'can discover in Christianity no point in the aspirations of Spirit that is not satisfied' (*The Philosophy of History*, p. 342). For this reason, Hegel understood his own study as a 'Theodicæa, a justification of the ways of God . . . so that the ill that is found in the World may be comprehended, and the thinking Spirit reconciled with the fact of the existence of evil. Indeed, nowhere is such a harmonizing view more pressingly demanded than in Universal History' (ibid., p. 15). For Adorno's philosophy 'after Auschwitz' this way of thinking was no longer viable. Just as Voltaire had been cured of Leibniz's theodicy by the natural catastrophe [of the Lisbon earthquake] (cf. *Negative Dialectics*, p. 361), Adorno was cured of Hegel's version of theodicy by the social catastrophes of the twentieth century. Adorno defined his own thought as an anti-system, and it is scarcely an exaggeration to regard it as a complete anti-theodicy. Where Hegel had declared that truth and history were one and the same, that the rational was actual and the actual rational, Marx had maintained that it was the insulted and the injured, their existence and sufferings, that signified the negation of Hegel's theory. However, while today Hegel's actualized reason seems like sheer mockery, Marx's 'realization of philosophy' has not taken place, the opportunity has been 'missed', to use Adorno's term (ibid., p. 3). The catastrophes that have occurred and those that are to come make any further waiting seem absurd. There is no 'reconciling knowledge' of history: 'the One and All that keeps rolling on to this day – with occasional breathing spells – [would] teleologically [be] the absolute of suffering. . . . The world spirit, a worthy object of definition, would have to be defined as permanent catastrophe' (ibid., p. 320).

Once he had returned from exile, and after all that had taken place in Auschwitz and elsewhere, it was anything but obvious to Adorno that philosophy could continue as before, as if nothing had changed. In the *Dialectic of Enlightenment* that he and Horkheimer had written in the 1940s, the authors had set themselves the task of discovering 'why humanity instead of entering into a truly human state, is sinking into a new kind of barbarism' (*Dialectic of Enlightenment*, p. xiv). This question never ceased to trouble them; it became the focal point of their thinking, by the side of which the traditional problems of philosophy had become irrelevant. Philosophy, which in Hegel's words is supposed to 'grasp its own age in thought', fails abjectly in the attempt to comprehend the rupture in civilization that has taken place. To a great extent it does not even bother trying, but contents itself either with vague reflections on the meaning of Being or with the analysis of the linguistic assumptions of thought as such and in general. Adorno criticized both these trends, both Heidegger and his associates and positivism. His criticism was by no means free of emotion. Recently we have seen the emergence of thinkers who see themselves as part of a post-metaphysical trend or who assume the vague role of a discussant, but who in fact are concerned with the abolition of their own role as philosophers. Adorno declined to play any of these games, but doggedly continued to reflect the actual processes of history and its rejects. In *Negative Dialectics* he inquired whether it is still possible to live after Auschwitz. The impossibility of an authoritative answer coincided in his thought with the impossibility of philosophy after Auschwitz.

Nevertheless, this does not mean that he ceased to be a philosopher; indeed, he insisted that philosophy was an indispensable activity, even if he had no illusions about the indifference with which it is commonly regarded by the rest of the world. What was crucial to Adorno's philosophy was the intention of memorialization, of taking things to heart [*Eingedenken*], something it shared with modern works of art such as Picasso's *Guernica*, Schoenberg's *A Survivor from Warsaw*, or Beckett's *The Unnameable*, works wrested from their own historical and philosophical impossibility. Books such as *Negative Dialectics* and the *Aesthetic Theory* have their legitimate place alongside these. If Adorno's practice of memorializing the recent past during the two decades after 1945 was not entirely without effect, its place meanwhile has since been occupied by a renewed interest in chthonic origins, the ideology of a 'new' mythology resurrected once again, as this was expressed in the revival of a misunderstood Nietzsche and in the impressive comeback of Heideggerian ideas. This return of theory to the Pre-Socratics went hand in hand with a retreat from actual history that blots out memory and negates experience. It ratifies trends that were anyway becoming prevalent in society. But the end of history celebrated or bewailed by the postmodernists has failed to arrive; instead it is historical consciousness that appears programmed to disappear. This will deprive philosophy not just of its best part, but of everything. From Adorno, in contrast, we could still learn today that without memory, without Kant's 'reproduction in the imagination', there can be no knowledge worth having. Memory, however, in contradiction of a theory that had been dominant ever since Plato and which Kant too accepted, is no transcendental synthesis, but something that possesses the 'kernel of time' of which Walter Benjamin was the first to speak. For philosophy in the age after Auschwitz, this 'kernel of time' is to be found in the screams of the victims. Since then, as Adorno has written, 'the need to lend a voice to suffering is a condition of all truth' (*Negative Dialectics*, p. 17f.). If philosophy is still possible today, then – and this is the message of Adorno's own – it can only be one that retains in every one of its statements the memory of the sufferings of human beings in the death camps. It will be a philosophy that recalls not the shadow of the tall plane trees on the banks of the Ilissos, like Plato's *Phaedrus*, but the 'shadow / of the scar up in the air' of which Paul Celan speaks.*

Adorno's philosophy constantly worked away at the interpretation of history so that one day the moment of its fulfilment might arrive. From almost the very beginning of his philosophical labours he displayed this interest in history and the historical. In the summer semester of 1932 he gave a seminar on Lessing's 'Education of the Human Race' together with Paul Tillich, who had supervised his second doctoral dissertation, his *Habilitation*. In Lessing's essay the *res cogitans* no longer stands opposed to the *res extensa*, but instead reason becomes conscious of itself through the unfolding of history. Even earlier, in his inaugural lecture of 1931, Adorno had declared that the question of Being as the idea of existing things was 'impervious to questioning', and floated the suggestion that 'it has perhaps faded from view for all time . . . ever since the images of our lives have been guaranteed through history alone' ('The Actuality of Philosophy', in *The Adorno Reader*, p. 24). From that time on Adorno's material works were dedicated to the interpretation of such 'historical images' as he called them, borrowing the term from Benjamin. His method, if we can call it that, was very close to Lessing's own, one that Ernst Cassirer had described as a '"micrological" immersion in the smallest detail' – this too a description that Adorno liked to use to characterize Benjamin but which fits his own writing even better.

As a topic, Adorno lectured on the philosophy of history on two occasions, in courses that he gave in Frankfurt in 1957 and then again in 1964–5. The first, the 'Introduction to the Philosophy of History', has survived only as the fair copy, probably made by Gretel Adorno, of a shorthand record. Although hardly complete, it nevertheless gives us a good idea of his lectures. His intention had been, he says, to attempt 'to establish the history of philosophy as the centre of philosophy in a radical sense' (Theodor W. Adorno Archive, Vo 1941). Although still slightly academic when treating traditional

---

*See Paul Celan, 'To stand in the shadow / of the scar up in the air . . .' in *Selected Poems*, trans. Michael Hamburger, Harmondsworth: Penguin, 1995, pp. 232–3.

philosophies of history, from St Augustine via Vico and Condorcet to Dilthey and Simmel, the lecture course of 1957 presents all the important motifs and themes of Adorno's own philosophy of history: the key phenomenon of the domination of nature, the criticism of the existentializing of 'historicity', the mystical relevance of inner temporality for the Absolute and, lastly, the opposition to a conception of truth as something permanent, immutable, ahistorical. Everything which philosophy concerns itself with under the primacy of the philosophy of history remains, 'a changing, virtually transient thing' (*Negative Dialectics*, p. 307). These ideas are only fully developed eight years later in the present lecture series, as well as in the first two 'models' of *Negative Dialectics*, where they are given their final form.

History in the sense used by Adorno is not the abstract other of nature, but what human beings make of nature. As long as this 'making' is unplanned and anarchic, humans remain in the 'kingdom of necessity' and there is no such a thing as a consciously created history alone worthy of the name. Freedom is one of the preconditions of such history: the free will of mankind to dispose of their own circumstances as they wish. It is this factor that has justified the inclusion of freedom in the philosophy of history, rather than in moral philosophy where it has traditionally been found. Adorno remarks halfway through these lectures, not entirely tongue in cheek, that 'almost without my having been fully aware of this when I set out – the concept that has turned out to be crucial for the theory of history, and incidentally also for the theory of progress, has been that of the *spell*' (p. 172f.). And he defines this spell that governs life as a whole as 'the eternal sameness of the historical process' (p. 183). History, however, was not an eternal sameness, but a process in which the new constantly begins. In the view of antiquity and its myths, eternal sameness was history seen as cyclical, the idea that history does not progress, but that, when it has run its course, it is back where it started. Cyclical views of history have repeatedly returned to haunt the history of the philosophy of history. They can be found in Vico and Spengler, and even in Toynbee, as well as dominating the theories of contemporary diagnosticians of the end of history. Opposed to such ideas is the Christian view, expounded most powerfully by St Augustine, that history represents a progress towards Christ, and that in Him there is redemption and history will be fulfilled. If cyclical theories are ruled out by the hopes of human beings who are unwilling to accept that Sisyphus is the last man, redemption through Christ is refuted by that 'immediate view' of history as a 'slaughterhouse in which the happiness of peoples, the wisdom of states and the virtue of individuals have been sacrificed', as Hegel, a good Christian, summed it up (*The Philosophy of History*, p. 21).

Marx thought of the history that, strictly speaking, had not yet begun as 'prehistory'. Adorno adopted this term. 'What Marx with a mixture of melancholy and hope calls prehistory is nothing less than the epitome of all known history up to now, the kingdom of unfreedom' (*GS*, vol. 8, p. 234). The spell that still presides over everything is prehistorical in nature, it is the spell of myth. Adorno's subject, one that he pursued with infinite persistence, is the afterlife of this mythical dimension in a world that seems to have been entirely denuded of myth, the 'prehistorical world of the present' that he rediscovered throughout the works of someone such as Goethe. At the heart of the persistence of myth Adorno discerned the exchange relation of a commodity-producing society, and in this respect too he follows Marx, who on occasion described the sphere of circulation as an archaic fate, as 'a power over . . . individuals which has become autonomous, whether conceived as a natural force, as chance or in whatever other form' (Karl Marx, *Grundrisse*, p. 197). Adorno refused to abandon the belief that, despite all the frustrations of the past, history was not doomed to remain futile for all eternity. Not least, it was the catacombs of the victims that prevented him from finalizing the construction of history in his philosophy once and for all. He held open the door for history to enter into the future; instead of an ending he believed that history should flow into a Hölderlin-esque *openness*. For all the differences that separated him from Ernst Bloch, he agreed with him on one point; he never played off a wretched reality against the idea of utopia, nor did he ever show the least desire to sabotage the concept of utopia. In his thought, utopia, the trace of the messianic, had what he called 'the colour of the concrete' (see p. 253) not that of abstract possibility.

In the winter of 1964, when Adorno gave his last series of lectures on the philosophy of history, the first signs of future disagreements with his students could already be seen on the horizon. The general disquiet of the post-Adenauer years was symbolized by the Auschwitz trials in Frankfurt, the proposed legislation on the Emergency Laws and, most acutely, the American war in Vietnam. Against the background of these restorative, reactionary developments, a powerful opposition, dominated by students, emerged for the first time in the history of Germany. Admittedly, from 1967 on this opposition in part adopted forms of protest that Adorno was to condemn emphatically as 'pseudo-activity' (cf. the contributions in *Frankfurter Adorno Blätter* VI, Munich, 2000). Not content with merely interpreting the world, the students called for social change, and Adorno's lectures represented something of an attempt to provide a theoretical analysis of this situation by refocusing attention on the relations between theory and practice. At the time, this aspect of his lecture course passed more or less unnoticed. The idea that the philosophy of history should be studied in the interests of practical intervention had always been implicit in Adorno's philosophy. As a programme, it could be derived from Marxist theory. However, Adorno dates what might be regarded as its anticipated critique back to the early modern age and, more specifically, to the problematic situation of Hamlet, whom he often called upon in support of his argument. In Shakespeare's hero 'we find the divergence of insight and action paradigmatically laid down' (*Negative Dialectics*, p. 228). And Adorno found himself confronted by the same divergence when the students demanded guidance for political practice. It was for this reason that he wanted to discuss the question of theory and practice yet again, quite explicitly, in the summer semester of 1969, at the height of the student protest movement. This was to have been in a course with the title 'Introduction to Dialectical Thinking', but he never gave more than a few lectures because it was repeatedly disrupted and he was finally forced to cancel it. All that survives of the course is his notes for three lectures (cf. *Frankfurter Adorno Blätter* VI, p. 173ff.). Nevertheless, at least some of what he would have said to the students, had they let him, has survived in two essays: 'On Subject and Object' and 'Marginalia to Theory and Praxis' (in *Critical Models*, pp. 245–78). These essays preserve his thoughts; they are a kind of epilogue to the student movement and at the same time an epitaph that the philosopher wrote for himself.

The text of the present lecture course is based on tape recordings that were transcribed in the Institute of Social Research directly after each lecture. Once the lectures had been transcribed, the tapes were erased and reused. The transcriptions are lodged today in the Theodor W. Adorno Archive with the classification numbers Vo 9735–10314.

   In order to produce the present text, the editor has attempted to adopt the same methods as those used by Adorno when editing talks given spontaneously. Where, that is, he agreed to publish them at all. In particular, the attempt has been made to preserve their spontaneous character. The editor has introduced as few or as many changes into the text as were essential. Anacolutha and elliptical formulations have been eliminated, as well as other errors of grammar and excessive repetitions, and a number of syntactical constructions have been simplified. Adorno used to speak fairly quickly and this often led to slips of the tongue; wherever it has been possible to make definite decisions about which words belonged where, the syntax has been retouched. Fillers, particularly particles such as '*nun*', '*also*', '*ja*', have been omitted where they added nothing to the meaning. Punctuation of course had to be inserted, and the editor felt that here he had the greatest licence to ignore the rules Adorno normally applied to his own written texts and to concentrate on making sure that Adorno's spoken words should be rendered as unambiguously and clearly as possible. Needless to say, no attempt has been made to 'improve' the original, but only to convey *his* text as faithfully as the editor knew how.

The notes provide sources for the quotations used in the lectures as well as citing texts that Adorno was referring to or might have had in mind. In addition, parallel passages from his writings have been provided where they help to clarify what he was saying in the lectures, but also to show the close links between his lectures and his published writings. 'One needs to develop a faculty for discerning the emphases and accents peculiar to a philosophy in order to discover their relationships within the philosophical context, and thus to understand the philosophy itself – that is at least as important as knowing unequivocally: such and such is . . .' – let us say, the philosophy of history or freedom (*Metaphysics*, p. 51). The notes are provided to assist a reading in the spirit of Adorno's remarks. In general, they are intended to bring to life the cultural sphere that is inhabited by Adorno's lectures but that can hardly be taken for granted any more today. Wherever they give the impression that they are coming close to offering an interpretation, this is entirely in tune with the editor's intentions.

*

Thanks are due to Michael Schwarz for his help in dealing with all sorts of problems that arose during editing.

July 2000

PART I

HISTORY

LECTURE 1

10 November 1964

PROGRESS OR REGRESSION?[1]

Adorno's notes for this lecture:

Refer to the special situation of this lecture course.[2]

From a book on dialectics, i.e., to be treated as completed sections of a dialectical philosophy; that is to say, *not* as individual phenomena independent of the overall conception.

Legitimate in the sense that the two complexes to be treated have always been at the core of a dialectical philosophy.

Thus in *Kant* the relation of the realm of freedom to history is mediated by conflict [*Antagonismus*].

While in *Hegel* history is regarded immediately as progress in the consciousness of freedom, such that consciousness for Hegel amounts to a *realized* freedom.[3]

This doctrine is extremely precarious. Shall concentrate on its problematic nature, i.e., the actual historical relation of universal and particular.

Even with the greatest generosity and with the aid of a spiral theory,[4] it is no longer possible to make the case for such progress *directly*:

objectively, because of the increasing dense texture of society both in the East and in the West, the intensification of the process of concentration and of bureaucratization which has the effect of reducing people more and more to the status of functions. Freedom is limited to self-preservation. Even the most highly placed are merely functions of their function.

subjectively, because of ego-weakness, addiction to consumption, conformism. Nothing seems less plausible than the claim that there is progress *in the consciousness* of freedom, even allowing for the progressive democratization of *formal* political institutions, since these find themselves opposed by both the substance of social power and human apathy. Indifference to freedom. Neutralization of mind. Depoliticization of science.

After Auschwitz, a regression that has already *taken place* and is not merely expected à la Spengler, not only every positive doctrine of progress but also even every assertion that history has a *meaning* has become problematic and affirmative. There is here a transformation of quantity into quality. Even if the murder of millions could be described as an exception and not the expression of a trend (the atom bomb), any appeal to the idea of progress would seem absurd given the scale of the catastrophe.*

[Interpolation] *Problem: what is the relation of progress to the *individual* – a question brushed aside by the philosophy of history.

Simply by asking what history is over and above the facts, the history of philosophy seems inexorably to end up in a theory of the *meaning* of history.

This applies even to so-called negative or pessimistic histories of philosophy such as Spengler's.[5]

Cultural morphology – overarching patterns = organic teleologies; cultures would then have at least as much purpose – 'meaning' – as the plants to which Spengler compares them; they would be living beings in their own right, a solace for individual subjects.[6]

Incidentally, where Spengler attributes the unity of a cultural sphere to its soul, it would be more logical to ascribe it to the unity of its modes of production.

Even in Spengler, the anti-idealist, there is a latent idealism in his explanation of history as arising from within human beings.

Question: is the philosophy of history possible *without* such latent idealism, without the guarantee of meaning?

10 November 1964[7]

[From Hilmar Tillack's notes][8] When one grows older and is forced to choose between one's duty as professor to give lectures and the desire to follow one's own philosophical bent, one develops a certain peasant cunning. In the case of this course of lectures, I shall focus on two complexes taken from a philosophical work in progress[9] that I have been engaged on for years, two core themes, samples of dialectical philosophy, concerned, on the one hand, with the relation of world spirit to the history of nature, and on the other, with the doctrine of freedom.

In Kant's philosophy of history, the essence of which is distilled in the 'Idea for a Universal History with a Cosmopolitan Purpose', the realm of freedom into which individuals might hope to enter is brought together with history. For his part admittedly, in his practical philosophy, Kant is inclined to think of this freedom as existing in the here and now. It is supposed to arise as a result of conflict [*Antagonismus*]. This resembles Hobbes's earlier view of a war of all against all, the savage conflicts in which mankind has nothing to gain and that result in the famous contracts founding the states.[10] Objectively, Hegel takes over the idea of working one's way forward through conflict but, by adding the idea of the cunning of reason, he intensifies it into a metaphysics, a theory of progress in the consciousness of freedom. History becomes a radical movement in the direction of freedom. 'Consciousness of freedom' does not refer to individual, subjective consciousness, but to the spirit that objectively realizes itself through history, thus making freedom a reality. This theory of progress, as an advance in freedom, is highly vulnerable.

I do not propose to give you a general introduction to the philosophy of history of the kind you will find in writers such as Mehlis,[11] Bernheim[12] or Georg Simmel.[13] Instead, my specific approach focuses on the relationship between freedom and the individual. This is in large part identical with the relation of the universal, the great objective trend, to the particular. This dialectical and logical approach is almost more important than the direct discussion of the structural problems of history. I may note, incidentally, that I agree with Liebrucks[14] here that Hegel's authentic statement of this dialectical philosophy of history is to be found in his *Logic* and *The Phenomenology of Spirit* rather than elsewhere. Without wasting time on the overworked notion of a spiral development in history, it can be said that a direct progress towards freedom cannot be discerned. Objectively, such progress is impossible because of the increasingly dense texture of society in both East and West; the growing concentration of the economy, the executive and the bureaucracy has advanced to such an extent that people are reduced more and more to the status of functions. What freedom remains is superficial, part of the cherished private life, and lacks substance as far as people's ability to determine their own lives is concerned. In reality they are only given free rein in limited activities because they could not stand it otherwise, and all such licence is subject to cancellation. Even in the sphere of consumption – significantly, this term has displaced what used to be called enjoyment – they have become appendages of the machinery. Goods are not produced for their sake and their consumption satisfies people's own desires only very indirectly and to a very limited extent. Instead, they have to make do with what the production line spews out. Freedom becomes impoverished, jejune, and is reduced to the possibility of sustaining one's own life. Mankind has reached a point today where even those on the commanding heights cannot enjoy their positions because even these have been whittled away to the point where they are merely functions of their own function. Even captains of industry spend their time working through mountains of documents and shifting them from one side of their desk to the other, instead of ignoring office hours and reflecting in freedom. Were they to pursue the latter course, their businesses would collapse in chaos. Where an optimum of freedom seems to have survived people cannot avail themselves of it. If you were to sit down, reflect, and make decisions, you would soon fall behind and become an eccentric, like the Savage in Huxley's *Brave New World*.[15]

Freedom is also a realm of subjective experience; that is to say, it is not just to be assessed by some objective standard. Where a subjective interest, a consciousness, is absent, there can be no freedom. Where objective conditions cease to favour a person or a category, or even obstruct and undermine them, there will be a corresponding loss of interest in them, and hence of the strength and the ability required to help them to prosper. Spengler says that Rousseau is starting to be a bore, and Marx even more so.[16] We need not discuss the truth of this claim here, but we can concede that the pathos of freedom in 1789 had its purely decorative side, one that continued to reverberate down to the middle of the nineteenth century. Nowadays, people are unable to get excited about it. They may fear losing the opportunities for consumption, but their interest in expanding freedom is absent. It is an illusion to imagine that freedom is a substantial value merely because words are long-lived. Freedom survives only in remote mountainous regions where there is still resistance to totalitarian tyranny. Elsewhere, it has long since acquired the odium of obsolescence. What is of significance for the internal structure of individuals today is a phenomenon identified by psychoanalysis. This is the phenomenon of ego weakness. David Riesman speaks of inner-directed and other-directed characters.[17] By the latter, the predominant type today, he means the social character whose actions are guided by outside influences. In his case the discrepancy between the development of his ego and the power of the forces that bear down on him has the effect that his ego does not reach the point of a dialectic between his internal and external powers. In consequence he simply conforms. The chaining of people to consumption is an index of this. Political apathy has also become the universal rule in all countries now, as long as direct personal interests are not affected. It should be thought of in the same context. The progressive democratization of political institutions will do nothing to mitigate the loss of a sense of freedom, the growing indifference or the enfeeblement of the desire for freedom because the socio-economic reality of even the freest political institutions stands in the way of such a sense of freedom.

People are not as bound to authority as was supposed as recently as some thirty years ago because of their identification with their father imago. What we are witnessing is rather a neutralizing effect resulting from the pressure to conform. This leads to a closing off of the entire horizon of freedom and dependency. Where no freedom is experienced, there can no longer be any authority. The vanishing of this conceptual pair, freedom and authority, is more significant today than the growing apathy. This process of neutralization is what we must be concerned with. Resistance to the routinization of science is another task that still remains to philosophy.

This process of neutralization should not be thought of as harmless. The loss of a sense of freedom tends to flip over into immediate terror, as is all too evident in Auschwitz. The catastrophe there was not just a disaster predicted by Spengler, but an actual reality, one that makes all talk of progress towards freedom seem ludicrous. The concept of the autonomous human subject is refuted by reality. By the same token, if freedom and autonomy still had any substance, Auschwitz could not have happened. And by Auschwitz I mean of course the entire system. Confronted with the fact that Auschwitz was possible, that politics could merge directly with mass murder, the affirmative mentality becomes the mere assertion of a mind that is incapable of looking horror in the face and that thereby perpetuates it.

What we see here is the transformation of quantity into quality – monstrous though it is to try to operate with the concept of quality in order to grasp the murder of millions. In fact, even to attempt to withstand such events mentally, to shed light on them with the aid of concepts, is to fix them with concepts. To speak of genocide as if it were an institution is to institutionalize it. We thereby assume a second burden of guilt. The change from quantity to quality here has this meaning: in bygone days exceptional situations were exceptions to the main trend. Alternatively, we might treat men such as Tamburlane and Genghis Khan as great natural calamities. Nowadays that has all changed. The horror of our day has arisen from the intrinsic dynamics of our own history; it cannot be described as exceptional. And even if we do think of it as an exception and not the expression of a trend – although this latter is not implausible, given that the atom bomb and the gas chamber have certain catastrophic similarities – to do so is somehow absurd in the light of the scale of the disaster. What can it mean to say that the human race is making progress when millions are reduced to the level of objects?

Such things have a kind of retroactive force and demonstrate the extreme precariousness of the affirmative view of history. It raises the question whether the view of history as a continuous progression towards higher forms does not include the catastrophes that we are experiencing today; whether the predominance of the universal, the broad tendency, over the particular is not a delusion; whether the consolation of philosophy that the death of individuals is the price paid by the great movement of history was not always the swindle it is today; whether the sufferings of a single human being can be compensated for [*aufgehoben*] by the triumphal march of progress.

In so far as the philosophy of history sets out to show something more than the facts, it implicitly contains the search for meaning, formally at least – without the need for philosophy to explain it. In the same way, negative, cyclical theories of history also have this affirmative side despite themselves, even though they do not claim that history has a definite meaning but instead substitute nature for history.[18] Spengler disastrously encouraged people to insert themselves into the machinery of history within the general framework of historical necessity at the same time as predicting the victory of that machinery. Frobenius's cultural morphology is an organic teleology that preaches the idea of an all-encompassing, coherent totality.[19] This implies at least as much meaning or purpose within cultures as the plants to which Spengler compares them. This leaves the poor unfortunate individuals with the consolation that they are part of a higher living being, which has the benefit of conferring some meaning on their otherwise pointless existence. The fact that Spengler later developed a political point of view is not inconsistent with his cultural pessimism. This is connected with the affirmative element in his teaching. Where pessimism is a general proposition, where it has a totalizing view, it implies that everything is fundamentally flawed, as Schopenhauer believed. Paradoxically, this means that it tends to leap to the assistance of individual evil in the world. It does so by arguing that attempts to change the world as a whole are doomed. This is also implicit in a negative philosophy of history.

It would be more logical to attribute the unity of a cultural sphere to the unity of a mode of production than – as with Spengler – to purely internal factors. It is not easy to see how something internal could put its stamp on an external form, like the 'shape that has been impressed upon evolving life'.[20] Spengler the anti-idealist becomes an idealist when he argues that the totality arises out of something internal to human beings, to the essence of humanity, without noticing that history is for the most part something that is done to people. He fails to realize that institutions have become so independent that individuals are scarcely in a position to impinge on them and are able to express their opinions about them only indirectly, through art, for example.

The question we must ask, therefore, is whether a theory of history is possible without a latent idealism; whether we can construct history without committing the cardinal sin of insinuating meaning where none exists.

LECTURE 2

12 November 1964

UNIVERSAL AND PARTICULAR

Last time I talked to you about the *philosophy* of history. I should like to continue today by saying something about history as an *academic discipline* [*Geschichtswissenschaft*].[1] In the course of this lecture I shall perhaps be able to go some way towards persuading you that – objectively – history is possible only as the philosophy of history, a view that is not wholly without foundation. Moreover, any history, historiography, that denies this is simply unaware of itself and its own requirements. Now what I have represented to you as a crisis in the idea of historical meaning can be seen in the postulates of historiography and, beyond that, in the majority of the humanities, which especially in Germany are predominantly historical in their methods and which resist every attempt to oppose that historical orientation. Let me remind you of the dominant positivist tradition in historiography which was first formulated in Ranke's dictum that the task of history, of historical research, was to 'tell how it really happened'.[2] The effect of this tradition was that increasingly it involved the outlawing of every attempt to understand history from above, and this meant the elimination of every element of history, every objective historical tendency, which I claimed last time was not derivative or secondary, was not merely the weird invention of phi-losophers of history, but was in fact what people immediately experience when they find themselves caught up in a maelstrom of the so-called great historical epochs. If I am not mistaken, the tendency of historians is increasingly to call into question all large concepts such as that of universal history itself, and then likewise to cast doubt, firstly, on the idea of the great trends that are supposed to be at work throughout history and, finally, on narrower concepts such as those of the different epochs. I need only remind you of the fact, well known to the historians among you, that the concept of the Middle Ages has – with very good reason – been undermined in a variety of ways. One line of argument has been to maintain that the crisis in the Middle Ages should probably be dated much earlier than the official start to the Renaissance. Scholars began to talk about the discovery of a kind of proto-Renaissance as early as the age of High Gothic – a period traditionally assigned to the Middle Ages. By way of contrast, there are other trends that challenge the concept of historical facts as such, so that the undermining of historiography even extends to its own opposite pole, the concept of the individual historical event, the *événement*. In France above all critical historians have attacked *événementisme*[3] as an approach in which too much importance is attributed to major, particular events. You may well be familiar with this yourselves if you have ever wondered whether the great battles of Napoleon or the Great Elector[4] really were as important historically as people said they were. This overweighting of the factual itself presupposes a theory that historical processes have some sort of meaning which then identifies its nodal points or crises in such *événements*. And the moment the idea of such a meaningful historical process is shaken, it begins to have an effect upon the counter-idea of the specific fact so that history begins to slide almost imperceptibly to a point where it becomes questionable whether we can say anything meaningful about it at all.

In these lectures I wish to deal only with one specific problem of history, namely the relation between the universal, the universal tendency, and the particular, that is, the individual. It is not my task here to enter into the detail of the way in which history is constructed. Even so, I believe that, if we are to treat certain fundamental questions of the philosophy of history, we cannot ignore such matters entirely; and I believe further that the knowledge of historical matters is in the first instance a question of distance. If we approach details too closely and fail to open them up to critical inspection, we will indeed find ourselves in the proverbial situation of not seeing the wood for the trees. On the other hand, if we distance ourselves too much, we shall be unable to grasp history because the categories we use themselves become excessively magnified to the point where they become problematic and fail to do justice to their material. I have in mind concepts such as the progress of freedom, about which I offered some critical comments last time. So I would say that we need to keep a certain distance. This will enable us both to dissociate

ourselves from a total theory of history and equally to resist the cult
of the facts which, as I have explained, have their own conceptual
difficulties. We can illustrate this by saying, for example, that we
cannot really speak of something like progress in general, as indeed
I have already argued. Incidentally we shall take a closer look at this
concept towards the end of the section in which we discuss the philosophy of history. But you should also be aware that there is always
something dubious about the talk of individual examples of progress
that have allegedly occurred in the course of history. This is because,
in the society in which we live, every single progressive act is always
brought about at the expense of individuals or groups who are
thereby condemned to fall under the wheels. Thus because of their
particularity, because they disregard the organization of society as a
whole, each of these progressive events means that there are always
groups who are their victims and who legitimately doubt their value.
Nevertheless, we may say – and I believe that even the severest critic
of history would not simply dismiss this view – that we can speak of
something like progress from the slingshot to the atom bomb.[5] It is
not by chance that I am willing to apply the concept of progress to
something as terrifying as the atom bomb, something that is so completely inimical to the progress of freedom, to the advance of the
autonomy of the human species. There is a good reason for this, or
rather it has a very bad and indeed catastrophic meaning. The fact
is that particularity will be the mark of all historical movements as
long as there is no such thing as what we might call a human race,
that is to say, a society that is conscious of itself and has its fate in
its own hands. As long as that remains true, all progress will be particular, not just in the sense that progress will always come about at
the expense of groups who are not directly involved in it, and who
have to bear the brunt of progressive changes, but in the sense that
progress has a particular character by nature.

I believe that a thinker such as Max Weber displayed a very proper
instinct for this when he reserved the concept of progress for rationality. Max Weber was of course a positivist thinker through and through
(even though it was a German version of positivism, one that had
passed through the sieve of critical philosophy). He postulated something like a universal structure of progressive rationality at least as a
perspective for humanity as a whole. To be sure, he exercised great
caution in so doing since he accepted that there were entire civilizations that were prevented by their traditionalist economies from
sharing in this progressive rationality and its associated social
dynamic.[6] It will astonish you to hear me speaking of a progressive
rationality immediately after talking about particularity in the evolu-

tion of the historical totality – since you might well imagine that, because reason is a pre-eminently universal category, for it to prevail would represent the polar opposite of any such particularity. However, I think it a mistake to conceive of this idea of a progressive rationality as something incompatible with particularity. I believe that if we are able to appreciate the particularity of the universal, in this instance of progressive rationality, we shall understand a little about the dialectics of the universal and the particular as a structure of history. This is because the universal principle contains a particular within it as a bad, negative element. And in the same way, the converse too holds good, as Hegel has shown with irresistible force, namely that the particular, the individual facts, embody the power of the universal in concentrated form. For from the very outset the rationality to which we commonly ascribe universality was a rationality of the *domination of nature*, the control of both external nature and man's inner nature. I should like to refer you here to the *Dialectic of Enlightenment*, by Horkheimer and myself, a book that at long last is due to appear again in the foreseeable future.[7] This domination of nature was not self-reflective but asserted its control over its so-called materials by subsuming, classifying, subordinating and otherwise cutting them short. By materials here we include the materials of nature, the human beings that are to be dominated, and even the subjection of one's own inner nature to the process of rationality. And this contains an idea that I think you should bear in mind since I believe that it is of key importance for our argument. It is the idea that the principle I have called the universal principle, the principle of progressive rationality, contains an internal conflict. In other words, this kind of rationality exists only in so far as it can subjugate something different from and alien to itself. We can put it even more strongly: it can exist only by identifying everything that is caught up in its machinery, by levelling it and by defining it in its alterity as something that resists it and, we may even go so far as to say, something that is hostile to it. In other words, then, antagonism, conflict, is in fact postulated in this principle of dominant universality, of unreflecting rationality, in precisely the same way as antagonism to a subservient group is postulated in a system of rule. And the stage at which self-awareness might lead this rationality to bring about change – that stage has still not been reached.

I should like to say more about this proposition that will probably seem to many of you to be wildly speculative, a piece of pure Hegelian idealism. Perhaps I can turn it the right way up so that it may appear a bit more plausible to you. But before doing so, I should like to add something in honour of the concept of universal history, even though

I remain of the view that this concept too must be understood dialectically. By this I mean that we can say neither that there is such a
thing as universal history, nor, as is the general fashion today, that
there is no such thing. Instead we shall have to say, and this is implicit
in what I have already told you, that universal history exists precisely
to the same degree as the principle of particularity, or, as I now prefer
to call it, the principle of antagonism, persists and perpetuates itself.
Ladies and gentlemen, I do not want to present you with such high-
sounding declarations without linking them to materials that will
help to illuminate them for you. This is particularly important, I
believe, at the start of these lectures. At the same time, I do not wish
to venture into the territory of what goes by the notion of 'examples',
something to which I have the gravest objections for a variety of
philosophical reasons.[8] I come back once again to Spengler, who was
adamant in his hostility to such universalist theories of history and
especially to such notions of a progressive rationality. In contrast, he
advocated a theory – one which was very striking in many individual
details – of self-contained cultures that occurred simultaneously, that
is to say, that succeeded one another and were nevertheless simultane-
ous. And he defended this theory until he was blue in the face. We
may not have enough time or space to explain just how this simultaneity is to be understood. However, I believe that it is explicable
without our having to have recourse to Spengler's own morphological
hypothesis. One idea that he advances is the theory[9] that Western
technology – which he calls 'Faustian' – was alien to the Russian soul
and the East Asian soul in general. It follows that it is simply inconceivable that the Japanese, for example, might be able to appropriate
this technology for themselves. Well, as things have turned out, Max
Weber's prognosis has been fully vindicated. We have seen how technology has succeeded in sweeping across the frontiers of the different
'national souls', if such things exist, and it has done so simply by
virtue of its own objectivity, its own inherent laws. You will all be
aware that the Japanese came within an ace of destroying the American fleet in the last war, thanks to their technically advanced use of
air power. And you will also know that today the Russians have
become the Americans' keenest competitors in the most modern
branches of technology. You can see something of a convergence
towards a kind of universal standard at the level of technical rationality, and this is particularly marked in countries which had previously
been excluded from what Germans think of as the pull of universal
history. You only have to travel abroad a little to see the uniformity
of the airports and compare them with the differences between cities
that lie far apart from one another. These differences then seem to

have an anachronistic air, almost like that of a fancy-dress ball. Once you experience this it takes little to convince yourself of the power of this trend towards universal history. To this extent there does seem to be an element of truth in the much criticized idea of universal history, at least in terms of its *telos*. And doubtless this element of truth can be traced back to periods in which such a universalist element did not yet exist, at least not one implicit in the processes indispensable for the reproduction of life and the social formations contained in them or in the forms taken by the forces of production.

I shall now come to the question that I put to you earlier and that really cannot be side-stepped now. The question is whether this process of progressive rationality has to be seen as an absolute. I should say that this question is particularly important in the context of the discussions in the *Dialectic of Enlightenment*. This would not involve denying that there are great countervailing tendencies. The existence of outbursts of the irrational is not in dispute, only we must qualify this by noting that the so-called outbreaks of irrational or primitive forces in our own age have almost always been the product of manipulation. They have almost always appeared in the service of domination, rational or irrational domination, and must be understood therefore as integral to the growth of the techniques of rational domination. Needless to say, this can be seen with especial clarity in the case of National Socialism, if you still have the heart to study that phenomenon. But I have something different in mind. What I have said does not imply that we are bound to ascribe this tendency of which I am speaking to spirit as the agent of rationality in the abstract, as was the case in the idealist philosophies. And I should like at this point to pay my respects to Hegel. Although Hegel talks constantly of spirit, the principle of the identity of subject and object ensures that this concept is organized from the outset in such a way that it remains distinct from what people thought of as spirit later on in the nineteenth century, and indeed in our own day, where it is generally defined as purely subjective thought. In Hegel's philosophy, thanks to a powerful theory, however open to question it may have been in certain respects, spirit embraces the entire realm of the historical, political and economic life of mankind. In Hegel's system, spirit is assigned a specific place in the real historical world.[10] Hegel would have vehemently repudiated the idea of spirit as a free-floating thing distinct from its opposite, the material life of mankind. Dilthey's conception of the humanities and everything connected with it regarded itself in a sense as Hegel's heir.[11] However, this is an utter misunderstanding and a lapse beneath the level of the discussion that had been attained in Hegel himself – but this is by the way.[12] The important point here is that you should not think of the spirit of which I am speaking as something absolutely autonomous. It is true that the spirit has made itself independent and it is equally true that, through its potent instruments, logic and mathematics, it has freed itself from the conditions that brought it forth. Because of the division of labour into mental and manual work, spirit even *appears* to itself as something absolute and autonomous – as a method that includes its opposite within itself. But we should not buy into this view of spirit. The evolution of spirit as rationality, as the reason that dominates nature, or as what I have called technical rationality – in other words, the evolution of the technical forces of production *in toto* – is the product of the material needs of human beings, of what they need for their preservation; and the categories of the spirit constantly and necessarily contain these needs as the necessary elements of their form. Spirit is the product of human beings and of the human labour process just as much as it informs and ultimately dominates human labour processes as a method, as technical rationality. It is vital that we should not hypostasize the concept of spirit, but that we should instead see it in its dependence upon a concept of life, upon the need to help sustain the human life in which it has its roots. Only if we do this will we be able to understand how spirit in the shape of technical rationality could have contrived to achieve such a unifying control over the life of mankind as has increasingly been the case. Spirit is no absolute first thing. The postulate that spirit is primary is an *illusion*, an illusion created, and necessarily created, by itself. But by the same token it is something produced by the reality of a life bent on self-preservation, something that postulates itself as primary only so that it may criticize existing reality or gain control over it. I spoke earlier of the absence of self-reflection on the part of spirit and of technical rationality, an absence of reflection that had the unfortunate consequence of forcing reason into a strange and paradoxical relationship with blind, historical fate. But this was caused not least by the fact that spirit misconceives itself as primary, instead of perceiving its interconnectedness with actual life.

The growth of rationality is something like the growing ability of the human species to preserve itself or, as we may also say, the growth in the universal principle of the human self. And the progress of this rationality in its unreflective form is at bottom nothing other than the exploitation of nature transferred to men and continuing to work in them. However, in so far as it is this exploitation and in so far as it is bound up with such concepts as exploitation as well as with what is opposed to it and subjugated by it, this progressive reason harbours within itself an element of self-destruction. I told you about this last time when I attempted to portray the experience of the course of history as it is available to us in the here and now as in essence the experience of its negativity, that is to say, as the experience of the way in which we are impotently dragged along in its wake. In other words, then, this progressive instrumental reason is the embodiment of the antagonism that consists in the relation between the supposedly free human subject, who for that very reason is in fact not yet free at all, and the things on which his freedom is built. The antagonistic character of progressive rationality is the aspect of it that turns the universal, the universal that is in the process of asserting itself, into the particular which causes such anguish to us who are likewise particulars. And this will perhaps resolve the contradiction – I mean theoretically, not in actuality; and not even *resolve* it in theory, but at least throw some light on it – the contradiction of which I spoke earlier when I told you how paradoxical it appears at first sight for the universality of the historical principle, which is supposed to be continuing and progressing and to be growing in strength, to be identical with blind fate. But if the enlightening principle of reason fails to become transparent to itself, if it fails to perceive its dependence on what is different from itself, it inevitably becomes transformed into the very fate that it thinks of as its own antithesis. This is the blind spot that acts as a jinx on the entire historical dimension of Hegelian philosophy. It brings me to the main difficulty of every theory of history for the pre-critical consciousness which forms my starting-point. I may remind you that I have already formulated this – and would ask you to be aware that in our discussions we have indeed gained this insight – by saying that in this pre-critical consciousness the dominant, prevailing universality can no longer be equated with the *meaning* of history or indeed with any *positive* value. This is indeed the difficulty to which almost every form of consciousness, every naïve form of consciousness, finds itself exposed: the danger of regarding as justified the supremacy of an objective power over human beings who always believe that they are in full possession of themselves and, because of their certainty on this point, are highly reluctant to admit the degree to which they are merely the functions of some universal. For the moment they were to concede that they would in a sense cease to be in their own eyes what their whole tradition tells them they are. This is a great paradox and I should like to encourage you to reflect upon it. On the one hand, the fact is – and I believe that I said enough about this last time – that our most immediate experience is that we are all harnessed to an objective trend, and it is hard to disabuse us of this. We may think, for example, of the situation of someone who is being persecuted, a typical fate in our time, who is being discriminated against and possibly exposed to liquidation because he is said to possess some characteristic or other that he doesn't even need. Or we may think of the much more harmless situation of someone who is looking for a job and who, at the very moment he hopes to find one that meets his own requirements and abilities, turns out to be biting on granite even in this age of glorious full employment and ends up having to do something that is not at all to his liking – such experiences I would say are absolutely fundamental. If there is any immediate experience, this is it. On the other hand, however, the moment you draw attention to this, the sciences, donning their full academic robes, so to speak, ask you what actually gives you the right to assume the existence of something universal; this universal is a metaphysical principle, it exists only in your mind; in reality there is nothing but spontaneous individual phenomena, the individual acts of individual human beings; and this universal is no more than an idea you have let others foist on you. Nowadays, there really is something like a perversion of consciousness, a reversing of what is primary and what secondary, which goes so far that, for purely epistemological reasons that have by now become automatic, we let ourselves be talked out of everything we experience at any given moment as the determining forces in our lives, and we are taught to regard them instead as a metaphysical sleight of hand. And in contrast to this, things that are really questionable, such as the primary character of individual human reactions, are treated by this so-called scientific mind as if they were truly primary and an absolutely secure foundation of knowledge, simply because they are supposed to be the basis of all our judgements. I believe that we would do well to obtain some clarity about this web of delusion if we are to have any hope at all of, if not acquiring a firm basis for our understanding of history, at least clearing a path towards it. And having seen through this web of delusion, we shall perhaps find it easier to think of the concept of universality as *negativity*, a concept I shall turn to next time.

LECTURE 3

17 November 1964

CONSTITUTION PROBLEMS

Ladies and gentlemen, I learned today of the death of one of my oldest and closest friends.[1] I find it almost impossible to concentrate my thoughts as much as I ought, both for your sake and my own. However, I did not wish to cancel the lecture and so ask you for your forbearance.

Last time, I talked about the difficulty of a theory of history that presents itself to the naïvely scientific but philosophically pre-critical mind. This difficulty is that of grasping that something objective has primacy over human beings who nevertheless think of themselves as the most certain reality. This fits in with the conception of history and the philosophy of history based on it as an assemblage of facts which then have to be interpreted in their indirect, derived *context*. It is held to be legitimate to investigate this context even though it really presupposes a larger framework that encompasses the individual subjects. Now, precisely because dialectics is necessarily and permanently concerned with the critique of mere facticity, of mere immediacy, I should wish not to ignore or neglect the element of truth contained in facts. Everyone who, like me, had the experience of having his house searched early in the National Socialist regime will know full well that such an event has an immediate impact that is greater than any attempt to seek out its causes, however convincingly these may be explained in the newspapers – explanations, for example, to the effect that the National Socialists have seized power, that the police have been granted certain powers, and other statements of the same sort. A fact like a house search in which you do not know whether you will be taken off somewhere or whether you will escape with your life has a greater immediacy for the knowing subject than any amount of political information, itself on the level of the facts, to say nothing of the so-called larger historical context to which only reflection and, ultimately, theory can give us access. At the same time, this immediate knowledge that we need to hold onto as one element, something that no theory of dialectics may ignore, is no more than immediate knowledge *for us*. In itself, the fact of such a house search, however unpleasant it may be and however horrifying the threats lurking within it, is no more, despite its immediate impact, than the expression of the change of government, the abolition of legal safe-guards under the emergency laws made permanent by the Nazis, and similar factors. In the final analysis it is the product of the changing social structures that had led to the fascist dictatorship as a result of the special conditions obtaining in Germany between 1929 and 1933. In all probability, the concept of the fact can itself only be grasped as an element in an overall process; individual facts can only be spoken of as part of a context which then manifests itself in these individual facts. The very concept of 'fact' ensures that it cannot be insulated from its surrounding environment – just as I could probably not have really *experienced* that house search if I had not connected it in my mind with the political events of the winter and spring of 1933. If all that had happened was that two relatively harmless offi-cials belonging to the old police force had turned up on my doorstep, and if I had had no knowledge of the complete change in the political system, my experience would have been quite different from what it was. And, in the same way, no one can appreciate the terrors of a totalitarian regime if he has not personally experienced that ominous knock at the door and opened it to find the police waiting outside.

I should like to take this opportunity of defending myself against an attack or a criticism to which dialectics is exposed when one simply takes it to mean what in fact it does mean in large stretches of Marx's writings: namely as something that is no more than a cri-tique of the immediacy of the immediate, in other words, as the demonstration that what appears to be brute fact is in reality some-thing that has become what it is, something conditioned and not an absolute. A further factor should not be overlooked, if the dialectic is not simply to degenerate into something like a superstition or a trivial pursuit. By referring something back to the conditions that prove immediacy to have been conditioned, you do indeed strike a blow against immediacy, but that immediacy survives nevertheless. For we can speak of mediation only if immediate reality, only if

primary experience, survives. It would therefore be just as foolish to
demand of history that it should concentrate solely on the so-called
context, the larger conditioning factors, as it would be for historiography to confine itself to the depiction of mere facts. The construction
of theoretical frameworks alone without confronting the facts really
can lead to large-scale delusions. We may think here of attempts to
explain the historical fate of mankind, the division into rich and poor
and such matters in terms of racial origins, as was attempted as early
as the nineteenth century by writers such as Gobineau.[2] So the point
about dialectics is not to negate the concept of fact in favour of
mediation, or to exaggerate that of mediation; it is simply to say that
immediacy is itself mediated but that the concept of the immediate
must still be retained.

Ladies and gentlemen, what I am saying to you here, and what
probably sounds to you like a chapter from a dialectical or speculative book on logic, is of the most immediate importance for the
subject of these lectures. For we have been concerned here with the
relations between the universal and the particular, the course of
history and the individual. And, needless to say, when confronted
with the general trend, the encompassing process, the individual
inevitably has something of the immediacy of individual human experience of which I have been speaking. And if, as will gradually emerge
from these lectures, we insist on this concept of the particular as
opposed to the universal, on the grounds that in its present form the
universal is no true universal, then the justification for doing so is
that, even if we accept that the individual is itself a manifestation,
that individuality is itself a historical category, we must likewise
accept that it is a historical category that cannot simply be set aside.
It is rather the case that the immediacy of individuality, that is to say,
of the individual being who is concerned to preserve his own existence, is just as truly an element of the dialectic as the predominant
universality. But it is only an element and one that should no more
be overemphasized abstractly than the universal. That is the reason
why I wish to insist on this point.

However that may be, in the dominant view the larger, encompassing context, the context that is not to be immediately grasped in, let
us say, factual accounts, is generally taken to be a form of theory,
and is therefore consigned to philosophy and the realm of controversy
in the spirit of the division of labour. It finds itself relegated by the
general scientific consensus to the status of a kind of sauce or the
final chapter in a historical narrative, one that does not need to be
taken too seriously. One instance of this can be seen in Simmel's book
on the history of philosophy[3] which I have now referred to several

times.[4] In this book every speculation about history, and indeed every attempt to conceptualize history, appears to be treated as a subjective stylization that may be unavoidable but one that is also exposed to all the risks of relativism. This is a view that seems to me to be worthy of criticism. It can also be found in an extreme form in Theodor Lessing's book *Geschichte als Sinngebung des Sinnlosen* [History as giving meaning to the meaningless],[5] a book that I nevertheless find remarkable in its own way and commend to you as an example of a negative philosophy of history. I should point out, however, that a chasm separates the so-called idealism of a semi-Kantian such as Simmel from Hegel's absolute idealism, and that it is in their theory of history that they can be seen to be at their most antithetical. Paradoxically, Hegel's theory of the objective nature of history has a far greater realism than Simmel's in the sense that this objectivity has a far greater validity in actuality. I would make only one general point in criticism of Simmel. This is that the entire problem presented itself in a manner that was typical of grand philosophy in the late nineteenth and early twentieth century. It manifested itself in the concept of the constitutum, what was constituted, in other words, the way in which both objects and the truth were constituted was not explored in a radical fashion in this philosophy. Instead, thinking took place in an already constituted world, in which already constituted human beings behave in various ways towards already constituted objects of knowledge, and where these forms of behaviour are investigated in their turn. We may say that this procedure is roughly analogous to so-called subjective economics, marginal utility theory,[6] in which exchange relations within an already constituted barter society are analysed without inquiring into the way in which the exchange relationship, its true objective meaning, has been constructed. At bottom, for all his subtlety, Simmel's analysis is lacking in reflection; he is concerned with the way in which an existing mind relates to already existing facts.

I want to confine my criticism purely to the essential issue, simply to clarify its relevance to our own problem here. The point is that what is secondary according to his theory, namely what we owe to the knowing mind, the course of history, the historical trend, the dynamic of history that prevails despite the efforts of human beings – that secondary aspect is in reality the thing that constitutes objective reality. It is in fact the objective nature of history in which individual subjects have their being that has primacy over all the human subjects that according to him are supposed to give shape to history. Simmel's entire philosophy, then, is marked by a methodological *hysteron proteron*, a putting of the cart before the horse. And I would say that this is one of the underlying experiences that have been engendered by the historical events of our own age. Simmel died in 1918 and so does not properly belong to our own period. He still tended to think of history in much the same way as the joke lines in *Faust* in which history takes place in faraway Turkey where 'armies come to blows'.[7] What in his lifetime could be shaped and inspected, like a collection of china in a glass case, has in the meantime come far too close for comfort. Confronted with this change, the very idea of the historian who can choose and shape events to his own taste and in accordance with his own interests has faded into myth, a myth which in the good old days Simmel could still mistake for the objective thrust of history itself. The fact is that we can only properly experience the objective nature of history, as opposed to its supposed subjective 'shaping', once we realize that we are its potential victims. And that has become possible for individuals only with the world wars and the emergence of totalitarian rulers. You can see from this how historical developments can influence our own attitudes to history. In a given situation a social system, and above all the dynamics intrinsic to such a system, has unconditional primacy over the human subjects who perceive them and who, according to Simmel, are the agents of primary historical categories. I would go even further and say that, just as in general historical events have retroactive effects, this also holds good in this instance. That primacy, in other words, also existed in Simmel's own day and only failed to make its presence felt because of the distance of the observer from the events of history. If there is any truth in the epistemological claims of naïve realism – as expounded by materialism in its vulgar phase – then we see it precisely at this point.[8] This was what was uppermost in the minds of dialectical materialists when they insisted upon the reality of society as opposed to psychological subjectivism. For this had been their own experience. Their mistake was merely that they tried to express their insight in the language of epistemology. For that brought about a relapse into the dogmatic assertion of a history that existed in itself, without showing any awareness of the problems of constitution I have been describing to you. This is what I should like to stress to you by way of salvaging the reputation of those so-called vulgar writers – who in many respects really were crude and epistemologically naïve and who admittedly look quite different in the light of the self-reflection and self-criticism of a traditional subjectivist epistemology. Even from a Hegelian point of view, the vulgar thesis, the no less vulgar thesis that history is purely subjective in constitution would be quite untenable.

Even the subject's resistance to the pre-existing categories facing him is mediated by the categories in which he is enmeshed. In

consequence, even in the high-bourgeois phase in which the sovereign
freedom of the perceiving human subject is at its greatest, his freedom
is vastly more circumscribed than appeared to be the case. By way
of illustration, I need only refer to Joseph de Maistre, the philosopher
of the Restoration in France. De Maistre is in general a very remarkable figure and it is certainly worth taking the trouble to look at him
more closely. At the time of the so-called Restoration in France, de
Maistre attempted, with extraordinary assiduity, we must say, to
develop a critique of democratic society. It can be shown, however –
and I have to restrict myself here simply to a passing reference – that
the highly rational and polished logic which de Maistre deploys in
his attack on rational and liberal society presupposes the entire
panoply of sophisticated ideas that had been produced by the process
of emancipation. In the eighteenth century, or indeed in an age when
the feudal system was secure in its own beliefs, thinking of the kind
seen in de Maistre would have been inconceivable. In his defence of
the *ancien régime*, he necessarily marshals all the rational arguments
that had brought about its demise, and, if we may say so after the
fact, he is helping to undermine the same conservative forces that he
is defending. This is because the ideas he advances in their defence
are of precisely the same kind as the necessarily egalitarian rationality
whose substance he assails. That, incidentally, is a situation that I can
only touch on here. I wish only to remind you of it since it is a situation of enormous importance and with widespread ramifications for
historical theory. Resistance to speculation or the desire to restrict it
epistemologically is merely derivative and secondary in the face of
this priority of the course of history to which we have been harnessed.
I would go so far as to say that today the resistance to speculation,
like the ideology of positivism in general, tends rather to become the
ideology whose adversary it imagines itself to be. The less free people
are in history and the more they feel themselves to be in the grip of
the universal necessity that, thanks to the coherence of the social
system of a given epoch, stamps its imprint on the dynamic of history,
the historical age, the more desperately eager they are to assert that
their own immediate experience is ultimate and absolute in nature.
It follows, too, that they have an altogether greater interest in turning
the situation upside down and misconstruing as a mere matter of
speculation or arbitrary thought what in reality is the *ens realissimum*
– except that we should take care not to confuse the *ens realissimum*
with the *summum bonum*, the greatest good, a common error in the
philosophical tradition. Pre-critical thought is aware of this and must
not allow its experience to be devalued by this confusion of the logical
ground [*ratio cognoscendi*] with the real one [*ratio essendi*].

I should like now, with your permission, to return to what I said at the beginning of this lecture, namely my experience when my house was searched. This was something that might have cost me my life, and in that event it would have been the thing with the greatest reality of all. Immediately, however, it was real only as the logical explanation of the horror that I felt quite drastically and directly, while of course its real cause [*Realgrund*] was not the fact that the doorbell had rung or that these particular policemen had appeared at my front door because they had received orders to do so, but in fact the nature of the system as a whole that had led them to act in that way. Hence when I object to false immediacy, to turning the immediate into an absolute, what I have in mind in the first instance is this confusion of the logical explanation or, rather, the immediate cause of an experience with the real cause, that is to say, with the total historical context and its direction, on which we are all dependent.

In Hegel we find that these ideas have at least been registered – in the shape of objective idealism. Because of its identification of all existence with spirit, objective idealism has as its object the freedom to concede to existence the actual power that existence has over us. In the final analysis, this is not the least of the reasons that enabled idealist dialectics to give birth to the materialist variety by virtue of a small adjustment. Just how small is something we can no longer imagine today. Feuerbach must have sensed it when he wrote his famous letter to Hegel, in which he attempted to demonstrate that Hegel was already an anthropological materialist.[9] Unfortunately, Hegel's response to this letter has not been preserved. Now, what Hegel calls the world spirit is the spirit that asserts itself despite people's wishes, over their heads, as it were. It is the primacy of the flow of events in which they are caught up, and it impinges on them no less than do the facts. Only it does so less painfully, and is therefore the more easily repressed. What is important here is that you should not regard this idea of the spirit prevailing over people's heads as a kind of speculative prejudice and hence dismiss it all too readily. It is important, I say, that you should realize that this is a process in which what prevails always passes not merely over people's heads, but *through* them. One of the most widespread misunderstandings of Hegel, in my opinion, is what I have recently termed 'the priority of the subject'.[10] This is a misunderstanding that must be eliminated if we wish to gain a proper appreciation of the problem we are discussing. It is essential that where such things as spirit or reason are under discussion you should not imagine that we are faced with a secularization of, let us say, the divine plan that floats above mankind, but minus the person of God. There is no suggestion here that there is such a thing as providence, but no provident Being, and that the divine plan is somehow fulfilled independently of mankind. Matters are not so simple. I believe that, if you want to understand what I am saying and what I think of as the real task of these lectures, you should not start thinking about such independent embodiments of the spirit separate from human beings, but quite simply about such things as what is meant by the spirit of the age. What I mean by this is that if you travel around Franconia or elsewhere in southern Germany or Austria you will be able to see how in the seventeenth century all the surviving Romanesque and Gothic churches and chapels were suddenly given a baroque facelift. It is as if they were all under the same spell. Or think for a moment of the way in which every little café suddenly becomes ashamed of its cosy atmosphere and tries to update itself by installing neon lighting so as to give itself a more functional look. If you think of the spirit of the age in these terms, you will come closer to what I have in mind than if you think of the influence of an objective spirit as something terribly meaningful and theological – although, needless to say, I would not wish to dispute that in its origins we undoubtedly are witnessing something like the secularization of the theological divine plan of the world. Nevertheless, Hegel and the dialectical view of history were far too considered and far too critical not to notice that, if such a process of secularization is to succeed, it cannot be achieved if the divine plan or the new objective reality are allowed to retain the same predicates that they once possessed in the theological scheme of things. In this respect Hegel was a genuine philosopher of mediation and also an Aristotelian in the sense that he attempted to define the spirit that prevails *over* mankind as something that also prevails *in* them.

I believe that it is very important – in so far as such matters have any importance at all, but since you have come here in such large numbers, you and I both indulge in the fiction that we are talking about very important matters, so that I can assume that this fiction remains valid – with this reservation, then, I believe that it is very important to remember that the objective course of history asserts itself over human beings – in such a way that no single mind and no single human will suffices truly and effectively to resist it. And, at the same time, it asserts itself *through* human beings. By this I mean that they appropriate and identify with what is expressed, slightly vaguely perhaps, by the English term the 'trend'. And even this is to define it far too superficially, for in reality – and this is where Hegel's philosophy of history coincides with classical economic theory and also with Marx – the fact that people pursue their own individual interests makes them at the same time the exponents and executors of that

same historical objectivity that is ready to turn against their interests
at any moment and thus may assert itself over their heads. There is
a contradiction here since it is claimed that what asserts itself despite
people's own efforts does so by virtue of them, by virtue of their own
interests. But since the society in which we live is antagonistic, and
since the course of the world to which we are harnessed is antagonistic too, what we might term this logical contradiction should not
be thought of as merely a contradiction, merely the product of an
inadequate formulation. It is a contradiction that arises from the situation. To put it in metaphysical terms, it states simply that the very
constraints that are imposed on people by the course of the world,
and that compel them to attend to their own interests and nothing
beyond them, is the very same force that turns against people and
asserts itself over their heads as a blind and almost unavoidable fate.
It is this structure of things that leads us to the point I have been
aiming at: namely, a conception of the philosophy of history that
permits us to *comprehend* history, that is to say, to go beyond its
bounds as mere existence [*Dasein*] and to understand it as something
meaningless. And this meaninglessness is itself nothing but the dreadful antagonistic state of affairs that I have been attempting to describe
to you. So the primacy of universal reason is not to be understood
as the primacy of some substantive rational force beyond human
beings that directs human actions – and this is something I should
like you to understand, since I regard it as of prime importance for
the theory of history. You can best understand it, perhaps, if you
think of various turns of phrase that you will have come across in
your own experience. I am thinking of such phrases as 'the logic of
events', or the phrase used by Franz von Sickingen that I have cited
in earlier lectures. As he lay on his deathbed having been mortally
wounded during a siege – something of a professional hazard for a
condottiere – he is said to have remarked, 'Nought without cause'.[11]
The belief that all things are proper and above board, that events can
be understood step by step, that even the worst and most meaningless
suffering can be comprehended as the product of overall circumstances – this and this alone is what we are to understand as the
world spirit of which Hegel spoke. And I can add right away that we
should put a large question mark here about whether this world spirit
is truly a world spirit, or rather its exact opposite. At any rate, all
facts are transmitted by virtue of the primacy of this process in which
things happen over people's heads and through them. Or, more precisely, what characterizes this primacy is that events assert themselves
over people's heads because they assert themselves *in* people's minds
themselves. And this primacy takes precedence over the facts; it is no

mere epiphenomenon. You can see this from the fact that it is mere chance whether someone who has his house searched in a totalitarian regime, as I did, escapes with his life or is killed. In contrast, the trend that ensures that people's houses are searched, that people live in constant fear and that they are unable to discover whether or not they will be caught up in such events, we might go so far as to say this random element, is *not* itself random. It is part of the objective tendency of which I have been speaking. It is this situation that we need to be able to penetrate, and to succeed in penetrating such mysteries is the truth of what is so frequently vilified as the metaphysics of history. At the same time, and this is something we need to bear in mind as well – I have already pointed this out, but would like to repeat it – such things are *impenetrable* because human beings are not, *pace* Hegel, *at home with themselves* [*dabei*]; because the meaning that history has as the logic of events is not the meaning of individual destinies. On the contrary, the meaning of history always comes across to the individual as something blind, heteronomous and potentially destructive. And this unity of the to-be-penetrated and the impenetrable, or, if I may express it differently, the unity of unity and discontinuity, is in fact the problem of the philosophy of history and how to theorize it.

LECTURE 4

19 November 1964

THE CONCEPT OF MEDIATION

Ladies and gentlemen, you will have noticed that the explanation I have given you of the nature of the history of philosophy has taken a somewhat paradoxical form – the paradox is that the kind of speculative thought of which positivism has accused the philosophy of history has become a kind of necessity. This is because the facts that have been advanced as a counterweight to mere illusion have themselves become a sort of cloak and so reinforce the impression of mere illusion. In the last lecture I gave you the necessary qualifications about this in my apologia for immediacy. But I should now like to give you a more detailed explanation of the view I put forward then so as to provide you with an immanent critique of positivism, that is to say, a critique of positivism on positivist assumptions. By this I mean the attempt to comprehend what is actually essential while rejecting or restricting the concept of the fact itself. Above all, I should like to make the concept of facts more concrete, for once you decide to reject the customary distinction between the so-called universal structures treated by philosophy and the concrete historical event, you commit yourself to an obligation to enter into the spirit of these events. Hegel honoured this obligation in exemplary fashion, and if I am unable to follow in his footsteps that is because I have to communicate certain fundamental ideas, not because I am lapsing into idealism as far as the form of thought is concerned, while disputing it in terms of its content. So the fact that facts become a mere cloak is itself a function of the growing power of the totality which imperceptibly reduces the facts to epiphenomena. By this I mean that the more a true dialectic between the universal and the particular is reduced in the world we live in today, and the more the particular is defined as a mere object belonging to the universal without being able to affect it reciprocally, then the more the so-called facts become a mere cloak veiling what really exists. And by facts here I mean the individual both in his understanding of himself and in his effect on another mind. In this context, I may perhaps refer you to my essay 'Titles', in volume 2 of the *Notes to Literature*,[1] where I discuss this demotion of the concrete to mere illusion as compared with the universal. This will spare me the necessity of expounding the idea as fully as it doubtless deserves. And if you do look it up, it will leave me with the space to do rather more justice to the subject matter of these lectures if I need to mention only those matters that I have not discussed elsewhere and if I can refer you to already existing publications that can reinforce what I have to say here. This is the only reason I am doing it and not because I think it essential for you to have read every sentence I have written. Someone like Karl Kraus could justifiably make such a demand, but it would be sheer arrogance for me to do likewise. So what I think is that only speculation which can penetrate external reality, and show what really and truly lies behind the façade of facticity that is asserting itself, can be said to do justice to reality, to use a phrase originating in psychoanalysis. The only way to capture reality and the true experience of it is to go beyond the immediate givens of experience. In this sense we can say that speculation remains an aspect of experience.

I shall explain this to you as follows. If you have ever had to serve on committees on whom important decisions depend, or are thought to depend, you will see how the worst and the basest instincts prevail over the better, more humane ones. I should perhaps say that you will perceive this unless you completely identify with what is going on and subscribe to its principles. This is a basic experience, even though you will not see a simple confrontation between the 'best' and the 'worst', but rather an infinitely nuanced chain of individual decisions, proposals and processes that focus initially at least on topics that seem utterly remote from such global judgements. Nevertheless, in questions involving individuals there is an overwhelming tendency not so much for the worse speech to triumph over the better one, but for the worse man to be appointed to the position that should have gone to the better one – and this is a common experience that has to be faced up to as frankly as any other experience. And only a concept of experience that is restricted in advance will enable you to avert your gaze from such events by focusing on the immediate matters under discussion. Needless to say, it is not helpful to dwell on such experiences. We have to go beyond them and ask how we can persuade others and ourselves that such things really do happen and that you yourselves will have seen them happen once you have disabused yourselves of the illusions attendant upon such processes. And if you have not experienced such things already because you have had the good fortune not to serve on any committees, then I fear I shall have to disillusion you because I predict that one day you will all remember my words on this subject, unless you succeed in repressing them – something I should like very much to prevent.[2] To explain this further I should like to bring to your attention a number of concrete considerations. In the first place, the better course of action is in general the more productive one, the more innovative one, the course of action that does not fit in with established opinion, to say nothing of established group opinion. As such it is suspect from the outset, particularly where there are groups and a more or less settled consensus. The resistance of the better way to a conformist view is almost always compromised by the fact that it appears to contravene some pre-existing rule or other. Take the example of a young scholar whose promotion is up for discussion, as they say. If he is really able, if he has opinions of his own and is not simply a careerist, and if he retains his intellectual independence from what-ever happens to him – then, when he comes to write reviews, he will not write that this or that book is a valuable contribution to a par-ticular branch of learning, as is almost universally the case in the current critical anarchy. Instead, he will decline to mince his words when criticism is warranted and he will not shrink from saying that a dull, unintelligent book is dull and unintelligent. This will instantly expose him to the rebuke that his polemical tone is improper, that it is incompatible with the academic tradition and God knows what else. And in committees such objections will generally find a willing ear; anyone who behaves in such a deviant manner will have com-promised himself by the mere form of his deviation. Those of you who are doing your teaching practice and take part in staff meetings will have plenty of stories of your own to confirm what I have been saying. A further factor is that, for reasons I cannot go into now, anyone who deviates from the consensus is not only in a superior position to what he opposes, but also in an inferior one in certain respects. This is partly because the support structures for a lone opponent are always more flimsy than for the compact majority. I have given a very circumstantial account of this in my *Introduction to the Sociology of Music*,[3] where I analyse what is thought of as official musical life, but I believe that what I am talking about is a very widespread phenomenon.

Perhaps I may insert here a few words about methodology. In formal terms, these remarks may remind you a little of what is generally thought of as formal sociology. You will find similar discussions in certain works by Georg Simmel, such as *The Philosophy of Money*[4] or the so-called great *Sociology*.[5] The only difference is that when I make such sociological points they only appear to be formal in nature. The social structures I am referring to are indeed phenomena with formal characteristics, but if one were to look a little deeper, certain social realities would come into view, such as the fact that ideas are being controlled by the socially dominant groups in power at any given time. Formal sociology and, by the same token, the formal structure of history are legitimate because they seem to operate with formal categories that remain constant and are continually encountered regardless of their social content. In reality, however, these formal categories are filled with a sedimented content that conceals the dominant relations and the dominance of the universal that forms the subject of our reflections on the philosophy of history. To return to the question of nonconformists, people who want things to continue as they are and who resist the introduction of alternatives are incredibly sensitive to this weakness in the advocates of change. The voices of the majority are no more than the echo of current opinion, and when they lean back in their chairs and give vent to what they imagine to be their own ideas, they merely reproduce the bleating of the many. I think that you cannot picture vividly enough just how sensitive such people are to any signs of difference – and that is what is such a matter of concern in what I am telling you. So here you have an example of the way in which the universal succeeds in getting its own way. The situation is that, when such touchy matters are at stake as those we are discussing at this moment, individuals may act unconsciously as *zoon politikon*, as social beings, as the organs of social control, but as the functionaries of universal opinion they will evince a degree of intelligence that I sometimes think is astronomically greater than anything the individual can muster. The consequence is that anyone who desires change is always in the wrong vis-à-vis the concentrated intelligence of the collective. I must emphasize that in this situation we are not talking about a lack of good will in those who resist improvements, or not necessarily so. Rather, we can really perceive here something of the objectivity on which Hegel insists so emphatically in opposition to the merely subjective mind. Subjectively, they almost always act with the best of intentions – 'almost always' may be a little optimistic. Perhaps I should say that subjectively they frequently act with the best of intentions, or they rationalize their intentions by arguing that they are acting only in the interests of the institution or the collective which they happen to represent at that moment. Intrigues then regularly put in an appearance, and that too seems to be an obligatory feature, but they can be thought of as an extra over and above the negative world spirit that is asserting itself. An example of this can be seen in the victory of fascism, which really was part of the objective trend in 1933, but which could be said to have been reinforced or promoted by a backstairs conspiracy in the house of a Cologne banker.[6] It would be rewarding for such a formal philosophy of history or sociology, albeit of a slightly different kind than is to be found in the textbooks, to explore further this additional role of what might be called a specious individuation which appropriates the objective disaster for its own advantage and reinforces it. Circumstances like these cannot be reduced to the totality of their various mediations, and in that sense they can never be made fully transparent, as indeed I am suggesting to you. I believe that you can clarify them for yourselves to a certain extent by reflecting that groups of the kind I have been discussing are reflections of the totality, of the universe. This is a theme that my former pupil Mangold has argued very persuasively in his volume on group discussions.[7] In other words, conflict situations inevitably lead to acquiescence in the opinions of the group, and in such committees or 'restricted groups' this acquiescence involves translating the general process of social adaptation into the specific situation. This is not to assert that these general processes of adaptation are no more than a symphony of such concrete group adaptations – that would be a far too innocent interpretation of the situation. In fact the reverse is the case. In reality the driving impetus, the thing that actually acts, is a far larger, more anonymous force. It consists of the dominant attitudes of society as a whole, attitudes that are difficult to grasp hold of but which unconsciously determine and give shape to group opinions and to which the group then adapts itself. These committees I have been speaking of are typical examples of such group opinions, but I could give you countless others. We may say, then, that global social relations reproduce themselves here at the micro-level, in the way in which deviants and nonconformists relate to the committees or groups with which they come into conflict. That is the situation, rather than the opposite scenario in which the totality of these groups are what comprise society as a whole. In the same way, the ideologies that are advocated in such groups and provide the basis for the phenomenon I have tried to explain to you are not confined to these groups. They are framed in such universal terms and possess such an abstract generality in comparison to the plethora of group opinions that this fact alone makes it implausible that the universe of group opinion, or public opinion, should emerge as a synthesis of the concrete attitudes of the group.

I hope now that I have been able to give you a more easily comprehensible idea of what I have called the prevailing universal. And I would add that my remarks do not just hold good for questions involving personnel, but are relevant to much more far-reaching decisions, economic decisions, for example, in the most influential controlling committees. I should now like to try and explain more concretely the complex issues involved in mediating between the universal and the particular, a question I have discussed up to now only on the level of the universal. Perhaps I can illustrate this with reference to a historical issue, since this might well seem appropriate in discussing a theory of history that sets out to comprehend history and not simply to chronicle it, while at the same time resisting the temptation to impute to history a positive meaning. This contradiction as I have now once again formulated it is actually – and I would like to remind you of this – what I intend to explore in these lectures, or at any rate in the first part of them, and to do so to the best of my ability. To illustrate what I mean I would like to say something about the French Revolution, the so-called Great French Revolution of 1789, and the problems it presents us with for an understanding of history. The first point to make is that in this revolution the political forms taken by the economic emancipation of the middle class were adapted to the principle of liberalism, by which I mean an uninhibited entrepreneurialism organized into nation-states. This revolution, then, was part of the great process of the emancipation of the middle class, and that in turn dates back, as you all know, to the emancipation of the city-states of the Renaissance. This process continued chiefly in England during the seventeenth century and in France in the eighteenth. I probably have no need to tell you about this process of emancipation, except for the slight reservation I have about the so-called rise of the middle class that is more or less automatically associated with it. The question whether the middle class did in fact rise as a consequence of its increasing power is one that cannot be answered as unambiguously by a critical theory as it is by bourgeois ideology itself. At all events, at the time when the Great French Revolution broke out, the crucial economic levers were already in the hands of the middle class. This means that production was already under the control of the manufacturing and the incipient industrial middle class. At the same time, as was pointed out by Saint-Simon, the great sociologist of the day,[8] the feudal class and the groups associated with it in the absolutist system had ceased almost entirely to have any influence over production in the sense of socially useful labour. This weakness of the absolutist system was the precondition for the outbreak of the revolution, and it will be difficult to deny, particularly in the light of more recent research, that what appeared in the self-glorifying accounts of bourgeois historiography to be an indescribable act of liberation was in reality more like the confirmation of an already existing situation. Nietzsche's dictum in *Zarathustra* that you should give a push to whatever is already falling[9] is a classical bourgeois maxim. That is to say, it contains the idea that bourgeois actions are almost always of the kind that are covered by the dominant universal, by the universal historical principle that is in the process of asserting itself. And this is connected with the fact that, because all bourgeois revolutions merely make official or *de jure* something that already existed *de facto*, they all have an element of illusion, of ideology, about them. This is an insight developed very perceptively for our understanding of the bourgeois freedom movement by Horkheimer in his essay 'Egoism and Freedom Movements', which at long last is soon to be made available again.[10]

On the other hand, what I have called the great process which led to something like the takeover by the middle class in the French Revolution would not have been conceivable without notorious mismanagement by the absolutist rulers of France. I am thinking here of the intractable problems of the budget and the financial crises which physiocrat reformers such as Quesnay – who as you know was close to Turgot – strove in vain to resolve. Without this specific basis in fact, namely the evident inability of the absolutist regime to align its own understanding of the economy with the current state of the forces of production, things would never have reached the point of revolt, let alone the mass uprisings of the initial phase. During those first critical years the genuine sufferings of the quasi-proletarian urban masses of Paris were the precondition for the revolutionary movement. And to a certain degree these masses spontaneously sustained that movement and contributed to the increasing radicalization of what was essentially a middle-class phenomenon. That such a negative factor was a necessary precondition can also be seen from the contrast with other countries in the same period where bourgeois, liberal and national tendencies established themselves, but without provoking a revolutionary uprising. We may even say that comparable trends made their appearance in Germany during the following decades, despite its economic backwardness. Moreover, similar tendencies can be observed in our own day in the way in which the

non-totalitarian nations have come to adopt some of the structural
forms of the administered world. I do not wish to sound pompous,
but the vulgar distinction between the underlying cause [*Ursache*]
and the proximate cause [*Anlaß*], a distinction which may be familiar
to you from school, may, fatuous though it may seem, have something
to do with the difference between the objective process and the specific condition that triggers it. An underlying cause is the element that
is crystallized in the global social process that tends to take over
everything else. This tendency to annex everything, even where the
individual components seem to diverge or to have nothing in common
with the overall process, is a phenomenon that can be observed even
today – and that is a contribution that empirical sociology can make
to the philosophy of history. It is quite certain that the bombing of
German cities during the last war was in no sense intended to con-
tribute to slum clearance,[11] the 'Americanization' of the city or other
sanitation measures. In its effects, however – no doubt because they
were more inflammable the older, in part medieval town centres could
be more easily destroyed – the bombing did result in that growing
similarity of German towns to American ones. This is all the more
striking because we cannot assume that this was part of any so-called
historical trend. Or, to take another example, it has been observed
and much has been made of the fact that the so-called refugee families
have resisted the general tendencies undermining the traditional sta-
bility of the family. In contrast to this, empirical sociology has produced ample evidence that, despite these countervailing tendencies
which emerged towards the end of the war and shortly after it, the
statistics show that the most important elements of that anti-family
trend, namely the increase in the divorce rate and the number of so-
called incomplete families, have continued unabated. It was the
achievement of my colleague Gerhart Baumert, who tragically died
young, to have pointed this out.[12] Thus you may see from these two
examples how the larger trends relate to the so-called immediate
facts. You should bear in mind, however, that so-called proximate
causes [*Anlässe*] such as Louis XVI's bankrupt financial policy represent the element of immediacy without which there could be no
mediation.

Now, ladies and gentlemen, I have just told you that, despite my
attempt to salvage the schoolmasterly distinction between underlying
cause and proximate cause, this distinction, this philosophical distinction, still retains a fatuous element, even if no attempt is made to
account for its significance. I should like to come back to this by
pointing to a third aspect of the French Revolution, one with a
bearing on the relation between underlying cause and proximate

cause, if I may continue to use these terms. No doubt these elements are to be differentiated, but the distinction I have drawn is, and remains, superficial; the two concepts are mediated *in themselves*. More specifically, throughout the whole of history as it is known to us, they are mediated in the sense that the universal, i.e., the underlying cause, takes precedence over the proximate cause. To explain this in more concrete terms: the mismanagement that triggered the French Revolution is not a matter of chance, a contingent fact, independent of the historical process. It was determined by the global situation. In the first instance, it was determined by the structure of a feudal, absolutist order which, if I may borrow terms from Werner Sombart's history of capitalism, and especially his book on the bourgeois,[13] was essentially an economy based on expenditure, rather than one based on acquisitiveness. It was therefore quite unlike capitalism. It follows that the very meaning of that ruling class and the essence of its behaviour was not to manage the economy in the same way that it would have been managed, and indeed was managed at the time by the middle class with which it was in conflict, namely in terms of balance sheets. On the other hand, however, thanks to the economic ascendancy of the middle class that I have told you about, the expenditure system of feudal absolutism was somewhat retrograde even then. It was behind the times when compared to the state of rationalization of the forces of production; when compared to that its mode of management was irrational and was therefore a function of the general trend. What I mean to say is that this particular factor which, like every immediacy, is an indispensable element in triggering the universal, as I explained to you in the last few lectures – this particular factor is itself mediated by the universal which would not exist without it. In this instance, it was mediated by the development of the forces of production in the hands of the middle classes. What this tells us about the theory of history, then, is that, taken in isolation, none of these factors would suffice to give even an approximate explanation of the course of history. In short you need to grasp the complexity of the pattern, by which I mean the overall process that asserts itself, the dependence of that global process on the specific situation, and then again the mediation of the specific situation by the overall process. Furthermore, in addition to understanding this conceptual pattern, you need to press forward to the concrete, historical analysis I have hinted at and that goes beyond the categories I have been discussing.

I should like to conclude for today by reminding you of that celebrated transition from philosophy to historiography that is implicit in Hegel's *Logic* and is explicitly called for in a famous passage in

Marx.[14] In all probability, the key to this transition lies in the fact that this particular configuration of categories, this dependence of the categories of historiography on actual history, is itself so much a question of categories, a conceptual process, that the traditional superficial distinction between essence and mere fact – 'worthless existence', as Hegel once termed it[15] – becomes quite irrelevant. You may regard this also as a very concrete illustration of the thesis that the separation of philosophy from disciplines with a substantive subject matter cannot be sustained for reasons intrinsic to philosophy, for reasons connected with the nature and structure of categories. And this of course brings you onto the terrain of a philosophical turn which I believe will have far-reaching consequences.

LECTURE 5

24 November 1964

THE TOTALITY ON THE ROAD TO SELF-REALIZATION

You will remember that last time I tried to explain the concept of mediation with particular reference to the mediated relations between the universal and the particular in history. I did so with the aid of a brief discussion of the aetiology of the French Revolution. I should now like to add something, a matter of fundamental importance, that I would ask you to take note of as a methodological or principled conclusion from the ideas we have been discussing – on the assumption that this entire line of thought does have some persuasive force in your eyes. What we have seen is that the historical construction of an event actually requires and presupposes the totality of elements, both their distinctiveness and their unity. My discussion of the French Revolution may well have been far too abstract and schematic. But if you follow my train of thought for a moment you will realize that, once you take all the relevant factors into account, the philosophy of history merges with the writing of history. In other words, you can really only do philosophy of history seriously if you enter into the subject matter of history itself with all the nuances and distinctions that we struggled with last time. I recollect that I gave a course of lectures on the philosophy of history some years ago[1] and felt very dissatisfied with it, even while I was giving it. Only later did I understand the cause of my dissatisfaction, and that it arose from the problem I have just described to you. Needless to say, it is quite impossible to tackle any genuine historical topic, even in a very limited way, in the course of these lectures – quite apart from the fact that I am no historian and would be able to make only very limited

comment on historical subjects. But what I can do, and what I have
tried to do, is to disentangle these various concrete factors in order
to show you how intertwined they are. I have tried to show you how
the philosophy of history, that is, the interpretation of historical
events and the philosophical understanding of these events, not only
presupposes historiography proper, but also moves in the direction
of history-writing in the process of explicating them. I should add
that I make no claim to this discovery; you will find this theory
already anticipated in Hegel. I have described the relevant aspects,
which I refer to as the 'narrative' [*episch*] aspects in part 3 of my
little book on Hegel.[2] As you might expect, there are also passages
in Marx where he explicitly calls for the transition from the philosophy of history to historiography proper.[3] Thus it is important to
realize that the philosophy of history does not fall outside the scope
of historical research, but that the constellation of historical events,
both as a whole and in detail, should regard itself as the philosophy
of history proper. But the converse is also true. By this I mean that
philosophy should have the tendency to become history just as readily
as history should become philosophy. I would like to emphasize the
importance of this in our day, that is, in a situation in which (as I
have repeatedly tried to show you) the world of facts has degenerated
into a cloak, a veil that conceals what is *essentially* real. I may
perhaps remind you of my own studies in music history. They deal
with such topics as the relations between classicism, romanticism and
modernism,[4] and they are intended to make the methodological point
that we must try to overcome the sterile dichotomy between history
and its philosophical interpretation. Those of you who have an
inkling of what the word 'science' [*Wissenschaft*] meant to Hegel –
and indeed to Fichte and Schelling before him – will understand what
I am driving at. I know full well that what I am saying is at odds
both with positivist epistemology and with current trends in the
positivistic knowledge industry, but I am firmly convinced that this
is the only viable approach. This means, then, that a history of literature that is not also philosophical history, in other words, a study
that traces the development of literature in terms of its own conceptual nature, would be entirely nugatory. In this connection, I would
refer you to Walter Benjamin's *Origins of the German Tragic Drama*,
and especially its 'Epistemological Preface', which develops a similar
argument, though from a very different point of view.

   Having noted this by way of a preface, I would like to remind you
that the abstract theorization of history from above is problematic
because it fails to address the specific configurations of historical
processes. I believe that I have given the idea of analysing history

from above its due, that is, the abstraction, the course of history in general, but it is a remarkable fact that if, as an observer of history, you simply go along with the flow of events, this ends up by committing you to giving your approval to whichever universal tendency happens to be gaining the upper hand. If I may again cite Benjamin in this context, you will turn out to be writing history from the point of view of the victors.[5] Perhaps I can put it like this: when Hegel asserts that history is rational, we must not hypostasize the concept of rationality; we must not speak of rationality in itself. Rationality always has a *terminus ad quem*, or, to use a less highfaluting phrase but also in Latin, it has a *cui bono*. This means that history can be called rational only if we know *for whom* it is rational. If rationality, a concept based on an understanding of the self-preservation of the individual, ceases to have a human subject for whom it exists, it will lapse into irrationality. The developments we witness today consist in no small degree of such a reversal of rationality into irrationality arising from the loss of this 'for someone'. To put the situation in a more down-to-earth fashion, this means that the question whether history is in fact rational is a question about how it treats the individuals who have been caught up in the flow of events. We can really talk about the rationality of history only if it succeeds increasingly in satisfying the needs and interests of individuals, whether it be within general historical phases or at least in its general trend. Hegel disagrees with this in principle when he states that the theatre of history is not the theatre of happiness.[6] In so doing, Hegel hypostasizes rationality and falls into the trap of thinking of rationality as the logic of things independently of their *terminus ad quem* in human beings, the very thing he had expressly called for with his realist interpretation of the concept of reason. The rationality, of the universal, then, if it is to be rational at all, cannot be an abstractly self-standing concept, but must consist in the relation of the universal to the particular. Now, as a logician, Hegel is very well aware of this and is even responsible for the extreme statement, as I am sure many of you know, that the universal is only universal in so far as it is the particular – and that the reverse is likewise true.[7]

Thus in a certain sense Hegel's approach is one-sided because he writes his philosophical history from the standpoint of the victor, because he justifies or vindicates the universal as it asserts itself. In so doing, he ends up adopting a class standpoint that obscures the implications of his own principle. Despite the dialectic of universal and particular for which he made such a powerful case, his own theory of history ends up leaning towards the universal. The particular is not given the credit 'in particular' that Hegel ascribes to it 'in general'. If nevertheless we speak of idealism in Hegel, we do not mean just his metaphysical assumptions such as the absolute subject or absolute identity, but rather the fact that the universal, which is always a concept, an idea, contrasted with the particular, ends up lording it over the particular. For all the talk of a dialectic between universal and particular, it is the universal that is declared the true reality. We see here a contradiction, a non-dialectical contradiction, in Hegel's philosophy. On the one hand, he calls for the dialectic of universal and particular and actually carries this through quite magnificently in many respects. But then he fails to take the particular quite so seriously and constantly threatens to go over to the side of the universal – if I may put it that way – so that the consciousness of non-identity which characterizes the particular is stripped of its own substantiality and survives only as suffering, as a consciousness of pain. Instead of concluding that what we have is a state of non-reconciliation, he behaves a little like a senior church official or a judge, at any rate like some high-up bureaucrat or other, who sees only the limited outlook of the lower orders who are unable to recognize the higher meaning in all of this. He is not deterred in this by the consideration that it is unreasonable to ask the victim, the individual who has to put up with the consequences, to find comfort in the circumstance that the irreconcilable principle of the way of the world should govern his own private fate. I should perhaps draw your attention to a methodological point here. Unlike the young Marx in his criticism of *The Philosophy of Right* – and I too have of course chiefly had *The Philosophy of Right* in mind here – the critical point I am making now is intrinsic to Hegel's own argument. That is to say, I am not proposing any yardstick other than to demand that he really follows through with the implications of the dialectic of universal and particular that he has himself proposed. In short, in the belief that he has rightly claimed that this dialectic is the only appropriate method, I wish to judge him according to his own criteria.

Having fired off this broadside at Hegel – military figures of speech tend to spring to mind when speaking of *The Philosophy of Right* – I should now like to add a few words in defence of Hegel. I am sorry if you find it confusing for me to set about obscuring a distinction that I have only just clarified, but it cannot be my task to make difficult and complex matters appear simpler than they are merely from a desire to present everything to you in an easily digestible form. The task of thought is to attempt to present this complexity to you in as precise a way as possible, even when the matter in hand is extremely difficult and complex. To put it in aesthetic terms, my aim is to present what is vague in a conceptually clear shape. The point I wish

to make is that Hegel's mistake or his inconsistency – and my hope
is that by now you will have grasped where the mistake lies – has a
certain justification. Perhaps you will recollect that, as I have suggested several times, the Hegelian programme paradoxically has a
positivist side, in the sense that he tries to 'fit in', that he would like
to adapt himself to the world as it is, and that he assumes the identity
of what exists with the spirit, the whole of idealism in fact. But what
this amounts to in the first instance – and I would ask you to set
aside these admittedly gigantic assumptions for the moment, and the
more gigantic they are, the more it is to be recommended that they
be set aside – is that he quite straightforwardly wishes to be guided
by things as they are, by what he sees before him. Now what makes
the problem so complicated is that the reality is – and this is hopefully
not too stale a conclusion to be drawn from our discussion of the
French Revolution – that the supremacy of the universal, the prepon-
derance of the universal that is then deified by Hegel, does in fact, as
the actual historical power, emerge as the stronger. As long as Hegel
simply theorizes the course of the world as it is by asserting that the
universal takes precedence over the particular, he is, to put it quite
crudely, a realist: this is the way the world is. He proceeds therefore
in the opposite direction to that taken by nominalism. Nominalism
believes that the universal is no more than a conclusion arising from
the countless particularities which are then brought together in a
single concept. And Hegel was incredibly sensitive to this, to what
he calls the course of the world [*der Weltlauf*][8] (I have borrowed his
term here). If anything about him was realistic it was precisely his
responsiveness to this dominance of the universal in the realm of
realities, the so-called facts. The only delusion lies in the way that he
interprets this primacy of the universal, this actual primacy of the
concept, as if it meant the world itself were concept, spirit, and therefore 'good'. Admittedly, he is in tune here with the main current of
Western philosophy in which, ever since Plato, the universal, the
necessary, unity and the good are all identified with one another.
    And here I have reached the point where it becomes clear that,
even though they are highly innovative, Hegel's philosophy of history
and his construction of dialectics really belong to traditional theory;
they remain imprisoned in a Platonic framework. Once reason – and
this is the counter-position I am attempting to present to you in these
lectures – once reason has lost its relation to the individuals who
are concerned with self-preservation, it degenerates into unreason.
And this reversal takes place objectively in Hegel, but it is not a
change that the Hegelian dialectic has made explicit. Moreover,
this is an idealist tendency that goes far beyond Hegel himself. The

identification with the universal enters deeply into the fibre of Marxism notwithstanding the much cruder epistemological positions of Marx and the Marxists. For there you find something like the belief that, when ultimately the universal takes over and the concept is victorious, individuals will indeed come into their own – and this factor will ensure that all the suffering and the wasted individuality of history will somehow be made good. This is an issue that to the best of my knowledge was first commented on critically by Ivan Turgenev in the nineteenth century. Turgenev maintained that even the prospect of a completely classless society could not console him for the fate of all those who had suffered to no purpose and had fallen by the wayside.[9] I have already said that when the concept of reason becomes abstract, when it becomes separated from individual interests craving fulfilment, it turns into unreason. However, you should try not to think of this change as pointing to the decadence of philosophy, of the philosophy of history, because here too there is 'nought without cause', and it is a process with deep underlying causes. In all probability we shall only be armed intellectually, philosophically, to withstand this tendency if we think of this not as a corrigible error but as a necessity. For the fact is that a genuine reality underlies Hegel's defence of that absolute reason that comes to understand itself. We might say that his hypostasization is the hypostasization of mankind as a species. It is the species that maintains itself as a whole as against the claims of individuals who are concerned with preserving themselves. For the principle of self-preservation is itself irrational and particular if it is restricted to individuals, to the particular individual rationality of individuals. The great bourgeois thinkers from Hobbes to Kant have always taken care to point this out – I mention these two names in particular because it shows you very clearly the beginning and the end point of this idea. It is therefore part of the logic of the self-preservation of the individual that it should be extended to embrace the conception of the self-preservation of the species. But that is also the problem. It is not a problem I would claim to be able to solve for you, but I should at least like to make you aware of it, since it seems to me to be a matter of extraordinary difficulty and gravity. It consists in this: because the self-preserving reason of the individual is converted into the self-preservation of the species, there is an intrinsic temptation for this universality to emancipate itself from the individuals it comprises. Kant himself had noted in his 'Theory of Right' that the universal freedom of all should have restrictions placed on it in so far as it called for the freedom of each individual from every other.[10] Thus, the idea of species-reason, that is, the form of reason that comes to prevail universally, already contains, by virtue of its universality, an element restricting the individual; and in certain circumstances this element can develop in such a way as to turn into an injustice on the part of the universal towards the particular, and hence in turn to the predominance of particularity. Thus, on the one side, reason can liberate itself from the particularity of obdurate particular interest but, on the other side, fail to free itself from the no less obdurate particular interest of the totality. How this problem is to be resolved is a conundrum that philosophy has failed to answer hitherto. Even worse, it is a problem which the organization of the human race has also failed to solve. It is for this reason that I do not think I am exaggerating when I say that it is a problem of the greatest possible gravity. This is probably connected with the fact that the concept of the species automatically involves the idea of the domination of nature. And this means, if I may borrow an expression from my friend Horkheimer, that the constitution of humanity as a species amounts to a gigantic public company for the exploitation of nature, without involving much alteration in the idea of particularity. In all probability, we would have to reflect far more deeply about the principle underlying reason, namely the principle of self-preservation, if we are to make much progress beyond the simple idea of gathering everything up in the notion of species. We may add a further point regarding that quite logical and consistent perversion of universality which involves the idea of the whole as opposed to the particular, while simultaneously converting the whole into a particular. We may point out that this perverse conclusion is what triumphed in fascist race theory according to which this universality was twisted into a natural relation, naturalized and thereby turned into a particular. Then, like all particulars, this one became increasingly intolerant of *other* particulars, choosing instead to beat the life out of them whenever possible. This will perhaps explain to you why the dialectic of reason or the dialectic of Enlightenment is a matter of such profound importance in history, so much so that we must conclude – and I perhaps exaggerate in order to make the point – that, in the historical form in which we encounter it to this day, reason is both reason *and* unreason in one.

The concept of the primacy of reason contains the idea that reason has the task of taming, suppressing, ordering and governing whatever is unreasonable, instead of absorbing it into itself in a spirit of reconciliation. Thus this notion of reason as domination is inherent in the concept of reason from its inception and the idea of conflict is implicit in it from the outset. Accordingly, we should not be too surprised if conflict continues to reproduce itself through reason; that is, if reason continues to flip over into unreason. The more powerful the world spirit is (and it has never been as powerful as it is today, when we have all been reduced to the status of its agents), the more powerful the world spirit is, the more we are justified in doubting whether the world spirit really is the world spirit, rather than its opposite. This leads us to conclude that the primacy of the totality in history represents anything but the victory of the Idea. We can formulate it like that or, alternatively, we might say – as I have already indicated – that the world spirit *exists* as the universal that comes to prevail; but that it is *no* world spirit, that it is not *spirit*, but that for the most part it is the negativity that Hegel had shifted from the universal to its victims, to what he refers to as 'worthless existence', to mere individuality.[11] We can find evidence in the great philosophies of spirit to support our belief in the dubious nature of the concept of spirit at the very point where it becomes so inflated that it identifies itself with the totality, where it lays claim to the totality. The evidence is so powerful that I would like to commend it to you. Far from encouraging, requiring and stimulating spirit to become a real force in the world, this philosophy of absolute spirit displays an almost universal tendency to discourage everything one might think of as spirit in a concrete sense, namely the ability of individuals to reflect, to understand and to criticize. This tendency started as far back as Kant, in whose writings the idea was first postulated. This disparaging view of the individual consciousness can be found in countless passages in Kant, for example, where he defends the categorical imperative against individual critical voices.[12] You will also have seen the same tendency at work in Hegel's diatribes against reformers and 'intellectuals' [*Räsoneure*]. You will find it in all the passages where he makes short work *a priori* of all criticism, that is, every concrete expression of what could be thought of as spirit, in the name of an allegedly higher conception of spirit – without its even occurring to him for a moment that this allegedly higher conception of spirit still has to prove its worth before the tribunal of the actual, living spirit of mankind. Furthermore, you will also find in Hegel that appalling academic rancour towards anything clever and witty [*das Geistreiche*] – in other words, towards those who know how to write. Later on, during the decline of German universities, this became the veritable signature of the spirit of so-called science, the so-called human sciences. So when we hear what Hegel had to say about certain representatives of the Enlightenment who, like Diderot, for example, were just too clever, it is altogether too painful to read.[13] We are thus contemplating a philosophy that on the one hand elevates itself to the plane of the absolute, while on the other shows signs of nerves as soon as it encounters a clever and witty thinker. Such a philosophy renders itself highly suspect. It may be that a well-informed Hegelian (incidentally, I think of myself as being fairly well informed about Hegel) will riposte that the spirit that Hegel was talking about and the spirit that Diderot really had are two very different things. But I would reply to any such well-informed person that the two things are not so different as all that. For if all links are broken between the living, critical spirit of the individual whose mind penetrates reality and the absolute spirit which is said to be in the process of realizing itself, between spirit as imagination, as a constructive and perspicacious faculty, *and* spirit as the world spirit that is coming to prevail objectively in the world – then spirit will rightly come under suspicion of turning into the ideology of its own absence. It will be comparable to that bourgeois tendency (or indeed that of class society as such) to elevate women into an object of worship, to speak of women as the Eternal Feminine that draws us onward[14] or, as does Schiller, as creatures who 'plait and weave'[15] in God's name, but at the same time to treat women in reality as minors and to hold them in permanent subjection. And this analogy between the role of spirit and that of women is not as arbitrary and formal as may appear at first sight.

The transfiguration of spirit, however – and I am trying to be as fair-minded as possible – the transfiguration of spirit about which I have now told you enough compromising things, this transfiguration of the *totality*, was only possible because the human race in fact can only survive in and through the totality. The only reason why the optimism of the philosophy of absolute spirit is not a mere mockery is because the essence of all the self-preserving acts that culminate in this supreme concept of reason as absolute self-preservation is after all the means by which humanity has managed to survive and still continues to do so. And it has succeeded in doing so despite all the suffering, the terrible grinding of the machinery and the sacrifices of what Marx would have called the forces and means of production. The infinite weak point of every critical position (and I would like to tell you that I include my own here) is that, when confronted with such criticism, Hegel simply has the more powerful argument. This is because there is no other world than the one in which we live, or at least we have no reliable knowledge of any alternative despite all our radar screens and giant radio telescopes. So that we shall always be told: everything you are, everything you have, you owe, we owe to this odious totality, even though we cannot deny that it is an odious and abhorrent totality. I believe that you can only understand the violence inherent in this view of history as a self-realizing totality if you understand that its truth, its almost irresistible truth, lies in the

fact that life and with it the possibility of happiness, and indeed even
the possibility of a differently constituted world, would be inconceivable without all the things that can be urged by way of objection to
it – its failings towards the individual, and all its senseless suffering
and cruelty. And I would say that if you wish to go beyond seeing
the theory of history as absolute spirit as more than a complementary
ideology, more than a piece of justification of the kind that I believe
I have been able to show you without any whitewashing, then you
will very definitely have to include this factor that I have just been
outlining to you. But I should like to say a few more words on this
subject next time.

LECTURE 6

26 November 1964

CONFLICT AND SURVIVAL

I have tried to show you something of the negative aspects of the universal as it asserts itself, both as an actual historical process and, if I may put it like this, in terms of its logical structure. I then went on – I say this so that you can see more or less where we are in these discussions – to show you what might be called the legal title underlying the affirmative construction of history as we find it both in Hegel's *Logic* and *The Phenomenology of Spirit*, on the one hand, and in his *Philosophy of History*, on the other. In the process I have emphasized that the 'course of the world' – to use Hegel's own expression once again[1] – does in fact possess a positive side, since it reproduces the life of the totality as a species. It achieves this by joining mankind together in societies, that is, in a totality. I have already talked enough about the lethal entanglement involved in this totality, and you will rightly ask me to comment on the relation between these two aspects. For it is strange that, on the one hand, the totality should oppress everything that is beneath it and, potentially at least, threaten it with destruction, while, on the other hand, it is a cohesive force to which society owes its survival. In this connection let me add that you will find that Marx too approves of this affirmation of the coming together of mankind as well as the idea that mankind reproduces itself notwithstanding its sacrifices and sufferings. And if we may look for an element of idealism in Marx, an idealist element in the precise philosophical meaning of the word, this would certainly be the place to find the truly affirmative strand in his thought. It is a strand, moreover, that fits with his predominantly optimistic view of history. The form this Hegelian theme takes in Marx is transformed almost out of all recognition, but retains extraordinary power. It is the highly obscure and difficult theory of the so-called law of value.[2] This is the summation of all the social acts taking place through exchange. It is through this process that society maintains itself and, according to Marx, continues to reproduce itself and expand despite all the catastrophes that may eventuate. I now believe that you are in a position to appreciate the difficulty of this question, which we can describe as the central question of any theory of the philosophy of history. But you can only do so if you take a further dialectical step beyond what I have already told you. Because if we look at the situation with the eyes of common sense, and indeed in accordance with what I have told you so far, it appears as though society is riddled with conflict and hence is irrational through and through, but that it nevertheless contrives to survive, though quite how, no one knows. It is very much in the spirit of the famous formula of the invisible hand, the empirical maxim which summed up the English approach to history until the process of integration made it impossible to encapsulate society in a single concept.

In my view, the crucial contribution to a theory of history is to be found in the idea that mankind preserves itself not despite all the irrationalities and conflicts, but *by virtue of* them. This idea, incidentally, was espoused at least twice before Hegel by the great bourgeois philosophers themselves. We find it first in Hobbes, in whose writings integration and the social contract are brought into being by the plight of individuals who are unable to survive in its absence.[3] It emerges once more in Kant, in his essay on the philosophy of history that I mentioned to you at the start of these lectures and that you ought all to read if you really wish to understand the concrete context, the philosophical horizon, of the problems I am explaining to you. I'll give you the title of Kant's essay once again; it is the 'Idea for a Universal History with a Cosmopolitan Purpose'. So what I wish to say is that society, the totality, does not simply survive *despite* conflict, but because of it. You will best be able to understand this perhaps if you reflect that in the developed bourgeois society all life is dominated by the principle of exchange and, at the same time, by the necessity – which is imposed on the many individuals – of securing for oneself as large a portion as possible of the social product in the course of this struggle of all against all. But, and this is something that was understood quite clearly by the old liberal theory of Adam Smith and David Ricardo, thanks to this antagonism, thanks to this conflict of interests, the machinery of society does in fact succeed in maintaining itself. This is to be understood in the sense that use values are produced not to satisfy human needs but for profit. I do not wish to involve myself in lengthy explanations of Marxist theory and so will just say that by use values I mean the satisfaction of needs, either natural needs or, as is almost universally the case, needs as mediated historically. The only reason why goods are produced is so that the producers, by which I mean those who control the means of production, should be able as a class to profit from them as much as possible. This of course is what sets up the principle of conflict: between those who pocket the proceeds and those from whom the profit is made in the final analysis, and who therefore miss out on it. But the life of human beings is reproduced only by going through this process which contains the conflict, the class relationship, within itself. Down to the present day life has succeeded in perpetuating itself only because of this division in society, because a number of people in control confront others who have been separated from the means of production. And given this reality, the needs of human beings, the satisfaction of human beings, is never more than a sideshow and in great measure no more than ideology. If it is said that everything exists only for human beings, it sounds hollow because in reality production is for profit and people are planned in as consumers from the outset. In short, it sounds hollow because of this built-in conflict.

If it is now asserted that this fact and this entire argument is all wrong and superfluous, that life would go on without it, the Hegels and, to some extent, as far as the construction of the past is concerned, even the Marxes and Engels will retort: the *possibility*, the world as we might imagine it, that is all very fine, but this is the *reality*. . . . Without that reality, that is to say, the reality of a class society that stands as the very principle of bourgeois society, there would have been neither the huge population increase that we have seen, nor the growth in transport, nor would there ever have been anything like enough by way of food supplies for the population. It will not have escaped your attention that the starting-point of a critique of this entire way of seeing is the idea (one that Hegel pursued with especial rigour right on into the heart of his *Logic*) that from the outset reality is given precedence over possibility. And of course, it is here that we see that unquestioned *parti pris* for the prevailing universal of which I have already spoken at some length. To recapitulate, then, the fact is that mankind has survived not just in spite of but because of conflict, and this fact has such weighty consequences for the theory of history because Hegel has inferred from it with a very great semblance of justice, a semblance of justice that cannot be dismissed out of hand, that categorically, in terms of the idea, when looked at from above, life can be reproduced *only* by virtue of conflict. And this has resulted in what might be termed the theodicy of conflict. Thus it may be claimed that Hegel's *Logic* amounts to the assertion that the world spirit or the absolute is the quintessence of all finite, ephemeral forms of conflict, of all negativities; the positive is the quintessence of all negativities. If that be so, then this thesis which at first sight may seem utterly arrogant and preposterous may be seen to have its foundation in the fact that the world has survived precisely because of this negativity, in other words, because society has been essentially conflict-ridden down to this very day. We can trace this tradition of conflict back to the most abstract ideas of unity, totality and even reason, and this is something I shall return to. This is why it is so vital for us to understand it. And this may enable you to see why the idealist form of dialectics was not so completely unworldly as all that, but that within the general process of idealization it also expressed something real that the theory of history cannot afford to ignore. At the same time, the moment this realistic element is accepted it becomes an affirmation that simply reinforces the negative, destructive side of society.

Now it is an open question – and one that I shall make no attempt to answer today – whether or not the human race could only have been perpetuated by means of conflict, whether conflict was historically an absolute necessity. In other words, does it make any sense at all to conceive of a course of history that does not involve this conflict? The most powerful evidence that things could not have been otherwise is to be seen in mankind's commerce with physical nature. For nature began by inserting humanity into a situation of lack, where people had too little, and it was only with the aid of those particular forms of organization that it was possible to cope with this situation. They could not have done so without the relations of domination that forced people to come to terms with shortages and to make them good. This was the factor that made conflict inevitable. Marx and Engels (and especially Engels, who devoted a lot of attention to this matter) gave the problem a highly idealist turn by providing a positive answer to the question of what we can only call the metaphysical necessity, the absolute necessity of conflict in the course of history. This takes a specific form in Marx and Engels, in particular in the argument they advanced very emphatically that domination, social domination, was a function of the economy, in other words, of the life process, the reproduction of life itself, and not the other way around. It will surprise you to hear that I have picked out this argument among all others to call idealist, but I believe that a very little reflection will show you just how idealist it is. For if history derives its antagonistic character from the economy from the outset, that is to say, from the need for life to preserve itself, then, at least in retrospect, social conflict is in a sense as legitimate as historical negativity is in Hegel's metaphysical logic. If, on the other hand, economic conditions and economic conflicts were themselves the product of a fundamental form of domination, then their necessity would be extraneous to the historical totality, the life process of society. They would be mere accidents, things that could easily be dismissed as inessential in principle.

Now, ladies and gentlemen, it is hardly possible to reconstruct the primitive conditions that form the object of this dispute. If there are any ethnologists and anthropologists among you, you will know how your disciplines have brought an infinitely complex body of knowledge to bear on these questions, to the point indeed where simple answers have to be ruled out. For example, I may remind you of all the research that has led scholars to derive the original structures of society neither from power relations nor from economic conditions, but instead from magical and religious practices. Admittedly, we must add that such explanations leave the question of the relationship between those practices and the nature of society open, and so far as I can see, unanswered. The chief sources of these controversies, by the way, are Engels's *Anti-Dühring* and his *The Origin of the Family*.[4] You can also find a lot of important material in Marx, in the great preface to the *Critique of Political Economy*, which is one of the – what should I call it? – chief theoretical sources for dialectical materialism.[5] What moved them to grapple with this prehistorical problem which must always remain something of a puzzle was certainly not to provide a realistic picture of primitive society – and, in general, the question of how things were in the beginning is a matter of indifference when seeking a solution to the pressing social problems of the present. It is merely one of the shibboleths of the traditional philosophy of history that I would invite you to think about critically. The fact is that people tend to regard what is older and pristine as somehow better because it comes from the inner nature of man, whereas any casual glance at the wretched existence of primitive peoples who have survived but who still live in Stone Age conditions ought to persuade us to abandon every such idealization of primeval society once and for all. But, as I have said, the interest of Marx and Engels in this question, which may appear somewhat pointless to you, was really quite different. The reason why they placed such enormous weight on the idea that the origins of conflict are to be found in the economy and in the historically necessary structure of human relations of production, rather than in power relations, was that otherwise their own point of view might have led them to believe that, in analogy to those mythical and legendary conditions of primitive society, it would only have been necessary to alter the existing power relations to bring about a rational society, without taking economic conditions into account. Thus the interest in such questions is not in the nature of origins, despite what the title of Engels's book might lead us to suppose, but in highly topical political issues. This becomes clear if you look closely at the debates between a strictly economics-based communism as taught by Marx and Engels and anarchism, which at that time was an extremely important competitor (if I can put it in such vulgar terms). Anarchism was highly influential, particularly in its impact on the masses and in many different countries such as Spain and Italy, and has remained influential right down to the threshold of our own age. So whoever regards power relations as primary and who therefore wished to alter those relations would be driven automatically to the anarchist side in this debate, whereas the socialists wanted to bring about changes in the economy. The changes they wished to introduce all lay in the direction taken by the economy itself, that is to say, in the direction of increasing rationalization, planning and the concentration of the economy.

I should like to take this opportunity to tell you that if you are seriously interested in socialist writings on the philosophy of history you will not be able to comprehend them properly if you treat them as a kind of contemplative theorizing about history, understandable as this would be, looking at them from our own situation. In this respect they differ from the reflections on the philosophy of history that I have been presenting you with. There is a structural distinction here whose importance cannot be overestimated. The driving motif of the socialist way of thinking about history was the idea that the revolution is just around the corner, that it can break out at any moment and that therefore everything, the entire construction of history included, should be interpreted retrospectively in terms of the requirements of the impending revolutionary situation. And since these thinkers were convinced, and rightly so no doubt, of the profound historical impotence of anarchism, they pursued the traces of anarchist thinking back into the dim and distant past, and they did so with a relentless rigour that makes one shudder, all the more so since we now know how this aspect of socialism later developed. At all events, we cannot simply dismiss the idea that history begins with a catastrophe of some kind, thanks to which this element of domination made its entrance, and this idea is not so very different from the view contemporary psychologists have of primal events that are to be reconstructed on the basis of unconscious memories. If in fact history turns out to be a permanent catastrophe, then we cannot simply reject the conjecture that something terrible must have happened to mankind right at the start, or at the time when mankind was becoming itself, and that this terrible event is like those that have been handed down to us in the myths about original sin and similar stories in which the origins of mankind and the growth of reason are associated with some disaster from the remote past. However, I leave such conjectures to your imagination. At all events, these are the themes that I have been trying to explore today – themes that put any aspiring social critique into such a weak position. Its position is weak not only because existing society can confront any criticism with its own power and glory, but also because it can be pointed out that there could be no *possibility* even of something different and better, that is, of a rationally organized society, without a means–ends rationality with its domination of nature. And it is precisely that means–ends rationality whose world-historical consequence has been all those disasters whose memory has been repressed or eradicated to a simply unimaginable degree by the victorious powers of history. Only an actually achieved identity would lead to the reconciliation of opposing interests – and not simply the comforting thought that the quintessence of all conflicts would, by making life possible, permit something like reconciliation among all mankind, namely their continued existence. And never can reconciliation be the merely asserted reconciliation brought about by the violence towards everything subsumed under it. To sum it up in a rather bolder way, an achieved identity, in other words, the elimination of conflict, the reconciliation of all those who are opposed to one another because their interests are irreconcilable, an achieved identity does not mean the identity of all as subsumed beneath a totality, a concept, an integrated society. A truly achieved identity would have to be the consciousness of *non-identity*, or, more accurately perhaps, it would have to be the creation of a reconciled non-identity, much as we find in the utopia conceived by Hölderlin, though to a degree that has been exaggerated by the current state of research in Hölderlin studies.

This is perhaps the point at which I might usefully say something about the twin concepts of conformism and nonconformism. This pair of concepts is based on our extraordinarily difficult relation to a course of the world to which we owe everything and that yet threatens to bury us all. I believe that in the present intellectual climate in Germany the concept of nonconformism is subject to a degree of defamation. It should be defended against cheap criticism. I regard myself as especially obligated to engage in this defence because many years ago, in a rather different situation, I published a piece in my *Minima Moralia*, which I would not wish to disown and still stand by today, in which I gave a fairly detailed account of the conformism of the nonconformists.[6] It does me no credit – though it probably does no credit to anyone else either – that it was this passage from *Minima Moralia* that was singled out for praise. It is easy to draw a parallel with all those people whose only knowledge of Marx is that he once wrote somewhere that he was no Marxist.[7] However that may be, in the present context, conformism would be either the assertion – not the explicit assertion, but the assertion implied in the objective spirit of the age, in its language, its mental household – that the reconciliation that has not been achieved really *has been achieved* or, on the other hand, to deny the *possibility* of that reconciliation at all. These two ideas – that we already find ourselves living in a utopia, and that no utopia is possible or even desirable and that it should not exist – these two incompatible ideas actually coexist peacefully together. The two together really express the idea that we have been discussing in this lecture, namely that, on the one hand, society only survives because of the conflicts it contains – which is then expressed in the affirmative doctrine that all is right with the world. On the other hand, despite this, people experience the present unreconciled conditions, and this comes to be expressed as a denial of the possibility of reconciliation in general. Needless to say, if you say of an unreconciled situation that reconciliation has taken place, this torpedoes the possibility of a true reconciliation in the future, since it undermines the very people who wish to bring about the very state of affairs that is supposed to exist, and makes them look like fools or rogues. The alleged conformism of the non-conformists, that is to say, the way countless nonconformists seem to display the same stereotyped thinking as you heard described yesterday in the lecture given by my friend Hans-Magnus Enzensberger,[8] who subjected this phenomenon to very incisive and legitimate criticism, criticism that I would wish in no way to soften or qualify – this nonconformist conformism is in great measure only a reaction to the prevailing conformism. By this I mean the general situation which is characterized by compartmentalism, rigid categorization and stereotypes coming from above. It is in general a situation that necessarily rubs off on those who resist it. The overwhelming power of rigid categories, the static, rigid categories of the universal that confront the critical mind, forces the critics to take on something of their rigidity – even if only so as to describe them in the course of asserting their own position. This is to say nothing of the fact that we all live in bourgeois society and therefore – even if we are not conscious of the fact and do not realize just how deeply it has penetrated into the darkest recesses of our souls even when we disagree – we remain the children of the condition that we oppose, and carry endless baggage around with us which we then reproduce, all unbeknown to ourselves. In this sense the nonconformists who are so criticized and derided today and who of course think it a sin to be pinned down to a fixed label or concept – in actual fact we can speak only of conformism; nonconformism is a *contradictio in adjecto* – would be justified in invoking the famous Brechtian plea for forbearance on behalf of nonconformism.[9] From what we might call a kind of perverse gratitude, the prevailing conformism confuses the grinding reproduction of life, which after all keeps us all alive, with the possibility of shaping life in a way that would genuinely be achievable today, given the advanced state of the forces of production and of human rationality. And this confusion is what marks the gap between conformism and nonconformism. Thus it is not a matter of the formal fact of agreement or disagreement with a given state of society. What is crucial is this substantive factor: are you prepared constantly to let your experience be guided by the concrete possibilities available in the present, in every respect, or are you not; that is to say, have you capitulated in favour of worshipping whatever happens to be the case? In comparison with this issue it is hard to make significant distinctions at the level of substance, to separate the sheep from the goats and to say this is conformist and that is nonconformist. I may mention the case of Max Stirner in this context. Subjectively, and in terms of his situation in the immediate social conflicts of his day, he was initially a nonconformist. His own theory, however, the theodicy of absolute individuality, was conformist.[10] This can be contrasted with works of art that refuse to take up any so-called concrete position with regard to current social questions, works that are not what we can call 'committed' (to take up Enzensberger's argument), and from which it is not possible to deduce any immediate forms of action. Such works therefore cannot be described as nonconformist, but from the way they conduct themselves with regard to existing reality they must be described as nonconformist. Such a person is Samuel Beckett, of whom Enzensberger also made mention in his lecture yesterday. Conformism and its opposite, nonconformism, belong to the categories of consciousness or of attitude, subjective categories that are falsified the moment they are isolated, torn from the totality, taken abstractly, independently of the historical moment and the function and constellation of individual motifs in a specific situation. I believe that in general this is something we can learn from dialectics, namely that there is no category, no concept, no theory even, however true, that is immune to the danger of becoming false and even ideological in the constellation that it enters into in practice.

Normally, I am very critical of the entire concept of ideology.[11] But if it has any truth[12] it lies in the suspicion that, precisely because spirit is in general dependent on the course of the world and its constellations, no isolated instance of spirit, no embodiment of spirit that sets out to oppose the course of the world, can be true or false in and for itself – or, rather, independently of its relation to that reality.

LECTURE 7

1 December 1964

SPIRIT AND THE COURSE OF THE WORLD

Last time, during my discussion of the dialectics of the universal and the particular, I took the opportunity to say a few words about the concept of conformism, more especially about the currently fashionable ways of dealing with it. In the light of our basic theme, the antithesis of society and the individual, the universal and the particular, it will have become clear to you just how difficult it is to pin down the idea of conformism to fixed categories. If you analyse the conformist elements in Hegel – there is no great problem involved in this – if you read the *Philosophy of Right* and take note of the conformist elements in it, you will soon see that his sympathies always lean towards the universal, and that the individual is fobbed off with the assurance that the universal, the absolute, the Idea, maintains itself by destroying him – an assertion that does nothing to restore his peace of mind. It reminds him of the consolation offered by the church to a man contemplating his own death, but thanks to secularization is incomparably feebler and less persuasive than the promises given by the church in times gone by when a dying man could be promised eternal salvation, whereas now the idea of eternal salvation is no more than a shape of consciousness. This shape of consciousness is of course essential and does provide the individual with a salvation of sorts, but you learn nothing of its substantive meaning from Hegel, while the individual is in fact supposed to be pleased if he or she dissolves into nothing *ad majorem dei gloriam*. Incidentally, categories generally become diluted to the point of absurdity in the course of secularization and this strengthens the tendency to rebel against the entire process. On the other hand, it is true in our day, as also in the 1920s, that conformism has insisted on the importance of the individual, a concept that had been inflated during the nineteenth century at the expense of all others. Now, in a situation such as existed then, in which socialism appeared to be an imminent possibility and in which the tendency of the communist state in Russia to repress the individual had just begun to make itself felt, the concept of the individual began to play a significant role as a reaction to socialism, in other words, in defence of existing society. This was the idea of the precious, immortal individual which was now in jeopardy, but which had played a similar role at other times, namely, during periods of the untrammelled, unrestrained ascendancy of the individual, such as the Romantic age in which Hegel had lived. In such times too the individual had assumed a conformist function. What I wanted to show you, and the real reason why I have introduced the concept of conformism, is not only to immunize you against a kind of formalistic thinking that asserts that, all right then, there is a conformism from a spirit of opposition as well as a conformism of the conformists – it's all as broad as it's long. That is an indescribably superficial way of thinking and my hope is that I will have put you off it for ever. But even more importantly, I should like to show you that categories may be subject to radically different interpretations within the dialectics of the universal and particular. This means that it is not possible to tell in advance what is conformist or nonconformist, that these concepts always call for analysis and, in fact, they presuppose the nuanced analysis of particular historical situations. On the specific point of the celebrated and also much denounced conformism of the opposition, it is perfectly possible, particularly when discussing intellectual, artistic products with an oppositional slant, to make quite precise distinctions and not blindly accept statements at face value in the spirit of a ticket mentality. If one can muster the energy and patience needed to make the necessary distinctions oneself without capitulating and making concessions to the dominant 'healthy' attitudes, then one can quite easily evade the allegedly so dangerous conformism of the opposition. I myself fondly imagine that I have been able to provide a small model of how this is to be achieved in my essay 'The Ageing of the New Music'.[1] I have tried to show there how a process of self-reflection can make it possible to resist the formation of clichés from within an oppositional intellectual movement. My hope is that this attempt will not have been entirely without its effect.[2]

I should like to make one last point about conformism. It too is one of the concepts that are falsified as soon as they are released from their context, or taken abstractly, as Hegel and Marx would have said. Such concepts only acquire their substantial meaning within the social matrix in which they appear. I should even like to venture the still broader generalization, one of some importance for a theory of history – in so far as it is at all possible to establish 'general principles' in a dialectical philosophy – that there is no category, no valid concept that might not be rendered invalid at the moment when it is cut off from the concrete context to which it really belongs. This applies with particular force to the concept of *ratio*, which is of such pivotal importance for the theory of history – and I believe that it will do us no harm to cudgel our brains a little on this subject before we proceed further. I have already told you[3] that the simplest way to construct something like a universal history is to create the history of a progressive rationality. Now it is extremely easy to hold this *ratio*, in other words, the unfolding of reason, responsible for the perennial catastrophes of history. We can indeed say with only minor exaggeration that all, and I mean all, the so-called Romantic intellectual tendencies do just that. But my own view is that it is also important not to hypostasize reason and its history (something that Max Weber tended to do). That is to say, it is important not to split reason off from the things reason is useful for, that it is there for, and in which it is embedded. I explained to you in one of the recent lectures[4] that the element of domination and thus the conflict inherent in reason was itself intrinsic to the process of history; that the concept of reason necessarily contains matter alien to reason, matter that has to be subjugated. I argued that the concept of reason only has meaning if there exists outside it material on which it can act – by abstracting, arranging or summarizing, etc. My intention (and I think it is important to clarify this) was not to talk you into a kind of idealist philosophizing; I did not mean the reason in which all this is embedded to be thought of as the *origin*, the absolute origin of the material it dominates and on which it works. It would be quite contrary to what I have been trying to tell you if you were to go away believing that there is a dialectic of *ratio* or, God forbid, enlightenment, in the sense of a dialectic of pure forms of consciousness, independently of the material to which it relates. What I would say – and I have hinted at this already, but I should like to repeat it quite explicitly – is that precisely the abstract nature of *ratio*, that is, its setting aside of concrete subject matter, points to social processes in which everything depends on who is equal with whom, or rather unequal, in the social hierarchy. That is to say, abstract reason ignores these specific concrete aspects of society. Specific class relations, for example, cannot be explained by an appeal to *ratio*, although they reproduce themselves in it. Instead, reason contains this amalgam of abstract thought *and* material that has to be subjugated, and this fact is itself merely the reflection of an attitude of thought, of reason, to reality,[5] which in its turn (and this too we must reiterate) does not remain external to reason. On the contrary, as Durkheim was the first to have pointed out, in an inspired, but also highly contentious way, reason becomes embedded in the forms of consciousness including its most abstract forms, such as the categories of pure logic and even the so-called intuitive forms of time and space.[6] However, I leave open the question of whether there is not a dialectic at work here in the sense that, for hierarchical social conditions to be deposited in subjective forms, there must always be an element of constitutive subjectivity which ensures that people experience things in one way rather than another. That is a complex matter that I really wish to mention only in passing and certainly do not want to resolve here. Thus we may speak of the irrationality of *ratio* in the present historical phase; we may point out that the pro-digious achievements of science benefit only a small group of people or that science seems to be moving towards the destruction of the human race. We may accuse reason of all sorts of other irrationalities. Indeed, I would not defend reason against these accusations; I would certainly not deny that, as the process of rationalization advances, it claims any number of victims. But we should not let things get out of proportion; we must be clear in our own minds that the responsi-bility for the threats that the advancing sciences unleash on mankind lies not with reason or science, but with the way in which reason is *entwined* with very real social conditions. Within these social condi-tions reason is directed at purposes that are irrational because of the irrational state of society as a whole. Thus while reason contains such a destructive element, thanks to its unreflecting persistence as stolid domination, the blame for this must not be laid exclusively at the door of the isolated category of *ratio*, but must be ascribed to the totality. It can really only be grasped in the relationship between the processes of rationalization – chief among them scientific and technical inventions – and the external purposes imposed on them and from which they cannot escape. For even though this advancing *ratio* impinges on and even modifies the *existing* relations of domina-tion, it is always tied into them.

Having said this, I should now like us to turn our attention to the problem of the subjective experience of the negativity of history, since this will be one of the principal themes with which we shall be con-cerned. I should like to read out to you a few sentences from Hegel's *Philosophy of Right* that I would like to explain to you and that have some bearing on our discussions. They are to be found in the Preface: 'That right and ethics, and the actual world of right and the ethical, are grasped by means of thoughts and give themselves the form of rationality – namely universality and determinacy – by means of *thoughts*, is what constitutes *the law*; and it is this which is justifiably regarded as the main enemy by that feeling which reserves the right to do as it pleases, by that conscience which identifies right with subjective conviction. The form of right as a *duty* and a *law* is felt by it to be a *dead, cold letter* and a *shackle*; for it does not recognize itself in the law and thereby recognize its own freedom in it, because the law is the reason of the thing [*Sache*] and reason does not allow feeling to warm itself in the glow of its own particularity [*Partikularität*].'[7]

Now, ladies and gentlemen, these statements carry conviction; they sound like statements that have something in them, and whenever people feel that they are hearing something that is backed up by the power of what *exists*, they generally react in a highly suggestible manner. In this instance, however, these statements are those of a demagogue. I should like to demonstrate this to you and to draw your attention to a few details. To begin with, then, it is claimed that conscience identifies right with subjective conviction. If Hegel has Kant in mind here, as we must assume, he ought to know, as someone steeped in the history of philosophy and Kant especially, that Kantian ethics and the Kantian conscience not only make no mention of the feeling that he is so scathing about here, but that Kant is just as hostile to this so-called ethical feeling as Hegel himself. In this respect he differs from earlier moralists such as Hutcheson and Shaftesbury,[8] for whom the idea of ethical feeling was seen in a far more positive light. This has a significance which goes well beyond questions of dogma. The fact is that what he criticizes here as subjective conviction constantly recurs in individuals – and this is why I wish to note it in Kant – and is perfectly rational in itself. Thus however isolated an individual may be, if he criticizes a historical trend which he feels powerless to change, this cannot simply be dismissed as the grumbling of the disaffected or the irrational protest of someone who feels pangs of emotion. His protest, if it has any substance at all, will contain an element of reason. Thus when individuals protested about the Third Reich, it was not just from a sense of moral outrage. If the protester was politically conscious, and I believe I may even claim this of myself and my initial memories of Hitlerism, then he must have been aware that the policies being introduced were catastrophic and that the National Socialists were launched on an adventurist path that could only end in disaster. The crucial factor here is that the awareness that Hegel tacitly and dogmatically ascribes to a collective consciousness can also be present in an individual. By thinking, the individual shares in the objective nature of thought, or can do so. To put it in a Hegelian manner, he shares in the objectivity of spirit, unless the objectivity of his own thought is determined merely by impulses and is completely unbalanced in consequence. Hegel simply ignores the element of objectivity, of universality, that lies concealed in the particular, in individuality, and that enables it to determine itself as thought, as a thinking monad. He thus fails to recognize an aspect of his own dialectic of universal and particular that he of all people should have emphasized more strongly. This is the idea that the figure of the universal in which the particular possesses the universal to a substantial degree is in actual fact the process of thought in which the particular is raised to the level of the universal. This thought is located nowhere but in the individual. Only individuals can think; blind collectives quite certainly cannot – and the contrast has become even more pronounced nowadays when collective reactions are being so blatantly manipulated.

You can see from this just how fuzzy Hegel's critique is. Linked with this is his avoidance of the main issue when at one point he denounces the sentiment of thinking oneself superior, where in reality what is at stake has nothing to do with feelings but addresses the question of thinking at the only point where it matters, namely as the thinking of the individual. We might say that there are historical situations in which the interest of the totality, in other words, the objectivity of spirit, can only be found in individuals, namely those who consciously and by design offer resistance to the trend. In contrast, what can be called the semblance of objectivity, the general consensus, is so much the mere reflex of social mechanisms that it actually lacks the objectivity commonly ascribed to it, and is really no more than subjective illusion. I believe that, particularly in a situation like the present, we have to drive the dialectic forward to this conclusion.

However, Hegel himself says at one point (if you think back to the passage I quoted) that when he looks at 'the law' 'with subjective conviction' he 'justifiably' regards its universality 'as the main enemy'. This 'justifiably' contains his whole position. Typically for Hegel, he would not say that the individual's resistance – we would add: the thinking individual's resistance – is purely a matter of chance; he would probably say that what the individual thinks is limited when compared to the objective process as a whole because he does not properly realize how everything is interconnected. My own view is that this 'justifiably' has to be taken much more seriously than even Hegel believes. It is characteristic of Hegel's thinking that he really wants to have it all ways; that he really wants to include everything, even things that simply cannot be reconciled. By this I mean that he adopts the standpoint of the universal; he tends always to claim, ideologically and in a conformist spirit, that the universal is in the right. But equally, almost as an afterthought, he would also like to be credited with wanting fair play for the individual. And he does this with a throwaway remark, in this case the single adverb 'justifiably', merely in order that the individual should get his just deserts, simply so that it does not look as if anyone is being left out. Incidentally, this comment applies with equal force to the entire Hegelian macro-structure since the whole point of his philosophy is that it not only teaches absolute identity, but also believes that non-identity – in other words, the very thing that cannot be included in identity – should somehow be incorporated into the concept of identity in the course of its elaboration. In this way, he could almost be said to be protecting himself at his weakest and most elementary point. I shall return to this particular problem at a later date. At the moment, I just want to take an even closer look at this 'justifiably'. Thus if, as I have suggested to you, the individual conscience regards right, rational right or, as Hegel calls it, 'the actual world of right and the ethical' as the enemy, then a philosophy that teaches the positive doctrine of the reconciliation of the particular and the universal should focus on this question instead of skating over it. The idea of absolute reconciliation [*Geschlichtetheit*], the idea that spirit should always be at home with itself and should rediscover itself, as Hegel phrases it,[9] and at the same time the emphatic admission that the individual mind is simply not at home with itself in its confrontation with objective institutions and the objective historical trend – there is a conflict here that he cannot simply ignore. The reason that he cannot ignore it is that this state of not being at home with itself is a kind of *methesis*, a kind of participation in the very rationality that is thought of as the achievement of the act of identification. It would be easier for an opponent of Hegel, it would be easier for Kant to react in this way, since Kant rigorously maintained a dualistic attitude towards empirical subjects, and hence would say: very well, individual conscience and the course of the world are absolutely incompatible. But then he would add: so much the worse for the course of the world. However, if, like Hegel, I say that the course of the world and individual conscience are each mediated by the other and that therefore the individual consciousness must discover itself in the course of the world, while *simultaneously* teaching that rightly and 'justifiably' it *cannot* discover itself in the universal – then in effect it reverts to dualism, to Kantian dualism, and even hypostasizes this as a kind of positivity. To cite the English proverb, he adds insult to injury. Thus not only is an injustice done to the individual by both the course of the world and the institutions, but if the individual recognizes what is happening and protests, instead of joining in and identifying with the process, he finds himself derided as stupid, narrow-minded, sentimental and God knows what else. People continue to wag their philosophical finger at him until he gives in. Anyone who, like Hegel, insists on mediation should refrain from introducing a *chorismos*, a separation, at a crucial juncture; he should refrain from representing the *chorismos* of reason and unreason, chance and necessity, as a positive. The absolute is treated by Hegel, and the entire philosophy of history that talks about the world spirit, as spirit, as a spiritual principle. But if this concept of spirit is not to degenerate into something vacuous it cannot be allowed to break every link with the living spirit, the spirit of individuals. For living individuals objectify and universalize themselves in it, while even Hegel, as my earlier quotation shows, demands that they should be 'at home with themselves'.

Hegel perceives the need for the separation and regards it as a dialectical necessity which he ought to criticize or supersede; but instead he tends to trivialize it and treat it as mere accident, simply to counter the resistance and the rights of the critical mind. And the downgrading of this separation *sub specie individuationis* corresponds to the theodicy of separation *sub specie aeterni* – that is to say, to the doctrine that, as the totality of life, this separation is the desired reconciliation.[10] However, whenever we ask this reconciliation to deliver, to show what is reconciled and how, we are only given the assurance that this is not what was meant. Reconciliation was the totality, and if you expect more from it, if you would like to achieve it for your own consciousness (and not even for you as a person), then you are simply small-minded, a petty philosopher of reflection [*Reflexionsphilosoph*][11] who has not yet reached the pinnacle of absolute idealism. . . . And this simply will not do. This kind of thinking sins against its own virtue, against the bourgeois virtue that one should pay the debts that one incurs – intellectual debts in this case – whereas Hegel tries to wriggle out of it at this crucial point. Incidentally, I do not believe that I need to explain to you just how much I admire Hegel's philosophy, despite such faults. But you can see here how even such a mighty edifice as the Hegelian dialectic not only demeans itself, but is forced to demean itself before the course of the world to which it has been harnessed. Karl Kraus's verse

'What has the world done to us?'[12] applies not just to us as individuals, to each of us, but it also applies to what we imagine has raised us above ourselves, namely our philosophy. Following this Hegelian argument, and having said to you that what you can find in Hegel is this suggestive power that everything has behind it, everything that exists; the entire force, I would even say, the entire machinery of history that everything has behind it – faced with all this, where can we obtain the courage as citizens to prevent us from knuckling under? Particularly if it is the case, as I explained to you in an earlier lecture,[13] that this life reproduces itself not *despite* conflict, but *because of* it. I believe that the answer to this is that the critical lever, the intrinsic critical lever, is to be found in the category of *objective possibility*. To a certain degree we must concede that Hegel is in the right, even though I have been critical of specific arguments, of course without wishing to trivialize them. In particular, he is right to assert that an abstract ideal that has nothing to do with the course of the world, that is to say, an ideal whose conditions of realization have no basis in the world as it is, is impotent and worthless. And you all know how an ideal of that sort has had such an extreme, and I may say extremely dubious, influence on Hegel's socialist disciples. But what we *can* say is that universal reason, which Hegel insisted on in opposition to all particularity, did actually bring about the possibility of reproducing the lives of all mankind at a more adequate, more human level. This happened quite straightforwardly, in the first instance, thanks to the growth in the forces of production, that is, by virtue of the increasing opportunities. These opportunities are so tangible and so concrete that they provide us with a legitimate platform from which to criticize the actual course of the world. This advance is evident not just in the context of a so-called welfare society, which after all is very limited numerically even now, when compared to humanity as a whole, but on a global scale. I should add, very speculatively and perhaps rashly, that this possibility of making a leap forward, of doing things differently, always existed, even in periods when productivity was far less developed, an opportunity that was missed again and again. This is something I shall perhaps return to later on. The point I want to make here is that this entire view of history contains a single strand, and this applies both to the Hegelian and the Marxian doctrine. Emancipation from this single-stranded view will only come when we refuse to accept the dictum that it has only now become a real possibility. It is important to realize that in all probability the opportunity we see today of a sensible organization of mankind was *also* possible in less complicated times, when there were far fewer people and social conditions were incomparably more modest. The assertion that it did not happen, that it was impossible, is one of the propositions that owes its plausibility to the fact that it was uttered by the victors, and so its importance should not be exaggerated. Hence I would say that the critical yardstick that allows reason, and indeed compels and obliges reason, to oppose the superior strength of the course of the world is always the fact that in every situation there is a concrete possibility of doing things differently. This possibility is present and sufficiently developed and does not need to be inflated into an abstract utopia that can be instantly scotched by the automatic retort that it will not work, it will never work. What you can see here is one of the most disastrous consequences of an idealist theory of history. By identifying reality and spirit, you conflate possibility and reality. Not only is reality identified with spirit, but spirit, mind, is identified with reality; the tension between the two is eliminated, thus quashing the function of spirit as a critical authority. Thus in idealist thought, with its emphasis on identity, the tendency is to equate reality and possibility, and to do away with possibility as the subjective element of tension that corresponds precisely on the subjective side to non-identical being on the objective one. It is this act of elision that makes it possible to denigrate possibility as such. Nowadays, when Hegel's philosophy has long since been forgotten, this tendency has been secularized – or, as I would prefer to say, vulgarized. It has become common prejudice to claim that utopia is not permitted and that therefore it is not possible. It follows that the spell under which most people live is not the spell of the materialism that is said to be so awful. The real spell that has taken root in this kind of thinking is that of a vulgar idealism that has long since forgotten its own assumptions.

LECTURE 8

3 December 1964

PSYCHOLOGY

I imagine that quite a few of you, having heard me talk so much in these lectures about the concept of the objective historical trend, the world spirit, the way in which this objective process comes to prevail and the negative nature of the universal – that quite a few of you will have an urgent question on the tip of your tongue: isn't all this a mystification of history? I would find it very easy to understand if you were to ask this question. After all, surely history is made, as has been remarked, by human beings; all historical events are tied to the human beings who bring them about. On the other hand, these events work themselves out at the expense of human beings, human beings are their victims, history stretches its hand out over all human beings. I have intentionally phrased this question in a slightly blunt and primitive way. But there is no doubt that it deserves an answer in a course of lectures on the theory of history, and of course this answer should take its proper place in the context of what I have been saying. In fact, looking at it in architectonic terms, we might say that we have reached the precise point in our discussion when it would be appropriate to attempt an answer. I should like to begin by reminding you of something I have tried to impress upon you, namely the coercive nature of history. It is not just that we are constantly exposed to its blind, overpowering events and also its larger tendencies. Nor is it just the fact that, in so far as we act as social beings, as socialized beings, we act as character masks (to use Marx's term).[1] By character masks I mean that, while we imagine that we act as ourselves, in reality we act to a great extent as the agents of our own functions.

When a businessman calculates his options and takes his decisions, he is guided not by his character, but by calculations, his balance sheet, his budget and his plan for the next business cycle in which the objective elements of the situation are concentrated. And other things being equal, the same may be said of almost all the functions that human beings have to carry out these days. Even the most powerful government minister will generally find himself limited to converting open files into closed ones. It is regularly the case – you can see this in any examination in the modest situation in universities where the interest in making sure that the files are in order, that the co-examiner has not forgotten to sign the examination form and niceties of that sort – that the interest in such matters takes precedence over the candidate's performance. Moreover, it does so to a degree that would shock examination candidates if they were to witness it, although it might also make them smile, and this might help to relieve them a little of their pre-examination anxieties. But I do not want to talk about all this today, that is to say, about the way in which objective social necessities come to assert themselves. I want rather to discuss a specific factor that really focuses our attention on the role or place of human beings in the history that they allegedly make. What I have to say about this is that, even in the realm in which according to convention human beings are really more or less in control, that is to say, in which they are not determined by their functions but enjoy a certain measure of freedom, they continue to be determined by the universal. So much so that even the most specific aspects of their individuality are preformed by the universal, and this includes even those elements that diverge from the universal. Let me add right away: this influence is in general negative.

In other words, individuals and even the category of the individual – which as you will recollect is a relatively recent development, dating back only to the beginning of the Renaissance in Europe – even individuals and the category of the individual, then, are the products of history. Given the nature of history, I would also ask you to reflect for a moment that this implies that the individual is also a transitory phenomenon. Please note that by individual here I do not mean the biological division into individual beings, i.e., the fact that human beings do not come into the world like coral colonies but as single beings or at best as twins, or less well as triplets or quadruplets with slighter chances of survival. What I mean is that individuality is a reflective concept, that is to say, we can only speak of individuality where individual subjects become conscious of their individuality and singularity, in contrast to the totality, and only define themselves as individuals, as particular beings in the consciousness of this opposition. In this particular sense, we can say that the individual is a product and, as I said, may be a transitory phenomenon. Of course, you should be aware that the natural form of individuation, that is to say, the physical separation of individual people from each other, does in a sense enter into this reflexive concept because the biological fact of individuality requires that just as people have come into the world singly, so they should perpetuate themselves as individuals. So it is true that the notion of individual self-preservation, which is the central feature of individuation and also of the development of individual character, does extend back into the realm of biology. In contrast, animals do not possess this self-awareness and a fixed self as an internal authority has not become crystallized. The fact that animals do not have this self-awareness suffices to explain why individuality can be considered a reflexive category and thus the product of history. The process of socialization to which human beings are subjected by history, the process of inclusion in society as a whole, is one through which the universal realizes itself in history and so can be described as a historical process. Now the fact of individuation is not merely a matter of a conscious attitude towards the universal on the part of human beings. It does not resemble extreme situations in which, for example, a recruit submits to a hostile force, namely orders, drill, or being ground down, by adopting the slogan: 'Man, you had better keep your head down', an attitude that enables him to survive as an individual separate from coercion at the hands of the universal. It is rather the case, and I believe this is fundamental to an understanding of the attitude of the individual human subject caught up in the historical process, that the historical coercion which moulds human beings enters into the very core of their psyche and their subjectivity is in a sense shaped by this socialization process. The sphere of psychology in which we imagine that we are ourselves is also the sphere in which in a certain, obscure sense we are furthest from being ourselves. This is because we are preformed by that being-for-others to the very core of our being. This being-for-others is what is most successful in breaking whatever part of the existence of the individual that has not submitted to that identity coercion. By this I mean that the more individuals identify with the universal – not consciously, but in their unconscious and preconscious reactions – the more they can be said to distance themselves in a sense from the universal by the fact that their identification with it is blind and defenceless because they are acting unconsciously, as a form of adaptation. It has frequently been maintained – with justice, I would say – that the realm specific to psychology is the realm of irrationality. This is true of psychology as knowledge as well as of the objects with

which psychology concerns itself. I believe that we see here the explanation of this irrationality. That is to say, at those points where
human beings strive to internalize the universal, the very thing that
should harmonize with their reason, they almost always act irrationally. For this universal is directed against their conscious interests
in the sense in which I have already discussed at some length and
which I shall perhaps be able to explain further during this lecture.
This is because the identification with the universal cannot be achieved
in any other way, through reason, for instance, which human beings
nevertheless stand in need of if they are to survive in an irrational
universe. For this reason they can achieve their own socialization only
in a way that is irrational, or even anti-rational in principle, or as we
could say in clinical terms: neurotic, or as a consequence of repression
or regression or by means of all those modes of self-mutilation that
psychology enumerates. The distinction between psychology and
reason has in addition to its subjective explanation, for example, in
the individual resolution of the Oedipus complex, an objective, historical explanation, though of course the entire Oedipus complex
could not be understood without the family and with it the authority
of the father as a social phenomenon.

The irrationality of psychology assigns the irrationality of the
course of the world to individuals against their own reason. This is
the source of the peculiarity that is so characteristic of our own
situation but which presumably already featured in Hegel's proposition of identity. What I have in mind here is the constant illusion that
reconciliation is a reality: in other words, the suggestion that, despite
all the horror and negativity of which I have tried to give you a not
wholly implausible picture, it always looks as if human beings and
the course of the world that is imposed on them are truly similar in
nature, are genuinely identical; it looks as if the world were so constructed as to be worthy of human beings and as if we had no right
to complain about the course of the world that has made people what
they are. This is because what the course of the world has made of
people is largely to ensure their affirmation of itself. It has modified
or shaped their social character to the point where they are willing
to sell their souls to the world, even where it is at its most irrational
and where it exacts senseless sacrifices from them. People are forced,
nowadays especially, to turn the realities that have been foisted on
them into their own business simply in order to survive. And then
Hegel comes along and glorifies the world spirit by asserting that it
is identical with what human beings are, adding only that people are
ignorant of this fact – and in this respect he is absolutely right. The
only problem is that this alleged positive knowledge is in reality a

negative. By this I mean that people simply do not know what the world has done to them because, if they did know, they would be different from what they are and could not be turned into whatever it is that the course of the world has made of them. Incidentally, such concepts as the objectivity of despair or the objectivity of happiness can be measured against such things. That is to say, their objectivity is of the kind that might have broken through the illusion of identity that has been created by a painful process of identification that is consistently and necessarily faulty and unsuccessful, and cast it off. For this identity is completely misconceived. We may say that the measure of its failure is one we can see everywhere today. It takes the form of that infantility among adults that surfaces at its most extreme where the adults are at their most grown up. That is to say, it manifests itself when they have rid themselves of the last trace of their childhood dreams and have completely surrendered to the business of self-preservation that has lost its ultimate purpose and become a fetish. At that point, the reason that has kicked over the traces, that has run wild and insists only on its formal fulfilment without following its rational purpose, merges with illusion and, psychologically at least, deteriorates into damaged goods.

In a somewhat cynical passage in the *Philosophy of History*,[2] Hegel remarks that as a general rule the course of the world ends up with people sowing their wild oats (his use of this idiomatic phrase suggests that he is distancing himself a little from this attitude), and in so doing, and in the process of socialization (although he does not call it that), people find their proper place and their proper situation in life. This should be contrasted with a statement by a very significant figure who did not conform to the course of the world even though he occupied a prominent position in it, more specifically in the world of art. I am thinking here of Gustav Mahler, who struggled for years to do away with lax conformism, by which I mean the wrong sort of socialization, in the world of music, a struggle which was probably to blame in part for his premature death. Mahler said (and his answer does seem to me to amount to a critique of Hegel) that the wild oats that we sow are really the best thing about us.[3] It is my belief that when you too find yourselves facing the need to sow your wild oats, you should reflect on what I have been saying here. If you find that you can slow down the process a little that might be far from the worst thing that could happen to you. But the disaster consists as a rule in the fact that people – today at any rate, in contrast to the still happy, individualist times of the late nineteenth century – that people are all rushing to sow their wild oats; or, as I once expressed it in *Minima Moralia*, most people today kick with

the pricks instead of against them.[4] But when you make a remark
like this you only prove that you have become a grumpy old man
who is naturally suspect to the serene young people of today. Even
so, I should still like to point out to you that this false identification
of an unreconciled universal with the particular is necessary in an
ironic and negative sense. We are not dealing here with arbitrary
subjective processes that can be avoided as long as you have a
modicum of insight, self-confidence and critical spirit. A necessity
rules here and you can count yourself lucky if you can keep your
head above water long enough to recognize it and give it a name. But
no one should imagine that he is immune to it or that a fortunate
intellectual disposition can make him independent of such mechanisms. Psychologically, it is scarcely possible to make good the narcissistic loss, that is to say, the constant injuries offered to the
narcissistically driven instincts whose violence cannot be exaggerated;
it exceeds everything that the imagination can grasp, and I would say
that this is true of *every* human being, without exception, in the world
in which we live. *Why* that is so is something I cannot explain here.
These lectures do not deal with social psychology, and I am speaking
today about the phenomena of social psychology only in order to
show you their place in the framework of history, and not so as to
provide you with knowledge of social psychology – that would be
quite impossible here. But if people really were to become fully aware
that their own selves – that is to say, the point where they believe
that they belong entirely to themselves – that their own selves belong
not to them but that they are, right down to and including their
idiosyncrasies and peculiarities, what might be called the negative
imprint of the universal, that would involve such a fearful loss of
self-esteem as one tends to call it in bourgeois circles that in all probability they would be unable to bear it.

When I say that people's peculiarities are the negative imprint of
the universal what I have in mind are, for example, the widely ridiculed stereotypes of the miser, that is to say, the kind of character
structure deduced and criticized by Freud.[5] This structure is nothing
but the mutilation, the deviation from the norm that arises because
people are forced to develop certain character traits in the course of
socialization. Given the striving for profit imposed by the universal,
this leads everyone who consistently obeys that instinct to develop
the deformations of pathological avarice. These can be seen in the
novels of Balzac, for example, whose inexhaustible and precise imagination depicts them with all their nuances. This is just one aspect
that I propose to you as a model. You will not find it hard to think
of others. So what I am talking about today are these problematic

identifications with the universal from a psychological point of view, that is to say, about what human beings actually mean for history in a specific sense, in their inner composition, and what the historical universal actually means for them. Without these problematic iden- tifications with the law that governs them objectively, that is to say, without the primacy of self-preservation and the forms in which this is reflected, the human subject would probably be unable to survive in this world. Whoever wished to exist immediately, absolutely imme- diately, without the psychological hardenings and stigmata through which we are transformed by the unreconciled universal, would be an entirely defenceless person, and probably a feeble human being without a self who would be completely helpless and powerless in the face of the world, an easy prey. The deepest reason for this is that, owing to the socialization process, that is to say, owing to our adaptation to the social and historical universal, we are forced to renounce our instincts – every day, at every moment, in a myriad of ways. We do so on the tacit assumption (one that was criticized as early as the ancient hedonists of the Aristippean, Cyrenaic school)[6] that, if we renounce momentary, immediate satisfactions, we shall prosper in the long run, that we shall eventually receive in full what we sacrifice now. In general, postponement is the basic model of social denial. The motto 'Jam tomorrow, never jam today' is the basic model according to which social and historical denial comes to prevail, from the most intimate matters to the construction of entire societies which exact sacrifices from people on that pretext that everything will be just dandy in three or four generations, even though the people directly affected have no real reason to believe this. These promises – promises that are implicit in the social contract itself, that is to say, in the exchange relationship – that we shall one day be compensated for our present sacrifices, or shall really gain greater security, these promises are doomed to disappointment over and over again. There are periods, the present is one such, in which the disappointment is not so much in evidence, and where certain needs are satisfied relatively easily; at other times this is less true. Even in our own age, I would say, without being able to analyse it in detail here, that this fulfilment of the social promise in the future for what we sacrifice in the present by performing our social roles calls for a psychological surplus value that is squeezed out of us in addition to the ordinary, economic one. This psychological surplus value is the difference between the expectation of happiness in the long term that is always being held out to us and the actual satisfac- tion that we generally receive. At bottom of course, everyone knows what I am talking about here – perhaps 'knows' is not the right word

– everyone is aware of it subconsciously. People manage to come to terms with this phenomenon, with the realization that their own rationality is irrational, and that they do not obtain what their rational behaviour promises, only by making an irrational response. It is to accept the irrational course of the world, to identify with it and to make it their own. You can see this every day, in discussions, for example, where people simply echo what others say and produce 100,000 arguments to prove that things can't be any different, won't be any different and shouldn't be any different. It is as if they are inwardly prepared to take the side of whoever will prevent them from embarking on the course of action that would be best for them. This fact too is well known to analytical psychology, admittedly from a very limited, that is, an abstract, subjective point of view, but nevertheless a stringent one. Anna Freud, Sigmund Freud's daughter, has made a special study of these questions and has introduced the concept of identification with the aggressor or with one's own enemy.[7] Incidentally, this should not be taken too personally as referring to one's own enemies, but should be expanded to one's identification with the course of the world just as it happens to be. This sets up a catastrophic vicious circle in which human beings have an objective interest in changing the world and in which this change is quite impossible without their participation. However, these mechanisms of identification have stamped themselves on people's characters to such a degree that they are quite incapable of the spontaneity and the conscious actions that would be required to bring about the necessary changes. This is because, by identifying with the course of the world, they do so in an unhappy, neurotically damaged way, which effectively leads them to reinforce the world as it is. And that, I would say, is the truth about the situation of human beings in history.

This has two consequences for the theory of history and I should like to summarize them for you briefly. On the one hand, the position is that the course of the world which is hostile to human beings asserts itself against them but with their approval – in pivotal situations it even prevails with their conscious, self-destructive acquiescence. To explain this in slightly more concrete terms, I shall say only that, as you know, at its lowest and in terms of its potential today, democracy is a system that would like to give mankind the form it deserves; it is a social form in which people are the subjects and not the objects of society. Accordingly, it is the socio-political form that expresses the self-determination of mankind. Nevertheless, it is alien to the masses and in critical situations it becomes the object of hatred. It is alien because as long as it is purely formal it appears further removed from people and more abstract than forms that at least appear to be immediately familiar and close by. The success of race theory, which is based on something as close as so-called blood relationships and, ultimately, the family, has exploited these elements by contrasting them with remote, objective mechanisms, even though it is to these that human beings are in truth connected. Its immensely profound appeal was based on the illusion of closeness that is echoed in such formulae as the term 'national community' [*Volksgemeinschaft*] and which went to the innermost core of the human unconscious. By speaking of the merely formal character of democracy, I have already suggested that in the world in which we live the possibilities that might be open to mankind are denied them in reality – instead they have to make do with the illusion of alterity. However, so as at least to point to a particular socio-psychological mechanism by way of illustration, there is a tendency – one that ought to be carefully analysed since it seems to be a constant factor – for situations where possibilities of improvement are visible but are denied to provoke the fury of those who are kept down. Where this happens this fury is directed not against evil, but against the imperfections of the good which find themselves ridiculed as a swindle simply because people choose to identify with the inexorable course of the world as it is. An instance is the fury unleashed against so-called bleeding-heart humanitarians by powerful populist forces proclaiming their yearning for the return of the death penalty. Given our current relatively peaceful domestic situation, this is a particularly frightening example of the mechanism I have in mind.

On the other hand, since the achievement of a proper identity cannot succeed because of the objective course of the world and because people's interests cannot be reconciled, people are necessarily crippled by this unconscious act of identification with the world. To an increasing extent, they find that they lose the inner, spiritual freedom which would enable them to detach themselves from the course of the world; they find themselves unable to rise above it as free, autonomous and critical beings. I can illustrate this tendency by referring you to an expression originally introduced to psychology by Carl Gustav Jung[8] but which I took the liberty of applying some years ago in sociology.[9] This is the idea of 'concretism'. This concept contains the idea of the displacement of the libido to what is immediately present to people's minds. Because they identify with the institutions, commodities, things and relations immediately familiar to them, they are incapable of perceiving their dependence upon processes at some distance from them, the actual objective processes. By way of conclusion, the inference I should like to draw from what

I have been telling you today is that, to a degree that is difficult to grasp, psychology has an immensely important role to play. This remains true even though objectively, and compared to the objective necessity of history, it is only a secondary, supplementary phenomenon. For were this not so, people would simply not put up with the situation as I have described it. Psychology has become the cement of the world as it exists; it holds together the very conditions that would be seen through rationally, if this irrational cement did not exist. This probably also explains why the most effective form of ideology today, namely the culture industry, is concerned less to transmit particular ideologies, propositions and attitudes than to reinforce and reproduce in an unending chain those same mechanisms that enable people to identify with the things with which they are not identical. Thus what I mean by this cement is the way in which human psychology has embedded the world *in* human beings in the form, moreover, of a perverse, deceitful consciousness; it is a deformed consciousness that knows only how to yield. It is independent of specific theoretical or political ideas, which for the most part it never even begins to formulate. Nevertheless, this consciousness is the only form in which ideology really survives today. Thus the form taken by ideology and by the false identity of subject and object in a world of radical discord is one in which a conscious-unconscious state is produced in people both objectively, and with their own connivance and the aid of their own instincts. This state of mind blinds them to the unreconciled nature of life and leads them to accept and adopt as their own the very conditions that they feel to be their exact antitheses. And this, ladies and gentlemen, may perhaps explain to you why, in a theory of history or a theory of society that is basically objective in nature, such a subjective science as psychology (which as you will know is commonly traduced in Russia) is able to make such a crucial contribution. Its task is to analyse the cement, the ideology, that exercises such immense influence over human beings, and is thereby able to reproduce the entire global situation. We may conclude, then, and this brings me back to my starting-point, that, at the very moment when people believe they are most themselves and belong to themselves, they are not only the prey [*Beute*] of ideology. We might even go so far as to say that they themselves have turned into *ideology*.

LECTURE 9

8 December 1964

THE CRITIQUE OF UNIVERSAL HISTORY

Since it is my undoubtedly laudable intention in these lectures to give you not just an introduction to the introduction, but also as much as possible of the relevant subject matter, I have decided to modify my argument a little. I should like therefore to confine my comments to giving you a few of what are in my opinion the pivotal categories needed for the construction of a theory of history. I shall then move from the concept of history to that of freedom so that I can discuss the concept of freedom in the second half of the semester. This means that there will be a little less time, and perhaps no time at all, to focus on a number of purely philosophical questions concerning dialectical structure which I had thought important. But it also means that I shall carry out a little more faithfully the promise that I had made in announcing this course of lectures. One of the countless causes of disappointment experienced in universities stems from the discovery that a lecture course with a highly promising title frequently yields far less in practice than one had been led to believe. If I cannot do away with this problem, I should at least like to show you that I am conscious of it.

Ladies and gentlemen, I have had a lot to say about the unity of the historical process, about the idea of the course of history as a totality, and I followed this up with some remarks on what I have called the negativity of the course of the world. I should like now to transfer this theme to the construction of history. This idea, this motif, which I have explained to you in philosophical terms – in earlier days people would have said 'in speculative terms' – can be found in Hegel, and indeed in the entire thinking of the Hegelian era, under the rubric of *universal history*. During the period of the so-called ascendancy of the bourgeoisie, this concept of universal history, by which I mean that of a continuous history of mankind, was generally conceived as an upward development, albeit not without setbacks. This idea formed something like the general climate of thought at the time – and, incidentally, you would do well to bear in mind when working on Hegel that what you find in Germany at this period is not so much the achievements of individual writers as the expression of an objective spirit as it developed in the course of living communication. This then found its most coherent expression in Hegel's thought. Under the influence of Dilthey's history of ideas, we still see these things in far too individualistic a way.[1] I just say this in passing so as to make you aware of a perspective from which you will perhaps find it easier to gain an understanding of Hegel. The path taken by history as a whole (if we may put it like this) ought in the spirit of Hegel's philosophy to be a thoroughgoing phenomenology of mind. It would not be difficult to read something like a theory of universal history from the *Phenomenology of Spirit*, which is what is generally thought of as one of Hegel's systematic works. These ideas are roughly equivalent to the conception of world literature which was of such great importance at around the same time, as we can see from Goethe. And not only Goethe, since we can see the same thing throughout the Romantic movement, from where it can be traced back to Herder. Hegel may have been at loggerheads with Herder, quite explicitly so,[2] in fact, but their disagreement was *mediated*, in particular by the way in which all the romantic motifs migrated into his philosophy and were absorbed there, but were at the same time reflected upon critically. The same may be said of this idea of a totalizing history that was both coherent and also broken down into its specific phases. It expressed this idea of a total history that was at the same time divided into distinct aspects. We may say that the notion of the joining together of the world was anticipated by the youthful bourgeoisie in this idea of universal history as a unity, as the single unfolding process of human nature, and that it arose at a moment in history when such a unity had not yet become a visible possibility. This idea was given its definitive expression in Wendell Wilkie's formula of 'one world'.[3] We need add only that at the time the antagonistic elements that determine this universality, this internally divided unity of a global society, had not yet become crystallized.

Nowadays, this idea of universal history is highly controversial and problematic. However, if what I have said to you about the unity of history in general, about the unfolding of a unified, historical process, has any plausibility, there is a lot that can be said in its favour. And it is my belief that, if you wish to say anything at all about the theory of history in general, you must enter into a discussion of the construction of universal history. This idea is under attack from two quarters. It is criticized by positivists who constantly point out that there is no such thing as a unified, continuous process of history, and they have good reason to do so. They point out, for example, that the immense rupture in Western history during the long centuries of the barbarian migrations, followed by the tentative rediscovery of the classical tradition, is the most dramatic illustration of this. But you can trace this element of rupture, this demonstration that it is not possible to speak of a unified progress of history, into its most minute ramifications. I need mention only one sphere of activity, one that has just occurred to me and that concerns a branch of knowledge with which I am conversant, namely music. The situation in music is that a particular development, the compromise between medieval polyphony and the newly discovered homophonic music, culminated in Bach. It was then interrupted by non-musical, as it were exotic, factors, namely social developments. The result was that following Bach's death a new style emerged that can be regarded as the negation of his music. We then see a musical tradition of quite a different kind, one that incorporates Bach's achievements only tentatively and with difficulty. Incidentally, this demolition of the Bachian tradition after Bach was an event that probably had extremely grave consequences – but it is not my concern here to give you a history of the philosophy of music. At all events, you can see here how a detailed knowledge makes it extremely difficult to produce a speculative account of universal history. It is interesting to consider Spengler in this context. Spengler had vigorously combated the idea of universal history, since he even denied the continuity of time, which he replaced with a concept of simultaneity. That is to say, he treated the chronological succession of so-called cultures synchronically, thus effectively denying chronological sequence. Spengler is regarded by historical positivists as a wildly speculative metaphysician because he demolished the unity of history by his insistence on the specificities of individual cultures. Nevertheless, because of his denial of historical continuity we must situate him likewise in the positivist tendency. This places him incidentally in the tradition he stems from and which goes back via Nietzsche to Schopenhauer. Schopenhauer too should be included among the thinkers who, in sharp contrast to what he thought of as the optimistic purveyors of universal history, effectively came around to a denial of history, to a conception of history as no

more than the dreary repetition of eternal sameness or perhaps even
as the history of decline. When I say that Spengler's theory of history
comes close to positivism, for all his opposition to positivism, in a
strange way this nevertheless chimes in with Spengler's own attitude.
His own habits of mind were strongly positivistic and he always gave
precedence to the inexorable facts over attitudes, will power or the
idea, or whatever else one is disposed to call it. As long as you do
not have too great a knowledge of historical detail – and this is a
factor that must for once be included in the philosophical discussion
– you not only have the benefit of a greater distance which enables
you to gain a better overview, but, by the same token, you are blinder
to facts that make things awkward for philosophical theory. In such
a situation one's own intellectual superiority thrives on one's own
deficiency, on the fact that one knows too little. It is all very well to
try and demonstrate one's ingenuity in devising a profound interpretation of history when one has only a passing acquaintance with the
details of the case. Philosophically, too, this is an aspect of the dialectic between universal and particular that we should not lose sight
of. It provides the justification, the element of truth, in the positivists'
constant sniping at philosophical interpretations of history. We may
say that in general philosophy, and indeed intellect as such, is more
naïve and, we might even say, more infantile than its otherwise inferior positivist adversary. At the same time, it must not allow itself to
be persuaded to part with the advantage that lies in this greater distancing, but must instead face up to the task of directing its constructive energies towards the details of history; and it must go on to
mobilize the forces required to construct the totality in the details
themselves. For if those forces remain unable to engage with the
details of history, they are all too likely to remain vapid, vacuous and
lacking in authority.

I believe, for example, that Benjamin's historical studies, or indeed
my own, if I may be allowed to talk out of school for once and speak
of my own efforts, both have their roots in this situation. That is to
say, they arise from the wish to hold fast to the speculative element
without which (as I have explained in an earlier lecture)[4] historical
knowledge that aspires to being more than superficial is hardly possible. On the other hand, both of us strove to immerse ourselves in
historical detail in order to avoid that specious mastery that arises
from not being too familiar with the facts. Something of this desire
can be seen in Benjamin's so-called defence of induction[5] and also in
my own tendency to immerse myself in highly specific individual texts
or other intellectual products, instead of seeking out broader contexts, and then to look for the broader interconnections in those

specific texts or products. You too, if you eventually end up in productive work of this sort, will perhaps experience the tension of which I am speaking and to the philosophical significance of which I am alerting you. I should like to offer you one further illustration of this, in an example taken from Hegel. In this sphere we find him combining the profoundest insights with a kind of inferiority, an almost childish reluctance to get to grips with the matter in hand. The specious mastery that results from this amounts to what we associate with the term idealism: the naïvety, the schoolmasterly naïvety with which history is judged en bloc, or constructed en bloc. There is a theory in his *Philosophy of History* – and many of you who are busy preparing yourselves for the so-called Philosophicum[6] will already have heard of this theory. It can be found in the *Lectures on the Philosophy of History*, that is to say, one of Hegel's supposedly easier books, and it asserts that in the oriental world – by which he chiefly meant China – only one man was free; in the world of the Greeks, which of course was a slave-owning society, a few men were free, and only in the modern world, or what he rather disastrously calls the Christian-Germanic world, is everyone free, potentially at least.[7] It is very easy to demonstrate the arrogance and folly of this thesis. I need only remind you of the simple fact that has long been familiar to us all that even oriental societies governed by an extreme form of absolutism never had such a pure, absolute single monarch at their head. In reality they were largely feudal societies, so that they contained no single free person but a class system, admittedly one that was hierarchically organized. But this fact is simply ignored in Hegel's theory, since he plays fast and loose with the facts for the sake of the brilliant symmetry of the argument (which with its logical progression: one, a few, all . . . was brilliant at least for his age which had rather more modest aspirations). This cavalier treatment of the facts can also be seen in Balzac, a near contemporary of Hegel's, who sometimes dealt with social reality in a similar fashion. This remarkable attitude of 'so much the worse for the facts'[8] was undoubtedly one of the factors leading to the emergence of positivism, but, on the other hand, it contains a power of the imagination without which the intellectual advances that were so characteristic of the age could not have been made. But, equally, it goes without saying that in the modern world the idea of the freedom of all has not become literally true, because in the meantime the critical analysis of society has demonstrated in countless ways that the formal liberty of all individuals in bourgeois society must be contrasted with their actual unfreedom in reality. In this sense, it is quite easy for any student of history in his very first term to criticize Hegel's theory. If he is content with this, he can go back home with a massive prejudice against philosophy and without ever feeling the need to come to grips with those windbags.

Well, I have been playing the devil's advocate here, but I have to tell you that in reality the matter is not as simple as all that. You need only to reflect briefly to convince yourselves how much truth is contained in Hegel's seemingly absurd – masterfully absurd – theory. As you are aware, the idea of freedom is the cornerstone of Hegel's philosophy of history since that philosophy understands history as progress in the consciousness of freedom.[9] But the idea of freedom is tied to the *individual*. Initially, the concept of freedom has its meaning only in so far as we understand by it individual freedom, the freedom of the individual to act spontaneously, autonomously, on his own responsibility, and to decide for himself – as long as he does not offend against the freedom of others, the freedom of his fellow human beings. This latter doctrine was formulated in exemplary fashion by Kant in his philosophy of right.[10] Thus underlying the doctrine of freedom in whose name Hegel developed that three-stage theory of the development of history is the individual himself. In fact, when he speaks of 'one', 'some' and 'all', this idea of freedom does refer directly to the freedom of individuals, and even the number of individual human beings. If you take Hegel's thesis literally, it leaves itself open to all the objections that I have been almost too embarrassed to explain to you because they are so commonplace and so obvious. However, if for a moment you look at Hegel's intended meaning in a slightly less literal spirit, from a greater distance and from the standpoint of the individual, you would perceive how much rationality, how much plausibility enters into this seemingly rash idea – and I do not think that one would need to do too much violence to the text to rescue Hegel in this way. In the East, in oriental society as a whole, the category of the individual, the category of individuation, does not stand at the centre in the same way as it does in Western thought. I think that one can say this without exposing oneself to the accusation of colonial, Eurocentric impertinence. The difficulties in communication, in mutual understanding between East and West are to be found essentially in the fact that we – and I believe that this 'we' has a scope that includes the most heterogeneous political and philosophical concepts – that we measure all the concepts of the universal, of the not-I, by their relation to the I. In contrast – and this extends to the very heart of oriental beliefs – the tendency in the East is to mitigate the suffering of the individual by identifying him with a totality that he is not, by identifying him with a not-I, rather than to judge existing reality against the yardstick of individuality.

Thus if you examine this Hegelian argument from the standpoint of the *principium individuationis*, the assumption that in China there was only one individual because only one person was the emperor does indeed sound nonsensical. However, it is by no means nonsensical to assert that in the oriental world the concept of the individual was not of central importance. Hegel may even have been aware – and the most recent historical developments seem to have proved him right – that this absence of individuation was itself a historical stage. By this I mean that in order to be able to endure the suffering imposed on him by barbaric rule the individual simply had no alternative but the unconditional identification with the not-I, and ultimately with nothing at all, the void. In contrast, the category of the individual is itself the product of history and only assumed a formative role at a much later stage. In antiquity – and here too Hegel had a genuine insight – the category of the individual remained a privilege simply because Greek and Roman society owed their reproduction to the slave system, to slavery. Only relatively few people in antiquity, then, if anyone at all, had the opportunity to develop into individuals. I should add at once that this is also the reality in our own Western society. There is something hollow and fatuous about telling people who are entirely ruled by the wants and deprivations of everyday life, an elderly cleaning lady, for example, that they should develop their individuality. That is not so much humane and universally human as universally cynical in my view. Nevertheless, there is a crucial distinction here. The conditions of formal equality mean that even this famous elderly cleaning lady receives something like a licence to be an individual, a right to individuality, however little she is able to avail herself of it and convert it into a reality. In antiquity, in contrast, the idea of such a right did not exist. In this respect, Christianity, with its doctrine of the absolute value of the individual soul as immortal and created in the image of God, did indeed bring about a world-historical change of incalculable proportions, and Hegel was right to emphasize this.

It can be said that in antiquity the idea of individuality was essentially privileged. This means that, where individuality was able to develop, it was somewhat restricted, particular, one might even say barbaric. This circumstance had a negative effect upon the notion of individuality as something of universal human validity in the Middle Stoa, particularly in thinkers such as Posidonius and Panaetius,[11] turning it into something very pallid and chimerical. On the other hand, there is a period of antiquity in which we can genuinely speak of an individualistic society. This was the entire period following Alexander the Great that we are accustomed to referring to as the

Hellenistic age. During this epoch individuality did not so much form the substance of society as a kind of incidental accompaniment. For even where it developed it was more of a private intermezzo, a protected reserve for individuals, than something that determined the inner nature of society, as was true of the new society later on. In this connection, it is no mere chance that one of the most famous Hellenistic maxims for the individual should have been: *ladei biosas*, in other words, 'Live in obscurity'.[12] In other words, wherever individuality emerges it really remains separate from society, which is more or less left to its own devices, that is to say, the great political potentates, first Alexander and the Diadochi, and then the Romans. The consequence is that individuality remains a particular even where its social impact is concerned. And Jacob Burckhardt, who had great sensitivity in matters of this sort, and to whom we owe the deepest insights on such questions, has come up with the very perceptive comment – this is in *The Greeks and Greek Civilization* – that, in this so-called individualistic Hellenistic society, the individual became atrophied, thanks to the separation of the individual from the political and social reality. He is speaking only of Greece in the period following Epicurus, that is to say, of the true age of individualism in Greek society, but his conclusion is that in this age no record of great individuals – whatever that might mean – has come down to us.[13] The concept of the individual becomes radical in the modern world, the bourgeois world, only when the form of the economy, that is to say, the way in which the lives of human beings are reproduced, is determined by initiative, by labour, a sense of responsibility, the autonomy of individual human beings standing in a relationship based on exchange. 'Radical' here means that for centuries, right down to the threshold of our own age, the individual has proved to be the figure through which the universal, that is, the reproduction of the human world, is mediated. Modern history begins with the discovery of the individual, and this has a quite different pathos and what might be called a quite different three-dimensionality from the manifestation of individuality in antiquity. We see it in Descartes,[14] for example, or in Montaigne's essays, or in its first truly great expression, in Shakespeare.[15] In this sense we can say that in the history of modern, i.e., bourgeois, society the category of the individual is socialized: in the first instance, so that formally at least it becomes the *decisive* form of the social process. We need of course to make this idea dialectical if we do not wish to talk nonsense. In this instance, because the bourgeois concept of individuality contained the call for its socialization, that is to say, its adaptation to social norms, and because that has been the case ever since the concept of individuality became dominant, it has had its shadow side, namely the *crisis* of individuality. Today, when the category of the individual seems to be in complete decline, this crisis has assumed extreme forms.

You can see, then, the value of reading a writer such as Hegel as I have generally suggested, that is to say, not just with the requisite precision, but also by making certain allowances. If we read him in that way, then even assertions that are as provocative as those I have focused on, because they are provocative, turn out to have far more truth and to be far more productive than might appear to a theory that is inclined to throw the baby out with the bathwater and to consign Hegel's entire theory of history to the rubbish heap of obsolete thought simply because of one absurd statement. To this degree, then, theories of universal history do have their validity, as I have tried to show you with the aid of this arbitrarily chosen example of the concept of the individual – although admittedly it is not quite as arbitrary as it may seem, since the individual is a crucial phenomenon of history. After all, we might just as well assert that history is the history of the rise and fall of the individual as make a similar claim under some other heading. However, the fact that we might make use of a whole series of other definitions – Hegel's idea of freedom or Marx's thesis of the struggle between the forces of production and the relations of production are obvious examples – this fact shows that history is a *constellation* that can really be grasped only with the help of an elaborate philosophical theory, and not by reducing it to individual concepts or pairs of concepts. However, the theory of history as universal history is open to objections of quite a different sort. These objections may be based on theological or socio-critical assumptions, and you can see them in their most extreme form in the theses on the philosophy of history of Walter Benjamin to which he gave the title 'On the Concept of History'. These come from his very last period and can in a sense be regarded as his testament. They may well be the last text that he completed. You can read about it in our edition of his writings.[16] I would be grateful, in fact, if you all were to do this if at all possible, so that in my next lecture I can assume that you are all familiar with these theses. At all events, I should like to anticipate that, by pointing out that the element of consent, of apologia, that is to say, the element that justifies history from the standpoint of the victor and defends everything that has happened on the grounds of its necessity – this element of consent is connected with the construction of a theory of universal history because the assumption of such a continuous *unity* in history seems to point to the idea that history has a positive meaning. In this respect it resembles the element of victory which is proclaimed in the name of the principle that has been the unifying factor in history down to the present day. It would be the task of philosophy to determine whether that unifying factor really is the positive, meaningful principle it appears to be. But let me continue with this discussion next time.

LECTURE 10

10 December 1964

'NEGATIVE'
UNIVERSAL HISTORY

Ladies and gentlemen, last time I tried to show you that theories of universal history such as Hegel's have a lot more to be said in their favour than we are inclined to think at first sight, even though from a positivist standpoint they may seem to be guilty of arbitrariness or naïvety. I should now like to go on to explore a number of what I like to think of as far more valid objections to the construction of universal history. I believe that I pointed out in an earlier lecture that these objections are to be found in Benjamin's essay 'On the Concept of History', an essay which still appears in the Benjamin edition under the title of 'Theses on the Philosophy of History'. Benjamin himself had evidently fixed on 'On the Concept of History' as the definitive title, although in his letters he always spoke of the 'Theses on the Philosophy of History'.[1] I believe that it would be a good idea for me simply to read out to you the relevant thesis, and at the same time to alert you to the fact that Benjamin is attempting here to formulate a materialist conception of history, albeit one that is shot through with theological ideas that are presented in terms of a highly negative dialectic. It is not possible for me to explore this amalgam of materialism and theology at this moment, although I am fully aware that by failing to do so I run the risk that the very things I wish to emphasize may seem, shall we say, somewhat arbitrary to you, and their utterly compelling logic will fail to make itself fully apparent. But when all is said and done, I have to make sure that I stick to the topic of these lectures so as not to stray too far from what you have every right to expect from them. Thesis XVII states: 'Historicism rightly culminates in universal history. It may be that materialist historiography differs in method more clearly from universal history than from any other kind.'[2] I should note in passing that there is something faintly naïve, or even usurpatory, about the expression 'materialist historiography', since the predominant, official form of materialist historiography, that is to say, the historical writings of Marx and Engels and their successors, is very much within the tradition of universal history that descends from Hegel. In fact it makes a virtue of it. This means that Benjamin is attempting to enlist the authority of a materialist conception of history for an approach, his own, that is just as heretical when looked at from the position of Marxist practice as it is critical of traditional historicism. 'Universal history' (i.e., historicism) 'has no theoretical armoury.' Well, that is not something that can be said of Marxism. Despite Benjamin's strong sympathy for Marxism, particularly in his late phase, it is astonishing to see just how undeveloped his knowledge of Marxist theory is. Instead he worked out a version of Marxism that it would be unfair to juxtapose to Marx's own theory. By the same token, however, he did himself no favours by thinking of himself as an orthodox Marxist. But these are dogmatic quibbles that we need not go into here. The only point worth making in this connection is to note that it is an absolute travesty to attempt, as we find in the Eastern bloc countries, to claim Benjamin in support of beliefs which for the most part fly in the face of ideas that have been elevated there to the status of dogma.[3] Benjamin continues: 'Its procedure is additive: it musters a mass of data to fill the homogeneous, empty time.' Of course, as I hope I have shown you, *no* such claim can be made for a universalizing philosophy of history in the broadest sense, such as Hegel's. But now we have reached the nub of the question, the really interesting bit: 'Materialist historiography, on the other hand, is based on a constructive principle. Thinking involves not only the movement of thoughts' – we might say the movement of the time-continuum – 'but their arrest as well. Where thinking suddenly comes to a stop in a constellation saturated with tensions, it gives that constellation a shock, by which thinking is crystallized as a monad. The historical materialist', Benjamin says, 'approaches a historical object only where it confronts him as a monad.' I may perhaps remind you of what I said last time about my own belief that, especially in philosophical speculations about history, it was far more important to immerse oneself in particular phenomena than to elaborate universal structures. I am sure that you will take note of the affinity between my own way of thinking and that of the principle stated here by Benjamin. 'In this structure' the Benjaminian materialist 'recognizes the sign of a messianic arrest of happening, or (to put it differently) a revolutionary chance in the fight for the oppressed past.' Of course, you might say that here we have a universalizing motif, since in these theses what Benjamin perceives is the uninterrupted history of oppression – although, on the other hand, this unifying aspect is perceived only as something *negative*, and as something that he persistently disputes in the thesis that I am reading to you here. 'He takes cognizance of it' – of this chance – 'in order to blast a specific era out of the homogeneous course of history; thus, he blasts a specific life out of the lifework. As a result of this method, the lifework' – let us say the artist's or thinker's lifework – 'is both preserved and sublated *in* the work' – that is, in the individual, specific work – 'the era *in* the lifework, and the entire course of history *in* the era. The nourishing fruit of what is historically understood contains time in its *interior* as a precious but tasteless seed.'

What we have here, I would like to add, is nothing less than a theory that makes its appearance in Benjamin in a dogmatic form, but one whose validity can be demonstrated very cogently. His idea is that, contrary to what traditional philosophy believed, facts do not simply disperse in the course of time, unlike immutable, eternal ideas. The truth is that, while the traditional view inserts facts into the flow of time, they really possess a nucleus of time in themselves, they crystallize time in themselves. What we can legitimately call ideas is this nucleus of time within the individual crystallized phenomena, something that can only be decoded by interpretation.[4] In accordance with this, we might say that history is *discontinuous* in the sense that it represents life perennially disrupted. However, because history constantly repeats this process of disruption, and because it clings to the resulting fragments instead of its deceptive surface unity, the philosophical interpretation of history, in other words, the construction of history, acquires a view of the totality that the totality fails to provide *at first sight*. At the same time, history detects in these fragments the trace of possible developments, of something hopeful that stands in precise opposition to what the totality appears to show. In Hegel this discontinuity is hinted at in his theory of the spirits of the peoples [*Volksgeister*] that succeed one another in turn, a theory I shall return to. We may say – and here Benjamin may be justified in claiming to be a materialist – that the awareness of discontinuity goes hand in hand with the growing doubts about the possibility of understanding history as the unified unfolding of the idea. In general, the continuous structure of history is based on the assumption that a particular idea runs through history in its entirety and that the various facts gradually come closer to it. The more this way of thinking is resisted, together with its tendency towards idealization, the less will historians be tempted to think of history as a continuum, a continuum in which the idealism, the affirmative element, lies in the belief that things are getting better all the time. Put in general terms, the consciousness of discontinuity is simply that of the prevailing non-identity. This non-identity is the opposition between whatever is held down and the universal domination that is condemned to identity. And if history is looked at materialistically, as the history not of victories but of defeats,[5] we will become incomparably more conscious of this non-identity than was true of idealism.

The task of a dialectical philosophy of history, then, is to keep both these conceptions in mind – that of discontinuity and that of universal history. This means that we should not think in alternatives: we should not say history *is* continuity or history *is* discontinuity. We must say instead that history is highly continuous *in* discontinuity, in what I once referred to as the permanence of catastrophe.[6] In Benjamin himself I have discovered a sentence that comes very close to this when he speaks of 'the angel of history', the Angelus Novus, 'who seems about to move away from something he stares at. His eyes are wide, his mouth is open, his wings are spread. This is how the angel of history must look. His face is turned toward the past. Where a chain of events appears before *us*, *he* sees one single catastrophe, which keeps piling wreckage upon wreckage and hurls it at his feet.'[7] In this image, a magnificent one, incidentally, which grandly encompasses history as a whole in a way that is easily compatible with the monadological viewpoint, Benjamin finds an authentic expression for the union of the continuity and discontinuity of history. It is similar to at least one aspect of Hegel's theory, and in fact the resemblance is much more than casual, even though we may suppose that Benjamin's knowledge of Hegel was not very detailed. The resemblance is to be found in Hegel's doctrine that identity is not simply identity, but the identity of identity and non-identity, in other words, of concept and thing, since for Hegel the concept is the identity.[8] Admittedly – and this 'admittedly' which sounds like a minor reservation actually embraces a world of difference – the opposite situation obtains in Benjamin; and if I may add without immodesty, the same thing may be said of my own theory. The position is not that an identity rules which also contains non-identity, but non-identity is a non-identity of the identical and the non-identical. Thus non-identity includes what gives history its unity, what enables it to accommodate itself to the concept as well as what doesn't. For the very things that subjugate and submit, these very acts of subjugation and submission in which identity is torn apart, forge the identity of history of which we speak and which we must describe as negative identity. Simply to erase universal history from our thinking about history – and in this respect I *disagree* with what Benjamin says explicitly, although the opposite is *objectively* implied in his writings – would be to blind oneself to the course of history, the 'storm' of history of which he speaks.[9] We would blind ourselves just as effectively as by doing the opposite, namely by subsuming the facts of history into its overall course (which is what I have shown Hegel to have done) without emphasizing the non-identical side of history, since to do this confirms the course of history by the way in which it ignores individual fates.

Thus the task is both to construct *and* to deny universal history or, to use yet another Hegelian term, one used to refer to public opinion in the *Philosophy of Right*,[10] universal history is to be *respected* as well as *despised*. The domination of nature – which incidentally is mentioned in one of Benjamin's theses[11] – welds the discontinuous, hopelessly splintered elements and phases of history together into a unity while at the same time its own pressure senselessly tears them asunder once more. I would remind you of the quotation from Sickingen that I mentioned to you at the start of these lectures: 'Nought without cause'.[12] We might say that in its development hitherto history is constructed like a gigantic process involving the exchange of cause and effect. It is as if the principle of exchange were not only the determining factor in the countless myriad of actions that constitute the life of human beings, but as if the macrostructure, the macro-cosmic nature of history, were itself just one great exchange relationship in which penance follows the act of taking so that in this sense history never escapes from the bonds of *myth*.[13] This was a presentiment, incidentally, that was not alien to the early philosophers. Look, for example, at some of the documents of the early Greek philosophers, of the pre-Socratics. If you take the famous saying of Anaximander[14] and also certain statements of Heraclitus, and look at them from the standpoint of the philosophy of history, and not just of ontology, as is the fashion nowadays, you will get something of a sudden insight into the exchange structure of history.[15] We might even define the need to escape from this process of exchanging like for like as the *telos* of history, namely as the goal of liberating history from everything that history has been up to now. If you read the newspapers and are able to imagine what is involved in the events in the Congo,[16] you can reflect on the balance of horror between the atrocities committed by the natives and those committed by the forces of civilization by way of revenge. This will give you a direct insight into a contemporary instance of this situation. Not even the sanitized reports that have reached us can conceal the reality entirely. The cheers that greeted the liberation of Stanleyville by the [Belgian] paras are just as revolting as the mendacious claims by the Eastern camp that liberating Stanleyville from the natives and their atrocities was manifestly an instance of European imperialism. This too ignores the facts by failing to see the dialectic of history here, this wretched exchange relation. The two positions are equally repugnant and despicable. I would say that if you have a free relation towards history – and I venture to say that in the sense in which I have tried to explain it to you, the philosophy of history *is* this freedom towards history – that would enable you mentally to rise above these two possibilities, above partisanship in this restricted sense. The definitive threat to organized humanity by other organized human beings that we can see approaching in our time coincides with absolute continuity because the history of the mastery of nature really does culminate in such conflicts, just as it goes hand in hand with absolute discontinuity, in other words, with the fact that here the thread of history threatens to break – and to break once and for all.

In a society that has become societalized through and through, this discontinuity becomes evident in a far more specific sense. It is not necessary here to raise the spectre of the ultimate catastrophe – over-precipitately, I should like to add. There is a certain hubris, an intellectual hubris, in evoking the possibility of a total catastrophe which we can barely imagine, only to leap in just when intellectual solutions seem exhausted and propose some universal formula, even a negative one. On the one hand, total nuclear meltdown satisfies a need that is not so very different from that of an abstract utopia. But when we say that history is the union of continuity and discontinuity, and not either one of the two, we can see something of the sort in our own day. For, on the one hand, we can see how the power of totalitarian societies is growing in a way that cannot be misinterpreted, even if it does not always coincide with political control. On the other hand, we simultaneously perceive – through the fog of these totalitarian systems – something like a collapse of crucial historical forces into irreconcilable particularities. My late friend Franz Neumann advanced an argument of this kind in his book *Behemoth*,[17] a book that I would like to commend to you as a significant source for the philosophy of history. His principal thesis there is that the National Socialist state appears to be the very model of the absolute unification of society among current dominant regimes. In reality, however, despite its leader-principle and everything that goes with it, the unity that had developed more or less anonymously in a liberal society permeated by monopolies now disintegrates into the rule of rival cliques or power bases that cannot really be brought together under a common denominator, a common unified state structure. It would be my view that this tendency for society to break down into a number of competing, overpowerful groups will continue for the foreseeable future. They have long since passed the point where they can be synthesized into a higher concept and nor is there any possibility of a reconciliation in sight. When people nowadays speak of 'rule by interest groups', to use the term coined by Eschenburg in the very important book in which he has analysed this phenomenon, they may well mean what I have in mind here.[18] And perhaps I may add a further point. The term 'pluralism' is acquiring increasing currency in our own time. It is presumably the ideology describing the centrifugal tendencies of a society that threatens to disintegrate into unreconciled groups under the pressure of its own principles. This is then represented as if it were a state of reconciliation in which people lived together in harmony while in reality society is full of power struggles. As a minor by-product of these lectures I would like to recommend that you adopt an extremely wary attitude towards the concept of pluralism which, like the similar concept of 'social partners', is preached at us on every street corner. To transfigure and ideologize the elements of discontinuity or of social antagonisms in this way is part of the general ideological trend. In the same way, it is very characteristic of our age that the very factors that threaten to blow up our entire world are represented as the peaceful coexistence of human beings who have become reconciled and have outgrown their conflicts. This is a tendency which barely conceals the fact that mankind is beginning to despair of finding a solution to its disagreements. But all that is really by the by.

I would like to add that under the rule of the one principle, namely the world spirit, in the *negative* sense that I have explained to you, the elements that elude the world spirit, that is to say, the elements that I have been trying to explain to you – the individual elements, the individual group phenomena into which the great historical process fragments, begin themselves to take on something of a contaminated, doom-laden aspect. It would be altogether too primitive – and I would explicitly like to warn you against any simplistic acceptance of what I have said up to now, since it would be all too easy for some of you to believe that this is what I had intended – it would be simplistic if you were to assume that, in what I have called the historical process or the world spirit that gives shape to the totality and draws it into itself, it is the particular that is in the right, and has the right of human destiny on its side, while the totality is in the wrong. If you reflect for a moment on what I said at some length previously, namely that the totality preserves itself and prevails through conflict, that is to say, through the enduring persistence of particularity, you will be able to dispel an illusion about particularity. It remains true that historical particulars are constantly the victims of the general course of history. As against this, the overall course of history is only possible because the particulars necessarily harden out and become inflexible, whether they will or no. In this sense, we can say that the particular deserves the totality in which it finds itself. This too is an idea that I have tried to explain to you from a different angle, namely from the idea that the social totality comes to prevail through the actions of individual human beings. I should now like to focus on this a little more closely. The situation is that where the non-identical still takes the form of what are more or less natural categories, which incidentally are not at all natural in actual fact – they are merely relics from older historical epochs – these non-identical elements that have not yet been absorbed into the historical process go rancid and become poisonous. They go rancid much as the universal principle does when confronted with them. This too we may test against the recent events in Africa – if indeed we can pluck up the courage to do so, something that is not altogether easy. It is really the case that, under the rule of the totality, even the particular that opposes it nevertheless collaborates in weaving the web of disaster. It does so not just by lapsing into particularity, but by degenerating into something poisonous and bad. That is to say, these natives who are running wild in Africa for the last time are not one whit better than the paras, than the barbaric paratroops who are struggling to make them see reason, i.e., to accept the benefits of a progressive civilization, in a manner that is familiar to all of you. This is a dialectic that we should all fix in our minds. We might go even further and say that whatever fails to fit in with the dominant principle finds itself reduced to the level of mere chance. The great historical trend sucks the marrow out of everything oppositional and recalcitrant, and what gets left behind is something insignificant, lacking in substance and thus a random affair.

I believe that in this context we should dwell on the idea of chance for just a moment. Chance plays a part in history because we always have to ask ourselves about the role of chance events in history. For example, during the recent world war one had the feeling as an outside observer that there were countless moments when the fact that Hitler was losing seemed to be attributable to chance. However, it then appeared that it was only through these chance events that the great trend, by which I mean the greater industrial potential of the Western world, succeeded in prevailing against Hitler's bid to conquer the world. If I may return to the concept of the *'spell'* that holds sway over history and that I have attempted to explain to you,[19] I would say that chance is the form taken by freedom under a spell. As long as the spell of history lasts, whatever is immune to this spell is mutilated and defeated; it is stripped of meaning, blind and therefore a matter of chance. All the non-identical phenomena that are expelled as a result of the domination of the identity principle are nevertheless mediated by the power of that principle. What persists are the stale remnants left over once the process of identification has taken its share. And even these stale remnants are left mutilated, scarred by the power of the principle of identity. The spell cast by the identity principle, by the world spirit, to formulate it even more emphatically, perverts whatever is different – and even the smallest quantity would be incompatible with the spell if it were still pure. This other then becomes something evil and pernicious. Because it is a random thing, this non-identical remnant then becomes so abstract that in its abstractness it converges with the law of identification. This is the truth implicit in Hegel's doctrine of the unity of chance and necessity, a doctrine which he intended positively, as praise of the world spirit, though to be sure he did not really intend to say what I am suggesting here. Chance coincides with necessity only where both are equally bereft of meaning, equally external and equally unreconciled. The replacement of the traditional laws of causality by statistics whose core, even in its own terminology, is the principle of chance can provide us with proof of the convergence of chance and a victorious necessity.[20] But what chance and necessity have, lethally, in common is what metaphysics refers to as *fate*. Fate has its place; it is a negative concept. I believe that this is the dividing line separating thought from all mythologizing notions of fate, such as Heidegger's in his Hölderlin interpretations.[21] Fate has its place in the sphere in which the thinking of rulers holds sway, as well as in the realm of those who fall outside that sphere and for those who, having been abandoned by reason, acquire an irrationality that barely differs from the irrationality of the necessity insisted upon by the subject. The scraps of a subjugated nature that have been spewed out by the process of domination are just as deformed as those that are ground down by the machinery. Only true understanding would be *superior* to the two. It would stand in for a state of the world – true understanding, which of course would not amount to actual reconciliation, because knowledge alone is not the same thing as reconciliation – but true understanding would *stand in* for a state of the world in which everything that exists would cease to exist merely for others. This is because it would no longer remain content with its own existence-for-itself, its separation and particularity. Thus reflection on difference would help towards reconciliation, what Horkheimer once called 'happy reflection'. This is what would help, rather than extirpation and the elimination of the totality.

Hegel, on whom we have to some extent been basing these remarks, was surely aware of this. Despite his praise of totality he always insisted on its abstract nature. In so doing, he wished to remind us of what is left out of the totality. The grandiose nature of Hegel's project, both its reprehensible and conciliatory aspects, lies in his attempt to include the non-identical in identity (as I tried to show in the quotation that I gave you a few moments ago).[22] Thanks to this attempt, the non-identical itself is taken possession of by the spell while, on the other hand, it becomes the factor that enables the abstract spell to be attenuated. I believe that we should now move on to make a closer examination of how this attempt to gain recognition for concrete reality in history looks in detail under the spell of the totality, under the spell of the principle of identification. We shall find that the Hegelian philosophy itself has provided us with a paradigm in the shape of the concept with which it sought to grasp the process of history, the concept namely of the *spirit of the peoples* [*Volksgeister*], who are supposed to succeed each other in turn and in which according to his theory the *world spirit* actualizes itself. We shall see, I fear I have to tell you, that this magnificent project to spell out his conception of history ends up in its very opposite, namely in a reinforcement, a theoretical reinforcement of the acts of suppression that characterize history. Next time, then, I shall talk about the concept of the spirits of the peoples and the philosophy of the history of the nation.

LECTURE 11

15 December 1964

THE NATION AND THE SPIRIT OF THE PEOPLE IN HEGEL

Adorno's notes for this lecture:

Transition to the *spirit of the people* [*Volksgeist*] as Hegel's attempt to individualize the overall trajectory of history.[1] [Insertion IIa]

[Insertion IIa:] 'This actual and organic spirit of a people actualizes and reveals itself through the relationship between the particular national spirits and in world history as the universal world spirit.'[2] NB the word '*universal*' that precisely marks the regression to extensional logic, with its additive approach.

'The principles of the spirits of peoples [*Volksgeister*] are in general of a limited nature and their deeds and destinies are the manifest [*erscheinende*] dialectic of these spirits [from which] the universal spirit produces itself and exercises its right – which is the highest right of all – over finite spirits in world history as the world's court of judgement.'[3]

[Addendum:] Like Spengler, Hegel speaks somewhere of the natural *death* of the spirits of peoples as of individuals[4] – he hypostasizes pseudo-concreteness, boils it down into individuality. This gives it an *archaic* flavour. – The individual consciousness reduced to something accidental. [End of addendum]

NB the fact that the spirits of peoples are necessarily destined to *decline and fall*.

But if each spirit of the people is limited and hence doomed, it is the form of each national spirit that is to be preserved, and absorbed into a higher one.

Reflection on this is *absent* in Hegel.

Incidentally, the *particularity* of the spirits of peoples is problematic.

It is above all the folkways,[5] *mores*, that are what is substantial in Hegel's view – they resemble one another to the point of *abstractness* – like the unconscious (NB music).

Psychoanalysis. Against the illusion that the archaic *is more concrete*. [There are] *older*, often harder forms of repression. [End of insertion]

[Addendum] Hegel in search of the anti-Cartesian; in opposition to abstract, national equality, he wishes to *salvage* the ideas of Vico[6] and Montesquieu, as well as Herder. Has its good side. This good side is not constant. [End of addendum]

With his concept of 'spirit of the people', Hegel is unreflectingly implicated in the idolization of the nation that emerged at the turn of the nineteenth century.

'Nation' itself a historical concept that arose in the eighteenth century (*les hommes de lettres ou riches*). The *thing* itself is likewise historical. Bourgeois form of organization regressing to tribalism. Nature suppressed and re-emerging in mutilated form.

Manifests itself in Hegel as an unchanging component of history, immutable in the changing procession of individual spirits of the people. – Hegel full of such constants as *prima philosophia*.

The simple consideration that we would soon run out of the spirit of the peoples that had not yet made their appearance does not occur at all.

The nation – supposed to tame the diffuse tribes, *gentes*.

But there is something retrograde about it in a developed bourgeois society. (NB such admixtures are *necessary* in bourgeois society; as a corrective to the mastery of nature in the service of the principle of lordship.)

This is fetishized because otherwise the people who are threatened by it would not fit in with it. [Insertion 12a]

[Insertion 12a] Nowadays, nations facing the real identity of historical processes, are largely ideological, conserved.

The experience in the Veltliner Keller.[7] Dialectic: to Americans concrete manifestations are merely masks, farce. But on the exchange principle, that is what they *really* are. 13 December 1964 [End of lecture][8]

[Notes taken by Hilmar Tillack:] According to Hegel's *Philosophy of Right*, the spirit of the people objectivizes itself in the nations, and beyond them in the state. At the same time, both the spirit of the people and the nation should be examined in the context of a theory of universal history or world spirit. More particularly, the relationship between spirit of the people and world spirit is such that the world spirit neither hovers above world history, nor does it become realized immediately in world history. Instead, it assumes the shape of the various spirits of the peoples and of their relations to one another, relations of waxing and waning. According to §33 of Hegel's *Philosophy of Right*, the 'actual and organic spirit of a people actualizes and reveals itself through the relationship between the particular national spirits and in world history as the universal world spirit' [p. 62f.]. A subtle non-dialectical contradiction in this points to the problems inherent in Hegel's philosophy of history: the world spirit 'actualizes itself through the relationship between the particular national spirits' – that is strictly dialectical. We find the same thing in the *Phenomenology* where the procession of figures or shapes is not separated from the particular figures. On the other hand, in terms of extensional logic, because the world spirit actualizes itself 'through the relationship between the particular national spirits and in world history as the universal world spirit', Hegel is appealing to a higher degree of universality. This is significant because, alongside the conception of the absolute as something concrete, there is a recurrent notion that the universal possesses a greater dignity than the particular. Hegel always wants to have it both ways at once: a radical dialectic from which nothing is left out, while at the same time he remains a Platonist who presents a theory of universal substance in which the national spirits are introduced as specific instances of this all-inclusive universal. There is no doubt that Hegel's sympathies lie with the universal, but he sticks with the idea of national spirits, shying away from the conception of a universal spirit of mankind and indeed even the concept of mankind as such.

In §340 of the *Philosophy of Right*, Hegel writes: 'The principles of the *spirits of nations* [*Volksgeister*] are in general of a limited nature because of that particularity in which they have their objective actuality and self-consciousness as *existent* individuals, and their deeds and destinies in their mutual relations are the manifest [*erscheinende*] dialectic of the finitude of these spirits. It is through this dialectic that the *universal* spirit, *the spirit of the world*, produces itself in its freedom from all limits, and it is this spirit which exercises its right – which is the highest right of all – over finite spirits in *world history* as the *world's court of judgement* [*Weltgericht*]' [p. 371]. The courts with their judges – that reminds us of the transcendental world spirit who presides over the individual spirits of the nations. This is undoubtedly a factor here, but what is even more important is the echo of Goethe's Mephisto: 'for all things that exist / deserve to perish and would not be missed.'[9] Because of their limited nature, the national spirits are fallible and finite. They wither and die, deserving their ruin because of their limited nature. The world spirit – more properly, the absolute – consists solely in their ruin. Later on, Spengler was criticized for his refusal to acknowledge progress, but there is a certain continuity between Hegel's metaphysics of history and the later nihilist of history. Admittedly, Hegel does speak of progress in the consciousness of freedom, but this progress consists only in the succession, senseless in itself, of the individual national spirits, a succession brought about by their finitude, culpability. Hegel speaks of the natural death of the national spirits as one might speak of the death of individuals.

The category of national spirits as collective individuals fits in very conveniently with Hegel's desire to give concrete shape to the relations between universal and particular, but it is essentially a pseudo-concreteness. The universal character of a people, a nation is regarded as an individual and hypostasized; it is even treated as something possessing an essence of its own. Despite the limited nature of the national spirits with their *mores*, their repressive customs and usages, they are endowed with an absolute right vis-à-vis actual individuals. The principle governing the decline and fall of the national spirits should have been the sublation of their form and their objectification, namely the actual nation, their elevation to a higher stage of being. In reality this has come to pass since nations have ceased to be the substantial units of history. The conversion of national spirits into particularities, the replacement of actual individuals by individual national spirits, is problematic. What is problematic is not just the repressive nature of the national spirit in its attitude towards individuals, but the individuality of the national spirit itself. Hegel reduces this individuality to specific national, natural constants. Interestingly, these include the concept of race, which, following his criticism in the chapter on 'Physiognomy and Phrenology' in the *Phenomenology of spirit*, should have been excluded. If we assume the existence of pre-individual societies, the primacy of the collective, we find that the structures of such national collectives are surprisingly similar to each other, that they are not so very individuated at all, just as folk melodies that antedate individuated musical composition do not differ all that markedly but seem all to have been stamped in the same mould. Psychoanalysis ascribes the basic mental processes to a minimum number of psychological patterns – the pervasive structures of totemism, the prohibition on incest, taboos, etc. In themselves, primitive and national characteristics as mere natural phenomena are no more differentiated than the unconscious, which Freud locates as prior to the process of individuation.

What Hegel describes as the particular feature of the national spirits is precisely *not* the element of nationality. The situation is not that the national spirits form a concrete manifold which is subsequently subjected to a rationalizing process. Primitive forms of mind are characterized by a certain abstractness, which comes as something of a surprise. So in reality the idea that history exhibits a progressive increase in abstraction is too simple. Individuation is an intermediate state between the archaic and the abstraction that arises from the process of exchange that subjugates the individual.

Hegel's philosophy of history is implicated in the cult of the nation. But this too has its progressive side, since the tendency is for the overall course of history to become individuated, in contrast to the philosophical tendency to construct an overall pattern from a small number of concepts. In this respect Hegel belongs to the anti-Cartesian trend, as exemplified by Vico's 'Scienza Nova', and Montesquieu, from whom Hegel took over the theory that institutions are the product of history, a theory that cannot be gleaned from abstract rationality, as well as by Hamann and Herder's speculations.[10] The progressive element in this is the more dynamic view of the national spirit in contrast with the previous static theory.

The concrete articulation of history as opposed to measuring it in general terms against the progress of enlightenment – that is Hegel's intention. In the early eighteenth century these categories were progressive, but their significance changed with the passage of time. The concept of a particular that has developed historically, of a concrete historical power such as the nation – can age and become obsolete. If it is retained despite further developments, it turns reactionary and violent, just as happened to Hegel's national spirit as opposed to Herder's.

The concept of the nation is a late arrival; it was alien to the Middle Ages. The turning point came in the eighteenth century when it was defined as a sort of class concept. 'The nation' became synonymous with the notables, with the rich and the educated. The concept of race only emerged when that of the nation no longer sufficed and it was necessary to become all-inclusive. Both the concept of the nation and the nation itself are products of history; they are not a natural category, but the attempt to create a bourgeois form of organization by regressing to tribalism. These tribal associations, natural associations, have gradually been forced to retreat more and more in the history of the West. The modern world wished to assist these associations which had been kept in check by feudalism and the Christian feudal world. It made a pact with these natural formations that had been suppressed and that were coming once again to the fore – this is the source of the savagery and aggression of national units: a mutilated nature is brought together with the nation by means of oppression. This mutilated thing continues to reveal itself in nationalism to this very day. Bourgeois rationality is combined with the return to the pre-bourgeois natural association. This is what constrained Hegel to confer on the nation that quality of immutability and to make it a fixed constituent of history.

Hegel's theory puts on the brakes at this point and brings the dialectic to a standstill. A theory that involves constants and dialectics simultaneously – that is something he contrived to harmonize ingeniously in the *Logic*, but it cannot be sustained in the long run. The nation was supposed to constrain the *gentes* and at the same time to honour them. However, that has repressive implications. The irrational elements in developed rational bourgeois society are not coincidental, but essential. Ends–means rationality predominates, but the ends, the organization as a whole, remain irrational. This explains the persistence of irrational institutions such as the nation and the family. Because the theory as a whole is not transparent, not compatible with the principle of rationality, the citizen always has a bad conscience when he operates with such concepts. Hence the rancour and rage in the concept of the nation, something that is perpetuated in the Eastern bloc countries, where 'cosmopolitanism' is a term of abuse. Sacrifice for one's own nation does not produce the increase in the standard of living that people expect. This is why the nation has to be a value for its own sake, independently of its relation to people. This mechanism prevails objectively. It corresponds to a need, but one that is concealed from people. The nationalism of the rulers is just as pig-headed and unthinking as that of the ruled. In comparison with the construction of a radically organized society based on exchange, the nation and the national spirit are anachronisms. The individual is supposed to derive his own substance exclusively from the spirit of the nation to which he belongs, although in Goethe Hegel had a contrary example before his very eyes. [End of Hillack's notes]

LECTURE 12
17 December 1964
THE PRINCIPLE
OF NATIONALITY

Last time, I started to tell you about the role of the nation in the construction of history. In view of the complexities of that concept, it seems only right that I should summarize what I said then in a more succinct and hopefully more authoritative form, and at the same time make a few additional points. We may say that the nation is the specifically bourgeois form of social organization; it is a form of organization because it has emerged historically in certain definite units, whether geographical or linguistic in nature, or whether otherwise defined. It does not simply exist, but has had to fight to establish itself in the course of historical struggles. In accordance with the economic principles governing bourgeois society, this form of organization has perfected itself today, in the late phase of bourgeois society. Nations, or many nations, are transforming themselves – or have done so at particular stages of history – into something like huge companies, vast economic entities, and remain like that even if free-trade tendencies may temporarily mitigate their strict organization, outwardly at least. These massive concerns, which today could be said to be characterized by common values, and by internal currencies, are the ultimate stage of this process. They may even be said to go one step further since traditional national frontiers are to some extent ignored. If we regard nations as a form of organization appropriate to the rational constitution of bourgeois society viewed as an economic system, this implies that they replace natural forms of association, which are then all brought together in the modern nation. Moreover, sacrifices are imposed on these natural associations, since nations, because of their size, no longer possess transparent links to individual interests, while in smaller social forms, in other words, feudal or smaller city-states, this relationship was rather more transparent, at least for the actual representatives of the economy. (This statement, too, needs some historical qualification, but it can stand, if you take it *cum grano salis*, without our being crucified by the economists.) The nation developed everywhere through a struggle against feudalism. Feudalism was a world-historical force, but because of its basis in the family it was an essentially natural form of organization. People cling to these natural bonds and to part from them always costs us an effort – just think back to what the first day at school costs a child who has been brought up sheltered by his family, and you will be able to imagine what a nation expects from such natural associations. Thus by retreating from these natural bonds, the nation also suppresses them, even though it takes over some of their features, and this forces it to act *as if* it were itself a natural form of society.

And this is the primal pseudos, the primal delusion implicit in the concept of the nation and which then finds expression in those ideologies of national spirit that I have already criticized in connection with the Hegelian texts, as you may recollect. In consequence, from the very outset – and by no means as late as the so-called age of Romanticism, but as early as certain writers of the sixteenth century – the idea of the nation has possessed what today we would call a romantic element that culminates in the delusions of racism. The delusion is that a form of association that is essentially dynamic, economic and historical misunderstands itself as a natural formation, or misconstrues itself ideologically as natural. This culminates in a belief in races, even though it is perfectly plain that under fascism the national groups that have imagined themselves to be defined by race have long since ceased to be so. I believe that these arguments make clear that this delusion, this fiction, strictly applies to the historical dynamic that is implicit in the concept of the nation. It is not sufficient, or rather it is too easy, to talk about the delusions of racism and to denounce them. What counts here is the ability to explain it and to recognize its place in the dynamics of history. I believe that only by doing so, only by uncovering the historical roots of racism, does it become possible to escape the persistent habits of thought associated with it. It is a delusion in a strict sense of the word. Mind has become estranged from nature and even from itself, so that in this situation racism represents the mind's compensation for what has been done to it, for the nature that has been suppressed in it. This nature then reappears in perverse form, namely as fiction, and in that guise it necessarily assumes the destructive qualities that we have seen in nationalism throughout its entire history from the end of the eighteenth century and through the nineteenth, passing through imperialism until it reached its apogee in fascism. We may say, then, that the concept of the nation gives us an insight into the mechanisms that Freud analysed on the level of individual psychology in his book *Civilization and its Discontents*.[1] Only here, they appear as collective powers or as achievements of the collective unconscious, if I may for once be permitted to use this expression. In the concept of the nation, repressed nature is mobilized in the interests of a progressive domination of nature, progressive rationality, and, as a regressive phenomenon, that is to say, as a return to something already rendered obsolete, it is just as contaminated by that as it is by its untruth, which compels it constantly to gloss over its failings and exaggerate its virtues. Precisely because the nation is not nature, it has ceaselessly to proclaim its closeness to nature, its immediacy and the intrinsic value of the national community.

Things have not always been thus – and I believe that it is important for me to add this. There have been periods when the nation had a highly progressive function. If it had not done so, if the populations and all other important interested parties had not benefited hugely from the national form of organization of bourgeois society, then the sheer tenacity of the idea of the nation, even in an age when its failings are as obvious as they are at present, would be completely incomprehensible. I need only remind you how much the development of communications, and hence of the forces of production in general, was advanced by the collapse of the barriers erected by the small feudal monarchies, the states generally referred to under absolutism as petty principalities. I need only remind you that it was only with the creation of modern nation-states that something like a universal legal system was established – for example, that of safe conduct and the like; and, above all, that it was only by bringing large territories together and combining them into a single political unit that it became possible to organize large bodies of people in a rational manner and in harmony with the principle of exchange. For previously, under the feudal system, groups of people were only loosely connected with one another and in those circumstances could not be welded together into the totality of a bourgeois society. It is difficult to overestimate these achievements on the part of the nation-state as contrasted with feudalism. And it is certainly no coincidence that it is the nation-state that has witnessed the great achievements of technology, the great technological inventions. Lastly, we should note that this progressive side of the nation (if I can call it that) extends to its cultural life. That is to say, in its earliest stages at least, the truly free and great intellectual achievements of modern, bourgeois society were all linked to the origins of national consciousness and the creation of nation-states. Above all, this holds good for the creation of a national language. The most famous instance of this is of course Dante, but we could no doubt say the same thing of Chaucer in English literature, and in Germany the Luther Bible probably had a similar function – although these are chicken-and-egg situations in which it is not clear whether the national language and hence the national consciousness are the creations of those great intellectual structures, or whether, as seems to me to be more likely, the historical development of the mind had reached a point where it could be crystallized in the great linguistic monuments which made use of a national language. We can say that even as late as Herder – I believe I may have said this to you already – the concept of humanity and the emergence of the principle of nationality go hand in hand. It would be an interesting and rewarding task, sociologically and philosophically, to analyse this in Herder's case.

But then, around the time of the political victory of the bourgeoisie over absolutism, something happened. At the same time as the curbing of absolutism blunted the last vestige of feudalism still surviving into the bourgeois era, nationality turned into that truly pernicious, destructive phenomenon that we have come to experience. This change was already visible to Franz Grillparzer, a poet of moderate views, wholly innocent of any political radicalism. His attitude was summed up in that dictum that I hope is known to all of you to the effect that the historical process leads from humanity via nationality to bestiality.[2] At this juncture, Hegel represents something of a watershed. I believe that, now that we are studying Hegel's philosophy of history, we would do well to look closely at those passages that make it clear that Hegel had more in common with totalitarianism than one might have imagined, but which also show that he still exhibits the features of bourgeois liberalism. I should like to read you a passage in this connection, which goes as follows: 'The naturalness of spirit ... progresses into the further particularization of these racial differences and so falls apart into the multiplicity of local and national spirits.'[3] The concept of race occurs frequently, and likewise the reference to his belief in the difficulty in modifying nationality, something he regards as a natural given without seriously inquiring into the *mechanism* that enables a national consciousness to persist even when it has been rendered obsolete by history. This is one of the moments in which we might almost say that the dialectical philosopher lapses naïvely into static ways of thinking. In this connection he says – and this is extremely interesting and we shall have to discuss it in some detail – that 'the spirits of the people or national spirits' (I am quoting this verbatim) 'belong partly to the natural history of man and partly to the philosophy of world history.'[4] I should like to bring to your attention – we shall probably come back to it after the holidays, when we shall discuss it in greater depth, but I do not want it to be overlooked – the fact that precisely this concept of natural history which Hegel introduces so emphatically in connection with the principle of nationality is then taken up by Marx,[5] although in a radically altered form, as is so often the case with Marx's adoption of Hegelian concepts. I should also add, in the interests of philological accuracy, that generally speaking 'natural history' was not used in the precise sense that I intend it to have in what I shall be saying to you. Rather, in this older usage, 'natural history' really meant no more than 'nature study' [*Naturkunde*]. But the very fact that nature is somehow regarded as having a history – presumably a legacy of the baroque period – is highly significant, and hence we shall have to insist on the point. As early as Hegel, then, we find this tendency to stabilize things that have been rendered obsolete by the passage of time and, if possible, to restore them. And the later Hegel had a strong inclination to intervene in threatened and obsolete situations with a view to restoring them by converting them into ahistorical constants. Looked at historically, such constants are always regarded as 'natural'. It is then simply from this functional point of view, without regard to any truth content it might have, that we have to view his use of the ethnologically untenable concept of race.

Today, the situation is completely different. And this brings me back to matters that I alluded to last time in connection with my observation in the Veltliner Keller in Zurich. This was that, while Hegel had some justification for speaking of the substantial nature of the national in his day, the nation has now been reduced to a mere façade by the uniformity of the organization of life on an international plane. If you have the opportunity to fly long distances and to see – just to mention the most obvious fact – how all over the world airports resemble one another, by which I mean the entire business of loudspeakers, hostesses and everything that goes with them, you will indeed find it hard to resist the impression that other differences between individual towns exist largely only to motivate passengers to travel from one to another, from Karachi to Naples or elsewhere. But for this marketing interest, what these airports all symbolize would be taken further, to the point where the cities they serve would likewise be ruthlessly – I almost said buried beneath it. In that event, the forms of human existence which even now provide us with only an illusory sense of diversity would plainly exhibit the fundamental equality of the exchange principle which dominates our lives. I should like to emphasize that I do not believe that we are dealing here with a superficial phenomenon of external trappings: in other words, that the airports may all be the same, while the lives led by the peoples are notable for their great diversity. I believe that for you simply to play down the force of these examples would be to mistake the situation. The contrary is the case. The phenomena I am highlighting here as illustrating a historical insight simply point to the fact that the modes of production, namely the primacy of industry, have come to prevail throughout the world and that wherever this principle obtains, both in practical terms and as far as its marketing value is concerned, these uniformities will emerge. In other words, and this is what we must say by way of criticism of Hegel, it is no longer the case that so-called cosmopolitanism is the more abstract thing in contrast to the individual nations; cosmopolitanism now possesses the greater reality. We can now see a convergence in countless spheres of life and forms of production, right down to clothing and all sorts of other things that are all based on American models. This convergence points to the convergence of the fundamental processes of life, in other words, the dominance of industrial production. Compared with this, the differences between nations are merely rudimentary vestiges.

So what we are seeing is a change of quantity into quality. At this point, Hegel can be said to be in the right against Hegel in so far as in the sphere of nations, the national spirits, which in his writings have the status of a principle, are conceived to be eternal; although he might well have asked himself whether the supply of nations might not be all too rapidly exhausted, given that nations only have their turn when the previous incumbents have been slaughtered. By a qualitative change I mean that the theory of history in terms of national spirits is now outdated. It is no longer possible to say that the world spirit inhabits a particular nation as Hegel could in his day – for example, when he once caught sight of Napoleon and imagined that he could see the world soul on horseback,[6] in other words, in the shape of the specifically imperialist French national spirit of 1806. History itself, then, has put paid to what Hegel imagined was a timeless principle. Hegel and even Spengler still believed that the world spirit passed the torch from one nation to the next. But I should like to add that one of the factors responsible for the gloomy outlook for the present age is that we can now see that there is something amiss with this belief. Incidentally, there are passages in Hegel where he prophesies that one day the Slav nations will take their turn in this system, which he persists in basing on the model of ruling and being ruled. Now, if this principle were to be perpetuated by the triumph of the Slav peoples, this would not be saying too much in favour of the world spirit, which is supposed to have become conscious of itself. So today, the task is not simply to conserve the concrete essence of human relations in the transitory form of the different nations – which incidentally has long since been unmasked as fraudulent – but to bring about this concrete state of human community on a higher plane. And by a superior state, I do not mean a mechanical union of superpowers joined together in even more gigantic blocs. This would, if anything, just worsen the disaster. What I have in mind is something that would change the form of society itself and put an end to the abstract organization that acts so repressively towards its members. This is by no means as utopian as it sounds on first hearing, if only because modern technology already opens up the possibility of decentralization that actually makes it unnecessary to bring societies together in gigantic hierarchical entities. This means that the historical form of progressive rationalization has ceased to be the most rational way of doing things and it survives only in the interests of the existing relations of production. In the meantime, however, it would already be possible to organize societies far more rationally in much smaller units that could collaborate peaceably with one another and from which all those aggressive and destructive tendencies would have been banished. But, oddly enough, it is precisely the technical advances towards decentralization that have been neglected.

What we see in their place is the fetishization of the concept of the nation. I have already said something to you about this. We may say that the fetishism of the nation is especially highly developed in countries where nation-building was a failure. This is particularly true of Germany. As you know, in Germany, unlike France and Britain, the conflict between the vassals, in other words the representatives of feudal power, and the centralizing head of state was never fully resolved. That failure was traditionally embodied in the collapse of the Holy Roman Empire at the turn of the nineteenth century. The concept of nation has always had its precarious and repressive aspects both internally and externally, but the fact that the Germans never succeeded in creating a nation turned that concept into a trauma. In a specific sense, we can say that National Socialism represented an extremely belated catching up with the organizational form of the nation. The power that National Socialism possessed over people in Germany was probably connected with the fact that the Nazis had achieved something that had previously been thwarted in Germany and that had been a traumatic experience for so many people. But in Germany, just as the bourgeois revolution came too late, so too did the process of nation-building linked to the principle of the bourgeois revolution. This belated arrival was no less fatal for National Socialism since it endowed that movement with the particular and terrible qualities that occur in history whenever, as Hegel puts it, something is abandoned by the world spirit. It is very similar to the way in which the witches' trials occurred not at the time when Thomism was flourishing but during the period of the Counter-Reformation, when the ancient organization of the church had been shaken and its recovery problematic. I believe then that you must think of the specific case of German nationalism, and no doubt also its virulent nature, as the product of a failed process of nation-building and of its productive function, both matters associated with its belated arrival on the world stage.

To return to Hegel, the concept of the nation always has the propensity to belittle the individual in comparison to the universal and then to defame him. When Hegel establishes the nation as the connecting link between the individual and the objective or universal configuration in which the national spirit manifests itself, he does so chiefly because the concept provides a splendid ideological handle with which to reinforce the predominance of the universal as it existed in pre-individual, repressive ages before the category of the individual had come into being and the blind rule of the collective prevailed. However, this concept of nation is no longer compatible with Hegel's own doctrine of progress in the consciousness of freedom, and even in Hegel's own day it already belonged in the realm of ideology. In this context we should remind ourselves of Hegel's famous eulogies of war in *The Philosophy of Right*.[7] These eulogies were heavily exploited by the National Socialists, and I believe they were the only Hegelian propositions that were popular under Hitler. Their lesson is that, while Hegel believed that in the state antagonisms were, if not eliminated, at least tamed, in his glorification of the concept of the nation, the elements of antagonism and repression did break through to the surface against his own intentions in his cult of war. The national spirits, the nations, are fundamentally inured to reason and to that extent they are incompatible with Hegel's own doctrine of progress in the consciousness of freedom. They are anachronisms – unless we go so far (and Hegel is himself not above the suspicion that he has gone so far on occasion) as to sever all links between the spirit or the world spirit and actual human reason and individual reason, and to hypostasize them. When discussing Hegel in the course of these lectures, I have often praised him for emphasizing the logic of the whole, the 'nought without cause', the necessary chain of reasoning, as opposed to merely subjective individual reasoning. I have suggested that there is something remarkably progressive and magnificent about this. And what is magnificent is his insight into the context of guilt or the web of delusion characteristic of society as a whole.[8]

However, we must add that this complete separation of the concept of spirit as an objective reality from every form of subjective reason, in other words, the absolute hypostasization of this objective logic of things as opposed to the sensuous actuality of the course of history as it is enacted by individual human beings, becomes in Hegel a means of justification, a way of justifying and finding excuses for things that are absolutely irrational and lacking in spirit. The tenor of what I have been saying up to now is that in Hegel the path of the world spirit seems to resemble nothing so much as a terrible entrapment, a kind of infernal machine. You will rightly be asking yourselves, and looking to me for an answer to the question of how it was possible for Hegel, who was by no means blind and who spoke as cuttingly of the horrors of the course of history as apart from him only Schopenhauer could – how it was possible for him despite all that to end up glorifying history.[9] Now, we have reached the point where you have the answer, or so I should like to think. What he does is to split the logic of the course of history, that is to say, the rationality of the necessity of development from one event to the next, from any confrontation with individual human reason, even though it is in that reason that all judgements about the rationality or irrationality of the whole have their roots. This enables him to disregard the rationality of individuals, in other words, the rational interests of individual human beings. Instead he can proclaim as positively rational the intractable tangle of historical events and processes that is actually at loggerheads with the legitimate rationality of individual human beings. I would say that this is the starting-point from which to construct systematically a philosophy of history that would be prevented by its own logic from sliding into ideology or making concessions to any ideology alien to it. However, this can only be achieved at the price that a concept of spirit that dispenses with any justification before the bar of reason thereby ceases to be comprehensible as spirit. This is similar to the way in which Hegel's concept of the subject – this too is a concept that runs through the entire Hegelian system – how his concept of the subject thinks of itself as being an absolutely objective thing over and above the actual subject. In other words, he thinks of it as an absolute that rises above the subjectivity of individual human beings. This procedure enables this subjectivism that has made itself absolute to oppress the individual historical subjects and to oppose them. We can also turn this around and say that Hegel's entire theory is based on a distinction between natural elements and historical elements, but that, in the final analysis, it fits in with the concept of *natural history* that he himself promulgated. And that brings me to a discussion of the concept of natural history, with which I should like to begin in the second half of the semester, and which will then lead us on to the problem of freedom.

LECTURE 13

5 January 1965

THE HISTORY
OF NATURE (I)

Adorno's notes for this lecture:

[Later addition:] continue here after the vacation. 5.1.65

Fundamental statement about the relations between nature and
history. Hitherto, history as natural history (p. 64)[1] – Proof: the
primacy of statistics in Durkheim. Hegel himself speaks of natural
history. But in his case, nature is essentially a *basis*, history is spirit.
Spirit itself is naturalistic: therefore, belief in nature where history is
thematic.[2]

(p. 64)[3] Marx quotation. The concept of natural history in Marx
taken over from Hegel and reinterpreted.

(p. 65)[4] The idea of the laws of nature also as a mystification.

The idea of natural growth [*Naturwüchsigkeit*] both real *and* a
socially necessary illusion.

Laws of nature not to be taken literally, not to be ontologized.

In other words, the laws of nature capable of being abrogated.

They are the blind *continuation* of eating and being eaten as the
principle on which reason is modelled and which it no longer needs
once it has achieved self-consciousness. That is the pivotal *transformation* [*Umschlag*]. No *other* reason, only the reason that knows
itself. *Explain* the C[ritique] of P[ure] R[eason].

Kant's distinction between the realm of freedom and the realm of
necessity to be applied to history.

Already [to be found] *in Kant* where the realm of freedom is taken
much more seriously, i.e., more freely than in Hegel. Freedom as
something that *creates itself.*

In contrast to the naturalistic approach of vulgar Marxism, natural
history is a *critical* concept.

History has as yet no global subject. The identification of the proletariat with the latter is, however, [text breaks off]

Ironically, Marx was a Social Darwinist. What the Social
Darwinist praises is what he regards as negativity.

p. 66[5] at the bottom; quotation from the *Grundrisse.*
Natural history means as much as the mythical character of history.
See the Hegel quote[6] above.

The cyclical as an archaic image of natural history.

p. 69 below, 'Looking into the abyss, Hegel perceived . . .',[7] then
quotation – 70 above.[8]

Read down to p. 75.[9]

[Later addition that should probably continue here:] On 5.1. 1965
down to the top of p. 70. Introduce the idea that the history of
nature = second nature.

[Hilmar Tillack's notes:] On the relations between nature and history.
Not concerned with the problem of the historical sciences versus the
natural sciences or history as opposed to external nature. The question of natural history is more specifically that of the inner composition of elements of nature and elements of history within history
itself. The theme of 'nature and history' seems to point to a contrast
between two antithetical concepts. We shall see with what right and
by how much. At issue, then, is the question of freedom or unfreedom
in history.

Hegel possesses the concept of natural history, but astonishingly
he fails to redeem the promise implicit in the term 'nature'. Nature
makes an appearance only as the natural basis of history, that is to
say, in the shape of the geographical conditions in which historical
events are enacted, or else in the elements of physical anthropology
which, ominously enough, come under the heading of 'race'. In their
execution, the dialectics of history and nature in Hegel fall short of
their own ambitions; he does not advance beyond the creation of
more or less separate spheres that are supposed to be transformed
into one another. The internal mediation between these categories is
neglected in favour of treating entire spheres en bloc. This introduces
a pattern, a mechanism, that is hardly compatible with dialectics.
Adorno is concerned with internal mediation, not with the foundation of history in nature. In other words, he wishes to define even the

sphere of spirit in Hegel as nature, since spirit is regarded as the quintessence of an unconscious domination of nature. At the very point where history unfolds in its most uninhibited manner, it takes on the qualities of blind nature instead of distancing itself from them, as Hegel's theory would reasonably lead us to expect.

The fact that until now history has been natural history and that, while seeming to be distanced from nature, it becomes ensnared in it, is evident from a glance at Durkheim's sociology. Durkheim is instructive because he combines a very specific construction of history and society with a highly emphatic claim about its naturalness. Durkheim's method was statistical. We may remind ourselves of Kierkegaard's mockery of suicide statistics that are in conflict with the autonomous individual of his theory. However, the theory of both men is absorbed by nominalism. The law of the greatest number is to be understood nominalistically: an average is extrapolated from the universe of observed cases. The law makes no claim to have any conceptual autonomy vis-à-vis the phenomena it represents. The law of the greatest number functions by defining objectivity as natural history in contrast to the independent individuals who rise above it subjectively.

Marx makes a point of confronting Hegel on this issue, even though he agrees with him in claiming that objectivity asserts itself over heads of individuals and through their actions: 'And even when a society has got upon the right track for the discovery of *the natural laws of its movement . . .*' or 'My standpoint, from which *the evolution of the economic formation of society* is viewed as *a process of natural history*, can less than any other make the individual responsible for relations whose creature he socially remains, however much he may subjectively raise himself above them' (*Capital*, vol. 1, Preface to the first German edition, p. 10). The idea of natural laws governing history, the idea that social entanglements are the natural outgrowth of history, goes together with the unfreedom of the individual. There is this to be said about the interpretation of Marx: in contrast to the prevailing belief that Marx had a positive view of the natural laws of society and that one needs only to obey them to obtain the possibility of the right kind of society – in contrast to this belief, Marx wishes to get beyond them into the kingdom of freedom, i.e., to escape from the notion of history as natural history. As Alfred Schmidt has shown, Marx is not concerned with Feuerbach's anthropological concept of nature.[10] On the contrary, he reinstated Hegel's dialectical idea of nature in explicit rebuttal of the young Hegelians. There is a contradiction here: on the one hand, Marx speaks with the scientist's passion of the inexorable laws of nature, in particular of the evolution of the laws of economics. At the same time, however, these laws are shown to be a mystification, an illusion. It is this twin-tracked attitude that provides the key to understanding Marxism as a critical theory, and not the thesis of the natural laws governing society that we need to understand if we are to gain a hold on them. It is that thesis that is the cause of the reification, the perversion and sclerosis that we discover when people appeal to Marx today. When we see in a passage late on in *Capital*, 'The law of capitalist accumulation, metamorphosed by economists into a pretended law of Nature . . .',[11] the contradiction is what constitutes the dialectical medium. Accumulation does not refer to a man hoarding money, but to the situation in which the profit of an economic cycle is turned into capital once again, is reinvested in the new cycle. The organic nature of capitalist society is both an actuality *and* at the same time a socially necessary illusion. The illusion signifies that within this society laws can only be implemented as natural processes over people's heads, while their validity arises from the form of the relations of production within which production takes place.

This should not be regarded ontologically as a doctrine of so-called human beings. In the kingdom of freedom these laws would cease to be valid. Kant's kingdom of freedom is confronted by the kingdom of necessity which [Soviet] dialectical materialism prolongs and dubs the kingdom of freedom. Just as individuals have not existed hitherto, so too there has been no global subject; the two are corollaries of one another. Hegel avoids the problem with the ruse, the cunning of reason: a global subject devoid of subjectivity. It is cunning because it is detached from all personality; it confronts human beings like an abstract calculus. In this way, the unconscious history of nature is continued. Through an irony, Marx in contrast was a Social Darwinist. He has a critical view of natural history. The *Grundrisse* contains a passage: 'As much, then, as the whole of this movement appears as a social process . . . so much does the totality of the process appear as an objective interrelation, which arises spontaneously from nature . . .'[12] The 'natural laws of society' are ideology inasmuch as they are claimed to be immutable. They are actuality inasmuch as they are hunted down in *Capital* as the phenomenology of non-mind. In the chapter on fetishism, Marx speaks of the 'theological niceties' of the commodity form.[13] He thus mocks the false consciousness that acts as a mirror to the parties involved in the process of barter, reflecting back to them as characteristics of things what in reality is a social relation. Here, ideology tells the truth about society as it is, denouncing it as heteronomous. But by elevating the truth about the false society to the status of positive knowledge, i.e., by abstracting from that denunciation, it turns into ideology. If you take dialectics with the seriousness due to it, ideology ceases just to perch on the sub-structure [of society]. The element of ideology is implicit in the exchange relation itself: abstracting from the specific circumstances between people and the commodities – an abstraction that is neces-sary in the process of exchange – gives rise to false consciousness. The essence of false consciousness is that it reflects mere postulates as qualities of the things themselves. Without this crucial factor the monstrous mechanism of exchange could not survive. We are speak-ing here of a violence that is perennially intrinsic to ideology, because ideology is not an extraneous false consciousness but is something that sustains the entire mechanism.

The idea that theory becomes a real force when it grips the masses proves to be valid not simply for the theory of the commodity, but all previously existing structures. Hegel had a flash of insight into this: 'But it is at any rate utterly essential that the constitution should *not be regarded as something made*, even if it does have an origin in time. On the contrary, it is quite simply that which has being in and for itself, and should therefore be regarded as divine and enduring, and as exalted above the sphere of all manufactured things' (*Philoso-phy of Right*, §273, p. 312). But his insight was blind [*bewußtlos*], since he idolized as something existing in nature something that had been manufactured. Hegel fails to expose it as an illusion. What Marx adds as a philosopher is the consciousness of this illusion. Hegel presents as *physei* [existing in nature] something that is *thesei* [has been posited]; he defines the constitution of the historical world as something belonging to the world of nature. State constitutions should not arise from the conscious act of individuals. Hegel's logic sets out to provide a radical dialectics, but without going so far as to overthrow the ideal of a *prima philosophia*. Hegel sympathizes with the idea of an immutable aspect of history whose totality is intact. Spirit and reconciliation transfigure the myth: 'Whatever is by nature contingent is subject to contingencies, and this fate is therefore itself a necessity.'[14] Occidental nature myths already rehearsed what Hegel predicted of history. The cycle is an archaic image. Hegel's philosophy of history still appeals to an automatism over which history has no power. The world-historical political drama is per-ceived as a second nature, but the first nature recurs in it. Criticism of Hegel is directed at the fact not that he perceived history as second nature, but that he would like to confirm its status as a zone of the spirit and that he naïvely identifies as a positive feature of history the very aspect that is incompatible with the freedom that he also intends. [End of Tillack's notes]

LECTURE 14

7 January 1965

THE HISTORY
OF NATURE (II)

Ladies and gentlemen, you will recollect that last time we discussed the concept of natural history and had arrived at the notion of a second nature and its ambiguous meaning.[1] I should like now simply to continue with my reflections on the ideas we have now established in connection with the Hegelian concept of a second nature. This, you will remember, was the spiritual that forms the substance and the definition of freedom; it is embodied in the legal system on which Hegel then confers the title of 'second nature'.[2] To the best of my knowledge, this concept was taken up again for the first time – and in a very emphatic way – in Georg Lukács's *Theory of the Novel*. Taken as a set of reflections on art, as aesthetic meditations, this is a highly problematic book, but it retains its fundamental importance as one of the first attempts at an objectivist philosophy of history, instead of a merely subjectivist one. I should like to encourage all of you to read it now that it has been reprinted,[3] even though the preface contains an attack on me.[4] However, I do not wish to address his criticisms because what Lukács says there has nothing in common with the quality of the work and, so I would like to believe, nothing in common with the quality of my own work. The concept of a second nature remains the negation of whatever might be thought of as a first nature. So it does not represent the recurrence of a nature that has been suppressed and is now being restored, but on the contrary it is the totality of whatever has been so completely trapped by social and rational mechanisms – the two cannot be distinguished – that nothing differing from it can manifest itself. And because there is nothing else outside it, it acquires the appearance of the natural, in other words, of what simply exists and is given. There is not even the possibility of something outside it becoming visible, something that is not caught up in the general inclusiveness. The exclusion of possibility which converts this second nature into the only reality is what also turns it into the substitute for possibility, and it is in this way that the semblance of the natural comes into being. Thus whatever is a *thesei* (if I may use this terminology), that is, whatever is posited, albeit not produced by individuals, as Hegel and Marx taught, but brought about, as both recognized, by its impersonal context, usurps the insignia of everything that appears to the bourgeois consciousness to be nature and natural. You can picture this to yourselves quite easily by reflecting on the fact that in the unthinking language of everyday (a language I had always rather disliked) a man is thought to speak naturally if he speaks like everyone else, that is to say, if he is a man who conforms to general linguistic conventions. In contrast, a man who does not speak like that, who insists on the individual aspects of his own personality, can easily gain a reputation for affectation and artificiality. I think that what people irresponsibly mean by a 'natural person' is a prime example of this concept of second nature, and you can all see what is meant by it without my having to pursue this discussion any further. The more relentlessly the process of societalization spins its web around every aspect of immediate human and interpersonal relations, the more impossible it becomes to recollect the historical origins of that process and the more irresistible the external semblance of something natural. Nothing that is outside appears to me to be outside – there is even a sense in which it has ceased *to be* what is outside – thanks to the total mediation that transforms even the elements of nature into elements of this second nature. And so – to return to my argument – if you think of the role played by nature today, in the ordinary sense of nature in a landscape as contrasted with our urban, industrial civilization, you will realize that this nature is already something planned, cultivated and organized. It is gradually turning into a nature reserve (if I may exaggerate somewhat) and – as the director of the Frankfurt Zoo has frequently pointed out[5] – it is already becoming a problem literally to protect the natural space that wild animals need if they are to be able to move around freely. In this sense, then – and I intend this only by way of explanation: I am sure that you are all aware that, when I talk about a second nature, I am not referring literally to the nature of a nature reserve – in this sense, we can see that what seems to be outside us is in reality not outside at all, but something that has been captured. This semblance of the natural is a function of the gap between the history of mankind and primary nature. And by primary nature – I say this so that you should not pick me up on this and say, you see, even Adorno has forgotten about the dialectic here – by primary nature I mean in the first instance no more than the elements, the objective elements that the experiencing consciousness encounters without his experiencing them as things he has himself mediated. Semblance is the prophetic warning of an increasingly powerful spell.

On this point I should like to read you a passage from Marx, from his early writings, in fact from *The German Ideology*: 'We know only a single science, the science of history. One can look at history from two sides and divide it into the history of nature and the history of men. The two sides are, however, inseparable; the history of nature and the history of men are dependent on each other so long as men exist.'[6] So here you have this insight into the reciprocal mediation of these two so-called spheres – but in contrast to Hegel, about whom I spoke in this connection last time, this mediation does not take place externally in the sense that history becomes a special realm built up on nature. But rather, as Marx suggests, the history of nature and the history of men mutually condition each other as long as men exist. But if you will allow me to extract a further conclusion from this – and teasing out the implications of this reciprocal mediation of nature and history constitutes the substance of the philosophy of the young Marx – I should like to add that of course there can no longer be any point in talking about an insulated sphere of nature as the absolute realm of being or as existence as opposed to history. Marx is in no doubt that, if we are to speak of priorities here, then precedence is to be given to society, to the historical sphere. But there too we should not let ourselves be tempted to ontologize. We should not argue, as has been imputed to me, wrongly I believe, that this means that in the beginning there was society which then created heaven and earth. For society itself is determined by the things of which it is composed and it therefore necessarily contains a non-social dimension. Critical, dialectical thought should repudiate the idea that these two concepts, history and philosophy, are isolated, entirely detachable strata. The traditional antithesis of nature and history is both true and false. It is true when it expresses what happens to nature; it is false when it simply reinforces conceptually history's own concealment of its own natural growth.

The distinction between nature and history is an unthinking expression of the division of labour that has directly projected the inevitable differences between scientific methods onto the objects of their study. The ahistorical concept of history that is cultivated in the resurrected metaphysics of Martin Heidegger, above all in what it has called historicity, would serve to demonstrate the complicity of ontological thought with naturalistic thought from which the former had so eagerly sought to distance itself. If history becomes the basic ontological structure of existence, or indeed a kind of *qualitas occulta*, a hidden quality of existence that is supposed to be essentially historical simply because of its temporal horizon, then history will be mutation as immutability and thus the imitation of a natural religion from which there is no escape. For there too there is eternal change (just think of the seasons) which constantly repeats itself and thus congeals into a constant factor. Thus to locate the concept of history in existence amounts paradoxically to an ontological inflation that does away with the concept of history by a sort of conjuring trick. Something similar happened in ancient times in the case of Hegel's favourite Heraclitus. While traditional historians of philosophy have always regarded the Eleatic philosophers, that is to say, the philosophers of being, as the polar opposites of Heraclitus, the philosopher of absolute becoming, modern classical philology has not been mistaken in its insistence that this distinction is not absolute and that the two extremes meet and merge. This ontologization of history makes it possible to transpose determinate historical processes at will into constant factors. The effect of this is to give a philosophical cachet to the vulgar notion that historical conditions, which once upon a time were thought to be the expression of God's will, are now to be regarded as natural. This is one of the ways in which existing reality can be justified as essential. The ontologists' claim that we have now moved beyond the divergence of nature and history does not hold water. The historicity abstracted from actual historical processes passes unscathed the thorn that bears the true guilt for the antithesis of nature and history, which itself ought not to be ontologized. In this respect, too, the new ontology is a crypto-idealism. It relates the non-identical to identity, and, by postulating the concept of historicity as the agent of history, it does away with everything that resists the process of identification by an all-dominant consciousness.[7] We might point out, however, that ontology is driven to ideology, to reconciliation in the mind, because no reconciliation was achieved in reality. Historical contingency and the concept are at odds with each other, all the more inexorably, the more they are intertwined. We might speak in this context of contingency, chance as the historical fate of the individual, a fate that is meaningless because the historical process itself has no global subject and therefore presents itself as contingent and meaningless in this highest sense in which meaning stands opposed to the contingent. What nature actually is, is not just obscured by the

totality of what is *thesei*, what is posited, but the question of nature
as the absolute first, immediate thing, as opposed to its mediations,
represents the object of its search in the hierarchical form of an analytical proposition whose premises control everything that follows
from them – but they do so according to the pattern established by
what has been postulated. Thus what exists from the outset becomes
a function of what is posited; and, in particular, the semblance of
something that exists in itself, that is natural, non-posited, an absolute first thing, turns out to be a function of the act of positing, thanks
to which this non-posited thing is unmasked as its opposite, as something that has been made. Through a sleight of hand, whatever is
thesei is converted by history, which gave it birth, into *physis*, into
nature, and in fact into second nature. Once the distinction has been
postulated, it can be made more fluid by reflection, but cannot be
ignored. Without reflection, admittedly, the distinction would render
harmless the quintessence of the contents of the historical process,
demoting it to the status of mere ornament, and on the other hand
it would enthrone as essence whatever has not yet come into existence. Accordingly, mind would see all nature, and whatever claims
to be nature, installed as history, and all history as nature.

   That then is the programme – if I may call it that – that philosophy
would have to postulate for the relation of nature to history. If I may
repeat myself here: because I believe that this programme is constitutive for all attempts to interpret the philosophy of history, or indeed
philosophy in general, I think that the attempt should be made to
behold all nature, and whatever regards itself as nature, as history.
Hegel would call it something that has become, or has been mediated.
Conversely, however, everything historical has to be regarded as
nature because thanks to its own violent origins [*Gesetztheit*] it
remains under the spell of blind nature, from which it struggles to
dissociate itself. I may perhaps here cite a passage from a lecture that
I gave here to the Kant Society.[8] This was over thirty years ago, in
1932, but in its broad outlines it has retained its validity: the task of
philosophy 'should be to comprehend historical existence in its extreme
historical determinacy, at the point where it is at its most historical,
as itself a natural form of existence . . . or to conceive of nature as
historical existence precisely where it is at its most natural.'[9] End of
quotation. The point at which nature and history meet is in the fact
of transience. Walter Benjamin acknowledged the truth of this in a
prominent place in *The Origin of German Tragic Drama*, and in
general this book goes far beyond the sphere of purely aesthetic questions. In this sense it belongs in the same tradition as Lukács's book
on the theory of the novel, which I mentioned to you earlier on.

Through the medium of aesthetics questions concerning the philosophy of history and even metaphysics become legible. It would be worth dwelling on these matters, and perhaps I shall at some point find time to explore the fact that for a whole series of thinkers the experience of art has become a sort of key to other branches of philosophy. This is something I am very conscious of. We are not speaking here of a naïve attempt to aestheticize philosophy, as Helmut Kuhn once accused me of doing.[10] What is at issue, rather, is a particular relation to the experience of structures that purport to be meaningful and that provide a model both of meaning that can be explored and of the crisis of meaning. In this context, for those of you who are interested in this aspect of things, I would refer you to passages that I inserted into *The Jargon of Authenticity* in the course of my attack on Martin Heidegger.[11] These were passages warning against the devaluation of so-called cultural philosophy and about the relationship between philosophy and so-called cultural philosophy. At any rate, to come back to Benjamin, here is the sentence that seems to me to provide a key not just to *The Origin of German Tragic Drama*, but to this entire philosophy: the poets of the baroque age had a vision of nature as 'eternal transience, and here alone did the saturnine vision of this generation recognize history.'[12] Not only their vision, however, for even today the history of nature still remains the canon for the interpretation of the philosophy of history. I quote Benjamin once more, a few pages earlier in the same book: 'When, as is the case in the *Trauerspiel*, history becomes part of the setting, it does so as script. The word "history" stands written on the countenance of nature in the characters of transience.'[13] Here too would be the place to consider such matters as the decoding of one of the primeval allegories, that of the death's head, but perhaps I shall be able to say something to you about that at some point in the future.[14] But I would also remind you of the most ancient instance of an allegorical and hermeneutic writing from the theological tradition of monotheism, namely the *mene, mene tekel upharsin*.[15] Benjamin goes on to say that 'the allegorical physiognomy of the nature-history which is put on stage in the *Trauerspiel* is present in reality in the form of the ruin.'[16] You can see how, in such motifs as the ruin mentioned here or the death's head or the writing on the wall, the transition to concreteness is adumbrated that I think of as something that philosophy must implement in all seriousness. It differs from the usual philosophizing about the concrete in that the concrete references here are apprehended allegorically in their specific meaning, instead of serving as examples or paradigms for more general concepts whose validity they are supposed to demonstrate. This is how the concrete appears in an older generation of philosophers such as Simmel.[17] I believe that this is the truly pivotal turn to a relevant philosophy, but one which has not yet been taken by philosophical theory or, better perhaps, by epistemological theory to the requisite degree. However, it is one which my own modest efforts are striving to promote. What you will discover in this programme – and this is connected with that special notion of concreteness – is the transmutation of metaphysics into history. It secularizes metaphysics into the ultimate category of secularity, that of decay. Philosophy interprets its code at the micro-level, in the shards that result from decay and that are the bearers of objective meanings. No recollection of transcendence is possible any longer unless it passes through transience in the spirit of the heretical speculation that makes the life of the absolute as dependent upon the finite, as the finite is dependent upon that of the absolute. Those of you who know their Hegel will be aware of his thesis that the absolute and infinite are arrived at by passing through the dialectic of the finite. Thus Hegel himself is not as remote from this half-mystical, half-heretical speculation as the official tenor of his philosophy might suggest. We may have greater hope of finding metaphysics in the realm of the finite – if for once I may speak plainly and even bluntly – than in the abstract sphere of eternity, with its vain efforts to shuffle off the coils of transience. And the task of traditional philosophy today is precisely to justify this philosophical turn *against* its traditional meaning. Eternity no longer appears as such, but only as refracted through the most ephemeral of things. At the point where the Hegelian metaphysics equates the life of the absolute with the totality of the transience of all things finite, it rises above the mythic spell which it absorbs and reinforces.

Now, ladies and gentlemen, that is what I wanted to say to you about the history of nature. I should like to use the remaining minutes to draw some inferences from what I have been saying with reference to the conception of philosophy about which I have already told you in connection with these ideas. There are motifs that have such deep roots in the historical process, in what used to be called the spirit of the age, that a certain common theme constantly reasserts itself beyond even extreme differences of opinion. An instance of such a common theme is the idea of philosophy as interpretation or hermeneutics, as it is called in the school of Martin Heidegger, following on from Wilhelm Dilthey. This theme has of course become established academically and has merged with an old-style first philosophy. This is not the place to explain to you the reasons for this transition from philosophical thought to hermeneutics. Nevertheless, I believe that in my remarks on natural history I have to some extent given you an example of this transition and, as it were, demonstrated it to you experimentally. Even so, I believe that it is the task of a lecture course such as this to *accomplish* this transition, this philosophical turn, and not simply to assume dogmatically that this has already been done. I should like at least to mention a few of the relevant motifs here by way of explaining to you *why* philosophy has been forced into this change – and this, I repeat, despite its otherwise mutually incompatible tendencies. One such motif is the pervasive insight into the increasingly problematic nature of philosophical systems, a motif that is not the monopoly of any one school. By this I mean the impossibility of deducing all phenomena from a single, unified principle, or interpreting them all on that basis. If the light of philosophy can no longer be kindled by a single thought or motif or unified method – and we may ask whether a unified method has ever really succeeded in shedding much light on anything – and if, on the other hand, philosophy insists on attempting to shed light in this way, and does not confine itself to issuing guidelines for the sciences, this will lead more or less inevitably to its looking for this light in the individual phenomena, the *disiecta membra*, remaining from the different systems. If you cast your minds back to those quotations from Benjamin about transience and decay, you will recollect that they should be understood as pointing to the fact that interpretation presupposes the decay of systems. Moreover, inasmuch as those systems contained any truth, that truth has now – if it has not evaporated entirely – retreated into the details, into the individual parts of the system, and now forms the object of study of interpretation or, God help us, hermeneutics. For fidelity to philosophy, the insistence upon the philosophical impulse despite the demise of the system – together with the statement handed down from one philosopher to the next that philosophy is only possible as a system – all that can no longer be sustained in the face of the needs of philosophy. This does not mean that, by sacrificing the overall principle that it should organize the totality of all phenomena, philosophy should also abandon intellect as such. On the contrary, the more we see the erosion of the constitutive character of mind that used to find expression in philosophical systems, the more insistent becomes the need not just to register existing reality, but to reflect upon it and understand it. And it is this that refers us in our search for a philosophical knowledge of individual things to the only source of knowledge that remains, given the present trend towards dispersion and fragmentation, namely towards interpretation, the art of deciphering.

Finally, I should add something about what my own experience tells me is an almost overwhelming need for interpretation. This is the part played by the fact that the avenues that might lead to a

practice that could bring about change are all blocked. The effect this
has is to ensure that all the energies that were formerly concentrated
in attempts to bring about a novel state of affairs now flow into the
process of interpretation. I am familiar with the argument that interpretation is merely a surrogate, a way of fobbing people off. I have
nothing with which to counter this objection, except for a recurrent
idea of Marx's to the effect that it is not open to any way of thinking
arbitrarily to escape from the historical situation in which it finds
itself. If thought finds itself locked into a situation in which practice
is blocked so that interpretation is the only activity left open to it, it
would be an illusion and pure self-deception for philosophy to react
otherwise. That would be a sort of justification of Alexandrianism of
which I am sure I am as well aware as any of you. The problem here,
however, lies not so much with thinking itself as with the relation to
the objective situation in which thought finds itself.[18] Nowadays, at
any rate, the joy of thinking lies in interpretation. The conception of
interpretation, the sudden moment of insight, is what everyone hopes
for when he philosophizes today, seriously philosophizes, as opposed
to 'studying' philosophy. Anyone who is unwilling to undertake this,
who has never experienced the pleasure of interpretation personally,
should leave philosophy alone, at any rate, the only philosophy that
seems to be possible today. I would say that interpretation is the only
thing that could inspire people to 'do' philosophy today. With this
shrinking of trust in theoretical system-building, it may be that the
need to philosophize has effectively focused entirely on interpretation. After all, the only thing that inspires philosophers of all shades
of opinion – and I consciously ignore the differences separating thinkers in the world today – is contained in the gesture: What does it all
mean? Is what we see really all that there is? Is there nothing more
to it than this? What makes this question objectively so irresistible,
this 'Is that really all there is?', 'Isn't there any more to it than this?',
is this complete state of shut-down in which we find ourselves. We
might say that the function of such questions as 'Is that all there is?'
or 'What does it all mean?' is that of an absence. In the same way,
the majority of the concepts that have a resonance in philosophy
today exert a fascination precisely because those other concepts are
missing, their underlying substance is absent. Thus the widespread
preoccupation with the metaphysics of time arises from the circumstance that our consciousness of time itself has gone into crisis. Time
has ceased to be something we can take for granted, it is no longer
substantial, and this explains why our minds seek literally to rediscover time – as the title of the greatest novel of the century suggests.[19]
Enrico Castelli, the Italian philosopher, has written a fascinating book

about the way in which the metaphysics of time is built on the loss of time.[20] Unfortunately, his book has remained largely unknown in Germany.[21] The emptier of meaning existing reality appears today, the greater the pressure or the desire to interpret it and to have done with this meaninglessness. The light that is kindled in the phenomena as they fragment, disintegrate and fly apart is the only source of hope that can set philosophy alight: for philosophy, as I have been suggesting in these lectures, is the Stygian darkness that sets out to unveil meaning. It would be much more important to explain this idea than to obey the impulse to deduce or to take philosophical possession of the totality. All that has now ceased to be philosophy; instead we have the immersion in the individual detail, that unreserved immersion in the individual, specific detail that Hegel called for but that he also repudiated in his actual intellectual practice. Heidegger comes very close to the idea of interpretation, but it is corrupted – so it appears to me – because it is committed to the distinction between the ontic and the ontological, while the ontological structure turns out to be something other than what we might truly think of as 'meaning'. At bottom, it is nothing more than the multiplicity of universal concepts to which specific phenomena are to be adapted. And it is this process of 'adapting' that philosophical interpretation is supposed to transcend. That, to put it dogmatically, is what distinguishes the art of interpreting the signs of the philosophy of history from the hermeneutics fashionable today. I should like to continue next time from the point we have now reached and then conclude what I have to say about the philosophy of history by giving you an even larger backdrop relating to one of its most central categories, one in which all our previous discussions can be said to culminate – and that is the concept of *progress*.

PART II
PROGRESS

LECTURE 15

12 January 1965

ON INTERPRETATION: THE CONCEPT OF PROGRESS (I)

Last time I had begun to tell you about the transition from philosophy to the concept of interpretation. Today, I should like to finish off what was inevitably an all too cursory account of that transition before moving on to establish a bridge between the two parts of these lectures – and of course there is no need to explain to wily dialecticians like yourselves that this bridging exercise does not create a link between the two parts, but must effect a mediation *within* the two parts *themselves*. If you reflect on what I have said to you about philosophical interpretation, you will perhaps be able to see why I have placed such great emphasis upon the theory of natural history. It is because this interweaving of nature and history must in general be the model for every interpretative procedure in philosophy. We might almost say that it provides the canon that enables philosophy to adopt an interpretative stance without lapsing into pure randomness. For it retains the polarity that is essential to philosophy, that is to say, the combination of the stringent, the authoritative, with the element of living experience or expression, even though these two elements can never harmonize entirely. The fragmentation of philosophy into so-called schools – of rationalism or empiricism – that are constantly at loggerheads with each other has as its background the insoluble nature of this tension, behind which the insoluble problem of dissolving non-identity into identity may well lie. The relationship of nature and history provides us with the primal image of interpretative behaviour, something that has been handed down through intellectual history in the form of allegory. It is hardly a coincidence that the first philosophy to have emphasized the concept of interpretation and to have developed it as a methodological principle on a large scale was that of the middle and later Schelling, who himself made extensive reference to allegory, a concept that has since fallen into disfavour in aesthetics.[1] Beneath this gaze, the profound gaze of allegory, which is perhaps the model for the philosophical gaze as such – because the attitude of melancholic contemplation may well be the attitude on which philosophical inquiry has been founded – nature stands revealed. Nature, I say, reveals itself beneath this gaze as history, just as in all allegory the death's head owes its central importance to the fact that as a natural object its own expression reveals its historical nature. Conversely – and I would remind you here of the passage from Benjamin's writings that I read out to you in one of the recent lectures[2] – beneath this gaze history stands revealed as nature in so far as it turns out to be permanent transience. Moreover, the recollection of the past, the memory in the phenomenon itself, is the mode of behaviour, or what we might almost, following Hölderlin,[3] call the scheme according to which interpretation can take place. At the same time, as a form of melancholy which perceives transience in everything historical, this attitude is also *critical*.

We might even say in general that the transition from philosophy to criticism represents something like a secularization of melancholy. This is a melancholy that has become active, not a melancholy that makes do, that remains stuck fast in an unhappy consciousness,[4] not at home with itself, but a consciousness that exteriorizes itself as a critique of existing phenomena. Such a melancholy is probably the pre-eminent critical, philosophical stance. In other words, if you read the phenomena of history as the cyphers of their own transience or their own natural deterioration, they will also always be defined by their own negativity. This element of negativity is the element of criticism in philosophy. Interpretation and critique come together at a profound level. This explains why I find it foolish to demand that we should *first* understand a thing and only *then* criticize it. For since the process of understanding and interpreting entails negation, a consciousness of the immanent demise of a phenomenon is at one with the criticism of what the world has done to it.[5] In general terms, we might say that interpretation means reading nature from history and history from nature. Interpretation teases out of the phenomena, out of second nature, out of what has been mediated, out of the world around us that has been mediated by history and society, the fact that they have evolved – in just the same way as it shows that there can be no evolution without the process being convicted of its own naturalness, while the evolution itself, mediation, must be understood as a prolonged state of immediacy, a natural condition. The two aspects belong together. You may say that each is present in the other; in other words, nature is present in history as transience, a proposition I spent the entire first part of these lectures explaining to you. Conversely, we shall also be able to say that history is present in nature as something that has evolved and is transient. At the same time, however, because these two aspects are indissolubly linked, every interpretation is also *posited* – and I believe that anyone who, like me, emphasizes the standpoint of immanent interpretation and criticism is obliged to refrain from making a fetish of this immanence. For in order to liberate this immanence, to appropriate its power, we need the knowledge of what is other. This means that the deep melancholic gaze of which I have spoken will be able to discover the element of becoming, or of having become, in what has evolved, only if it can bring to the contemplation of phenomena the consciousness of that process of becoming. In my writings I have illustrated this with an example from Hölderlin and I would like to refer you to his poem *The Shelter at Hardt*,[6] the meaning of which only becomes completely clear when you understand its specific references – the fact that this was the allegorical place where Duke Ulrich of Württemberg is reputed to have hidden while making his escape, and that, according to Hölderlin, the place itself is made to speak of this. Only when you know this is it possible to understand the poem completely; whereas this reference [to Duke Ulrich], as Friedrich Beissner has explained it,[7] has some of the disturbed character that people were more likely to see in Hölderlin's poems than their specific content.[8] On the other hand, however, this vanishing of history into nature that we have seen in Hölderlin's poem is also an element of expression assumed by nature. This means that only because these pragmatic [historical] elements have disappeared, only because the poem has acquired this enigmatic character, has it succeeded in assuming the expression of transience that points beyond itself and constitutes its greatness. I should like to ask you all to read *The Shelter at Hardt*, this late poem of Hölderlin's. There is, I believe, no better model for what I mean by the interlocking of nature and history in a phenomenon, in this instance from the realm of poetry.

Interpretation, I said, is criticism of phenomena that have been brought to a standstill; it consists in revealing the dynamism stored up in them, so that what appears as second nature can be seen to be history. On the other hand, criticism ensures that what has evolved loses its appearance as mere existence and stands revealed as the product of history. This is essentially the procedure of Marxist critique (if I may briefly make mention of this here). Marxist critique consists in showing that every conceivable social and economic factor that appears to be part of nature is in fact something that has evolved historically. Thus there is always an element of reciprocity: what appears to be natural is discovered to be historical, while things that are historical turn out to be natural because of their transience. Behind this phenomenon stands the historicized dialectic of subject and object which cannot be reduced to their pure state. To destroy immediacy means dissolving the appearance of naturalness [*Ansichsein*] through the critical process. It means demolishing the claim that phenomena that have evolved [in time] are just what they are [in the present]. I have not drawn your attention to all the specific arguments in Hegel that have formed starting-points for my own remarks, but it seems to me that here Hegel has fallen victim to a certain illusion inasmuch as he has given his theory of the way in which immediacy constantly reasserts itself an excessively positive reading. He is undoubtedly in the right when he maintains that, in phenomena that have finished evolving, the process of evolution, its history, disappears or – to use the expression of Hegel's that I quoted in these lectures a few hours ago – becomes second nature. The more thoroughly this process of evolution disappears, the greater the appearance of a second nature, of sheer natural existence. You need think here only of the realm of pure reason, pure logic. What characterizes logic in the first instance is that the traces of its evolution, that is to say, the subjective aspect of synthesis, are scarcely visible any more and an extreme mental effort is called for if they are to be perceived and retrieved. Having said this, however, which anyway is rendered more or less self-evident by the Hegelian arguments, we should add that this evolved immediacy, this second immediacy, is still only an *illusion*. By this I mean that it hides something, that because it is a congealed history it seals off the dynamism contained within itself. The mistake Hegel makes here, if I may speak in this schoolmasterly way, is that, because this second nature is impenetrable, he is tempted to place it on the same logical plane as the first. In other words, he is tempted to treat it as something immediate without any reservations whereas, precisely because it postulates itself as immediate without actually being so, it inevitably conceals its own history and thus degenerates into ideology. We might even say that – setting aside the familiar but superficial political and ontological distinctions between the two men – this is the real difference between Hegel and Marx. Marx always takes the historical nature of the second, third and fourth immediacy, that is to say, of second nature, far more seriously than Hegel, who tends simply to accept that something that has evolved then disappears into the evolved reality. So that for Hegel all this means is that, with the demonstration of mediation, immediacy ends up at every stage as no more than a piece of subjectivity, as an instance of mind, as something postulated by mind. With Marx, on the other hand, the tendency is for the negativity contained in the very naturalness of immediacy, of a later, mediated, evolved immediacy, to come to the surface; he assigns to the reflective mind the task of dispelling this illusion of naturalness and, in contrast, of uncovering the true reality in the hidden laws of motion, in what lies concealed, what does not lie on the surface – while the façade shrivels into mere illusion. If it does not sound too pompous, we might say that this is a kind of metaphysical and dialectical interpretation of the relationship between dialectic and ideological critique. Besides, it is not by chance that the sphere of *art* should be the sphere in which something that is most perfectly *thesei*, that is to say, something that has become or has been made, presents itself as *physei*, i.e., as natural. Nor need we be astonished that the sphere of art which is remarkable for the fact that in it objects that have been created should present themselves as purely immediate, as being, should have declared itself to be the realm of semblance, illusion, while actuality, where we find the same encapsulation of the production process as in art, fails to acknowledge its own status as semblance. Indeed, if I may be allowed to exaggerate the position, it is in a sense far more illusory than art, since art turns the relationship between appearance and reality into a focus of attention and gives it expression.

Ladies and gentlemen, I have spoken of the joys of interpretation. Now that I am coming to an end of my discussion of this topic, let me say another few words about this. Perhaps what I have said about the joys of interpretation will by now have become a little clearer to you. These joys consist in refusing to be blinded by the semblance of immediacy, and instead in uncovering the process by which the work became what it is so that we may transcend that semblance. At the same time, they refer to the power of the mind to retain its self-control in the face of the sorrow that is aroused by the contemplation of the past. Kant had noted, in one of the profoundest passages in the 'aesthetics of the sublime', that what a common-or-garden aesthetics customarily thinks of as aesthetic 'pleasure' is in reality a state in which the mind remains in control of itself in the face of the overwhelming power of nature, in the face of total transience.[9] Thus the joy of philosophy – and philosophy should not deny this pleasure, but shed light on it and make it its own – is connected with the activity of interpretation. In fact, we are capable of experiencing this pleasure only in so far as we are capable of this act of interpreting. When it comes down to it, the source of this pleasure lies in the fact

that the phenomena – and I mean the phenomena in their most concrete form, the form in which they have all the colourfulness that
children desire, that children focus upon, for all happiness comes
from our childhood – our pleasure derives from the fact that the
phenomena always mean *something* different from what they simply
are. Thus interpretation leads us to break through their surface existence. The deepest promise interpretation makes to the mind is
perhaps the assurance it gives that what exists is not the ultimate
reality – or perhaps we should say: what exists is not just what it
claims to be. We might say, then, that the negativity of natural history
– which always discovers what phenomena used to be, what they
have become and, at the same time, what they might have been –
retains the *possible* life of phenomena as opposed to their actual
existence. In this sense, the interpretative stance in philosophy is the
prototype of a utopian stance towards thought. And philosophies
that remain true to this utopian motif have always had a soft spot
for interpretation. Interpretation in fact means to become conscious
of the traces of what points beyond mere existence – by dint of criticism, that is to say, by virtue of an insight into transience, and into
the shortcomings and fallibility of mere existence.

Ladies and gentlemen, this is really all I propose to say to you
about the relationship between the philosophy of history and interpretation. I should now like to conclude this part of the lecture course
by discussing a category that both encapsulates the entire problem of
the philosophy of history and also forges a link between it and the
theory of freedom. The concept I have in mind is that of *progress*. I
should just like to remind you that Hegel had described history as
progress in the consciousness of freedom, and that in Kant's philosophy of history progress had served as the mediating link between the
spheres of necessity and freedom in the sense that the natural antagonism between human beings, the fact that *homo homini lupus*, man
is a wolf to other men,[10] compels people to throw off the mechanism
of compulsion and to establish something that might be called a
'realm of freedom'.[11] But instead of attempting to provide a theoretical underpinning of these ideas on the philosophy of history that I
have tried to explain to you, or to synthesize them with the theory
of freedom, I would prefer to say something about progress – by way
of a conclusion and so as to give you a somewhat concise idea of this
view of history.

In order to give an account of the concept of progress, I shall have
to subject it to a scrutiny close enough to ensure that it loses its
obvious meaning, both positive and negative.[12] After everything I
have said about interpretation as the insistence on what phenomena

and even concepts say over and above *what they do say*, this probably does not call for further explanation. We must therefore put the concept of progress under the microscope, as it were, so as to strip it of its semblance of naturalness, its semblance of being a second nature. But examining it in close-up makes a proper assessment difficult. More even than other concepts, that of progress evaporates as soon as you begin to specify what actually progresses and what doesn't. The more you insist on knowing this, the less remains of the concept. I should like to take advantage of this for a philosophical or conceptual digression. The fact is that the function of nominalism has undergone a far-reaching change – this has to be said if we are to make a meaningful criticism of nominalism. Nominalism is tied to the tradition of enlightenment and the history of enlightenment since the Middle Ages is identical with nominalism. That is to say, it is denied that concepts have a natural existence and this means that they are to be treated as no more than the summation of particular characteristics. In consequence, there has been a growing demand that concepts should be able to give proof of their identity; we must be able to say what a concept means and how it is to be used. I hope that you will all have long since abandoned the vulgar practice you will constantly come across in naïve discussions of saying, 'Well, if you want to talk about progress or freedom, you will have to begin by defining what you mean by them.' This habit is an extreme distortion of a venerable enlightenment motif and I hope that I have managed to put you off it. It is a distortion because nowadays this nominalist insistence on defining your terms has long since ceased to serve the purpose of stripping concepts of their magic aura, their character as shibboleths. Instead, pedants who insist on doing this deprive others of the use of whatever true, substantive elements are contained in concepts, of the essential, structured aspects of phenomena that lie within concepts. To give you a drastic example of what I mean you have only to imagine a sociological discussion in which someone makes use of the word 'class'. In no time at all, someone will say that you can no longer use the word 'class'; nowadays you have to talk about different strata, and these strata have to be defined very precisely, and so forth. It then becomes clear that what used to be an attempt to make more careful distinctions has ended up as the wish to sabotage the critical function of concepts by claiming that their negative aspect simply does not exist. Quite recently Herr Ludwig Marcuse published an unfavourable critique of my writings in the *Welt der Literatur*.[13] In this he pretended not to know the difference between true consciousness and false, and demanded that I give him a definition. He seemed to be attacking me because I had

failed to provide him with such a definition – even though in reality
I certainly could give him one. It is a simple matter of distinguishing
between truth and ideology, in other words, between a consciousness
that is appropriate to the current state of society and one that
conceals it. However, his real motive was not to seek information but
to deny me the use of that distinction with the aid of a farrago of
pseudo-epistemological reflections. That is the only thing that forces
us into a certain wariness when objections are raised in a nominalist
spirit instead of tackling the substance of the question at issue. That
is to say, such objections attempt to deny us the use of a concept by
disputing that the phenomena it covers really constitute a unity. As
an experienced paterfamilias I would strongly recommend you in
such cases to reply to people who demand to know exactly what
freedom is, or progress, that they know precisely what these things
are, and that, however vague the general notions about such concepts
are, they contain a great deal more truth than attempts to evade the
concepts and to deny their validity. The best remedy when confronted
with such questions – my home-made medicine chest, so to speak –
when someone asks what freedom is, is to tell him that he needs only
to think of any flagrant attack on freedom. In most cases this is
enough to deflate epistemological exercises that have degenerated
into self-justifying sophistry. In the first instance, I am content to be
able to say of freedom – by this I mean political freedom, not the free
will – that being free means that, if someone rings the bell at 6.30
a.m., I have no reason to think that the Gestapo or the GPU or the
agents of comparable institutions are at the door and can take me
off with them without my being able to invoke the right of habeas
corpus.[14] I believe that this is in general the way to deal with objections of this sort.

The concept of progress is particularly prone to such acts of sabotage. It dissolves more readily than others as soon as we have to
specify what it actually means; what progresses and what does not.
Let me say right away that, in the case of progress, this has its justification. In other words, there are things that progress and others
that do not. I would like to apply this to our reflections on the history
of philosophy. In particular, the course of history as a whole thinks
of itself as progressive in many respects, and actually is so. Nevertheless, as I believe I have shown, in its natural course it remains constantly the same. The question, therefore, of what is progress and
what is not goes to the heart of our reflections about the concept.
But whoever wishes to define the concept more precisely risks destroying the very thing he aims at. The subaltern cunning that refuses to
speak of progress before we can distinguish between progress in

what, of what, and in relation to what, displaces the unity of different elements that constantly modify each other in the concept; this cunning reduces that unity to a mere juxtaposition that is supposed to separate them out from one another in a purifying process of sharp definition. A self-opinionated epistemology that insists on precision where it is not possible to iron out ambiguities, sabotages our understanding and helps to perpetuate the bad by zealously prohibiting reflection upon whether progress is taking place or not – a question to which all those caught up in an age of both utopian and destructive possibilities would dearly like an answer. Like every philosophical term 'progress' has its ambiguities; but, as in every term, these ambiguities testify to a common element. What we should think of progress in the here and now is something we know vaguely, but also quite accurately. I am no friend of Brecht's injunction, one that he often put forward in my conversations with him, that what was wanted was simplification. On the contrary, I believe that it is not for nothing that the term simplification is associated with Jacob Burckhardt's *mot* about the *'terribles simplificateurs'*.[15] And I believe that whoever wishes to resist totalitarian habits of thought must resist the temptation to simplify. But there are quite definite concepts where you cannot get by without a certain measure of simplification if you want to avoid the pitfalls of ideology. It is necessary to employ these concepts with the same simplicity and brutality as the reality to which they refer. We must differentiate as much as we can, but where the bestiality and the primitive nature of reality speak, we should take care not to lend them a helping hand by indulging in an excess of differentiation. I can still remember the early days of fascism in Germany when a sociologist[16] who later became very famous sought to persuade me of all sorts of distinctions between fascism and National Socialism. I won't even say that these distinctions were wholly lacking in validity, particularly since the two phenomena arose in different societies at different times. But ultimately these distinctions were superseded by the actions of Hitler and Mussolini and exposed for what they really are, namely, an evasive manoeuvre. Similarly, today, one of the core stratagems of ideology when you offer a trenchant critique of something is for people to reply, 'Yes, but things are not really like that, you must take this and that factor into consideration' – and they end up wriggling out of it. It is my view that, instead of always trying to cut off every individual head of the hydra, we should pay heed to the general principle at work. That is what I mean when I speak of the common factor in the ambiguities of the concept of progress.

LECTURE 16

14 January 1965

ON INTERPRETATION: THE CONCEPT OF PROGRESS (II)

We had started to explore the debates about the nature of progress, and I took the opportunity to make a brief digression on the subject of the mentality that always responds to everything – how should I describe it? – by saying 'that's not possible!', with the intention of thwarting the discussion of serious matters by resorting to the tactic of disputing that a concept has a recognizable referent, by denying the existence of the object denoted by the concept. If I have let fall a few scathing remarks about the concept of synthesis[1] you will be able to see from my comments on this phenomenon that synthesis can be quite a ticklish business. On the one hand, the universal dominance of synthesis – that is to say, the attempt to supply, to identify, to cobble together a concept for everything – is highly problematic. On the other hand, if you attempt to deny a concept any substantive meaning and endeavour to reduce it simply to what it happens to cover, then this will no more lead to knowledge than will the practice of dissolving everything that exists into pure identity with its own concept, to the point where in the last analysis the concept contains no more than itself. I believe that if you picture these two poles for yourselves, that is to say, on the one hand, the self-sufficient, absolute concept and, on the other, the absolutely empty concept which is no longer capable of grasping anything at all – you will come to see the sort of predicament philosophy has fallen into, a predicament that means that it must not surrender either to ontology or to positivism, but must regard these twin schools of thought as interrelated. And that no doubt is what common sense tells us is meant by the term dialectics.

I would say that if we apply the term 'progress' all too pedantically, that is to say, if we look too closely at the word, we will find ourselves cheated of what it promises – namely, of its answer to our doubts and hopes about whether things will ever improve and whether human beings will ever be able to breathe a sigh of relief.[2] I believe that you should start by taking progress to mean this very simple thing: that it would be better if people had no cause to fear,[3] if there were no impending catastrophe on the horizon – if you do this, it will not provide a timeless, absolute definition of progress, but it will give the idea a concrete form. For progress today really does mean simply the prevention and avoidance of total catastrophe. And I would say that, if only it can be prevented and avoided, that would in fact be progress. If only for this reason we cannot say with any precision what we should understand by progress; it is because an aspect of the present crisis is that everyone feels what I have just tried to explain to you while the words that would break the spell are missing. In other words, we can find nothing in reality that might help to redeem the promise inherent in the word 'progress'. This absence of a concrete, immediately obvious potential is what makes it so difficult to answer the question whether or not progress is possible. The only reflections about progress that have any truth are those that both immerse themselves in the idea and yet maintain a distance from it, standing back from the paralysing facts and specialized meanings that prevent us from understanding what actually is intended. Today, as I have already remarked, all these reflections come to a head in the question of whether mankind will succeed in preventing a catastrophe. Humanity's survival is threatened by the forms of its own global social constitution, unless humanity's own global subject becomes sufficiently self-aware to come to its rescue after all. The possibility of progress, of averting the most extreme total calamity, has migrated to this global social subject alone. And I have no need to tell you that what I mean by this global subject of mankind is not simply an all-embracing terrestrial organization, but a human race that possesses genuine control of its own destiny right down to the concrete details, and is thus able to fend off the unseeing blows of nature. On the contrary, the mania for organization, be it for an enlarged League of Nations or for some other global organization of all mankind, might easily fall into the category of things that prevent us from achieving what all men long for, instead of promoting that cause. To repeat, the possibility of progress, the avoidance of total catastrophe, has migrated to such a real, not merely formal, global social subject. Everything else involving progress would have to crystallize around it. Material want which long seemed to mock progress has been potentially eliminated. Thanks to the current state of the technical forces of production no one should need to suffer privation any longer. Given the current state of technical development, the fact that there are still countless millions who suffer hunger and want must be attributed to the forms of social production, the *relations of production*, not to the intrinsic difficulty of meeting people's material needs. This has particular force when we consider the possibilities of a truly rational organization of agriculture throughout the world. Whether there will be further want and oppression – the two things are identical: humanity must and will, certainly *will*, continue to be oppressed until the question of material needs has been resolved – will be decided solely by the avoidance of a calamity through the rational organization of society as a whole in a manner befitting humanity.

Kant's sketch of a theory of progress too was anchored in what he called the 'idea of man'.[4] I quote from his *Idea for a Universal History with a Cosmopolitan Purpose*:

> The highest purpose of nature – i.e. the development of all natural capacities – can be fulfilled for mankind only in society, and nature intends that man should accomplish this, and indeed all his appointed ends, by his own efforts. This purpose can be fulfilled only in a society which has not only the greatest freedom, and therefore a continual antagonism among its members, but also the most precise specification and preservation of the limits of this freedom in order that it can co-exist with the freedom of others. The highest task which nature has set for mankind must therefore be that of establishing a society in which *freedom under external laws* would be combined to the greatest possible extent with irresistible force, in other words of establishing a perfectly *just civil constitution*. For only through the solution and fulfilment of this task can nature accomplish its other intentions with our species.[5]

Thus the concept of progress is linked to that of a fulfilled humanity, and it is not to be had for less. I would draw your attention in passing to a problem that arises here, namely, Kant's use of the term 'nature'. Obviously, 'nature' here is not intended in the sense of nature as constituted, in other words, nature as it is seen in the objects of the natural sciences. Nature here involves something for which there is not really any space in the official edifice of the Kantian critiques, not even in the *Critique of Judgement*. What I have in mind is a teleological idea of man whose disposition is such that what he really is, is something that he has first to *become*. This concept of human nature is neither a basic anthropological given in Kant, nor is it identical with the constitutum 'nature of man', as a thing among things; but it is a concept that must (and I hope: will) soon be energetically worked out. But all of this is simply by way of elucidating the direct impact of Rousseau on this question. The concept of history which has space for progress is emphatic; it is the universal or cosmopolitan concept that appears in Kant, not a concept concerned with particular life spheres. The dependence of progress on totality – the fact that progress exists only if mankind as a whole can be said to progress, and not if it represents progress in particular spheres of life – turns against progress itself in so far as it concerns humanity itself.

An awareness of this animates Benjamin's polemic against the coupling of progress and humanity in his theses 'On the Concept of History', perhaps the weightiest criticism of the idea of progress held by those who in crude political terms may be included among the progressives. For those of you who have taken a particular interest in Benjamin's philosophy, I should say in general that, from a relatively early stage, one of its underlying motifs was Benjamin's attempt to differentiate himself from Kant. Benjamin had been deeply impressed by Kant, and it is clear that he is striving to distance himself from a thinker who impressed him and appeared very powerful, but was also, I should like to add, something of a threat. Benjamin does not make this act of separation explicit or articulate it in philosophical terms, but it is one of the themes underlying his thought that we must be aware of if we are to understand him. Almost all his writings, at least his mature writings, are influenced by the fact not that he disputes the crucial Kantian concepts, but that he passes them over in silence, that he fails to mention them explicitly. The passage from Benjamin I have in mind is as follows: 'Progress as pictured in the minds of the Social Democrats was, first of all, progress of humankind itself (and not just advances in human skills and knowledge).'[6] In order to understand this passage properly you must be aware of the context in which it was written. It goes without saying that he does not believe that progress is to be sought in advances in human skills and knowledge, rather than in humanity itself. But what he ascribes to politically reformist attitudes is in fact (if I may extrapolate from his statement) the view that they, namely, superficial, middle-of-the-road thinkers, have equated this particular progress in skills and knowledge, in other words, progress in technology in the broadest sense, or, as Horkheimer and I have called it, progress in the domination of nature,[7] with progress itself. Whereas the truth is that particular advances in the techniques of domination contain the potential for the very opposite of the progress that I set out to describe at the beginning of this lecture. Just as mankind *tel quel* does not progress in line with the advertising slogan of 'better and better' that Benjamin criticizes in the increasingly superficial propaganda of the workers' movement of the period between 1870 and Hitler, so too there can be no idea of progress without the idea of humanity. In Benjamin progress derives its legitimation from the theory that the idea of the happiness of unborn generations – without which we cannot speak of progress – inevitably includes the idea of redemption.[8] He thus confirms that the idea of progress is inseparable from the survival of the species. No progress may be supposed that implies that humanity already existed and could therefore be assumed to continue to progress. Rather progress would be the establishment of humanity in the first place, the prospect of which opens up in the face of its extinction. It follows, as Benjamin continues, that the concept of universal history – which we have discussed at some length – cannot be salvaged.[9] That idea was plausible only as long as we could believe in the illusion of an already existing humanity, coherent in itself and moving upwards in a unified manner. If humanity remains trapped by the totality it itself creates, then, as Kafka observed, no progress has taken place at all,[10] while mere totality, the idea of totality, allows progress to be entertained in thought. This dialectical moment in the concept of humanity as a totality can best be clarified by the definition of mankind as that which excludes absolutely nothing. If humanity were a totality that no longer contained any limiting principle, it would be free from the coercion that subjects all its members to such a principle. It would thereby cease to be a totality so that it might finally become a totality. It would cease to be an imposed unity. The passage from Schiller's 'Ode to Joy', if my memory serves me right, contains the lines 'And he who knows nothing of this, let him steal away / Weeping, out of this company'.[11] In the name of an all-encompassing love it banishes anyone to whom such love has not been vouchsafed. The poem involuntarily admits the truth about the bourgeois conception of humanity, at once totalitarian and particular. In these lines what the one who is unloved or incapable of love undergoes in the name of the idea [of humanity] unmasks that idea with the same affirmative violence with which Beethoven's music hammers it home.[12] By using the word 'steal', the poem joins in the humiliation of the man who is joyless and who is therefore refused joy for a second time. It is scarcely a coincidence that associations from the realms of property and crime should be evoked in this way. As in totalitarian political systems, a constant antagonism forms part of the concept of totality. This is how evil mythic festivals are defined in fairy tales – by the guests who have not been invited. The principle of totality sets limits, even if it be only the commandment to resemble itself. Only if that principle were to disappear would humanity, and not its mirage, come into being.

Historically, the conception of humanity was already implicit in the theorem of the universal state proposed by the middle Stoa.[13] Objectively, at least, this amounted to an idea of progress, alien though it may have been to pre-Christian antiquity, which was dominated by cyclical ideas of history – as indeed were the Stoics. The fact that this tenet of Stoic philosophy also served to buttress Rome's imperialist ambitions tells us something of the impact on the concept of progress of its identification with human 'skills and knowledge'. The existing generation of people is substituted for those as yet unborn; history is turned directly into soteriology. That was the prototype of the idea of progress right down to and including Hegel and Marx. In St Augustine's *civitas dei* this idea of progress is still linked to redemption by Christ, as the historically successful redemption. Only a mankind that has already been redeemed can be seen, once it had been chosen and by virtue of the grace that had been vouchsafed it, as if it were moving within the continuum of time towards the kingdom of heaven.[14] It was perhaps unfortunate that later thought about progress should have inherited from St Augustine an immanent teleology and the conception of humanity as the subject of all progress. You all know about the links between him and Kant, and thereafter between Kant and later, secular theories of progress, while Christian soteriology – in other words, the science of salvation, the doctrine of salvation – gradually faded away in a welter of speculations about the philosophy of history. In this way, the idea of progress was completely absorbed into the *civitas terrena*, its Augustinian counterpart. Even in Kantian dualism, this *civitas terrena* was supposed to progress in accordance with its own principle, in accordance with its 'nature'. Such enlightenment places human progress in the hands of humanity itself and so concretizes progress as an ideal to be realized. However, within it still lurks the conformist confirmation of existence as it is. This receives the aura of redemption even though redemption failed to occur and evil persisted unabated. From the standpoint of the philosophy of history such a modification of progress, with all its incalculable consequences, was unavoid-able. Just as the emphatic claim of successful redemption turned into a protest in the face of post-Christian history, so, conversely, the

Augustinian doctrine of an immanent movement of the human species
towards a blessed state contained the motif of irresistible secularization. The temporal nature of progress, its simple concept – for progressing is simply inconceivable outside time – binds it to the empirical
world. Without such a temporal dimension, in other words, without
the hope that things might improve with time, the heinous aspects of
the world and its ways really would become immortalized in thought
and creation itself would be turned into the work of a gnostic demon.
In Augustine we can discern the inner constellation of the ideas of
progress, redemption and the immanent course of history, ideas that
risk mutual destruction if they are allowed to dissolve into one
another. If progress is equated with redemption as the transcendental
intervention par excellence, then it forfeits, along with its temporal
dimension, all intelligible meaning and evaporates into ahistorical
theology. However, if progress is channelled into history, this threatens to convert history itself into an object of idolatry, and with this,
both in the reflection of the concept and in reality, we are faced with
the absurdity that it is progress itself that inhibits progress. Expedi-
ents such as a concept of progress that is both immanent and transcendent – such as the one produced by the late Siegfried Marck[15]
– condemn themselves by their very nomenclature.

The greatness of the Augustinian theory was that of its originality
at the time. It contains all the abysses that beset the idea of progress
and strives to provide theoretical solutions for them. The structure
of his doctrine brings out the antinomian nature of progress without
attempting to soften it. In his teaching, as also later on at the climax
of secular philosophy of history since Kant, and above all, therefore,
in Hegel, conflict is placed at the heart of the historical movement
that is thought of as progress because it is a movement directed
towards the kingdom of heaven. For Augustine this movement is the
struggle between heaven and earth. Every subsequent idea of progress
has derived its profundity from the mounting burden of historical
calamity. Whereas in Augustine redemption was the *telos* of history,
the latter does not lead directly to the former, to redemption, nor is
redemption the direct consequence of history. Redemption is embedded in history by the divine plan of the universe, but has been at odds
with it since the Fall – both things hold good, then. Augustine saw
that neither redemption nor history can exist without the other, nor
can they exist in each other; they are suspended in a tension whose
accumulated energy ultimately aims at the transcendence of the historical world itself. In the age of catastrophe the idea of progress
cannot be conceived of as settling for less. Progress should no more

be ontologized, unthinkingly ascribed to the realm of Being, than should decline, with which, admittedly, modern philosophy appears to be more comfortable. Too little that is good has power in the world for the world to be said to have achieved progress, but there can be no good, not even a trace of it, without progress. If, in accordance with a mystical doctrine, worldly events, right down to the most insignificant occurrences, are to have momentous consequences for the life of the absolute itself, then something similar may be claimed for progress. Every single element in the web of delusion is nevertheless of relevance to the possible demise of that web of delusion. The good is what struggles free, finds a language and opens its eyes. As something that struggles free, goodness is part of the texture of history which, without being unambiguously set on reconciliation, in the course of its movement illuminates the possibility of reconciliation in a momentary flash.

According to conventional thinking, the features in which the concept of progress has its life are partly philosophical, partly social in nature. Without society the idea of progress would be quite vacuous; all its features are abstracted from society. If society had not advanced from a horde of hunters and gatherers to agriculture, from slavery to the formal freedom of the subject, from the fear of demons to reason, from want to the discovery of ways with which to ward off epidemics and famine and to the improvement of living conditions in general, if, in short, the idea of progress had been kept philosophically pure, if it had been spun out from the nature of time, it would have had no content at all. But once the meaning of a concept compels a move into the realm of facts, of historical reality, this necessary transition cannot be halted arbitrarily. The idea of reconciliation itself, the transcendent *telos* of all progress, cannot be freed from the immanent process of enlightenment which banishes fear, and, by erecting mankind as the answer to the questions posed by man, it reaps the concept of humanity which alone rises above the immanent state of the world. For all that, progress is not tantamount to society, it is not identical with society; indeed, given the nature of society, progress may at times even be its opposite. As long as philosophy was at all useful it was also a theory of society. However, by surrendering without demur to its power, it is reduced to rhetoric to assert its independence. The purity – Hegel speaks of the 'revolting purity' [*ekle Reinheit*][16] – into which philosophy relapsed is the bad conscience of its own impurity, its complicity with the world. The concept of progress is philosophical in the sense that it articulates the movement of society as a whole at the same time as it contradicts it. Having arisen from within society, progress calls for a critical confrontation with society as it actually exists. The element of redemption it contains, no matter how secularized, is indestructible. The fact that it can be reduced neither to actual reality nor to ideas points to its own contradictory nature. For the element of enlightenment in the concept, the impulse towards demythologization which, by assuaging the terrors of nature, ends up in reconciliation with it, is twinned with the element of the domination of nature. The model of progress, even if transposed into the godhead itself, represents the control of nature, both inner, human nature and nature outside man. The oppression practised by such control, and mirrored in the mind in the identity principle of reason, reproduces this antagonism. The more identity is postulated by the spirit that dominates, the more injustice is meted out to the non-identical. Injustice is passed down to the non-identical, feeding its resistance. This resistance in turn reinforces the principle of oppression, while, at the same time, poisoned by oppression, the oppressed limp on. Everything advances within the whole, only the whole itself fails to progress, or at least has failed to progress up to now. Goethe's 'and all urgency, all conflict, is eternal rest in God the Lord'[17] codifies this experience, and Hegel's doctrine of the development of the world spirit, the absolute dynamic, as a returning into itself or even a game with itself, comes very close to Goethe's apophthegm. We need add only one footnote to their summation: the fact that this totality is motionless in its motion because it knows of nothing beyond itself does not mean that it is the divine absolute, but rather its opposite, rendered unrecognizable by thought. If I were to finish on a theological note, I would have to call it: Hell.

Kant neither acquiesced in this deception nor did he make an absolute of the rupture. In the most sublime passage in his philosophy of history he taught that antagonism, the entanglement of progress in myth, in the hold of nature on the domination of nature itself, in short, in the kingdom of unfreedom, tends to move by virtue of its own law towards the kingdom of freedom. Subsequently, this insight formed the basis of Hegel's 'cunning of reason'. But if that is the case, then it means nothing less than that the possibility of reconciliation is rooted in its own contradiction, that the precondition of freedom is the unfreedom that precedes it. Kant's doctrine stands at a watershed. It conceptualizes the idea of reconciliation as intrinsic to the antagonistic 'development' since he derives it from a design that nature is said to have conceived for man. On the other hand, the dogmatically rationalist inflexibility with which such a design is ascribed to nature – as if nature were not included in this development and as if its own concept would not be modified by it – is the mark of the violence that spirit inflicts upon nature in its desire to postulate identity. The static quality of the concept of nature is a function of the dynamic concept of reason: the more reason appropriates elements of the non-identical, the more nature is reduced to a residual *caput mortuum*, and that is what makes it easy to furnish nature with the qualities of eternity that justify its ends. The very idea of 'design' can only be conceived if we allow that reason can be ascribed to nature itself. Even in the metaphysical use that Kant makes of the concept of nature at this point and which brings it close to the transcendent thing-in-itself, nature remains the product of spirit, much as it does in the *Critique of Pure Reason*. If spirit vanquished nature by following Bacon's programme and making itself the equal of nature at every stage, then at the Kantian stage it projected itself back onto a nature which is conceived as absolute and not merely constituted. It has performed this act of backward projection in the service of a possible reconciliation in which the primacy of the subject is to be preserved undiminished. At the point where Kant comes closest to the concept of reconciliation, namely in his assertion that antagonism culminates in its abolition, we find the key phrase about a society in which freedom is said to be 'combined . . . with irresistible force'.[18] But even this talk of force reminds us of the dialectic of progress itself. If a sustained oppression continually arrested the progress that it had unleashed, it was also, as the emancipation of consciousness, the first to recognize the fact of antagonism and the totality of delusion, a recognition which was the prerequisite for overcoming all conflict. The progress engendered by eternal sameness is that at long last progress can begin, at any moment. If the image of an advancing humanity reminds us of a giant who, after sleeping from time immemorial, slowly bestirs himself and then storms forth, trampling down everything that gets in his way, his rude awakening is the only potential for maturity. By maturity, I mean that the imprisonment within nature in which progress itself is implicated does not have the last word. For simply aeons it made no sense to inquire about progress. The question became meaningful only after the liberation of the dynamic from which the idea of freedom could be extrapolated. Ever since St Augustine, progress has meant transferring to the species as a whole the idea of the natural course of life of the individual between birth and death. If progress is as much a myth as the idea of the path fate has ordained for the constellations, the idea of progress itself is the anti-mythological idea par excellence. It disrupts the circle of which it formed a part. Thus progress means escaping from the magic spell, including the spell of progress that is itself nature. This happens when human beings become conscious of their own naturalness and call a halt to their own domination of nature, a domination by means of which nature's own domination is perpetuated. In this sense, we might say that progress occurs where it comes to an end.

I should like to break off at this point.

LECTURE 17

19 January 1965

ON INTERPRETATION: THE CONCEPT OF PROGRESS (III)

I should like to continue with my discussion of the questions I broached in connection with the concept of progress. Perhaps you will recall that last time I finished with the assertion that progress means – or, I should no doubt say, that progress would mean, if it were to be genuine progress – escaping from the magic spell. This includes the magic spell of progress which is itself part of nature; and I argued that humanity becomes aware of its own naturalness and this enables it to call a halt to its own domination of nature, a domination which enables that of nature to be perpetuated. I shall now move on from there. In earlier lectures I explained the motif of naturalness [*Naturwüchsigkeit*] and history, and in general the idea of history as a natural process, so I have no need to say anything further about that now. We might say (and this is how I finished up last time) that progress occurs where it comes to an end. This heterodox and even heretical view of progress would undoubtedly be unanimously condemned throughout the world. Nevertheless, it can be found in coded form, it is implicit in a concept, that is if anything even more taboo than what I have been saying about progress. The concept I have in mind is that of *decadence*. This concept was explicitly adopted by the artists of the *Jugendstil* period to whom we either condescend or else whom we treat as a sort of museum piece with the somewhat faded charm of the recent past. The fact that they adopted it can only partly be explained by their wish to define their own historical situation, a situation which may well have appeared to them to possess some of the features of biological morbidity. Their impulse to capture or immortalize their historical situation in an image – and in this there were profound similarities with the Philosophers of Life [*Lebensphilosophen*] – implied the conviction that the truth, what really mattered, was only preserved in whatever appeared to prophesy their own demise and the demise of their culture. In general, the entire art of *Jugendstil* was marked by a peculiar configuration of the worthless and the utopian. If, for example, you look at the writings of Henrik Ibsen, the greatest writer of *Jugendstil*, you will discover that the truth, what really mattered, was salvaged. In his work, the image of utopia consistently ends in nothingness, in destruction. This is true of *Rosmersholm*, of Johannes Rosmer and Rebekka West, who plunge to their deaths from the bridge in the belief that this will bring them fulfilment; it is true likewise of Nora with her belief in the 'miracle' that can never become reality, and also of Hedda Gabler with her fantasies about Eilert Løvborg appearing 'with vineleaves in his hair'; or of Master Builder Solness who builds the tower on his house which is supposed to embody his vision and the absolute, even though it has no function and would undoubtedly be judged a monstrosity according to the criteria of modern architecture.[1] This aspect of *Jugendstil* calls for very close analysis. It is undoubtedly closely connected with *Jugendstil*'s attitude towards ornaments, which it viewed both as worthless, superfluous, and cut off from reality, and *nevertheless* as the refuge of the beautiful. I am just pointing out a few of the motifs of the philosophy underlying *Jugendstil* here; I believe that we could learn an enormous amount from it.

This relationship of decadence, of the passion for death, and utopia, and thus the idea of a genuine progress, is nowhere expressed more forcefully than it is by a man who will be no more than a name to most of you, but who exercised a huge influence on the *Jugendstil* generation, or the Secession, to give it its Austrian name. This influence reverberated in radical modern art down to the period of my own youth. Among the artists of the avant-garde he was widely revered and even had a cult following. His name was Peter Altenberg, and Karl Kraus has published a selection from his numerous books.[2] These books deserve to be read very attentively though, to be sure, with x-ray eyes, since on the surface they are full of banalities and lapses of taste – but if you look more closely you come across quite extraordinary things. Here is an aphorism of Altenberg's on the subject of progress. I cite it in the form it has in Kraus's selection:

> Maltreatment of horses. This will only cease when the passers-by have become so irritable and decadent that, abandoning their self-control, they fall into a rage at the sight of such things and in their desperation

commit crimes and shoot down the dastardly, cowardly coach-men ... The inability to bear the sight of horses being maltreated is the act of the neurasthenic, decadent people of the future! Up to now, they have had just enough strength to enable them to mind their own business ...[3]

I would like to mention incidentally Altenberg's critique of one of the constants of bourgeois anthropology, namely of the coldness that permits a person to watch even the most extreme actions because in accordance with the principle of individualism it is felt to be of no direct concern to himself or herself; an attitude which culminates in Auschwitz and everything associated with it, events that would not be possible in the absence of such a principle.[4] In a similar experience, Nietzsche, who condemned pity, had his final breakdown in Turin when he saw a coachman whipping his horse. Decadence was the mirage of the progress that had not yet begun. However narrow-minded and wilfully obdurate the ideal of a remoteness from pur-poses, an ideal that renounced life, may have been, it was the reverse image of the false instrumentality of a busy activity in which every-thing exists only for something else. The irrationalism of *décadence*, which is how the movement liked to designate itself, represented a denunciation of the unreason of the dominant form of reason. It is quite mistaken to equate a happiness that is separated off, arbitrary and privileged with this irrationalism – a very specific form of irra-tionalism, incidentally. Such a happiness, separated off, arbitrary and, if you like, privileged, is sacred to this idea of decadence because it alone guarantees that one has escaped, whereas every direct form of universal happiness, in accordance with the fashionable liberal formula of the greatest good of the greatest number, sells out to the self-sustaining apparatus, the sworn enemy of happiness, even when happiness is advertised as the goal to be attained. It is from such a cast of mind that it dawns on Altenberg that extreme individuation is the stand-in for humanity. I quote him once more: 'For inasmuch as an individual has ... a legitimacy of whatever sort, it can only be that of being the first person in some respect, a precursor in some organic development of the human that is part of the possible, natural development of all human beings! To be the "only one" is worthless, a mere whim of fate. To be the "first one"' – and we are speaking here only in temporal terms – 'is everything! ... The first person will know that the whole of mankind will follow him! He has only been sent out in advance by God! ... One day, all human beings will be sensitive, tender, and loving. ... True individuality means being the first to be all those things that everyone, everyone will have to become later on.'[5] In passing, I would ask you to note the similarity between this idea of individuality and Hegel's. In Hegel the artist's individuality is supposed to prove itself in the demise of individuality, of the artist's being thus and so [*Sosein*] in the work he creates.[6] And Hegel's general view of the individual is not so far removed from the one expressed by Altenberg, except that Hegel has a certain tendency to move towards a kind of contempt for the individual in favour of the world spirit. In contrast, Altenberg's idea of the individual that is nothing contains the notion that, in his nothingness, which in *Jugendstil* often takes the very unfortunate form of the individual as victim, the individual is the locus of a real state of affairs, one that is supposed to redound to the benefit of all, in other words, all individuals. In this sense, we may even say that the apparently superficial and much criticized ideal of the greatest good of the greatest number can be said to have been salvaged by its negation at the hands of these *Jugendstil* artists and thinkers. Only through this extreme – and this has something infinitely salutary in the face of the cult of the collective that simmers on beneath the surface today – only through this extreme of differentiation, of individuation, and not as an all-inclusive generic term, is it possible to conceive of humanity today.

The prohibition imposed by the dialectical theory of both Marx and Hegel on a detailed blueprint for utopia senses the betrayal of the idea. Decadence is the nerve centre at which the dialectics of progress are, so to speak, physically appropriated by the mind. Whoever inveighs against decadence inevitably takes up the defence of taboos on sex which the antinomian, even heretical, ritual of decadence sets out to flout. In the insistence upon those taboos in support of the unity of the ego that dominates nature, we hear the rumbling of a blind, unthinking progress. Wherever voices are raised denouncing decadence and insisting on collective progress, the denigration of sexuality is an infallible accompaniment. This unthinking progress, however, can be convicted of irrationality on the grounds that the methods it uses are transformed by a sleight of hand into goals which are themselves then blocked off. To be sure, the counter-position of decadence remains an abstraction. Hegel would call it abstract negation, and this is one reason why it has become something of a laughing stock. Decadence confuses the particular happiness it is forced to insist upon with an immediately realized utopia, a humanity fulfilled, while it remains deformed by unfreedom, privilege and a class rule that it openly admits, but also glorifies. Once unleashed, erotic availability would spell perpetual slavery. We see this in Oscar Wilde's *Salome*, where the beautiful princess treats the attractive prophet as an object wholly at the mercy of her will. Incidentally, in *Hedda*

Gabler, Ibsen, whose dialectical force was truly without precedent, provided a striking image of this affinity between utopia and inhumanity in a scene in which Hedda, who is an icon of the *Jugendstil* world, appears with her aunt, an elderly woman who has been kind to her and who is the only person in this environment who shows any human feeling. In this scene Hedda makes her aunt look foolish simply by drawing attention to the fact that she is wearing a ridiculous hat that doesn't suit her.[7] If we read Ibsen or even Wilde and Altenberg, for that matter, with the aid of such categories we can learn a tremendous amount about such things, I believe, and I would be happy if I could inspire you to attempt it. These problems, incidentally, were then put aside and forgotten with the onset of expressionism – just as whole realms of knowledge in the history of the mind are forgotten. Expressionism was concerned essentially with the protest of human immediacy against reified and sclerotic institutions. It may have been one step ahead of the illusions of *Jugendstil*, since it found a voice for far more drastic experiences, and was able to devise a far more drastic world of forms to express them. Nevertheless, despite such advantages, expressionism sacrificed a great deal of subtlety in comparison to *Jugendstil*, and thus opened the door to a certain coarsening and primitivism. It is conceivable that the most durable products of modern art will prove to be those that have benefited from the new developments that began with expressionism and cubism, but have preserved some of the subtlety of which you will have perhaps got the flavour from the two brief passages from Altenberg that I have read out to you.

The explosive tendency of progress is not simply the flipside of the movement towards the progressive domination of nature; it is not the abstract negation of that tendency, but calls for the development of reason through the domination of nature. Only rationality, the principle of social rule as applied to the subject, would be capable of eliminating that domination. The possibility of the emergence of such a principle is brought about by the pressure of negativity. On the other hand, reason, which would like to escape from nature, is what shapes nature into the very thing it has to fear. What makes the concept of progress dialectical, in a strictly non-metaphorical sense, is the fact that reason, its organ, is just *one thing*. That is to say, it does not contain two strata, one that dominates nature and one that conciliates it. Both strata share in all its aspects. It is for this reason that we can speak of a dialectic of progress in such a rigorous sense. In reason, the organ of this dialectic, these two strata, which I have called the one that dominates nature and the one that conciliates it, do not just subsist alongside one another, but both go to make up the unity of reason in equal measure. The one element only turns into the other, or can only turn into the other, literally by reflecting on itself, in other words, if reason is applied to reason, and if through this act of self-limitation it emancipates itself from the demon of identity. The incomparable greatness of Kant consists not least in the way in which he incorruptibly held on to the unity of reason even in its contradictory form: reason as the domination of nature, or in what he called its theoretical, causal-mechanical aspect, and reason as the conciliatory power of judgement that moulds itself to the contours of nature. He rigorously translated the difference between them into the self-limitation of the rationality that dominates nature. A metaphysical interpretation of Kant should not impute to him a latent ontology, but instead should decode the structure of his philosophy as a whole as a dialectic of enlightenment. This was something that Hegel, the dialectician par excellence, failed to appreciate because, in his belief in a *single* reason, he erased this boundary line and so drifted into the mythical totality that he thought of as 'sublated', 'reconciled', in the absolute idea. Progress does not just define the scope of what is dialectical, as in Hegel's philosophy of history, but is dialectical in its own concept, like the categories of the *Science of Logic*. Absolute domination of nature is absolute submission to nature, and yet rises above nature when it reflects upon itself. It is myth that demythologizes myth. The protest of the subject, however, would cease to exist as theory or as contemplation. The idea of the rule of pure reason as something existing in itself, in isolation from practice, subjugates the subject too, moulding it into an instrument to be used towards an end. With the assistance of self-reflection, however, reason would achieve its transition into practice: it would perceive itself to be an aspect of practice, instead of consciousness or reason turning itself into something existing in its own right. Rationality would recognize that it is a mode of behaviour as opposed to misinterpreting itself as the absolute. The anti-mythological strand in progress is inconceivable without practical action which curbs the delusion of an autarky of the spirit. This explains why it is so difficult to define progress through a process of disinterested contemplation.

This provides a dangerous pretext for the ancient assertion, that it [progress] has no right to exist, an assertion that constantly reappears in a new garb. This excuse thrives on the fallacy that, because there has been no progress up to now, there will be none in future. It proclaims that the dreary recurrence of the same is the message of Being that must be heard and taken to heart. In reality, Being itself, which has this message foisted on it, is a cryptogram of myth, and if we could free ourselves from it, it would be something of a liberation. In elevating historical despair into a norm that must be adhered to, we hear the echo of that revolting adaptation of the theological doctrine of original sin, the idea that the corruption of human nature legitimates domination, and that radical evil[8] legitimates evil. This obscurantist conviction makes use of a catchphrase with which to bring the idea of progress into disrepute in modern times. This negative slogan is: faith in progress. The attitude of those who decry the concept of progress as superficial and positivistic is for the most part positivistic itself. They declare the course of the world which has constantly thwarted progress, even though it was progressive itself, to be the proof that the universal plan does not tolerate progress, and whoever does not abandon the concept commits sacrilege. In self-righteous profundity – and here you gaze into the abyss of profundity itself, or, if you prefer, into its shallows – such people take up sides with everything that is dreadful. They malign the idea of progress in accordance with the belief that, if human beings have failed at something, it must have been ontologically impossible. In the name of their finite existence and their mortality it would be their duty, so they imply, to embrace that finite existence and mortality wholeheartedly. A sober response to their false reverence for Being, their existential piety, faith in Being or whatever slogans are current nowadays would assert that our progress from the slingshot to the megaton bomb may well provoke satanic mockery, but that the age of the bomb is the first in which we can envisage a condition from which violence has disappeared. At the same time, a theory of progress must absorb the kernel of truth contained in those invectives against the belief in progress. It must do so as an antidote to the mythology from which the theory of progress ails. The last thing that would befit a theory of progress that has been made conscious of itself would be to deny the existence of a superficial theory, simply on the grounds that the ridicule of such a shallow conception belongs in the arsenal of ideology. Condorcet notwithstanding,[9] the much maligned idea of progress that held sway in the eighteenth century is far less superficial than that of the nineteenth: in Rousseau we find the doctrine of radical perfectibility combined in a highly dialectical manner with that of the radical corruption of human nature. As long as the bourgeois class was oppressed, at least in terms of political forms, it made use of the catchword 'progress' to show its opposition to the prevailing static condition of society. The pathos of that catchword was the echo of that condition. Only when the bourgeoisie had taken over the decisive levers of power did the belief in progress degenerate into the ideology that ideological profundity accused the eighteenth century of fostering. The nineteenth century came up against the limits of bourgeois society; it could not realize in practice its own rationality, its own ideals of freedom, justice and humane immediacy, without risking the abolition of its own order. That forced it to credit itself, falsely, with having achieved what in reality was left undone. This lie, which the educated classes then used to criticize the belief in progress held by uneducated or reformist labour leaders, was the expression of bourgeois apologetics. Admittedly, when the shades of imperialism began to gather, the bourgeoisie promptly abandoned that ideology and resorted to the desperate measure of transforming the negative outlook that the faith in progress had tried to refute into a substantial metaphysics.

Whoever rubs his hands in glee and mock humility at the thought of the sinking of the *Titanic*, on the grounds that the iceberg dealt the first blow to our faith in progress, forgets or suppresses the fact that this calamity, which incidentally was not decreed by fate, led to improvements that prevented unforeseen natural accidents to shipping (as opposed to the intentional sinking of ships in wartime over the following half-century). It is an instance of the dialectic of progress that the historical setbacks that are themselves the product of the progressive principle – what could be more progressive than the race for the Blue Riband? – create the conditions for humanity to discover the remedies that will prevent them in future. The web of delusion surrounding progress extends beyond itself. It is entwined with the order in which the category of progress might first gain its justification, and which in Kant's philosophy goes by the name of mankind, in that the devastation wrought by progress can be mended, if at all, only by its own resources, never through the restoration of the previous conditions that were its victim. The progress in mastering nature that in Benjamin's metaphor[10] runs counter to true progress, which has its *telos* in redemption, is not entirely without hope. The two concepts of progress communicate with each other not simply in averting ultimate catastrophe, but also in every current instance in which universal suffering is eased.

The antithesis of faith in progress is faith in interiority. But interiority, man's capacity for improvement, is no guarantee of progress. Even in Augustine the idea of progress – the word was not yet available to him – was as ambivalent as the dogma of a successful redemption in the face of an as yet unredeemed world. On the one hand, progress is historical, traversing the six epochs corresponding to the ages of man; on the other hand, it is inward or, to use Augustine's term, mystical. *Civitas terrena* and *civitas dei* are invisible realms, and no one can say – or so Augustine asserts – who among the living belongs to the one or the other. To decide that is the prerogative of the secret election to grace, the same divine will that moves history in accordance with its plan. Yet as early as Augustine – according to the perceptive comment of Karl Heinz Haag[11] – the interiorization of progress permits the world to be signed over to the powers that be and therefore, as subsequently in Luther, Christianity is to be commended because it preserves the state. Platonic transcendence, which in Augustine is merged with the Christian idea of salvation history, makes it possible to cede this world to the principle that represents everything that progress is designed to overcome, and only on the Day of Judgement, in defiance of all philosophy of history, to allow the resurrection of an unspoilt creation. This ideological mark has remained engraved in the interiorization of progress to this day. In contrast to this mark, interiorization itself, as the product of history, may be a function either of progress or sometimes of its opposite. The nature of man is no more than one aspect of inner-worldly progress, and nowadays it is certainly not the primary one. The argument that there can be no progress because none occurs inwardly is false because it posits the bogus idea of an immediately humane society, in its historical process, whose law is based on what human beings are. However, it is of the essence of historical objectivity – this is an idea I have recently tried to explore in the course of a debate with Arnold Gehlen[12] – that whatever human beings have made, institutions in the widest sense, make themselves independent of them and come to form a second nature. That fallacy makes possible the thesis that human nature never changes, a constancy that may be welcomed or deplored. Progress within the world has its mythical side, as Hegel and Marx recognized, in that it takes place over people's heads and forms them in its own image. It is foolish to deny the existence of progress merely on the grounds that it cannot quite cope with its objects, namely human beings. In order to halt what Schopenhauer calls 'the revolving wheel',[13] what would be needed would be the human potential that is not completely absorbed by the necessity of historical movement. The idea that progress offers a way out is blocked today because the subjective aspects of spontaneity are beginning to atrophy in the historical process. The desperate idea that we find in the French existentialists, that an isolated, ostensibly ontological conception of subjective spontaneity can have any hope of defeating the omnipotence of society, is, I repeat, too optimistic even as an expression of despair. A spontaneity that might turn the tide cannot be conceived of outside its entanglement with society. It would be an illusion of idealism to hope that a spontaneous gesture could prove effective here. Such hopes are entertained simply and solely because at the moment there is no basis for hope in the objective

historical trend. Existentialist decisionism is merely the reflex reaction
to the seamless totality of the world spirit. Nevertheless this totality,
which I referred to in the first part of this lecture course, is itself mere
appearance. The ossified institutions, the relations of production, are
not absolute Being, but man-made and revocable, however powerful
they may be. In their relations to the subjects from which they origi-
nate and which they hold in their grip, they remain antagonistic
through and through. It is not merely that the totality demands
change, if it is not to perish, but also, because of its antagonistic
nature, it finds it impossible to impose that full identity with human
beings that is depicted in negative utopias. This explains why progress
in the world, the arch-enemy of that other progress, nevertheless
remains open to the possibility of it, no matter how little it is able to
assimilate this possibility into its own law.

Against this, it can be plausibly argued that intellectual spheres
such as art, and, even more convincingly, law, politics and anthropology, do not advance with such vigour as the material forces of production. Hegel said as much himself, and Jochmann reiterated it in
even more extreme terms.[14] The idea that the superstructure and the
base do not move in tandem was formulated by Marx in his assertion
that the superstructure is transformed more slowly than the base.[15]
Evidently, no one was surprised by the idea that spirit, which is fluid,
volatile, should be static in contrast to the *rudis indigestaque moles*
[shapeless uncoordinated mass] of what was known, and not for
nothing, even in the context of society, as 'matter'.[16] Similarly, psychoanalysis taught that the unconscious, from which the conscious
realm and the objective shapes of mind were nourished, was supposedly ahistorical. To be sure, whatever is considered, as the product
of a brutal classification, to be 'culture' and which even contains
subjective consciousness raises a perennial protest against the eternal
sameness of mere existence. But its protests are perennially thwarted.
The eternal sameness of the totality, mankind's dependence upon the
necessities of life, the material conditions of self-preservation, hides
behind its own dynamism, the growth of ostensible social wealth.
Ideology profits from this. Spirit, however, which, as the truly dynamic
principle, would like to transcend this state, is told that it has failed,
and this pleases ideology even more. Reality creates the illusion that
it is moving onwards and upwards, while remaining at bottom what
it was before. Spirit aims at something new, in so far as it is not just
part of an existing apparatus. But in its hopeless attempts to create
it, it vainly batters its head against the old, much as an insect attracted
to the light flies into the windowpane. Spirit is not what it aspires to
be: the Other, the transcendent in all its purity. It too is a piece of

natural history. Because natural history appears in society as something dynamic, spirit ever since Plato and the Eleatics has imagined
itself to possess the Other, that which is removed from the *civitas
terrena*, in an immutable self-same sphere, and its forms – above all,
those of logic which are latent in all intellectual activities – are tai-
lored accordingly. In these forms, spirit is taken over by that immobile
something that it has resisted while still remaining a part of it. The
spell cast by reality over spirit prevents it from soaring above mere
existence, the very thing that its own concept wants it to do. As
something more fragile and evanescent, spirit is all the more susceptible to oppression and mutilation. As the repository of everything
that progress might be over and above all progress, spirit stands at
an angle to the progress that actually occurs, and this does it credit:
through its less than wholehearted complicity with progress, it proclaims what progress really amounts to. However, wherever we have
reason to say that the conscious spirit progresses, it means that spirit
is complicit in the domination of nature. And this happens because,
instead of being *choris*, separated off, as it imagines, it is in fact
entwined in the life process from which it had parted company in
accordance with the law of that process. With this observation I
should like to finish today. Next time, I shall continue by saying
something about the ways in which spirit is caught up in the domination of nature.

LECTURE 18

21 January 1965

ON INTERPRETATION: THE CONCEPT OF PROGRESS (IV)

I should like to begin by finishing off, as quickly as possible, my observations on the concept of progress. These concerned, as I expect you will recall, the question of the part played in progress by spirit, and, in particular, the much noted fact that the role of spirit in progress does not mean that we can simply assert that the products of the spirit have just got better and better. The fact that such an assertion would be highly dubious in the arts scarcely calls for comment, and in any case the point has been made with great force by Hegel in the *Aesthetics*.[1] As far as philosophy is concerned, simply in order to point out the problematic nature of such notions of progress in philosophy, I go no further than inviting you to consider, if you know anything at all about logical positivism, whether we can speak of progress in philosophy from Hegel to Carnap.[2] On the other hand (and I said as much to you last time), spirit, by virtue of its own ideas about eternal, unchanging verities, a preoccupation that has never really vanished from the idea of mind ever since Plato's time, has developed a certain static aspect that has repeatedly shown itself in a reluctance to engage with its own evolution. And this aloofness has even deeper causes. Spirit is the most susceptible and, if you like, the weakest, frailest link in the chain of being. It is particularly prone to the temptation to put itself at the disposal of rulers and to reproduce existing circumstances, but also, and this is perhaps a far graver cause for concern, under that spell it tends to become impotent, ephemeral and feeble. It is this that largely prevents it from evolving the way spirit ought to evolve. Thus spirit is said to have as part of its definition the ability to soar, as naïve people put it, in other words, to rise just as Plato's *enthousiasmos* [enthusiasm] envisaged, instead of staying put under the spell of conditions as they are. But as matters stand, spirit finds itself constantly paralysed by this weakness; it lacks the courage to follow its own nature and, instead, remains imprisoned in the spell of existing circumstances. Let me remind you of the implications for spirit of its function in established academic activity. Let me remind you of the thought control[3] practised by the professional guild in so-called academic philosophy (to remain in the narrow confines of our own subject); think of the resentment towards the imagination and indeed towards anything that floats freely, that sets itself apart and refuses to join in. What this led to was that even the most subaltern representatives of the discipline imagined themselves superior to Nietzsche at a time when he had already written *Zarathustra*, and they prevented him from taking up a teaching post in Leipzig.[4] I mention only the most egregious and thus little-known example of such incidents. This will enable you to understand readily that, while spirit is the medium in which you would actually expect to see progress, the reality is that we see astonishingly little of it precisely because spirit is enmeshed in contemporary society and is forced to fulfil a function that conflicts with its own nature, namely to reinforce society in its current form; it renders itself suspect as soon as it raises any protest. Its suspect nature is not just the invention of hostile outsiders. The weakness that prevents it from being different and raising itself above the present penetrates to the core of its being. In countless scholars, for example, it takes the form of their endorsing the expectation, quite without being invited to do so, that their activities should continue a tradition, even when this tradition has proved to be sterile in the extreme, as is the case in many of the humanities. Another aspect of the thought control of the spirit is that it is constantly expected to prove its grasp of facticity; spirit is supposed to be an authority on demonstrable facts, something that is quite alien to the whole concept of spirit since spirit is defined as something other than mere fact. A task of criticism that would be well worth the trouble of undertaking would be to show just how little spirit contributes to progress. This is not just in the sense that there are so few progressive minds or intellectuals, for the number of so-called progressive people in general is extremely small, and it is a mistake to identify intellectuals with progress. But above all, we need an explanation for the fact that the actual content of spirit – that is to say, what it produces – turns out to be so hidebound and in great measure so sterile as is in fact the case. If what we call cultural criticism is to have anything more than an elitist and reactionary meaning, this meaning must consist in exposing these aspects of spirit, in showing just how little of its own substance spirit contributes to that progress by way of resisting it, of fighting free of it.

As the repository[5] of everything that progress might be over and above all progress, spirit stands at an angle to the progress that actually occurs, and this does it credit: through its less than wholehearted complicity with progress, it proclaims what progress really amounts to. And – if I may correct and make more specific what I have already said to you – it goes without saying that spirit also participates in progress in so far as it is, as its pre-eminent organ, implicated in the process of dominating nature. Thus in art, too, we can assuredly speak of progress, in the measurable sense, moreover, that we can talk about the astonishing progress made in the mastery of the materials used in the different arts. However, there is no direct relationship between the progress involved in the mastery of the materials of art and the quality of particular works. In certain circumstances, the two may even be in conflict with each other. However, wherever we have reason to say that the conscious spirit progresses, it means that spirit is taking part in the domination of nature. And this happens because, instead of being *choris*, separated off, as it imagines, it is in fact entwined in the life process from which it had parted company in accordance with the law of that process. All progress (I said earlier) in cultural spheres is that of the mastery of material, of technique. The truth content of spirit is not indifferent to this. A quartet by Mozart – and we have to state this so that what I have been saying to you does not appear too crude and undifferentiated; these matters are highly complex and it is not my task to conceal these complexities from you, but rather to help you to understand them and, as far as possible, to articulate them so that they shed their bewildering aspect – a quartet by Mozart, then, is not merely better made than the works that preceded his stylistically, in other words, the symphonies of the Mannheim School, but, because it is better made and more consistent, it also ranks higher in terms of value [*im emphatischen Sinn*]. On the other hand, it is questionable whether the discovery of perspective means that the painting of the High Renaissance is intrinsically superior to the works of the so-called primitives. We may ask whether the greatest works of art may not be the product of a situation in which the mastery of the material is imperfect or as yet inadequate, in which something is produced for the very first time, something that makes its appearance abruptly and that fades away as soon as it turns into a readily available technique. Progress in the mastery of material in art is by no means identical with the progress of art itself.[6] However, if the gold background had been defended against the introduction of perspective in the early Renaissance, that would have been objectively untrue, as well as reactionary, because it would have been contrary to what its own logic called for. The complexity of progress reveals itself only in the course of history. That is to say, only with hindsight, only when you have followed the logic which you cannot escape, do you realize that this coercion is not identical with an improvement in absolute quality, and that you cannot just call a halt to it. *À la longue*, what in all likelihood will assert itself in the afterlife of works of the spirit is what I have called their truth content, in other words, their quality, as opposed to technical facility. This even takes priority over the stage reached in the mastery of the material that they have achieved for their own age. But even this ability to take priority, to prevail, is only possible in the course of a process of a consciousness that is progressing. The idea of the canonical status of Greek antiquity which still survived even in dialectical thinkers such as Hegel and Marx is not merely an unresolved vestige of the cultural tradition, but, for all the dubiousness surrounding the cult of Greek civilization, it is still the product of a dialectical insight. In order to express its contents, art, and, as I have already indicated, not only art, but also philosophy, must inevitably absorb the growing domination of nature. This means that it secretly works against the very thing it wishes to describe, namely a condition beyond that of the mere domination of nature; it distances itself from the very things that, using neither words nor concepts, it upholds in opposition to the growing domination of nature. This may explain why the apparent continuity of so-called intellectual developments frequently breaks off, often indeed with a – misconceived – slogan of a return to nature. I have tried to offer something of an explanation in the *Introduction to the Sociology of Music* of the ways in which social factors are connected to disruptions in the continuity of historical developments, and I would like to refer you to this.[7] The blame in this instance lies in the fact that – in addition to other, above all, social factors – spirit panics at this contradiction in its own development, that is to say, the contradiction between what spirit actually wants and the domination of nature without which it cannot exist. And it attempts, vainly of course, to rectify this contradiction, by having recourse to the very thing from which it had distanced itself and which it therefore mistakes for a constant reality.

The paradox that progress both exists and does not exist – and that is something I should like to explain to you in these lectures, or rather in this section of the lectures – is one that appears nowhere so vividly as in philosophy, where the idea of progress has its natural home. The transitions from one great philosophy to the next, as

mediated by criticism, are or may appear to be compelling, at least
during certain self-contained periods such as the seventeenth century
or at the turn of the eighteenth to nineteenth centuries. Nevertheless,
to maintain that the evolution from Plato to Aristotle, from Kant to
Hegel, or towards a universal history of philosophy, represents progress is highly dubious. Those of you who take part in our philosophy
seminars[8] will recollect that we kept coming back to the perennial,
unresolved disagreements between Kant and Hegel, disagreements
that are not to be overcome in any one-dimensional manner. The
same idea could be extended to all great philosophies, where we see
how a price has to be paid for every advance, and where, for every
problem that is solved, another has to be allowed to fall by the
wayside, something that is always made plain wherever we can talk
of thinking in an authentic sense. The blame for this should not be
sought – as one might easily suppose, in Schopenhauer's well-known
dictum about the conversation of great minds across the millennia[9]
– in the allegedly unchanging nature of the subject of philosophy, of
true Being, a notion which has now vanished from the history of
philosophy for ever. Nor is it possible to defend a purely aesthetic
view of philosophy that would place a greater value on imposing
systems of thought or the ominous-sounding 'great thinkers' than on
the truth that is by no means identical with the intrinsic coherence
and rigour of these philosophies. To assert that the advances made
by philosophy simply lead it away from what the jargon of bad philosophy designates as its true concern would be completely pharisa-
ical and misguided. We find a judgement of this kind in Heidegger's
philosophy, where the entire history of philosophy is devalued, as if
it were the expression, to use a new-fangled phrase, of one long
'obliviousness of Being',[10] and as if philosophy had only recently succeeded in remembering it. This meant that the need for philosophy
to concern itself with specific questions, such as the question of that
ominous-sounding Being, would become the guarantee of its truth
content. In reality, however, in a discipline whose limits are set by its
theme – that of limits – the unavoidable and questionable instances
of progress are posited by the principle of reason without which
philosophy cannot be thought, because without that principle no
thought at all is possible. It is the Hegelian 'fury of destruction',[11]
which hurls one concept after the other into the abyss of the mythical,
just as the Sphinx had been dashed to pieces by the word 'man'.[12]
Philosophy thrives in symbiosis with science; it cannot part company
with science without lapsing into dogmatism and, ultimately, without
regressing to mythology. Its substance should be the articulation of
what has been omitted or cut off by science, the division of labour

or the forms of thought governing the business of self-preservation. For this reason the progress of philosophy simultaneously recedes from the goals towards which it should be progressing. The power of the experiences that it registers is enfeebled, the more it is ground down by the machinery of science – or else these experiences are left floating like globules of fat in the watery soup of a scientistic philosophy. The movement of philosophy as a whole is that of the pure self-sameness of its principle. It is constantly achieved at the cost of what it is supposed to comprehend, and can comprehend, exclusively by virtue of the reflection upon itself which would force it to abandon the standpoint of pigheaded immediacy – or what Hegel termed the philosophy of reflection. Philosophical progress dupes us because the more tightly its arguments are interwoven, and the more compelling and unassailable its statements become, the more it turns into identity-thinking. It spins a web around its objects that leaves fewer and fewer gaps for everything that is not itself. In this way philosophical progress presumptuously forces itself on our attention at the expense of its object of inquiry. In the last analysis, in tune with the genuinely retrograde tendencies of society, it seems that the progress of philosophy is forced to pay the price for having not been much of a progress at all. To assume that the journey from Hegel to the logical positivists, who dismiss him as obscure or meaningless, has been progress is simply laughable. Not even philosophy is immune to such regression, whether into pig-headed scientism or the denial of reason, which is certainly not a whit superior to the much derided faith in progress.

Ladies and gentlemen, I may perhaps take this opportunity to say to you that what I have been telling you in the context of the philosophy of history – one which focuses on the so-called history of ideas – seems to me to lead quite clearly to what we might well think of as the *programme* for a philosophy today. According to this programme, philosophy might achieve through reflection on its own activity the consciousness that could lead it out of this web of delusion in a non-arbitrary manner. Instead, by using its own methods, philosophy would be enabled to understand the ways in which it is embroiled with forces that are in conflict with what it truly desires. In this sense, philosophy is literally in the same situation as Baron Münchhausen when he succeeded in pulling himself out of the mire by tugging at his own pigtail.[13] Well, there are very many philosophers who act in this way without reflecting much on it. They deal with the problem of actual existence by turning existence itself into an ontological category, and this enables them to sidestep the issue.[14] You will perhaps take it on trust that I don't see the matter quite so

simply. What is at stake is that, given that philosophy is faced with
the challenge of transcending itself, if I can put it in this somewhat
portentous way, this task should not simply be reflected on, but
should really be carried out rigorously through the medium of
thought. This is a task that really makes you rack your brains, and
I do not know whether it can be satisfactorily solved. But anything
less than that would really amount to no more than going through
the motions and seems to me to be quite meaningless – even though
such thinking may imagine itself to be fantastically metaphysical and
God knows what else besides.

Bourgeois society created the concept of progress, and the convergence of the concept with the negation of progress originates in
the principle governing society, namely the principle of exchange.
Exchange is the rational form of mythical eternal sameness. In the tit
for tat of every exchange, each act revokes the other; it's a zero-sum
game. If the exchange was fair, then nothing has happened, everything stays as it was, people are quits, things are just as they were
before. At the same time, the assertion of progress, which conflicts
with this principle, is true to the extent that the doctrine of tit for tat
is a lie. It always was a lie, and not just since the so-called capitalist
appropriation of surplus value in the course of which the commodity
of labour power is exchanged for the costs of its reproduction. For
one of the parties to the transaction, the more powerful party, always
received more than the other. Thanks to this injustice, one that had
been codified as early as Aesop's fable about the lion,[15] something
novel takes place in the course of the exchange; the process that
proclaims its own stasis becomes dynamic. We might say, then, that
progress originates in the fact that the justice that amounts to a repetition of sameness is unmasked as injustice and perpetual inequality.
The truth of the expansion feeds on the lie of the equality. Social
actions are supposed to cancel each other out in the overall system
and yet they do not. Where bourgeois society satisfies the concept it
cherishes of itself it knows no progress; where it knows progress it
sins against its own law in which this offence is already present, and
with this inequality it perpetuates the wrong that progress is supposed
to transcend. This wrong, however, is also the condition of possible
justice. The fulfilment of the contract of exchange, whose terms are
constantly being broken, would converge with its abolition; exchange
would disappear if the objects exchanged were truly equivalent.
Genuine progress is not simply quite different from exchange; it
would be exchange worthy of the name. Marx and Nietzsche were
agreed on this, despite being at opposite ends of the spectrum in other
respects. Zarathustra proclaims that man will be freed from revenge,

or, rather, he does not proclaim it, he preaches that man shall be freed from revenge.[16] For revenge is the mythical prototype of exchange; as long as domination persists through exchange, the myth will continue to prevail too. The intertwining of eternal sameness and the new in the exchange relation manifests itself in the imagos of progress in bourgeois industrialism. What seems paradoxical is that these imagos grow old and that anything new should ever make its appearance at all, given that technology ensures that the eternal sameness of the exchange principle is intensified to the point where repetition prevails throughout the sphere of production. The life process itself freezes into immobility in the expression of eternal sameness; hence the shock-effect of photographs from the nineteenth and the early twentieth centuries. They explode the absurdity that something happens when the phenomenon tells us that nothing more can happen; their ageing is shocking. In that shock the terror inspired by the system crystallizes into visible form; the more the system expands, the more it hardens into what it has always been. *Plus ça change, plus c'est la même chose*. What Benjamin called 'dialectics at a standstill' is probably less of a Platonizing residue than the attempt to raise such paradoxes to philosophical consciousness. Dialectical images are the historical and objective archetypes of that antagonistic unity of movement and immobility that defines the bourgeois concept of progress in its most general form.[17]

Both Hegel and Marx have argued that the dialectical view of progress stands in need of correction. The dynamic that they promulgated is conceived not as a dynamic *tout simple*, but as one in union with its opposite, with something fixed, which alone makes it possible to read a dynamic in the first place. Marx of course dismissed as fetishistic all ideas of the natural growth of society. As against Lassalle's Gotha Programme, he also refused to make an absolute of the dynamic in the doctrine of work as the sole source of social wealth. Furthermore, he conceded the possibility of a relapse into barbarism.[18] It may be more than pure coincidence that Hegel, too, notwithstanding his famous definition of history,[19] failed to elaborate a theory of progress, and that Marx himself, so far as I am aware, appears to have avoided the word, even in the constantly cited programmatic passages from the preface to the *Contribution to a Critique of Political Economy*.[20] The dialectical taboo on conceptual fetishes, the legacy of the Enlightenment's antipathy towards myth during its self-reflective phase, extends to the category that had previously softened up reification, namely 'progress' which turns out to be fraudulent as soon as it, a single aspect, usurps the whole. The fetishization of progress is identical with its particularity, with its restriction to technique, or, more generally, to techniques. If progress were in fact to become master of the whole, a concept which bears the marks of its own violence, it would cease to be totalitarian. It is no ultimate category. Its function is to thwart the triumph of radical evil, not to triumph itself. We can conceive of a situation in which 'progress' might lose its meaning, but which would not be the same as the universal regression that is allied with progress today. In that event progress would be transformed into a corrective to that precarious situation, the perennial risk of a relapse. Progress is this resistance to regression at every stage, not acquiescence in their steady ascent.

With these words I bring to a conclusion my remarks on the concept of progress. Perhaps I may add, for those of you who are interested in these matters, that the arguments that I have just put to you and that stem from a lecture I gave two years ago at the so-called Philosophy Congress in Münster – admittedly, somewhat more briefly and without the additional comments that I was able to offer you today – can now be found in the *Festschrift* for Joseph König that has recently appeared.[21] In the same context and with particular reference to the dialectic of the static and the dynamic, which I could only touch on here, I may perhaps also refer you to my article 'On Statics and Dynamics as Sociological Categories', in volume 2 of the *Sociologica*.[22] I regret that I have to refer to my own texts; you must take my word for it that I greatly disapprove of the academic habit of telling students about one's own writings in this way. But with increasing age, when one has committed to print a significant portion of the things one has thought, one cannot entirely dispense with such references, since what one has to say in a lecture is really no more than a drop in the ocean, which one then attempts to transform into an argument suitable for the printing press.

Ladies and gentlemen – if I may use this form of address, which was the way people used to talk in lectures 150 years ago. I am very well aware how old-fashioned it is and do not speak like this out of naïvety. I should like now to move on to a discussion of the doctrine of *freedom*. But here too a declaration of intention[23] is not enough. The least I can do is to give you some indication, or to remind you, of the main points that have led us from the discussions we have had up to now to the problems raised by the concept of freedom. I should like to begin by reminding you that in these lectures – almost without my having been fully aware of this when I set out – the concept that has turned out to be crucial for the theory of history, and incidentally also for the theory of progress, has been that of the *spell* [*der Bann*]. The concluding sentence of the *Dialectic of Enlightenment* states that all living things are, or seem to be, under a spell[24] – and both statements, i.e., that they *are* under a spell and that they *appear* to be under a spell, are probably equally valid. This idea is really an unspoken premise and it could be said that my efforts here, and my own philosophical work more generally, are concerned with what we, that is to say, Horkheimer and I, called a spell, and with our attempts to explore this concept of the spell in all its implications. The fact is that, once you have experienced such an insight – and let us assume for a moment that it is not quite without merit – it frequently turns out to contain far more possibilities than is evident at first sight, possibilities that reveal themselves only gradually, over time. You all know that it is extremely difficult to identify the positive defining features of a doctrine of freedom or of the concept of freedom. To convince yourselves of this I need only point out that today completely heterogeneous systems, incompatible political systems, lay claim to the concept of freedom for themselves in one way or the other. Even the National Socialists once held a party congress of freedom[25] – which of course was a sheer travesty of everything that might rationally be described as freedom, by which I mean the freedom of individual human beings. This Nazi claim to freedom did not sound as absurd then as it does today, particularly since at that time Hitler was celebrating his great triumphs in foreign affairs. What was meant then was more or less the freedom of all those who were held to be ethnic Germans according to the ideology of the day and who were supposed to join together freely in opposition to the heteronomy of socio-political systems imposed on Germany. If for a moment you make the mental experiment – and this does call for some strength of mind – of imagining that this ideology has been more or less well thought through, then the idea of such a party congress of freedom, by which I mean the freedom *of* the collective and not freedom *from* the collective, does not seem so utterly outlandish. You will also be clear in your minds about the glib way in which people talk of freedom in the Western world. You will likewise be well aware that the limits of individual freedom are very tightly drawn, particularly at points where you would like to test this freedom, simply to see just how free you really are. And finally, as far as Russia is concerned, or the entire Soviet realm, the situation there is just as it has been ever since the famous programmatic statements of the theoretician Manuilsky,[26] statements incidentally that were formulated while Stalinism still held sway. That is to say, the official theory is that of a humanist socialism which, in theory at least, was in favour of enabling the individual to develop so as to fulfil his full potential. This theory thus retained the idea of freedom that is implicit in such a development of the individual even though the practice of collectivism directly contradicts the development of individual human faculties. You can see from this example that every positive definition of freedom comes up against the very greatest difficulties because it has been appropriated by incompatible conceptions.

I wish to say that the section of my lectures that I am now beginning will have roughly the same form as the first part. By this I mean that I shall not treat the concept of freedom in its entire breadth and problematic nature. I shall not explore all the substantive political implications of the idea of freedom – tempting though this task would be. Instead, I intend to focus on one single, what shall I call it, antinomian point, a single contradictory point. What I have in mind is the question of free will, in other words, the inner freedom of the individual human subject, and this is because I believe that to focus on this particularly difficult problem will enable you to gain a much clearer overview than if I were to pursue the concept of freedom through all the channels of political history from John Locke on. However, I should like to make one point today, at the end of this lecture. If you agree with at least some of what I have told you about history as natural history, about history as spell, and if you are prepared to take seriously what I have also said about resistance, then this does provide a pointer to what might be meant by freedom. For if you agree with me on that point, then freedom is nothing but the quintessence of resistance to the spell that I have been trying to explain to you. I hope to be able to promise you that once I have worked my way into the dialectics of the intelligible character, and thus into the dialectics of free will, I shall return to the assertion that the positive meaning of freedom lies in the potential, in the possibility, of breaking the spell or escaping from it.

PART III
FREEDOM

LECTURE 19

26 January 1965

TRANSITION TO MORAL PHILOSOPHY

I shall continue with my summary of what we have gleaned about a theory of freedom, or, more simply, about the problem of freedom, from the discussions of the philosophy of history that we have undertaken up to now. I should like to begin by reminding you that we have defined freedom as escaping from the spell or working our way out of the spell. So, if you like, you can think of it more as a tendency than as a given of whatever kind. We might also say that there is no such thing as freedom as a positive determination; that there is no such thing as freedom in a succinct form. We can say only that freedom is something that has to be created or that creates itself. The difficulties raised by Kant's doctrine of freedom[1] are linked, as you know, to an antinomy from which it never really escapes. These difficulties arise from the fact that Kant perceived or suggested that, on the one hand, freedom is the only possible defining feature of humanity, but that, on the other hand, freedom cannot be treated as something present, as a fact. But if freedom remains merely in the realm of ideas, without any foreseeable or definable prospect of its being made real, it degenerates into something vague and insubstantial. And all the infinite labours that Kant expended on the concept of freedom arise in the final analysis from the fact that, put quite simply, this is a concept we cannot dispense with. That is to say, without this concept of freedom we cannot conceive of a situation in which human beings can live together, can live together in peace, even though, on the other hand, this very freedom is something that cannot be found in the realm of factual reality. Kant was extremely persistent in his efforts to purify freedom, as the foundation of ethics, from every empirical taint, and if we wanted, paradoxically, to uncover its empirical, factual roots, it would lead us to a void, a deficiency – namely, to the experience that freedom has never yet been made a reality in the entire realm of historical and natural experience so far as this is known to us. All the difficulties of Kant's doctrine of freedom are based on our need, on the one hand, to respect the non-existence of this freedom but, on the other hand, not to deny freedom, because the fact is that it is a concept we cannot dispense with. Lastly, we need to establish some sort of mediating link between this non-existence and the fact of our dependence on the concept. And we should take note that the problems raised by this need for a mediating link led Kant into antinomies and aporias that go far beyond those that are treated in the Third Antinomy of the *Critique of Pure Reason* and that incidentally supply the foundation of both the entire Kantian doctrine of freedom and his system of ethics. I should like to ask those of you who are not yet familiar with these matters to study closely the Third Antinomy of the Transcendental Dialectic of the *Critique of Pure Reason*, inclusive of the thesis and the antithesis, together with the notes and everything that goes with them. For the fact is that I cannot give you an account of all that here but have to assume in what I shall have to say that you are familiar with it.

A further consideration emerges from our observations in the realm of the philosophy of history – and with this we travel some considerable distance from Kant. This is that freedom is not to be understood as something purely individual. It is true enough that freedom or its absence from the personal experience of the individual, as we think of it today, appears predominantly as a characteristic of the individual, as an individual characteristic. But we need to be aware that the idea of freedom as something purely individual is itself an abstraction from the contexts in which we find ourselves as living, social individual beings; and in the absence of these contexts, freedom has no meaning at all. Freedom can only ever be defined in these contexts or, depending on circumstances, as freedom from them. We may also express it by saying that, without the freedom of the species, without the social species in general, there is no such thing as individual freedom. The concept of individual freedom remains imperfect and incomplete, as long as it remains particular, as long as and to the extent that it presupposes the unfreedom of other human beings – a definition, incidentally, that is very similar to those given repeatedly by Kant, although I have formulated it in ways that are somewhat removed from his actual words. Now, you may object that even in an unfree society there are individual free human beings. I shall leave open the question of what that freedom amounts to. When I was young, I was often very surprised to see what little use some of the very wealthy people I knew actually made of their wealth. That is to say, just how little they set out to acquire of all the things that one imagines as being available to the wealthy. And I soon realized that something very like class discipline is an integral part of individual freedom. What I mean by this is that, if very rich people use their money for purposes that do not fit in with specific, very restrictive notions of what is approved of by bourgeois society, they find themselves ostracized in a way that is quite at odds with their social position in other respects. Even when people seem to be largely independent of external circumstances, their freedom in fact exists to an unimaginable degree only on paper. This is even truer when you consider that in general people who are independent materially, and who of course form a relatively declining proportion of the population, are actually no more than a function of their own possessions, and that this in itself constitutes a significant barrier to their enjoyment of their freedom. I need only remind you of people like Rockefeller whose social character is so strongly determined by the Puritan work ethic that, even when they have billions, the only benefit they seem to derive from them is that when old beggars cross their path they give them a cent by way of a present. This gives us an idea of the restrictions on the freedom of even the freest in an unfree society. On the other hand, however, in an unfree society, even the exceptional freedom of individuals is essentially private in nature. By this I mean that this freedom consists essentially of acquisitions at the expense of others, in a specific kind of sovereignty in which the freedom of others is always offended against *a priori*, and which therefore contradicts the meaning of freedom from the outset. If we wanted to make a connection between the question of freedom and the sociological problem of the upper bourgeoisie, we might say that the so-called freedom and sovereignty of the upper bourgeoisie is always distorted by their attitude of 'I think I'll have that'. Members of the upper crust always have something of the attitude of people who say, 'Well, we are not nobodies, we don't have these little anxieties, we just take action'. It is this very attitude that turns these people into the agents of the social process in which they find themselves, and thus into the antithesis of their own freedom. On the other hand, it would be quite wrong – and I believe that I should add this in view of the very strange distortions that all these concepts are being subjected to in the East – on the other hand, then, we must add that we cannot speak of a freedom of the species or a freedom of society unless it means the freedom of individuals in that society. The

individual is to a certain extent the touchstone of freedom. If people
point to the freedom of the totality, of society as a whole, and if this
simply reinforces the unfreedom of individuals, then you can be sure
that even societal freedom, objective freedom, is in a bad way and
that genuine freedom has degenerated into ideology. And this (as I
have tried to show you) is what has actually happened almost
throughout the world (we might even say simply: throughout the
world) to the point where one finds it difficult to utter the word
'freedom' without a pang of shame. We shall have an opportunity to
explain why (and this is closely connected with what we have been
saying) the idea of freedom and the concept of freedom are beginning
increasingly to disappear from our intellectual horizons; and why,
furthermore, simply to speak of freedom makes us sound old-
fashioned or over-professorial. We shall have to give some account
of what can be done to oppose this tendency.

What also emerges from what we have said about freedom is that
it is a *historical* category par excellence. This means that we cannot
formulate and define the concept of freedom once and for all, as
philosophers have almost invariably done, so as to be able to confront
the changing events of history with this immutable concept. The
concept of freedom is itself the product of history and has altered
with history. I have referred you to the simplest illustration of this,
namely, that in totalitarian societies – I shall not even mention a
society built on slavery – the concept of freedom has appeared as the
privilege of a few people, but that this definition of freedom as a
freedom from inner and outer coercion has had such force that it has
never been possible to restrict it to a minority. What we might call
the socialization of the concept of freedom has made people realize
that they can significantly influence their own destinies by playing an
active part in public affairs. This would give us a completely different
view of the concept of freedom, that is, of political freedom, as it
concerns us most immediately. We may describe the structure of such
concepts by saying that they have a core meaning that remains constant, but that, at the same time, it constantly changes. It is a mistake,
a misconception, to extract this identical core from the variety of
changing meanings and to adjudge it to be universal and unalterable.
But it would be equally misguided if, like the historicists, one were
to attempt to dissolve this identical core into a process of endless
change. This is the problem of a philosophy of history of freedom –
and, for that matter, of all such profoundly historical concepts;
and the challenge facing such a philosophy of history must be to
preserve the identity, the permanent component, of such concepts
throughout the changes that they undergo, and not to contrast these

changes abstractly with something permanent. But by saying this, I really express nothing more than the principle that governs dialectical thinking in general. In the final analysis, we must say that we should not think of freedom as a merely abstract idea – which is what seems to be suggested by the statement that it does not yet exist. It is not a mere abstraction suspended somewhere above the heads of human beings who snatch at it without being able to jump high enough to reach it. Instead, we can only speak meaningfully of freedom because there are concrete possibilities of freedom, because freedom can be achieved in reality. And in contrast to the entire dialectical tradition of Hegel and Marx, I would almost go so far as to say that actually this has always been possible, that it has been possible at every moment.

I have hinted to you on a number of occasions now that the possibilities of freedom within a state of unfreedom are growing, that they are on the rise; and I do not want to go back on this. But I should like at least to plant a few doubts in your minds about the truth of it, particularly when we learn, if we study Marx or Hegel, that the Spartacus uprising in ancient Rome or the peasant movement in Germany [in 1525] or Babeuf's conspiracy under the Directory in France – that none of that would have worked because the historical conditions were not ripe. Whether historical conditions are ever ripe enough to let something happen is always judged after the fact, with hindsight. And it is very hard to say whether, given the extremely complex and often irrational structure of history, things might not have turned out differently for once, and mankind might have been able to raise itself out of the mire. I myself believe that I did once experience such a moment in my youth, when a change really seemed close. That is why I am not entirely convinced by that dialectical doctrine that I have dutifully passed on to you. I should like at least to add a question mark to the tradition from which I have come and which I have been teaching you – even though, needless to say, nothing has come of it up to now and it is always easier for the philosophy of history to take sides with the bigger battalions than to join the weaker ones. Of course, the question is highly speculative and it is in all likelihood not really possible for us to decide what might or might not have been possible. I should only wish to issue a general warning against automatically putting yourselves on the side of the victors, and joining in when people say what people always say when liberation movements are defeated, namely, that it happened because the conditions were not right. Hegel did indeed excoriate appeals to abstract possibility, as did Marx. But there is also such a thing as an abstract impossibility after the fact in which people try to persuade us on quite general grounds that a failure to achieve something proves that it would never have worked – and this inference simply won't do on its own. So the entire thing is really concerned more with the use of these categories than with our ability to make definite, positive judgements about whether something might or might not have been possible. Or at any rate, different. This means, then, that the concept of freedom cannot be salvaged as an imperishable internal quality of man in the manner attempted by the French existentialists, above all Jean-Paul Sartre. For that turns it not only into something quite vague, but even into an illusion, as seems to me to be the case in great measure in the case of Sartre himself.[2]

The concrete possibilities of making freedom a reality are to be sought – and I think this is a very important point – in the way in which we define the locus of freedom, namely, in the forces of production. By this I mean the state of human energies and the state of technology which represents an extension of human energies that have been multiplied through the growth of material production. The growth of freedom is not to be sought in the relations of production, which is the solution proffered by superficial minds. Thus when we say that freedom can be achieved today, here and now, or in a hundred years, this does not mean that everyone should be sent to better schools, or that everyone should have enough money with which to buy a fridge and to go to the cinema, something that can only increase their unfreedom rather than their freedom. The potential for freedom lies elsewhere; it consists in the fact that the state of the forces of production today would allow us in principle to free the world from want. In so far as unfreedom is *necessary*, that is to say, in so far as unfreedom can justify its existence by pointing to society as a whole, it can do so only by pointing to want. By this I mean that it is argued that without the pressure brought to bear on people they would not perform the work needed to produce the necessaries of life, or that without pressure they would not be willing and able to acquiesce in the want from which they are already suffering. In this context all the talk about a consumer society in which a greater equality is achieved and similar epiphenomena concerning mechanisms of distribution seem trivial compared to the fundamental changes that have taken place. What has really changed quite centrally is that technology has developed to the point where it would be possible to satisfy human needs so that there is no longer any need for privation. If want could be eradicated, repression and oppression would become superfluous. This would create a situation in which a degree of freedom might be established of which we could say as philosophers that it might not be a state of perfect freedom, but that such an imperfect freedom would be a whole lot better than a perfect and radical unfreedom. If want could be banished, all the instruments of oppression would come to appear superfluous, to the point where the machinery of oppression would be unable to survive in the long run.[3] This process would ultimately extend to the unfreedom of human beings, in other words, to their so-called adaptation to their social situation; that is to say, in the absence of want they would no longer need to conform.

On the other hand, however, the interests of those who profit from repression would be so threatened by such a development that the general effect must be to reduce the prospects of any real improvement in the concrete scope for freedom. And the proposition about the growth of unfreedom within freedom has as its underlying philosophical kernel the very insight that I have been trying to convey to you. This is that the closer the kingdom of freedom comes, and the greater the prospects of eliminating want and hence repression for good and all, the more radically those who are interested in the maintenance of repression will attempt to perpetuate it. This is doubtless directly connected with the factor that I have already mentioned to you, whereas the probable outcome would be that the eternal sameness of the historical process that I have attempted to explain with the aid of the concept of the spell would go into reverse at the point at which want was abolished – and I mean eradicated in all seriousness, not just on the surface, but for all mankind, universally and on a global scale. I believe that, after what I have said, you will be prepared to allow that I have not attempted to follow the philosophical custom of discussing freedom as the 'essence' of individual human beings, but that I regard it as something social. In accordance with what I have said, unfreedom must be viewed increasingly as the function of a superfluous form of domination whose attempts to maintain itself are therefore irrational. This leads me to something of a rehabilitation of an idea that I have subjected to severe criticism elsewhere in these lectures, namely, the idealist equation of reason and freedom. Freedom is quite certainly not immediately identical with reason; as a form of thought, reason is on its own, to begin with. For it to become freedom reason requires something further, something that I have elsewhere termed 'the additional factor' [*das Hinzutretende*], and I shall have more to say about it shortly.[4] On the other hand, however, the persistence of unfreedom today contains, in its intrinsic unreason, a reference, an appeal to reason, that in a certain sense vindicates the idea – the same idea as the idea conceived by idealism – as a created rationality. In a different sense, admittedly, from the vindication we find in Hegel, where the identity

of freedom and reason is purchased with the renunciation of real
individual freedom, so that he surrenders the very feature of freedom
that I have described to you as the quintessential one, namely, that
individual, actual human beings should themselves be free.

With this line of reasoning, ladies and gentlemen, I believe that I
have completed the transition from my reflections on questions of the
philosophy of history to those of moral philosophy, which I now
intend to begin and which will be devoted specifically to the concept
of freedom. Analogously with what I did in the first part of the course
in my discussion of the philosophy of history, my intention is not to
plough through the entire terrain of what is meant by the problem
of freedom, but here, too, I should like to choose a canon which will
enable us to focus on these matters – or, if not a canon, then a *model*.
Those of you who were present at Bloch's lecture[5] will have noticed
that, even though Bloch is strongly opposed to positivism, he nevertheless made use of the concept of a model that was in actual fact
developed by the positivists. I myself did likewise some time ago, for
example, in the *Interventions*.[6] Perhaps I may say a few words about
this concept of a model at this point by way of justifying the method
I propose to use. It is closely connected with my critique of system.
If you believe it is not possible to provide a system based on identity
philosophy, that is to say, a system in which existence is deduced
somehow or other from consciousness, then it is hard to resist the
attractions of the idea of a model. A model involves the analysis of
a specific, selective and, if you like, restricted complex of problems,
in such a way that light falls on all the aspects that cannot be treated
fully if one is reluctant, as I am, to elaborate a total, comprehensive
system. I must say – if you will forgive me for dwelling for a moment
on the objective forms of what I am attempting to think – that this
idea of the model has always been present to my mind in the sense
that I try to think my way deeply into specific phenomena in order
that light will fall from them onto the totality, not just on what I
happen to be discussing at any particular moment, but on things that
simply cannot be thematized by any philosophy that is so aware of
its own fragmentary nature. On the one hand, if what is at stake is
a type of thought that does not follow the procedures of identity
philosophy and that defines the concepts it employs only by virtue of
the *constellation* in which they obtain a specific value, then it follows
necessarily that dialectical thinking will not just apply to the phenomenon it scrutinizes but will also point beyond it. Just as the constellation always consists of individual phenomena, so too light can
fall on individual phenomena only from the constellation. Moreover,
I should like to add that the illuminating force of such models and

model concepts is all the greater, the more intensively you immerse yourselves in the details of individual phenomena. Those of you who attend the sociology seminar[7] that takes place immediately after these lectures will perhaps have already noticed, if you don't mind my commenting on it, that, of the individual seminar papers on specific social situations that we have studied, it is always those with the greatest amount of precise detail that have proved to be the most productive for our understanding of society; in other words, it is they that have gone furthest in transcending pure singularity. This suggests that there is a kind of reciprocal interaction between the constellations, on the one hand, and events on the micrological plane, on the other. If you look behind the scenes of what I am telling you here, it will perhaps be helpful to you to realize that it is this interaction between constellation and model that I am concerned with.[8]

You will now be eager to hear what model I intend to use as a focal point for our discussions of freedom. The model is that of *free will*. By this I mean in the first instance the problem of free will in its straightforward, pre-scientific sense. That is to say, it asks whether human beings are free to make their own decisions and, more particularly, whether they are internally or externally free or whether they are determined. Initially, at least, we can ignore external determination because the traditional view[9] ever since Locke has been that the internal ability or freedom of decision is supposed to be independent of external pressure. One of the tasks that will fall to me in these lectures will be to provide a critique – an immanent critique – of whether the monadological construction of the free will – and every theory of free will or unfree will begins life as monadological theory, as a theory of subjectivity – whether such a theory is tenable or not. This separation of inner and outer, as you will already suspect, cannot be sustained, but I shall be obliged here too to present you with the concrete mediations so as to explain why such a separation is not possible. However, I should like to say right away that there is something schematic about the distinction, since empirical science has long since shown that external pressures are continued internally. The theme that this therefore poses as a central theme of any doctrine of freedom is that of interiorization. And I should like to alert you to the fact that, in the discussions that you will have to put up with, the concept of interiorization will not simply shine forth bathed in the golden sunset which normally surrounds it in these parts. I would not wish to deny the enormous importance of interiority, without which the notion of freedom could not have been conceived. Its value can only be grasped in an age and a situation in which it is disappearing along with a whole series of other things of equal importance for the individual and society. In his book *The Lonely Crowd*, the American sociologist David Riesman[10] described the other-directed character who has succeeded the inner-directed personality type in the age of advanced industrialism. Whereas the latter becomes capable of autonomous action on the basis of behaviour patterns internalized in childhood, the other-directed personality type is influenced exclusively by his competitors and the mass media. Even earlier than this, in the *Dialectic of Enlightenment*, Horkheimer and I explained the dialectic at work in the interiorization of repression and its impact on the bourgeois character.[11] Needless to say, it is important to be aware that the concept of interiorization contains a social dimension, and that if you define interiorization as an absolute in contrast to that social dimension, and use it as the basis of an idea of pure human beings as such, you will then have embarked on an irretrievable decline into ideology.

LECTURE 20

28 January 1965

WHAT IS FREE WILL?

Adorno's notes for this lecture:

The separation of outer and inner is generally naïve, pre-critical. Even though the distinction should be retained, since it presents itself in primary experience (i.e., to the actually alienated), it should not be made absolute.

The internal to be radicalized as external: actual human beings together with their interiorization themselves belong, as actually existing, to the external world to which they know themselves to be contrasted and counterpoised. Inner and outer, too, are dialectical categories. The outer conversely mediated by the inner, never *knowable* as existing purely in itself.

The critical, scientific solution must be: the will has to be a constitutum, the unity of characteristics, whether of promptings, impulses or decisions guided by reason (even though these decisions are *determined* by it).

Thus we should not hypostasize the will, and the same holds good for the freedom that depends on its existence. Its position is exactly the same as the Kantian thing-in-itself, as he himself says.[1]

The question of freedom is a pseudo-problem [*Scheinproblem*] because [to pose it] turns it[2] into an independent problem as opposed to the phenomena it includes.

This objection lacks rigour because it simply pushes the problem back from the superior concept to the things of which it is composed. That aside, difficulties in the concept of the *regulative nature* of phenomena of the will.

a) Are there in fact irreducible impulses[?] (NB nothing is achieved with the *abstract* assertion of reducibility, it is purely regulative; what is needed is to carry through the business of *making determinations*, not simply to give assurances – so that these determinations could be seen to be *constitutive*.)

b) Can reason *interrupt* causal sequences? (Evidently, *yes*, but with the problem of the constitution of a second causal series of determinants.)

(1)[3] On pseudo-problems in general.

Changing function of the term; at one time enlightened. 'Scholasticism', angel's ladder.[4] Nowadays, to prevent discussion of what is of interest, a form of prohibition on thinking.

Concepts that are not clearly defined, 'semantic taboo'.

Question of 'freedom' of the 'will' as relevant as it is difficult to state clearly what the two terms mean.

Hence what a pseudo-problem means marks the *beginning* of reflection, not its end.

Relevance obvious: justice + punishment; the possibility of morality or ethics. This real interest not to be fobbed off with dismissive remarks about 'pseudo-problems'.

(2) However, philosophy may not simply bypass semantic criticism. Its theory must include

a) the impossibility of pinning down 'freedom' and 'will'

b) the necessity of discussing them after all.

Kant satisfied this requirement in a sense (give a brief account) but without fully resolving the conflict; it survives unanalysed. 28 January 1965.

[Extract from 'Determinism: Paraphrases of Kant':] The talk about pseudo-problems was once inspired by the Enlightenment. This wished to prevent the flow of ideas from the unquestioned authority of dogmas whose truth could not be adjudicated by the very philosophies to which it had been submitted. The pejorative overtones of this can still be discerned in the term 'scholasticism'. In the meantime, pseudo-problems have ceased to be questions that defy rational judgement and rational interests. Nowadays, they are questions that make use of concepts that have not been clearly defined. A semantic taboo has become prevalent that stifles questions of substance by converting them into questions of meaning. A pre-emptive prior consideration expands into an embargo on the discussion of certain questions. What may or may not be reflected upon, however crucial it may be, is governed by rules modelled on the current methods in the exact sciences. Established procedures, the means, are given priority over the substance, the goals of cognition for which they are supposed to exist. Disturbing experiences that impinge upon people prior to their articulation in language, and that sometimes baulk at being confined in unequivocal signs, are reprimanded, as if the difficulties encountered in expressing them were the fault purely of a lax, pre-scientific linguistic usage. The relevance of the question of whether there is free will is as great as the technical difficulty of stating clearly just what is meant by it. Since justice and punishment depend on this question – to say nothing of what the entire philosophical tradition has understood by morality and ethics – common sense refuses to accept that we are faced here by pseudo-problems. A self-righteous defence of tidy thinking responds by offering us stones instead of bread. Nevertheless, semantic criticism cannot simply be casually dismissed. The fact that a question is urgent does not mean we can compel an answer if no true answer is available; even less can a fallible need, however desperate, show us where to look for one. It would scarcely be possible to state simply, in terms that are *claire et distincte*, just what will is and what freedom, and the same common sense that insists on these categories would be the first to argue that, if we could discover no existing 'will' and no existing 'freedom', it would be a waste of time to consider whether the will is or is not free. We should not be concerned to reflect upon objects by judging their existence or non-existence, but by expanding their definition so as to allow both for the impossibility of nailing them down and also for the necessity of continuing to think them through. This is what is attempted under the conditions of Kant's transcendental idealism in the antinomy chapter of the *Critique of Pure Reason* and throughout extensive passages of the *Critique of Practical Reason*, although Kant does not entirely succeed in avoiding the dogmatic usage that he, like Hume, exposed in other traditional concepts. He settled the conflict between the world of phenomena – nature – and the intelligible world by having recourse to an all too Solomonesque dichotomy. But even if freedom or the will cannot be said to be entities, then – by analogy with simple pre-dialectical epistemology – this does not prevent specific impulses or experiences from being synthesized by concepts. There may be no underlying thing-like reality to correspond to these concepts, but they can nevertheless unify those impulses or experiences much as the Kantian 'object' can synthesize its phenomena.

LECTURE 21

2 February 1965

FREEDOM AND BOURGEOIS SOCIETY

I should like to begin by repeating some of the conclusions we had reached last time – following my principle that definitions are not simply to be dismissed out of hand as false, but, where they are used, they should follow from philosophical reflection, rather than preceding it with a view to keeping it under control. I told you that *will*, at least in traditional epistemology – what it is in reality is the problem we are battling with – was analogous to the Kantian 'object', the ordered unity of all impulses that are found to be both spontaneous and rationally determined. Please accept the definition for the moment, or for the present hour, with the same spontaneity as I have shown in employing it here. It contains – as I hope to show you in detail – problems that have a profound connection with the question of the will; but that is not something I wish to anticipate here. Freedom would be the word to describe the possibility of such impulses: the fact that such impulses are possible.

I also explained to you that this solution of relying on clear and distinct ideas is unsatisfactory because it assumes that there is a valid distinction based on form: either there is a will or there is not; either the will is free or it is not free. The fact is that we are inclined to adopt such procedures because we have been impregnated with logic, because we have been trained to equate philosophical thinking with logical thinking. Whereas, to take up a claim of Nietzsche's,[1] nothing real ever submitted to the laws of logic, since these laws are thought patterns that have been conceived in line with the needs of reason to dominate nature. If philosophy has a task, it is one you may well

think highly paradoxical, namely, to make use of the methods of
reason, among which we must include logic, to define those elements
in the object and to reflect on those elements that for their part do
not abide by the laws of logic, or submit to logic. And if you do
accept this for a single second, you must free yourselves – I believe I
have not yet stated this so clearly and so would like to repeat it so
that you do not become confused by what I shall go on to say. You
must free yourselves from the idea that such questions as: either the
will is free or else there is no such thing, or: either the will is free or
it is not free, must be capable of such simple, succinct answers as
their form seems to suggest. But the fact is that we simply do not
know whether such solutions, such succinct solutions, actually exist.
Let us for a moment set aside the fact that the Kantian doctrine of
the categories is essentially to do with the theory of reason, that is
to say, with the use of reason and the problems that such usage
throws up. Setting this aside, I should like to say that the antinomian
representation of the problems of freedom in Kant emphasizes the
objective aspect of freedom and that it has the extraordinary merit
that it too points to the fact that a succinct, unambiguous solution
cannot simply be assumed, but that we are faced with the possibility
of contradictory solutions – no more than a possibility, one that
should probably not be made to depend upon the transcendental use
of reason so much as upon the nature of the object. Inner perception
– and this is something I should like to say by way of criticizing the
idea of the will, as a kind of internal thing, by analogy to external
objects – inner perception, self-consciousness, the consciousness that
we have of ourselves, whether immediately or through a process of
reflection, does not encounter the will in the same way that our
external perception encounters objects that occur in various shades,
but that remain identical throughout these shadings.[2] But the assumption of such a will is very much an intellectual construct; this means
that, even on the assumptions of an idealist epistemological critique,
we cannot ascribe to it the kind of substantiality that we are inclined
to attribute to the objects of external reality. And if, earlier on, I discussed with you the possibility of pseudo-problems,[3] that possibility
refers precisely to the fact that the will is not a datum for us in the
sense that objects are givens in the external world; it is not something
that retains its identity and is perceived by us in a variety of shades
or nuances – so that we may feel fully justified in doubting whether
we can make such a distinction at all.

The reality underlying this alternative, the thing that is meant by
it, has something peculiarly intangible about it, something that eludes
our grasp, that we cannot pin down. And then again, it is something

to which we are constantly referred in the same realm of experience
in which we speak of human character, of people with a strong or
weak ego, or of a person's temperament, which may be sanguine or
melancholic or phlegmatic. All these things are qualities that have
made an extraordinarily powerful impression on the collective mind
without its having been proved possible to discover scientific rules
with which to identify objective correlatives for these things. That
means, however, that the real problem is that this definition of the
will, this concept of the will, is mediated by the very thing from which
it has been strictly distinguished by the original question. This remains
the case even if you agree that there is such an ordered synthesis of
spontaneous and rational impulses as I have postulated in this definition of the will. For the will or the substrate of freedom, or, if you
prefer, of unfreedom, is defined in the first instance by the monadological structure of individual human subjects; in other words, by
the fact that human beings find themselves confronting the non-
mental world (as it used to be called) which manifests itself as a
coherent and other totality, and they do so by means of their consciousness in the broadest sense, which here includes their emotions
and impulses. In disagreement with this – and I believe I have drawn
your attention to this several times – this supposedly monadological
being is intertwined with the very thing from which it is separated,
with both the sphere of experience coming from outside and the
impulses that arise within the individual and impinge on the external
world. Furthermore, the will itself and the ways in which it separates
itself – and this is the dialectical salt that adds spice to these observations – are likewise modelled on the external world and the relation
to the external world. Consider what I understand by the will and
equate it for a moment with a strong, single-minded ego, an ego that
does not let itself be distracted by momentary impulses or drift to
and fro, but firmly holds its course. We may undoubtedly agree with
common usage in claiming that there is an immediately obvious connection between a strong will and a strong ego. If that is the case,
we must conclude that this ego-authority has itself developed genetically as a means, an instrument, through which the biological human
being, the empirical, biological human being, tests himself against
reality and learns how to assert himself in the face of the external
world, the overpowering external world that assails us human beings,
and to survive. And if we assume that this identity, this hardness, this
opaqueness and impenetrability of this ego-authority is modelled on
something external, we may reasonably conclude, without wasting
too much time on idle speculations, that the hardness that characterizes the will viewed as a strong ego has been derived from the hard-

ness and impenetrability of things over which we have no control. As a primitive initial approximation, we might say that this quality of impenetrability is the stratum at which we become conscious of an otherness that is not subject to us, that is something that we are not. We might almost say that the monadological principle is itself the product of a quite primitive, primary experience of things that stand opposed to our own subjectivity. This means that subject would be object in the very precise sense that the solidity and persistence of the subject is a mimesis of the very things that are not intrinsic to the subject. Precisely because they elude us, these things acquire the hardness and solidity that we, as firm characters, and perhaps even as the embodiments of will power, set out to master. You can see from this that, by relating the concept of will to an isolated subjectivity that exists for itself, we end up positing in this separation, this separation of inner and outer, this relation of will to subjectivity, a relation to external reality as well. Not only that, our very model of the human subject turns out to be the non-self; we have the non-self as the model of the self. So that, if I believe that we may speak of a certain primacy of the object in the foundations (or whatever you would like to call it) of epistemology,[4] it is probably this curiously objective dimension of the self that we come across – although I have no wish to conceal from you the fact that all reflections of this kind conceal a cloven hoof. This is that, for such an objectification of the subject to occur, for the sphere of the subject to be assimilated to the sphere of the object in this way, means that something like a sphere of subjective reflection, of subjectivity, must exist. For if there were no such thing as a subject, there could be nothing capable of the self-objectification that I have attempted to show you in the concept of the will. In addition – and this is something I should like to pursue a little – I would draw your attention to the fact that the concept of the will did not make its appearance until relatively late as a philosophical concept in a precise sense, that is to say, in the form of the choice between the freedom or non-freedom of the will. Furthermore, when it did appear, it did so in close connection with the realm of intersubjectivity, in other words, with the involvement of human subjects with one another, and hence with the social sphere.

In more modern philosophy the problem of freedom and determinism did not become a topic of discussion until the seventeenth century, principally in the thought of Spinoza and then, explicitly in the context of the problem of determinism, in John Locke. There can be no doubt that the question of freedom, including inner freedom, the freedom of human beings, arose in connection with the emancipation of the bourgeoisie. The bourgeoisie, in contrast to the feudal class, postulated freedom in a highly external, objective sense. It meant freedom from the restrictions and dependencies that the feudal system had imposed on the bourgeois order, the bourgeois class. In raising the question of freedom, the youthful, increasingly self-confident bourgeois class felt it essential to ground freedom in the nature of man. From there it is but a step to inquire whether human beings are essentially free or not free. This rational justification of man proceeds from man's actual liberation, but attempts to ground this actual liberation in his own nature, that is to say, in man's nature as subject. It is an attempt that addresses itself to philosophy at a very early stage – remarkably enough, we should note – rather than to the empirical sciences or psychology. We shall have to ask ourselves how this remarkable situation came about. For at first blush it would seem more sensible to say that the question of whether human beings are free or not is one that should be resolved by the empirical science of man, in other words, psychology. But that is not what happened, and this was not simply because, as you all know, psychology was not so highly developed as the natural sciences during the early bourgeois period, by which I mean the seventeenth and eighteenth centuries. The fact is that, as early as Kant, the justification of freedom was not only seen as the province of philosophy, but it was explicitly set up in opposition to psychology. Take a look at the Kantian doctrine of the antinomies – and particularly the Third Antinomy, where, as I have pointed out ad nauseam, the question of freedom or determinism is of central importance – and think about it for a moment in the context of 'The Contest of Faculties', the question of the competence of the different sciences. If you do this, you will see that this Third Antinomy amounts to something like an antinomy between speculative philosophy on the left side of the page, on the side of freedom, and science as represented by psychology, which stands on the other side of the page.[5] And it is evident that Kant's own sympathies lean heavily towards the side of philosophy. In *The Critique of Practical Reason*, freedom is no mere theoretical concept, but one that is related to practice. Here, where freedom plays a decisive, positive role, Kant's writing is full of invective against psychology. We can even say that the entire anti-psychological tradition in speculative philosophy goes back to Kant himself. Hegel too may be said to have had his part in it, and it flared up again some seventy to eighty years ago in Husserl's campaign against so-called psychologism; the tradition experienced its nadir in the abuse hurled at psychology by Karl Jaspers.[6] We may say that this prejudice against psychology is not just a prejudice but an attitude that is connected with very serious questions. Only, in Kant's case (if I may add a few words about that),

he begins by defining the sphere of freedom as one radically opposed
to that of psychology, and reserves freedom entirely for the definition
of reason. This means that he ends up abandoning psychology to the
realm of the empirical and to determinism. Kant would have vigorously objected to the intervention of psychology in what he termed
the speculative business of philosophy. But since he thought of psychology as an empirical discipline, he would have granted it a place
in the cosmos of the sciences that recent obscurantists seek to deny
it. This is connected with the transformation in the attitude of
the bourgeoisie towards all enlightenment during the last 150 or
200 years.

But I had drawn your attention to the striking and even anomalous
question of how it came about that the doctrine of freedom had fallen
victim from the very outset, and had even – and it makes me a little
sad to have to say it – become the preserve of philosophy. I believe
that the answer is that from the very outset the interests of the bourgeois class were never so unambiguously served by the concept of
freedom as reflection on it suggested and, above all, as they appeared
to be following its decisive ideological manifestations in the struggle
against feudalism and then absolutism. For in its efforts to subdue
nature the bourgeois class needs the progressive process of rationalization as an instrument. Disenchantment (as Max Weber called it),[7]
making the world scientific, the increasing encroachments of science
on the world, a process that subjects the phenomena of the world
incrementally to the laws of science – all that is a mortal threat to
freedom. On the other hand, as I attempted to explain to you at the
start of this lecture, the bourgeois class has a no less vital interest in
maintaining the concept of freedom. This account smacks somewhat
of the history of ideas. If we go over to a more realistic description,
we might say that from the very outset bourgeois society was an
individualistic society that had established formal freedom, but had
not envisaged one free from coercion of every kind. Thus bourgeois
society always possessed this dual proclivity: on the one hand, it
postulated freedom, and in this respect it tended to look back, historically; and on the other hand, it tended to restrict freedom, especially
any demands that threatened to go beyond the bourgeois order. These
demands, which went hand in hand with a radicalization of the
concept of freedom, cut the ground from underneath the bourgeois
categories of exchange, free competition and whatever else formed
part of bourgeois ideology. In other words, the bourgeois attitude
towards freedom was antinomian through and through. And you
may, if you wish (and this too is a possible reading of Kant's Third
Antinomy), deconstruct it socially, by arguing that the contradiction

that Kant has formulated with such admirable frankness contains the dual interest of the society that is objectively defined by it in this way without any ideological slant or malign intent. This contradiction became philosophy in the shape of the Third Antinomy. This means that the Thesis represented the interest of the emancipated bourgeois class in freedom, while the Antithesis incorporates what has recently been expressed accurately, repeatedly and in various places all over the world as the fear of freedom.[8] And in general – I do not know whether I have already drawn the relevant passage to your attention – the Proof of the Antithesis of the Third Antinomy explicitly formulates the argument that would later become so popular. This is that, if we were to release nature from all rules by postulating an absolute beginning, we would escape not just from coercion, but 'from the guidance of all rules', and indeed there would no longer be any order at all.[9] For profound reasons, for reasons connected with the structure of society, the general bourgeois consciousness has always been vacillating and ambivalent in the sense that it fears the limiting of freedom and the constraints placed upon it, while at the same time it takes fright at its own courage and fears that a freedom made real might lead to chaos.

This may enable you to understand a phenomenon that lies very much at the heart of the history of the doctrine of freedom and that will show you just how dialectical the entire complex of freedom really is. We might well begin by thinking, the ordinary man in the street might well imagine, that the interests desirous of freedom, including social freedom, social liberation, that these interests might well hasten to endorse theorems concerned with human freedom. Whereas, conversely, we might assume that those who wish to keep human beings in a state of dependency would define human beings as dependent, necessarily unfree creatures, making use of categories drawn from nature. This was in fact common practice in the very early stages of bourgeois philosophy, in Hobbes, where the vindication of absolute monarchy went hand in hand with the definition of man as a purely natural creature.[10] This rather primitive explanation may well have appeared plausible, but the fact is that, in the history of ideas and the internal logic of such concepts as freedom and unfreedom, history does not always choose the most plausible route that you might expect. I believe that you can well understand why the bourgeois thinkers of the Enlightenment set such curious limits to the idea of freedom. These limits can be seen in the way that freedom was turned into the monopoly of philosophy, and this brings me, so I should like to believe, very much to the heart of the substantive problems of freedom (even though I am speaking in historical terms). For it turns out that the more theory urges the need for freedom, and the more theory insists that human beings are essentially free, that their will is absolutely free and that they have absolute responsibility for themselves, then the more readily theory lends itself to repression. You can easily explain this to yourselves if you consider the theory of criminal law, which provides us with something of a key to all serious thinking about the subject of freedom. In the theory of criminal law, it is the idealistic, Kantian thinkers, the ones who insist upon the freedom of man, free will, autonomy, self-determination, who infer from all this the unconditional responsibility of individual human subjects. It is they who, if I may put it in these terms, tend to reject all talk of mitigating circumstances and always seem to be on the point of ensuring that the (oh so free!) human subjects are made to feel the full weight of the law at every opportunity: precisely because they are free. You can see from this that ideas that originally had a utopian complexion and a critical complexion tend, notwithstanding their truth content, to degenerate in the course of history into ideologies. We can say that the doctrine of freedom really has degenerated gradually into mere declamations kept for high days and holidays. There is an infallible sign for this ideological distortion of the idea of freedom, one that will enable you to recognize it wherever and whenever talk about freedom lends itself to the justification for restrictions on freedom, in other words, where talk about freedom is perverted into the exact opposite of what it is supposed to achieve. What I have in mind are all the propositions that assert that freedom originally consisted in nothing other than voluntarily accepting a compulsion that human beings cannot escape anyway. Wherever it is maintained that the substance of freedom is that you are free when you freely accept what you have to accept anyway, you can be certain that the concept of freedom is being abused and is being twisted into its opposite.

So if we may take up another phrase of Kant's and speak of the *interest of reason* in this conflict,[11] we may say that this interest is by no means simply man's insistence on his inner freedom as the foundation on which to build his outer freedom. In certain circumstances, man's interest may be the very opposite, namely, whatever preserves him from adopting the cause of unfreedom and making it his very own – all in the name of freedom. This is the situation we have again arrived at in our own day. I have only recently read a product of the ideology of the Eastern zone [of Germany],[12] in which it is said almost literally with the same words – of course, in the name of dialectical materialism, but with the same end effect – that the freedom that is allegedly to be introduced there consists in people doing of their own

free will what they have to do anyway as part of the great movement
of history. Of course, this is an old story [olle Kamellen]. I mean, the
fact is that the theoretical ideology of the Eastern bloc closely resembles the traditional values of the petty bourgeoisie; these values are
duly conserved and then put in an appearance from time to time – just
as in the realm of art, as you are all well aware. Freedom, then, the
concept of freedom, has changed its function. The protestation of
freedom now enters into the service of repression, of actual unfreedom. This means that extreme vigilance is called for, particularly if
you are of the opinion that talk of freedom and unfreedom is not a
purely contemplative matter, but real, or, to invoke Kant once more,
in accordance with the idea, that is to say, in accordance with the
idea that freedom *should* exist. This is because an attitude to freedom
and unfreedom in the abstract tells us nothing about what a theory
or a political system has to say about making freedom a reality. In
general, the fact that human beings are *inwardly* free reinforces the
sanctions of the state. On the other hand, we can also say that the
determinism of the individual sciences has shown itself to be unequal
to the problem of freedom. I should say right away that on this point
psychoanalysis has adopted a highly curious ambivalence – curious
because it has perhaps gone furthest beyond mere assertion, the
abstract assertion of determinism, and has attempted to elaborate it
in concrete terms. For, on the one hand, it criticized the authority of
moral autonomy, the super-ego, or, to put it in ordinary language,
the conscience, as, in origin, a mental equivalent of unfreedom, and
in its heroic phase psychoanalysis even called for the dissolution of
the super-ego, in a noteworthy essay by Ferenczi.[13] But at the same
time, psychoanalysis was terribly afraid of what might happen if
people no longer had a super-ego. So psychoanalysis went on to say
that we must draw a distinction between a conscious super-ego and
an unconscious one. However, in the light of Freud's analysis of the
super-ego, this is a manifest absurdity, since the super-ego only has
any power because it is unconscious. An alternative that I once came
across in America was to distinguish between a healthy super-ego and
an unhealthy one – which is much like efforts to distinguish between
healthy patriotic feeling and a morbid nationalism. We all know what
distinctions of this sort amount to. The consequence of all these
things, and this may help you to understand why I am making such
heavy weather of this question of freedom of the will, is that this
problem has been betrayed ideologically by philosophy, while the
sciences, the individual disciplines, even the most progressive ones,
have failed to do it justice. It may also help to explain why this
problem, why this entire approach has ended up in a completely

wishy-washy world-view. If, for example, you take a look at current debates on criminal law, debates about the foundations of criminal law, you will find either appeals to a philosophy that is not equal to the task; or else, the participants in the debate arrive at their conclusions on the basis of their own world-view or, to use the term that people favour nowadays, according to the commitments or lack of commitments they happen to have at the moment. Thus what ought to be the most necessary and objective decisions of all, given their extreme seriousness, are made to depend on the most adventitious circumstances, namely, the ticket that just happens to have been chosen by a man who does not just have a working life, but who also keeps his brain active even when work is over. And this leads me to my conclusion, which I hope will give you something of an idea that philosophy does have a contemporary relevance and is not merely the twaddle to which it threatens to degenerate today. This conclusion is that a serious dialectical analysis of freedom is needed, because it is only through a process of philosophical reflection that would include all these elements that the question of freedom can be rescued from the vague waffle that in the long run can have only one consequence. This is that decisions about the legal or constitutional implications of freedom will hide behind these vague ideological commitments and will then be arrived at not through the exercise of autonomous reason, but simply in accordance with the power relations on which so-called world-views lean for support.

LECTURE 22

4 *February 1965*

FREEDOM IN UNFREEDOM

I attempted the day before yesterday to convey to you something of the complexity of the debate about freedom and determinism within society as it exists at present and to explain to you that the paradoxes of the situation have become so entangled that the very people who insist on freedom as a given of human nature generally interpret freedom as responsibility and place it in the service of repression – and the converse is equally valid. I went on to explain why the debate about freedom threatens to degenerate into ideological caprice at the very point at which it acquires genuine relevance, namely, on the crucial issue of the foundations of criminal law. Perhaps I may be allowed to amplify this a little. You may be in some doubt about whether the debate about criminal law really has the relevance I have attributed to it – simply on the grounds that it raises only a few issues and these could be said to be rather marginal. But my belief is that to think in this way is to think altogether too abstractly. This is because these marginal cases, precisely because they raise questions of ascription or responsibility, really do provide something in the nature of a touchstone because, as in all highly individuated situations, the relationship between individual and society appears in an especially sharp focus. For that relationship can best be seen where matters become critical, where it 'hurts', rather than in less aggravated circumstances or in the countless situations where things still seem more or less to function. One feature of this peculiar decline in the debates about freedom – which have actually degenerated from the heights of philosophy to the level of a *Weltanschauung* in the course of a process that would really repay close examination – is that the concept of freedom itself, as well as countless other concepts from the early phase of bourgeois emancipation, has an old-fashioned ring to it, something both venerable and archaic; and that, if the truth were told, people are no longer able to imagine anything specific by the idea of an appeal to freedom. I can remember very precisely at around the time when the fascist threat was becoming acute that a social-democratic organization (or just a plain democratic organization) chose 'Freedom' as a slogan – at first they said 'Free Salvation' [*Freiheil*], but decided that was just too silly and opted for 'Freedom' [*Freiheit*]. But even 'Freedom' was laughed out of court by the Nazis. And the slogan attracted this ridicule not just for the obvious political reasons, but because the term freedom no longer possesses the power it used to have, for a whole host of reasons. Chief among them was the fact of the great slump and the universal unemployment, which made a call for free-dom, which implies self-determination, including economic self-determination, seem like an unintended irony, much in the vein of the famous statement of the local Frankfurt poet Friedrich Stoltze, 'Come to eat if you can and if the door isn't locked.'[1] In other words, freedom was exposed as the freedom to starve; people had direct experience of their dependence on society, a dependence that made a mockery of a freedom that was defined in purely formal terms. Nowadays, such experiences are no longer typical, but they survive in people's minds as possibilities and could be said to have seeped into such concepts as that of freedom. I believe, then, that if we are to update the concept, the biggest mistake we could possibly make would be to issue appeals to freedom, to popularize the idea of freedom as a slogan or to appeal to people's autonomy. The better approach would be to take the question of what has become of freedom and what threatens to become of it in the future and to treat such questions as the precondition of any serious reflection on freedom – whereas every other attitude, such as taking freedom as a given, is to reduce it to the level of a cliché. This is not the least of the reasons why I believe that the limitations on freedom and the problem of freedom should be taken so extremely seriously as I have done in these lectures up to now. And I hope that you will all understand my intentions in this regard. People who desire freedom may not appeal to it or presume it in advance, but must above all give an account of the *problem* of freedom – whereas appeals to freedom, simply because they are appeals that involve an emotive dimension, contain the very aspect of heteronomy and dependency that contradicts the meaning of the word.

The entire problem of freedom as it confronts us today contains a possible paralogism. A paralogism is essentially a fallacy, though the fallacy I should like to talk about now has no direct connection with the so-called psychological paralogisms you find in Kant.[2] Dealing with the situation that most of us associate with the concept of freedom – and every such concept forms part of a constellation – always means dealing with a series of other categories with which it is intertwined; it is this that is implied in talk about concreteness. The context that has become indelibly linked with freedom is the threat of the absolute negation of freedom, which is what is evoked by the memory of the concentration camps. We might say, therefore, that there must be freedom so as to ensure that Auschwitz never happens again, simply because Auschwitz must not be allowed to happen again. I am the last person to resist the force of attempts to discover a rational formula in this argument. But if this idea really contains a fallacy that must mean that it misses its mark and would therefore fail to achieve the very thing it sets out to achieve, namely, the prevention of a repetition of Auschwitz. I would reply to this in the first instance by saying that, if Auschwitz could happen in the first place, this was probably because no real freedom existed, no freedom could be regarded as an existing reality. In other words, the misdeeds of Auschwitz were only possible, firstly, in a political system in which freedom was completely suppressed and, secondly, in a general social context that permits all that to happen, and, finally and more particularly, because the people who committed, and were able to bring themselves to commit, these atrocities were essentially unfree, and truly were the servants [*Knechte*] who claimed they were just carrying out orders. Unlike Heidegger, I am not in the business of language mysticism and have no desire to explore the roots of words. However, I believe that you can learn an awful lot from taking a closer look at the actual meanings of words and the ways in which language is used. The fact is that language speaks of 'torturers' and, more specifically, the original German term *Folterknecht* really referred to executioners' assistants. Thus language has reserved the use of 'servants'[3] [*Knechte*] for torturers, of all people, long after society had ceased to have servants, and this shows clearly enough that we really are concerned here with the actions of unfree men. This feature surely does make its appearance in Kant's antinomian treatment of the problem of freedom. For the fact that his argument calls for an infinite regress in order to arrive at an absolutely free ultimate cause underlying the chain of cause and effect implies that freedom is something that has not yet come into being. It means that freedom is to be treated as a possibility that has still to be *implemented*. No one has set about this task with as much energy as Kant himself in his resistance to the contamination of freedom with existing reality, that is to say, to the idea that freedom should be regarded as an immediate defining factor of reality. If you were to interpret the experiential content of Kant's doctrine of the antinomies in metaphysical terms, then what that doctrine would mean would be that we must abandon the illusion that freedom is a reality so as to salvage the possibility that freedom might one day become a reality after all.

The evil is not – as it must have seemed to Kant – that free human beings act in a radically evil way,[4] but there has been a change in the sense that, since we do not yet have a world in which men no longer need to be radically evil, the spell of the unfreedom which holds them in thrall has not yet been broken. It is my belief that this is a finding that brings the executioners into the diagnosis of entanglement and guilt, and even conceives of them as victims and not *just* as murderers, which is what they *also* are. I believe that only an approach of this sort would create enough breathing space to enable us to escape from the vicious circle that characterizes everything that is connected with these horrifying events and actions. I say this very cautiously and would ask you not to misunderstand me on this point. I do not have even the slightest intention of suggesting that reflections on freedom might provide any scope at all for evading a confrontation with such experiences, that is to say, with everything that Auschwitz represents. I believe that every thought that fails to measure itself against such experiences is simply worthless, irrelevant and utterly trivial. A human being who is not mindful at every moment of the potential for extreme horror at the present time must be so bemused by the veil of ideology that he might just as well stop thinking at all. However, this very situation and reflection upon the facts that are at issue forces us into a radical process of interrogation that leaves far behind us such naïve questions as 'Are you responsible or not responsible?' Freedom in the sense of moral responsibility can only exist in a free society. And a free society will have to be conceived as one which has ceased to produce people like Boger and Kaduk – at least in significant numbers.[5] I believe that their behaviour consisted of acquired, internalized modes of social behaviour – the term internalization, interiorization [*Innerlichkeit*], really comes home to roost here. God knows that it would be a task worthy of criminology, if only criminology were to be mindful of its proper tasks for a change, if it could demonstrate for once that, and to what extent, the utterly asocial attitudes that we encounter in such individuals are in fact social attitudes, namely, the extension of the principles of a society that has really always been based on direct, naked force and continues to be so based to this day. The responsibility in question amounts to something like our ability to intervene. We can only think of ourselves as responsible in so far as we are able to influence matters in the areas where we have responsibility. Everyone can learn the truth of this within his own limited sphere of activity when he perceives that there are frequently situations in which he is given responsibility for something by some institution or other, but without at the same time being given the authority to impose his will and to exercise control over what falls within his remit. This is the antinomy of authority which is caught between the twin poles of responsibility and the ability to impose one's will. It will be familiar to everyone who has been given some authority in the administered world and who occupies any position of responsibility in it. I would say that this is the antinomy par excellence, and it gives everyone who has experienced it something of an insight into the tangled nature of the real world.

Responsibility, then, is the touchstone by which freedom can be measured in reality, by which freedom can be imputed, as the lawyers put it. But if responsibility truly is the critical zone of freedom, we must say that today there is a complete mismatch between responsibility and influence – not merely in so-called official circles with regard to people who have authority to issue directives in a particular, defined area, but who then for a hundred different reasons issue instructions that do not reflect their own understanding, or do so only to a very limited degree. But over and above this, there is the so-called sovereign nation, in other words the people who cast their vote in the polling booths in order to determine their political and social destiny. These people have neither objectively nor subjectively the possibility and influence needed to ensure that their actions will shape the world as they would like it to be. These things have been said so often that I have no need to repeat them here. I would remind you only of the controversy that arose in connection with Niemöller,[6] who described this situation with a quite extraordinary integrity and frankness. I mention it only because it enables you to understand an insight we owe to Hegel. This is that, while freedom appears to us as a subjective quality, as if the judgement about whether freedom exists is one that falls exclusively to the subjective mind, this insight enables us to see how dependent freedom is on objective realities and to gauge the extent to which we are capable of influencing the real world with its overpowering, structured institutions by what we do as formally free subjective agents. It is only in this context that I wish to invoke all the assertions that have been made about the decline of the political process and the political impotence of individuals, assertions that are familiar to you all and about which a very large and very spirited literature has grown up in the meantime. What I wish to emphasize is something that each of you has experienced in all its subtleties in your awareness of the excessive demands made on you, and probably on everyone without exception, even if we ignore such matters as people's class membership. It is the experience that more is constantly demanded of you than you can possibly achieve. This is a highly paradoxical situation if I am right in assuming its general prevalence. And I would ask you to consider whether there is any truth in what I am claiming here. It is a very curious fact that we constantly feel that excessive demands are being made on us, even though advances in technology have rendered such vast amounts of work superfluous; that we ought all to find things a whole lot easier, and the difference between what social norms expect of us and what we are capable of achieving ought to be shrinking all the time, or even leaving us in credit on the subjective side. But there is no question of that happening. If I am not mistaken – I do not wish to exaggerate this – but my belief is that we all feel under constant pressure. This feeling is not a matter of particular causes. By this I mean that it is not so much the fact that many of you feel you have to learn too many things for your examinations, or that I feel too many demands are being made of me in the sense that I have to perform too many administrative duties and that these keep me from what I regard as my most important tasks, tasks I can find time for only by stealing time from unavoidable chores – so that I have to do countless jobs that others could do just as well as I or even better. All these things are probably no more than a cover for the fact that we live in a society based on formal freedom, and in return for this formal freedom it demands that we wholeheartedly devote our efforts to whatever has fallen to our lot, while at the same time preventing us from doing so because of the overwhelming power of its institutions and the overwhelming power with which it confronts us at every moment. This, I would say, is the concrete form in which we experience the question of freedom and unfreedom today. I hope that someone will one day decide that this phenomenon of excessive demands might be worthy of serious analysis. What marks out this feeling of chronic overwork is that it always contains, in a concealed form of course, something like a memory of freedom. That is to say, unless we felt that we ought by rights to be free, that we ought as free persons to be able to cope with all the demands that have been made, we would not have this chronic feeling of being overstretched, a feeling that is undoubtedly far keener than the feeling of 'care' [*Sorge*] and similar ideas that the existentialists tell us about.[7] The term 'excessive demands' [*Überforderung*], incidentally, is one that has only come into general use in our own day. It may have occurred in the period before Hitler, but

only in specific situations where you could say that this person or
that was having too many demands made on him, but the general
socialization of the term 'excessive demands' that one encounters
today is undoubtedly to be laid at the door of the present situation.
We should make one further point, namely, that it quickly results in
a vicious circle. The fact that every individual feels excessive demands
are being made on him; the fact that every individual discovers that
his so-called, i.e., formal, freedom and responsibility constantly
impose demands upon him that he is unable to meet, and that we
feel the whole time that we are bound to fail because of objective
circumstances – all this leads to a kind of resignation and indifference
which, if anything, only encourages our acquiescence in what is
imposed on us from outside and the shoulder-shrugging indifference
to everything associated with the concept of freedom.

If what I have attempted to explain to you has any truth in it, this
means – and I should like to emphasize this – that evil, unfreedom,
is not to be found where old metaphysicians of the satanic looked
for it, namely, in the idea that some people use their freedom of choice
to choose evil. We should include the philosophy of history here, since
we are talking about the theory of history and freedom – but in all
probability, and especially where the social trend, that is to say, the
total process of societalization, is furthest advanced, we should say
that one of the relevant factors here is that wicked people of the kind
you meet in literature no longer exist, Iago, say, or Richard III, to
name only the most famous literary prototypes. Such radically evil
people are no longer to be found, for the radical evil of the kind
postulated by Kant presupposes a strength of character, energy, and
a substantiality of the self that is made impossible by a world that
calls for more or less dissociated achievements that are separated
from the self. It is a world in which I almost wish to say that not
even a wicked man can survive. It may seem a consolation that utterly
evil people are perhaps no longer to be found, any more than I would
suppose that there are any misers left. But any such consoling thought
will be cancelled out by the corollary that it has also become impossible to imagine really good people. In the bourgeois age, an independent merchant would show some generosity to every beggar who
crossed his path – but in these busy, tangled times good men have
become just as unimaginable as truly evil ones.

This brings us to a point which I had believed would be at the
centre of the clutch of problems that I have been presenting to you
in these lectures. I believe that I have not just shown you that the
content of the moral principle, the categorical imperative, constantly
changes as history changes – this is a bit of a truism that I would be

a little embarrassed to have told you about; but also we have
approached a threshold at which we must ask whether the entire
moral sphere (not just the good, not just what can be thought of as
good), whether the entire sphere in which it is meaningful to speak
of good and evil, has not approached a threshold at which it is no
longer meaningful to apply these terms. If that were the case, it would
undoubtedly help to explain some of the antinomies and aporias that
we constantly encounter in discussions of Auschwitz. One such is
that here we necessarily apply yardsticks of good and evil to behaviour that, as if in fulfilment of a dreadful prophecy, already belongs
to a state of mankind in which, negatively, the entire sphere of morality has been abolished, instead of being elevated, positively, into a
higher sphere that is equally free of both repression and morality. Let
me add, or remind you, that freedom and unfreedom are not primary
phenomena, but derivatives of a totality that at any given time exercises dominion over individuals. If I may take up this dialectical idea
to which I have ventured forward, and pursue it a little further back
in the opposite direction – what I have told you about the obsolescence of our categories of morality, and the terrible threat of the
ageing of good and evil that is a kind of infernal reflection of the
utopia of which Nietzsche had dreamt[8] – all that has its prehistory;
it is not something that has just appeared out of the blue. It is a
product of history in the sense that the categories of freedom and
unfreedom are themselves the products of history; and in the sense
that the entire sphere of morality only came into being historically
together with the human subject. If we consider the amorality of the
world of myth, we can see that what matters is not the idea that
people used to have different ideas about morality – that is the kind
of claim made by trivial popular psychology and the like – but that
at that time, thanks to the global situation of the human species and
the stage of development reached by human society, the entire sphere
of a stable, self-contained and responsible subjectivity had not yet
emerged. Therefore there was nothing to which moral categories
might have been applied. On the other hand, we cannot simply deny
the existence of a separation, a historically caused separation of individual and society, which ultimately led to the problem of individual
freedom. The fact that a gulf has opened up between individual and
society is not only – and this is something that must be emphasized,
particularly nowadays – is not only the negative phenomenon it has
been misrepresented as, above all by the Romantic movement, as well
as a host of stale ideologies and recycled versions of Romanticism. It
is not merely the negative side of that loss of unity, meaning, and the
feeling of safety [*Geborgenheit*] that Bollnow likes to talk about[9] –

and all those supposedly lovely things. But Hegel rightly perceived, and it is perhaps one of the most brilliant achievements of the *Phenomenology of Spirit*, particularly the middle sections, in which he deals with all the topics we are speaking about here – that the rift between individual and society is a necessary element of the emancipation of the individual. Without this rift, the idea of freedom, which points the way beyond both this rupture and the undifferentiated state of affairs, would be inconceivable. At this point we come very close to – what shall we call it? – the gnostic, antinomian implications of dialectical thought.[10] Without evil – that is to say, without that modern term of abuse 'alienation', which has acquired such an alarming degree of popularity nowadays – there would be no good; without this rift to provide mankind with its substantive security within a given society, the idea of freedom and with it the idea of a condition worthy of human beings would not exist. This insight is swiftly joined by the suspicion that what were said, even in Hegel, to be substantial ages in which the individual lived in harmony with the collective of which he was a member,[11] were in reality far from providing the settings for a happy and harmonious existence. More likely, they were ages characterized by a repressiveness that was so powerful that what has come down to us from them is merely the end result, namely, the triumph of the universal, without our being able to give an account of the excesses of suffering and injustice without which these so-called meaningful times, as Lukács once called them rather romantically in his youth, would not have existed.[12] We may be quite safe in stating that the self naïvely immersed in the so-called substantial society would have found the distinction between freedom and unfreedom entirely alien. And in this way the link between history and the question of freedom must be seen to be more than a matter simply of an ever-changing content. The link between the two must lie instead in the constitution of the problem of freedom itself. If that is true, and if the alternative between freedom and unfreedom is alien to that individual, not just at the level of reflection, but also in his entire mode of behaviour as he naïvely and directly obeys the rules of the universal, then we must conclude that this allegedly happy time before the divorce between freedom and unfreedom had taken place can only have been an unfree condition for the individuals who were born into it.

LECTURE 23

9 *February 1965*

ANTINOMIES OF FREEDOM

It will perhaps not be entirely unproductive for the problems that we are exploring if we were to ask a question that Kant would undoubtedly have condemned as a genuine act of *lèse-majesté*. This question is: what possible interest might the human subject have in emphasizing that his own freedom is a positive given? It will then immediately become obvious – I am well aware that such a psychological approach is a *metabasis eis allo genos* [a transition to another kind], but it will become clear to you why I resort to it – it will then become obvious that the human subject's interest in his freedom is narcissistic. By this I mean that the suggestion that human beings are merely creatures of nature, and hence, in the last analysis, automata, as Descartes' *animalia* are supposed to be,[1] is felt to be a major slight. In general, humanity as a species feels an extraordinary revulsion from everything that might remind it of its own animal nature, a revulsion which I strongly suspect to be deeply related to the persistence of its very real animality. Probably one of the most intractable problems of Kant's conception of man and human nature lies in his attempt to differentiate it, and together with it man's dignity and everything that involves, and to mark it off from animality. We can readily understand this interest historically if we picture to ourselves the indescribable efforts and the sacrifices that it must have cost human beings in the course of their development to muster the strength to master their inner and outer nature. For it was only thanks to these efforts and these sacrifices that it became possible to distinguish themselves from nature and that this strength could be reflected back to them as a

divinely gifted quality, the quality of freedom. It is a remarkable and
striking fact that, even though Kant would have found such considerations anathema, he was able if not to illuminate theoretically the
secret of this interest in freedom, the subject's narcissistic interest in
freedom, at least to let it slip out in passing. This can be seen in a
passage in the *Groundwork of the Metaphysic of Morals*, in the
section entitled 'How is a categorical imperative possible?'. In the
course of a discussion of the possibility of a practical philosophy in
general, he expresses himself in such a way that what I have called
narcissistic interest breaks through to the surface. I should like to
show you this remarkable passage. The 'he' that Kant uses here is
the subject as such. Significantly, he at once identifies this subject as
a scoundrel in order to show that even such a scoundrel – needless
to say, the archaic sound of the word will not have escaped you – that
even such a scoundrel cannot dispense with the supposition of
freedom. By pointing to the driving force at work he gives expression
to this narcissism, in all innocence, I hasten to add:

> By such a wish he [the scoundrel] shows that having a will free from
> sensuous impulses he transfers himself in thought into an order of
> things quite different from that of his desires in the field of sensibility;
> for from the fulfilment of this wish he can expect no gratification of
> his sensuous desires and consequently no state which would satisfy any
> of his actual or even conceivable inclinations (since by such an expecta-
> tion the very Idea which elicited the wish would be deprived of its
> superiority); all he can expect is a greater inner worth of his own
> person. This better person he believes himself to be when he transfers
> himself to the standpoint of a member of the intelligible world.

– Intelligible world [*Verstandeswelt*] here means the world we can
understand, in other words, the world of freedom –

> He is involuntarily constrained to do so by the Idea of freedom – that
> is, of not being dependent on *determination* by causes in the sensible
> world; and from this standpoint he is conscious of possessing a good
> will which, on his own admission, constitutes the law for the bad will
> belonging to him as a member of the sensible world – a law of whose
> authority he is aware even in transgressing it. The moral 'I ought' is
> thus an 'I will' for man as a member of an intelligible world.[2]

The necessity that is ascribed here to the consciousness of freedom is
so peculiar because, as something narcissistic, that is to say, as the
mere consciousness of being a better person, it is defined by Kant in

precisely the psychological manner that the anti-psychologism of the *Critique of Practical Reason* ought to preclude.

But we are now confronted with a curious fact in connection with this tremendous narcissistic need to assert one's own freedom and sovereignty. I believe that I am not exaggerating when I say that the impact of German idealism, the political and also the social impact of German idealism, would have been inconceivable without that element of narcissism. But what is remarkable is that this interest in freedom runs in tandem with the opposing interest, namely the denial of freedom. I remember how as a child my parents were shocked to hear a housemaid telling me that I had to do what I was told, and this doing-what-I-was-told was presented to me as a sort of categorical imperative, without its being explained to me *why* I had to do what I was told, and *in what respect* I had to do what I was told. Of course, this is the ideal of conformity that plays such a major role in bourgeois society and that was originally determined by the coercion of the market economy. By this I mean that the man who produces for the market needs to adapt his supply to the prevailing demand because otherwise he will not be able to dispose of his products. The idea was then projected onto nature in the shape of Darwinist biology, no doubt for good reason, since you will remember that history is an extension of natural history. And having been naturalized in the shape of Darwinism, the idea was reimported into the society from which it had sprung. Incidentally, an intellectual or social history of conformity would be a project that would really give us an insight into the very heart of bourgeois society, especially if we think of the theory of conformity as the dark side of the theory of freedom. The two theories are corollaries of each other and between them they express the conflict that sustains bourgeois society itself. This conflict means, on the one hand, that human beings have to prove themselves through the work ethic, that is to say, they are evaluated in a double sense in terms of the socially useful work that they perform. They have to display independence, autonomy and initiative, in other words, all the qualities that bourgeois modernity championed in opposition to feudal notions, whether those of beggars or of great lords. These then are the virtues of freedom. If the single, atomized, isolated individual fails to insist on his own being-for-himself and his own autonomy, if in other words he fails to prove himself as a free being, he will be punished socially, he will fall under the wheels in one way or another. On the other hand, however, the same individual must define himself as a being-for-others; he must constantly mutilate himself because society as a whole is unfree, because in its content society as a whole is a heteronomous thing as far as he is concerned, and because he can only assert himself by this process of adaptation. The difficulties, the theoretical difficulties connected with the concept of freedom ultimately represent something like an interiorization or sublimation of that very real conflict between the doctrines of freedom and conformity in bourgeois society itself. You can find a vulgarized version of this in the ideology of the contemporary culture industry. In my essay 'Second-Hand Superstition', which appears in volume 2 of the *Sociologica*,[3] I have shown in great detail – and this could easily be replicated with reference to the astrology columns in German magazines – that two pieces of advice always go together and mutually reinforce one another. On the one hand, there is the advice: stand on your own two feet, use your own initiative, take your courage in both hands! *And*, on the other hand: keep in with your superiors, don't be too cheeky, don't make trouble, don't try always to get your own way! The pieces of advice that are to be gleaned from the stars – which basically just reiterate what life imposes on human beings anyway – merely attempt to strike a balance between the conflicting demands made on people, between the morning and the afternoon, or between the day and the evening, in accordance with a two-phased temporal scheme. You can perhaps see this most clearly in the dominant American ideology, in what is known as the American way of living.[4] In this ideology we find cheek by jowl the demand for a rugged individualism,[5] that is to say, the energetic, unruly individual who is not afraid to use his elbows, and on the other hand, the insistence on adjustment,[6] in other words, on the conforming individual. At the same time, there is a peculiar dialectic at work in which, because force is at bottom the principle governing society, the man with the most powerful elbows is generally the man who is also the best adjusted to society. We may say, and this is doubtless one of the reasons for the growing disenchantment with politics, that the trend, the general trend today, leans heavily towards the side of adjustment.

Connected with this is the fact that, in so far as people truly are free and autonomous (as I have already tried to explain to you in one of the recent lectures,)[7] freedom overtaxes them, just as the insistence upon their freedom simultaneously flatters them, or has flattered them in the past. Today in contrast we may well ask whether people are as flattered to be told: you are free, be proud that you are free, as they have been for the past 150 or 200 years. I should like to bring to your attention a fact with which we shall have to concern ourselves. If the process of societalization continues to advance, and if therefore the elements of freedom that I have told you about are progressively swallowed up by the elements of adjustment, then

freedom and what we might call the impulses of freedom, spontaneous actions, will come to appear increasingly old-fashioned, or even
archaic. This is not a superficial fact and that is why I have launched
out into these conceptual or, if you like, general historical observations. For it seems to be the case (and I note this in the first instance
as just one of the crucial themes of a doctrine of freedom) that a
certain archaic element is required for there to be such things as free
impulses, or spontaneous modes of behaviour that are not triggered
by reasons. This stands in contrast to the entire philosophical tradition, especially since Spinoza, Leibniz and Kant, in which freedom,
free behaviour, is equated with behaviour *in accordance with reason*.
This archaic element is a much older phenomenon, one that I should
like to call an *impulse*. It is undoubtedly closely connected with
mimetic phenomena. Mimetic behaviour is not causally determined
by objective factors, or factors that are seen to be objective, but
involves instead an involuntary adjustment to something extra-
mental. Because of its involuntary nature there is something irrational
about this adjustment that theories of freedom generally refuse to
acknowledge but which is part of the definition of freedom. This is
something that I regard as crucial to what I want to say to you about
freedom. The more the ego obtains control over itself and over
nature, then the more it learns to master itself and the more questionable it finds its own freedom. This is because its archaic, uncontrolled
reactions appear chaotic. We might almost go so far as to say that,
while something like freedom becomes possible only through the
development of consciousness, *at the same time* this very same development of consciousness effectively ensures that freedom is pushed
back into the realm of archaic, mimetic impulse that is so essential
to it. We might say, then, that the situation with freedom is like that
of so many other things in the world in the sense that, the more it is
translated into the imagination, the more it distances itself from its
own immediate reality. I say this only to show you that what is at
first sight a historical or psychological conflict between freedom and
conformity is in fact meta-psychological. That is to say, it reaches
down into what we may designate as appropriate to the prehistory
of individuation as such.[8] The concept of freedom could not be formulated in the absence of recourse to something prior to the ego, to
an impulse that is in a sense a bodily impulse that has not yet been
subjected to the centralizing authority of consciousness; while on the
other hand, its trajectory terminates in the strength of the ego itself.
In other words, it contains a conflict within itself.

When I speak of a dialectic of freedom I hope that I have been
able to show you that we are talking of dialectic in a very strict sense,

that is to say, of a contradictoriness that is integral to the concept we are investigating. You know that Kant – and then post-Kantian philosophy – makes use of a concept that really holds the key to the concept of freedom and that at the same time provides a starting-point for post-Kantian idealism. This is the concept of *spontaneity*. When you read the *Critique of Pure Reason*, you make the acquaintance of spontaneity as the consciousness's faculty for the activity of thought: in other words, everything that forms part of reason and the understanding, in contrast to receptivity, the ability to be affected, to the passive qualities of sensibility [*Sinnlichkeit*]. I would ask you now to consider a question that goes beyond the so-called branches of philosophy such as epistemology, metaphysics and ethics and that can justifiably be described as speculative. This is to inquire what Kant actually meant by spontaneity. If you do so, you will probably encounter a very similar duality in what he regarded as the most profound category of his philosophy to the one to be found in the concept of freedom, as I have just tried to demonstrate in the course of my attempt to give you a history of the individual. Thus on the one hand, spontaneity is active, thinking behaviour, and as such active, thinking behaviour, something that Kant argues at length in the Deduction of the Pure Concepts of Understanding, it is this behaviour by means of which something like a unity of consciousness comes into being, and with it the unity of the world. Thus this spontaneity is evidently connected to the ego; it is the true determining factor of the fixed ego, identical with itself. It becomes a unity as the unity of the activity that it is able to muster. But if you examine it more closely, you will find – and this is one of the dimensions of the *Critique of Pure Reason* that have in general been very neglected – that by spontaneity Kant is not really thinking here of the achievements of individual thought. If, God forbid, I were to solve some equation or other, or perform some other mental act of that sort, Kant would argue from within the theory of knowledge that such acts were simply the achievements or efforts of empirical consciousness within an already constituted empirical reality. What he understands by spontaneity is an activity, to be sure, but at the same time – and this is what is expressed by the dialectical nexus that I have been trying to explain to you – it is something involuntary: it is something that occurs without my being too clear about what is happening 'in the depths of the human soul', as Kant phrases it in the schematism chapter.[9] The actual conceptual achievements, by which I mean the achievements thanks to which the world becomes for me the world in which our experience has its being, these achievements are not so much my acts, in other words, conscious activities, but are more like objective, involuntary functions that occur even before any particular mental activities have taken place within the world as constituted. You can see this at its clearest in the very mysterious concept that represents the first stage of the first version of Deduction of the Pure Concepts of Understanding, namely the concept of 'apprehension in intuition'.[10] Thus the fact that something is perceived intuitively and retained in the mind as a unified entity coincides with what is an immediate, passive given. Nevertheless, in his view this process involves the intellect because the postulated unity is a substantive one. It goes beyond the merely formal determinants of time and place because it represents the organization of a specific perception into the thing that is perceived in it.

Thus both things are involved in Kant's concept of spontaneity. It means both the simple, straightforward concept of an activity and also the concept of an unconscious or, as we might put it, involuntary activity. I suggest once again that you should do what is always advisable in philosophy, namely to pay heed to the very simplest linguistic usage. In this instance, I would ask you to reflect on what is meant when we say that someone has acted spontaneously. If you reflect on it for a moment, you will see that this duality does exist. A person is spontaneous if he performs an action in a particular situation; but we only call his action spontaneous if it does not follow logically from prior considerations but instead has something sudden or abrupt about it; we might even call it something indeterminate. You can see, then, that this peculiar duality of ego and impulse, which I can only imagine as something somatic, something physical, extends into the sublimest reaches of Kant's theory of knowledge. And the incomparable greatness of Kant, I would remind you, consists in his ability to give expression to such complexities without regard to any particular thesis that he wishes to prove, simply by virtue of his fidelity to the facts of the case. I should like to add just one brief comment on this matter. You will undoubtedly find it surprising that post-Kantian philosophy, post-Kantian speculative philosophy, in particular in the development starting with Fichte, should have given Kant's own philosophy such a strange turn. Kant believed that he had succeeded in defining our acts as *our* acts, simply by analysing the mental activities of human beings as they are – entirely in the spirit of English empiricism. Yet in the hands of post-Kantian philosophy these acts became the acts of an absolute subject, and ultimately of the Absolute as such. This Absolute then turned more or less explicitly into the heir of the God who had been overthrown by nominalism. I believe that you will be able to see how things reached this pass if you reflect upon what I have attempted to explain to you today – unless you prefer to regard this development simply as a mere hypostasis, a hypostasizing abstraction from the activity of individual human subjects. What I have tried to clarify, then, is this element of feeling in our thought that our most profound acts, our so-called constitutive acts, are not those in which I am present as a thinking subject, but that an 'it' is thinking in me and that an 'it' is at work mentally even before we may say that the ego has been constituted – and this feeling represents an age-old, at bottom, archaic experience. It is a feeling that makes possible the transition through which to constitute whatever it is that thinks in the individual mind as it constitutes our world, prior to all individual thought, and to constitute it as something not individual but transcendental. By 'transcendental' I mean not something that formally comprises individuals, but something that actually establishes individuation and makes it possible. In the same way, the concept of the transcendental contains a memory of the transcendent, in other words, of a consciousness that should be more than merely individual consciousness.

I believe that if you are willing to entertain these ideas they will give you an entry into the mysteries of the concept of freedom in which the extreme exaltation of the ego goes hand in hand in a very strange way with the abyss of the self. But over and above that, it will enable you to understand something of the motives underlying German idealism, and in particular what is meant by 'the depths of the human soul'. It is here that you have to look to discover the sources of the concept of inwardness [*Innerlichkeit*] in its specific meaning, a term that played a great role as early as Hegel. It is interesting to note that this concept of spontaneity is of central importance not just in Kant, but also in the Marxian theory of socialism. Moreover, both in Marx and more generally in socialist theory, it has the same dialectical quality, the same dual character, that I have drawn your attention to in Kant. For the spontaneous action that Marx ascribes to the proletariat is supposed, on the one hand, to be an autonomous, free, rational form of action, action on the basis of a known and comprehensible theory. At the same time, however, it contains an irreducible element, the element of immediate action that does not entirely fit into the factors that theoretically determine it; and, above all, it does not fit smoothly into the determining factors of history. On the contrary, even though it is determined *by* these, it seems to be a way leading *out of* them – in extreme contrast to all mechanistic interpretations of the course of history. You can see from this how this curious duality of spontaneity has continued to thrive, until it finally underwent the strange fate, on the one hand, of simply vanishing; that is to say, it too succumbed to the blind conformity to dominant power relations. On the other hand, in the minds of all those who have opposed this development, spontaneity has made itself independent in a strange way, and has split itself off from reason, as a protest against a mechanical determinism through cause and effect, and this protest applied to the presence of that determinism in socialist thought too. In this way it came close to anarchism even though anarchism had been subjected to astringent criticism in socialist theory. The greatest example of this protest is Rosa Luxemburg. But you will also discover traces of it in the thought of Jean-Paul Sartre, even though he has long since discarded any immediate application to politics. Thus, to sum up this part of the argument, the concept of spontaneity, which might be described as the organ or medium of freedom, refuses to obey the logic of non-contradiction, and is instead a unity of mutually contradictory elements. It points, therefore, to a strict conception of dialectic. When I told you that the ego had conceived the idea of freedom for egoistic reasons, this contained the idea that the ego has enormous difficulty in grasping the elements of its own dependency. This is not merely a matter of psychology which strives to keep narcissistic traumas at bay because they entail a loss of self-respect, but it arises, we might say, from the *principium individuationis* itself. As the human subject separates itself off and becomes a single being, and defines itself as a single being, it must of course, if it is to defend its individuality against others that crowd in on it, insulate itself against the consciousness of its own entanglement in general. In the *principium individuationis*, individual beings appear in a society that reproduces itself through conflicting interests – and this reinforces their tendency to blot this out, thus strengthening the individual's belief that he is merely a being for himself.

You can picture to yourselves this remarkable connection between the semblance of freedom and what might be called the monadological veil; you can gain a clear idea of what is meant – and I try to the best of my ability to make these speculative concepts a little more concrete, not by means of examples, but by focusing on critical points, on contentious issues – you can best concretize the matter for yourselves, if you dwell on a pathological phenomenon for a few moments, one in which the ego becomes aware of its own nature as something determined, in a perverse manner I should add. I am thinking here of obsessional neuroses. These are psychological illnesses – in earlier days we would have spoken of nervous disorders – rather than proper mental illnesses or psychoses. People afflicted by them find themselves compelled to perform certain ritual-like actions without knowing why. If they fail to perform these actions they are overcome by the most terrible anxieties and even physical pain. I am thinking

here of the sleep rituals practised by many neurotic people, in which
they feel compelled to arrange their pillows in all sorts of complicated
ways in order to get to sleep – and there are all sorts of other comparable obsessions. Incidentally, everyone has obsessions of this kind.
I believe that if you think about it you will all become aware that
every individual has some obsession or other. But they are not called
obsessional neuroses unless they make it impossible for the individual
to function properly in ordinary life or lead to really serious unhap-
piness; but that is a relatively arbitrary distinction. If you do suffer
from such an obsessional neurosis, the way it works is that you give
in to the obsession and then defend it with a huge expenditure of
libidinal energy. You even look for reasons – often very absurd ones
– to explain why you cannot manage without performing the obses-
sive actions concerned. But what these explanations have in common
is that the obsessions are always seen as ego-alien (as psychology puts
it). That is to say, you experience the obsession as caused by a dependence on something in oneself, but something that ought not to be
there. The significance of these obsessional neuroses is that they have
at least torn a rent in what I have called the 'monadological veil'. In
other words, they teach people that they are not simply what they
are in their own intrinsic nature, that alien elements enter into them,
that freedom is denied them in what Hegel calls their 'native land',[11]
namely the realm of consciousness of self. The feeling one has is
'That's not really me', and this feeling that is experienced when you
are in the grip of an obsessional neurosis has both something illusory
and something true about it. It is an illusion because the ego that we
regard as something substantial and given turns out not to have an
existence of its own but to be highly precarious, and its vulnerability
is deeply exposed by these neurotic experiences. On the other hand,
however, the feeling is true because the ego knows that the *possibility*
of its own existence is its true being and it is against this that the
obsession offends. I could put it this way: the human subject knows
that the inner causes underlying his impulses are not part of himself.
And where the human subject comes across these inner causes underlying his impulses, this realization collides with his own consciousness
of himself – and this too is the expression of the real contradictoriness
of freedom of which we are speaking. I should like to bring together
everything that I have been telling you today by saying that the contradictions and antinomies of freedom that in Kant's view could be
explained as the product of a wrong-headed use of reason are in fact
antinomies that are inherent in the question itself. By this I mean that,
in a very real sense, we are simultaneously both free and unfree.

LECTURE 24

11 February 1965

RATIONALITY AND THE ADDITIONAL FACTOR

The day before yesterday I discussed with you the aspect of the consciousness of freedom that has its roots in the fact that the human subject has no knowledge of the internal causes of its own impulses, of what we might call its inner causation. In the process I placed great emphasis on one element connected with the ego-principle itself. This was the element of narcissism, since of course – and I might add: from a psychological point of view – the mechanisms of repression discovered by depth psychology play a vital role, and in a psychogenetic sense an even more essential one. This is because the conditioning factors, the blind conditions, at which the subject baulks are in fact the powers of the id, the repressed instinctual impulses. 'Repressed' in this context means keeping something at a distance from the subject. This disguising of the unfree elements of subjectivity from subjectivity itself is caused, as you know from your reading in psychology, by the ego. A further factor is that the ego, which, as you know, has come into being as the authority of the personality as a whole, and which is responsible for overseeing reality, that is to say, it has the task of testing external reality to make sure that nothing bad happens to a person – a further factor, then, is that because of this task this ego-authority assumes something of a propensity to externalize. This is so closely identified with its ego impulses, in other words the impulse to self-preservation, that it is only relatively late and only after a very high degree of differentiation has taken place that the ego arrives at a self-reflexivity that can be taken for granted every bit as much as the schoolmaster's statement in the Latin lesson

(to take an example from everyday life) that 'the general conquers
the city'. It is my belief that we ought not to take this primacy of the
ego for granted even though it has become something of an article
of faith among philosophers. We might say that the fact that the ego
operates coercively on the external world, that it operates in an
extroverted fashion (if I may use this psychological term), prevents it
from becoming aware of its own compulsive nature and the unfreedom of the principle governing its own freedom. I would remind you
in passing that this compulsive nature of the subject, its unfreedom,
has what I might even go so far as to call its ontological roots in the
fact that, in its solidity and its determinate nature, the ego imitates
the coercion that is imposed on it from without, so as to be able to
combat it. I believe that this is something I have already told you
about in some detail.[1] In short, then, the subject's consciousness of
freedom, his naïve consciousness of freedom, is something like a web
of delusion. The subject is trapped within itself. The name of the
resulting delusion is that of its freedom as something that exists in
the here and now, a quality that it ascribes to itself like other qualities. We could say that the human subject is bewitched by the idea
of its own freedom as if by a magic spell. And this condition of being
spellbound by one's own freedom, this inability on the part of the
self-preserving subject to perceive the way it is conditioned as a consequence of this mechanism of self-preservation – this is something
we might well describe as the meta-psychological or, if you like,
metaphysical truth of the Freudian doctrine of repression.

I would remind you that the ideas of freedom and unfreedom
within the subject, as subjective qualities, are both based on extra-
mental models. Freedom arose or was crystallized not merely by
naïvely postulating an authority that dominates nature – which is
what the ego turned into. It was constructed also as the positive
counterweight to the experience of social coercion. In the light of the
social coercion to which the ego succumbs, the self forms the idea
that it would be better to be different, that it would be better to be
free. In this web of delusion it adopts a kind of compensatory role
in the sense that, having once surrendered to external compulsion, it
imagines that it can still define itself as a free being, inwardly at least.
This is an ancient, even archaic tactic, and you can still find it in all
the ideologies, particularly those of a petty bourgeois kind. These are
still very widespread and can perhaps best be summed up in the idea
of an 'inner kingdom' of the kind cherished by the silent majority.
This inner kingdom consists in the idea of an internal life that is supposed to be a haven of peace and quiet, largely independent of the
factors that determine the external world. In reality, however, at the

very point where such inner kingdoms are to be found, we also tend to discover that they are really a kind of rubbish bin full of all sorts of elements of external life that take flight into the imagination only because they are pipe dreams that have no prospect of being put into practice in the real world. But in the same way, unfreedom, too, that is to say, determination, has its extra-mental roots. They are situated in the dependent circumstances in which the subject finds himself: those of nature in archaic times that overwhelmed mankind, and then and above all the dependence upon social conditions, dominant groups and cliques. These are hypostasized as internal determinants and thus become a matter of human inwardness. To give you an example, you will find this mechanism by means of which unfreedom, inner unfreedom, becomes a sort of reproduction of external unfreedom in Protestantism. For Protestantism uses the determinism of the will to justify the subordination of the human subject to alien authorities, in other words the ruler's will. You can see very clearly from this that the theory of the *servum arbitrium*[2] that Luther defended against Melanchthon is itself a reflex, an ideology or a vindication of external coercion, and that this kind of theology was indeed concerned to produce a vindication of that coercion.

The truth is that in contrast to these two illusions, these two illusory roots of both the theory of freedom and the theory of unfreedom, we should remind ourselves that the subject is not what it is explicitly called as recently as the phenomenology of Edmund Husserl, namely the sphere of 'absolute origins'.[3] Instead, we should remember that this view that the subject *could be* the sphere of absolute origins mistakes the ground of knowledge for the objective ground – in other words, the idea that phenomena are mediated by the subject and that the subject can only come to know them by turning them into its own innate truths; the two propositions are almost tautologous. The subject thereby elevates itself into the sphere of pure origins. Even the definitions which uphold the subject's claim to sovereignty stand in need of what according to their own self-understanding ought to need nothing but them. One aspect of this is that the sphere of absolute origins of which philosophy speaks is secretly still the sphere of the subject – and this remains true however much it speaks as if it were located beyond the distinction of subject and object. Thought couched in terms of absolute origins of the kind we see in the unambiguous thesis, the *undialectical* thesis, of both the freedom of the self and the unfreedom of the self is based on the delusion of a subjectivity that falsely assumes that everything that exists can be said to have derived from it. Whenever we think we might have discovered such a sphere of absolute origins what we find is that the absence of

ambiguity, the identity, that such a sphere assumes, in contrast to
whatever is claimed to derive from it or to be subsumed under it,
turns out to be no more than the metaphysical hypostasization of the
principle of identity, which is what the subject is. But whether the
subject is autonomous in reality, whether it is able to decide one way
or the other, as is imagined in the mechanism of the web of delusion,
depends on the opposite of this subjectivity that has inflated itself
into an absolute in this fashion. That is to say, it depends on objective
reality. For it is this, the organization of the world, the nature of the
world, that actually determines the extent to which the subject
achieves autonomy, and the extent to which it is vouchsafed or
denied. Detached from this, the subject is a fiction, or else such a thin
and abstract principle that it can be of no assistance in telling us
about the actual behaviour of human beings.

Again and again in the history of philosophy, attempts have been
made to apply the concepts of freedom or unfreedom to make definitive assertions about the actual behaviour of human beings. In particular, thought experiments, *experimenta crucis*, have been devised
in order to decide unambiguously whether or not man is free and
how to arrive at absolute decisions about the freedom or unfreedom
of man. The best-known, although slightly comical example, no
doubt intentionally so, was conceived by the Scholastics. It was the
famous ass belonging to Buridan which found itself having to choose
between two identical bundles of hay. The question of which one it
would turn to, which one it would eat, or eat first, was supposed to
be the proof of its freedom to choose.[4] I believe that by their nature,
by the way they are designed, these thought experiments undermine
the very logic to which they lay claim. For they always strive to reduce
the empirical context to the point where the example becomes incompatible with reality. All that is left is the abstraction, in this case, the
bundles of hay, but when you think of situations involving living
people, they always turn out to be different. Such identical bundles
of hay that are supposed to provide us with a test of free will may
perhaps exist for asses – but even there this won't happen often, for
what farmer would take the trouble to provide his ass with two
identical bundles of hay equidistant from the animal, unless he has
already been corrupted by philosophy? Nor will such things be discovered in the context of human society. The logical error lies, I
believe, in failing to recognize that such a thought experiment would
only be compelling in empirical conditions in which real people exist,
while, on the other hand, as soon as you introduce a degree of reality
into the experiment, you inevitably introduce elements that would
deprive the example of its cogency. In other words, all the elements

that come from empirical reality and that form the basis for rational decisions become arguments, motives, for the human subject that has to make these decisions. This means that the determining factors come from outside, the very factors that ought to be stripped away on the grounds that the question of freedom in all these experiments is supposed to be an internal matter. This condemns these experiments to absurdity, to a pointlessness that will not have escaped you but that we shall encounter again in Kant (I say this now to prepare you for the shock). I should also like to take the opportunity to point out that the epistemological problem I have sketched here recurs with experiments throughout the social sciences. The situation there is that you might create chemically pure conditions to enable you to explore some problem or other, let us say, the problem of human aggression – I have in mind here a particular experiment that our institute here in Frankfurt was involved in a few years ago.[5] By the time you have done that, you have made certain decisions and thus reduced the available facts to the variables that can be strictly controlled (as they phrase it in the social sciences), with the result that the experiment will be so far removed from every possible empirical reality as to lose all validity.

Now, it is truly remarkable that Kant, in his eagerness to justify freedom and the validity of the moral law together with everything that goes with it, simply rides roughshod over all these objections even though he must have been fully aware of them. Instead, he allows himself to undertake a whole series of such mental experiments. I shall read one of them out to you from the *Critique of Practical Reason* – it can be found in chapter 1 of part I, the chapter on the 'Principles of Pure Practical Reason' – and shall then comment on it briefly. Before doing so, I can perhaps point out that the examples Kant uses – and I think that such matters are anything but trivial – are all characterized by a peculiar irritation, not to say fury. This fury is aimed as much at the presumed subjects of the experiment as at anyone who begs to differ or who declines to be impressed by such experiments. We are speaking here of a certain philosophical tone that is to be found first in Kant. It continues in Fichte, where it takes on what can only be called paranoid overtones. And, regrettably, it is even to be found far more frequently in Hegel than Hegel's admirers would like to believe. The first example is as follows:

> Suppose someone asserts of his lustful inclination that, when the desired object and the opportunity are present, it is quite irresistible to him; ask him whether, if a gallows were erected in front of the house where he finds this opportunity and he would be hanged on it

immediately after gratifying his lust, he would not then control his
inclination. One need not conjecture very long what he would reply.
But ask him whether, if his prince demanded, on pain of the same
immediate execution, that he give false testimony against an honour-
able man whom the prince would like to destroy under a plausible
pretext, he would consider it possible to overcome his love of life,
however great it may be. He would perhaps not venture to assert
whether he would do it or not, but he must admit without hesitation
that it would be possible for him. He judges, therefore, that he can do
something because he is aware that he ought to do it, and cognizes
freedom within him, which, without the moral law, would have
remained unknown to him.[6]

If Kant can construct such a piece of casuistry, empirical casuistry,
he must also put up with having it analysed according to the rules
he himself accepts. If we do that, we see that quite obviously his
example won't stand up. It is not necessarily true that the immediate
prospect of the gallows will deter men from obeying their instincts.
I would remind you of the countless instances in the Third Reich
where people offended against the race laws. They were not necessarily deeply in love, and were often enough just acting on the impulse
of the moment, only to find themselves subjected to a horrifying
punishment.[7] In the meantime, psychologists have long since shown
that actions that lead to such punishments are themselves based on
a motive – that of the so-called need for punishment – that goes back
to infantile fixations. Thus in reality things turn out to be quite different. Of course, you can say that all this is just psychobabble and
does not have the least connection with the purity and sublimity of
these furious thoughts of Kant's. But having proffered the example,
and having called upon us to accept it, as evidence for the existence
of the moral law as an effective empirical reality, he has no right
suddenly to appeal to pure *a priori* propositions: he can't have his
cake and eat it too.[8] Either he must remain within the confines of
the intelligible world – with the consequence that his moral law
would have no application to empirical reality, that it would therefore
be invalid. Or, if he wished to include the relation of the *mundus
intelligibilis* to empirical reality in the scope of his argument, he
would have to submit to the criteria that apply to that reality. In this
instance, the supposed cogency of the decision is either no more
than a function of the super-ego, in other words, something that is
itself determined by other factors, or, more likely, something heteronomous in the Kantian sense, namely, something that simply follows
its own self-interest and has little connection, therefore, with the
moral law.

A further example is to be found a few pages later. Here, too, we see the same bizarre aggression; a psychologist would probably say that the punitive urge in Kant is so powerful that it always leads him to make use of abominable deeds as examples so that by comparison with such crimes his morality will show him in a better light and enable him to enjoy a clear-cut triumph. It was for reasons of this sort that Nietzsche criticized Kant.[9] It would have been good for us to have been able to go into this question in depth, particularly since what is at issue is the true content of the formal imperative, and it would be valuable if we could really get to grips with the true meaning of this idea of the absolute validity of the imperative. However that may be, here is the passage in question:

> He who has *lost* at play can indeed be *chagrined* with himself and his imprudence; but if he is conscious of having *cheated* at play (although he has gained by it), he must *despise* himself as soon as he compares himself with the moral law. This must, therefore, be something other than the principle of one's own happiness. For, to have to say to himself 'I am a *worthless* man although I have filled my purse', he must have a different criterion of judgement from that by which he commends himself and says 'I am a *prudent* man, for I have enriched my cash box'.[10]

I understand nothing of gambling as it was customarily practised in the eighteenth century, when it had a very important social function – just read Casanova and *Manon Lescaut*, you find people engaged in gambling the entire time. But I believe that we can say that it is highly unlikely that a genuine card-sharp would bring himself to say 'I am a worthless man'. On the contrary, he will generally be content to believe that he is a clever man; or else that at least he is living in accordance with his own professional code, in other words, in accordance with what swindlers generally agree is legitimate or illegitimate. In all probability he will think it wrong to cheat another swindler. All in all, he will manage things in such a way that he will never have to utter the words 'I am a worthless man', a statement to be expected only in plays by Sudermann, but unlikely to be found anywhere else.[11] The true attitude of such a swindler is probably better captured by the anecdote of the burglar sitting in a pub deeply immersed in a newspaper. When a colleague asks him what he is reading, he replies with a straight face: 'I am just reading the review of my latest break in'. Here, too, we see that, if you let your imagination roam a little and apply just a little psychological insight to these illustrations that Kant presents with such aplomb, everything turns out to be quite different. As a final point, by way of criticizing these *experimenta crucis*, I should like to say that it is always assumed that the moral law has psychological force. Its validity is always presupposed, even though this *a priori*, ineluctable validity is supposedly to be demonstrated by these examples. It is because of this circularity that these Kantian examples seem so curiously inconsistent and unconvincing. I have already remarked that Buridan-like situations are not often witnessed, just as card-sharps are not in the habit of following up their actions with great moral reflections. They may indeed be extraordinarily moralistic, like criminals in general, but psychologists are well aware that their moralizing is always applied to other people whom actual criminals cannot condemn severely enough, while at the same time displaying a remarkable ingenuity in exempting themselves from the same strictures. I would say, and this is something that could perhaps be taken up by students of criminal psychology, that there are mechanisms at work here that seem to exempt them from a sense of their own guilt, psychological mechanisms that are of course capable of explanation. But in that case, situations like the two contained in the Kantian examples I have told you about would be entirely irrelevant to the lives of ordinary human beings.

Of far greater interest than these *experimenta crucis* is the need to make use of such experiments to assure ourselves of our freedom or lack of it. This need should not be dismissed as merely psychological; it has its own basis in knowledge. It testifies to the fact that, however much the theory of freedom or unfreedom aspires to achieve an *a priori* status, it nevertheless has something like the feeling or sense of its dependence upon the ontological, on actually existing reality. There is an aporia here that forces people, philosophers, into these experiments, which are then doomed to failure. In the absence of any relation to empirical reality of the kind that such experiments are supposed to generate, at least marginally – and if you look closely you can see that neither of these Kantian examples is lacking in empirical references – without such a relation to empirical reality, all talk of freedom would be null and void. This is because there would then be no way in which we could imagine how freedom might manifest itself in reality, even if an intelligible character is ascribed to it. However, the moment empirical reality is introduced, it becomes a determining factor and thus impairs the principle of freedom itself. This in turn leads to a reduction or misinterpretation of empirical reality that deprives that relation of its fruit. The concept of the intelligible character, a very strange, even absurd, and yet not unconvincing concept, is one that asserts that people have an essence that enables them to act freely, such that their actions represent the beginning of a 'new' causal chain, on the one hand, while, on the other, it lifts them out of the mechanism of cause and effect in nature. The introduction of this concept, this extremely difficult and fragile concept of the intelligible character,[12] is connected precisely with the problem I have been discussing with you today. It is the idea that the will cannot, as in the tradition of these experiments, be inferred as an existing, internal reality from the world of phenomena, but that it must be postulated as their precondition. And that involves all the difficulties of a naïve realism of inwardness, the naïve assumption of an existing inner world with its freedom or unfreedom. This is an idea which Kant subjected to a withering critique in other contexts – I have in mind his criticism of other reifications of mind such as the indivisibility, the indestructibility, of the absolute unity of the empirical soul in the paralogism chapter of the *Critique of Pure Reason*.[13] In general, and perhaps I may throw this out to you as a suggestion for academic research, it would be a rewarding task to examine the entire theory, not so much of Kant's *Groundwork of the Metaphysic of Morals* as of his *Critique of Practical Reason*, and to confront it with the arguments contained in the paralogism chapter. It seems to me that in very many respects the *Critique of Practical Reason* regresses to a point that the chapter on paralogisms had superseded. Nevertheless, I believe that something does emerge from Kant's experiments, and that is the reason, the *substantive* reason, not the epistemological reason, the critical reason, but the substantive reason why I have spent so much time and effort on these experiments and these Kantian examples. As I say, something does emerge from all this, and it is something of decisive importance for the problem of the will or unfreedom, for both, in fact, and without which all the discussions one can have about this topic have something rationalistic, something intellectual in the dubious sense – I hope I can use these words like this without running the risk of being misunderstood. It is as if the sphere of pure thought – I should like to give you a precise idea of this concept of the rationalistic or intellectual – as if the sphere of pure thought were directly and seamlessly identical with the sphere of action. In this sense the Kantian theory is rationalistic. It is in this sense that it goes back essentially to the ideas of freedom to be found in the older rationalism, particularly the rationalism of the seventeenth century, where it always seems as if only the intellect is capable of lifting itself out of the natural context; as if it were only as rational creatures that human beings could raise themselves just one little bit above nature, and that men are only free because they are thinking beings, *res cogitans*. In contrast to this,

these thought experiments – and I would like to return to the ass
belonging to the worthy Buridan – bring us face to face with something new, something that has been elided in the intellectualist conception of the will that in Kant is really nothing other than pure
reason itself. This something is what I call the 'additional factor' [*das
Hinzutretende*].[14] The decisions of the human subject do not simply
glide along the surface of the chain of cause and effect. When we
speak of acts of will, we experience a sort of jolt. The most basic
example of this, the story of Buridan's ass, does in fact give us an
inkling of this when we consider that even the ass, stupid though it
may be, still has to exert itself, to make a gesture of some sort, to do
something or other that goes beyond the thought-processes or non-
thought-processes of its pathetic brain. That is to say, it experiences
some kind of impulse, I would almost say a physical impulse, a
somatic impulse that goes beyond the pure intellectualization of what
is supposed, in the theories we have been discussing, alone to constitute the will. And the memory of this additional factor that we shall
have to discuss in some detail is preserved in these *experimenta
crucis*.

LECTURE 25

16 February 1965

CONSCIOUSNESS AND IMPULSE

Ladies and gentlemen, you will perhaps recollect that last time I spoke in some detail about the *experimenta crucis*, the thought experiments we encountered in connection with the question of freedom, and that this had led to two negative results. First, the inadequacy and lack of cogency in the conclusions reached by these experiments as such, particularly in the experiments conducted by Kant. And second, the problematic nature of this approach in general. Despite this, I believe that these experiments and, perhaps even more strongly, the need to conduct such experiments does lead somewhere, and, in particular, it has led to what I referred to last time or in the preceding lecture as '*the additional factor*', a term somewhat arbitrarily chosen, but one I feel comfortable with for that very reason. Sterile though these experiments may be, they do reveal one insight. This is that the decisions of the human subject do not simply glide along the surface of the chain of causality, but are pulled up short with a sort of jolt. I had already said as much to you, and even Buridan's ass – assuming that he finds himself faced with that rather luxurious choice – needs a bit of a jolt if he is not to starve to death. In the classical theory of freedom of the will, that is to say, from Leibniz and Spinoza on, this additional factor is interpreted as the intervention of consciousness. Consciousness alone is supposed to make it possible to alter the direction of a causal sequence by adding extra motives. Kant's card-sharp, for example, is motivated by his natural greed. Let us assume that despite everything he happens to reflect on the moral law or, even more simply (because according to Kant he does not even have to know the moral law), that he happens to recollect what he has been taught, in other words, 'Always be faithful and true / until you are in your cold grave.'[1] Perhaps our mythical card-sharp will be swayed by this to resist the causality of greed and to restrain the hand stretching out to seize the money. This may be true, although there is always a not entirely unfounded fear that any such change of mind may have been the product of reason, but in a quite different manner. Our card-sharp may well have said to himself that the risk of being caught was too great in this particular situation. Even so, there may be a grain of truth in this equation of the will with consciousness, and it would be a mistake simply to deny it in the interests of a purely voluntaristic theory of spontaneity. The way in which these two aspects are linked is something I hope to be able to explain to you in this lecture.

Without consciousness, there can be no will, that is evident. And no action that we could describe as an act of will could be an action without consciousness. In this connection I would draw your attention to the way in which – and this is an argument *against* the realm in which all these arguments take place – we are constantly forced to engage in the analysis of concepts (very much *contre coeur* in my own case), instead of being able to concentrate directly on matters of substance. Hence I had to tell you (and I could not have done otherwise) that when we speak of the will we necessarily speak of consciousness, and that in doing so we are concerned with phenomenology, with the analysis of meanings. Of course, these various meanings tell us nothing that is compelling about these complex matters of substance. At most they tell us that, if we wish to use the concept of the will, we cannot dispense with the concept of consciousness. I simply mention this in passing. The actual relationship between the analysis of meaning and the analysis of substance is not something we can pursue here; it belongs in a course of lectures on the theory of knowledge. Of course, such meanings always convey something of the underlying substance, so they are not to be despised, any more than they are to be made a fetish of. But I cannot go into this now. Unconscious action, an action in which consciousness does not intervene, of the sort we find on the part of the dying, or very sick people or the mentally disabled, is purely a matter of reflexes. It cannot be distinguished from other natural processes. Our entire experience of freedom is tied up with consciousness. Whenever we know ourselves to be free agents, however misguided or problematic our actions may be, we confront our actions with the consciousness with which we act – in contrast to the series of motives that I referred to a few lectures ago as 'ego-alien',[2] a term taken from psychology, but which I would like to think of as meta-psychological here. The human subject can know that he is free only when his actions seem to him to be identical with him as subject. That is the case only where his actions are mediated by his consciousness, are indeed essentially induced by his consciousness. This, then, is the legal justification of what might be called the rationalist theory of the will in the broadest sense, one that also includes Kant.

But consciousness is not simply identical with free action. Consciousness is not simply to be equated with the will, as is the case in Kant where ultimately the will is nothing but the capacity – or the quintessence of the capacity – to act as reason dictates. I believe that I can explain the distinction most easily, or, if you prefer, most vividly, with the aid of an illustration that is familiar to all of you and that was formulated at the birth of the modern age. What I have in mind is what literary scholars tend to call the problem of *Hamlet*.[3] You all know about how Hamlet, Prince Hamlet, is completely sane, but that he acts the madman in order to be able to avenge the murder of his father and to put the state of Denmark, in which something is rotten, again to rights. You all know too that this problem by no means exhausts the problem of Hamlet. The distinction between sanity and madness expresses itself in a further distinction that goes much deeper. The huge influence of this Shakespearean play and the fact that its relevance has endured over the centuries could not be adequately explained by the intrigue based on this act of dissembling. The real problem is that this man is incapable of performing an action that he believes to be right. This problem becomes entangled with the question of insanity because he finds himself cut off from reality in a way that really does possess structural similarities with madness. For it involves the same kind of withdrawal of libininal energy from external reality that is one of the most typical symptoms of schizophrenia. You all remember this situation, this chasm that opens up between inner and outer – you all recall his words about 'the pale cast of thought', thanks to which 'enterprises of great pitch and moment' are 'sicklied o'er'.[4] That is the substance of Hamlet's famous monologue. Its content, however, is philosophical in nature. And its modernity is probably connected with the fact that Hamlet's inner conflict stands at the beginning of the age of the bourgeoisie and of rationalism, the age of reflection. Hamlet is an outstanding example of a reflective person, and, as has been shown, knew his Montaigne inside out. Thus the chasm that has opened up between consciousness and action has to do with the philosophy of history and it is connected with the gulf between inner and outer that must have come as a great shock at around this period, a shock that we can scarcely

imagine and that has been reflected in philosophy in the writings of
Descartes, Shakespeare's near contemporary. Descartes drew a sharp
distinction between the two substances, the inner, 'thinking' substance and the outer reality to which action belongs, and only by
means of an artificial and superstitious contrivance was he able to
explain the way in which one of these might impinge upon the other
– this was the so-called *influxus physicus*, as he terms it.[5]

At the time when the medieval world refused fundamentally to
recognize this gap between inner and outer it was itself a self-
contained totality. The individual did not see himself as an autonomous thinking being whose reason stood opposed to an external
order. On the contrary, he regarded himself as an integral part of that
order. It was in this sense that he felt at home in the world. Incidentally, this is also the basic motif of all backward-looking speculations
about the Middle Ages, beginning with Novalis's essay *Christendom
or Europe*, and continuing down to our own day, with Georg Lukács's
magnificent *Theory of the Novel* deserving particular mention. It
should be noted, however, and I cannot speak of these matters without
pointing this out to you, that such writers failed to perceive the necessity for the demise of the medieval cosmos. This means that all these
retrospective reflections have something romantic and untrue about
them because these writers were so enamoured of the idea of a unified
culture, something Hegel called 'substantiality', an idea that plays a
central role throughout his writings and that he developed on the
model of the Greeks. These writings, I say, were romantic and untrue
because their authors were so enamoured of this unified quality or
substantiality that the question of the truth or untruth of the transcendental reference points, of the spiritual reference points on which
such an order rested, never even arose. Such writers then go on to
declare that what is genuinely or supposedly beneficial for mankind,
namely what Mr Bollnow would call the 'sheltered nature' [*Geborgenheit*][6] of such a constitution, is to be made the *index veri*, regardless of whether the state of our knowledge has undermined the
assumptions of such a medieval cosmos. We might almost go so far
as to criticize Romanticism by pointing out that it is profoundly
pragmaticist in its assumptions, in other words, the very opposite of
what it believes itself to be. By this I mean that romantic thinkers
infer the legitimacy of a spiritual order from the effect that it has,
without paying attention to its truth or untruth. Incidentally, this
development, which was magnificently codified for the first time in
Hamlet and Descartes, has a long prehistory in medieval nominalism.
The only difference is that, just as Hegel represents it as resembling
the petals that still lie concealed beneath their protective sepals,[7] so

too do these rational reflections begin by remaining within this medieval *ordo*, only to burst forth suddenly, at the time of the Reformation, and transform reality at a stroke. This change brought about by processes within the philosophy of history meant that, as a knowing, rational being, the conscious human subject withdraws his actions from the realm of the irrational, corrupt, bad reality confronting him – but it also means that the entire relation of the individual to this reality becomes problematic. Wherever the subject wishes to move to action, he finds himself in the grip of a *horror vacui*, unsure about how he will ever succeed in emerging from his own rationality so as to transform into reality what he has perceived to be rational and what actually constitutes the substance of a reflecting subjectivity. For the fact is that this reality whose meaning has been sucked out of it and has become wholly concentrated in the human subject itself no longer provides the basis for an intervention, and, indeed, has become so radically alien and opposed to the human subject that the latter prevaricates while attempting the simplest task and finds himself unable to cope. Thus in a philosophical sense Hamlet's feigned madness is also his true madness – one of the most inspired creative acts [*Innervationen*] in the history of art, but in all likelihood one that was only possible, like the later instance of *Don Quixote*, because its author was unaware of the philosophical background but simply codified the experiences that were triggered by that underlying shock.

If you think back to the plot of Hamlet – and I assume that you all have a thorough knowledge of the play – one fact will perhaps have struck you. This is that at the end, in the final scene, events, and here this means the most horrific killings, suddenly crowd in on us in a way reminiscent of puppets on a string. Up to now Hamlet, whose thoughts have prevented him from carrying out the deed that follows from his thoughts, and who has not succeeded in breaking the spell of thinking and escaping from his *monologue intérieur*, as we might put it nowadays, has suddenly, and I would add, irrationally, in a manner that leads directly to his own death, gone on a killing spree and has stabbed everyone who crosses his path. I believe that it is easy for us to criticize the improbability of these circumstances, in which events, poison and daggers seem to conspire together and bring about a conclusion that could not be attained by the conscious human will. But, as always with supreme works of art, it pays to reflect a little on what this denouement really *means*. For unless you want to reduce works or art to a sort of fetish, to plaster busts standing around in some museum or other, it is not enough for us to declare ourselves satisfied with the vague effect they have on us. We should instead try to discover the underlying reason for this effect. In the case of *Hamlet* I would suggest that what I have called the additional factor – and I hope that you will forgive me for this term – makes its appearance in the play, both inwardly and on the surface, in just as striking a manner as in the case of the rupture between inner and outer in the history of philosophy. The situation is that Hamlet has, rightly or wrongly, felt himself to be under an obligation to obtain revenge. This obligation itself is a relic from the Middle Ages, from feudalism, rather than a rational duty, but you can see from this too how the two epochs stand on a knife's edge in the play. Once he has felt this obligation, he can only succeed in carrying out his intention with the aid of a sudden, violent impulse that in the play stems from the fact that he himself has been wounded. And the Prince's action at this point seems to be unconnected with the complex, elaborate and rational reflections that have preoccupied him throughout the drama hitherto. The additional factor, that is to say, the element in his taking action that goes beyond rationality, can be studied here as in a test tube. And it is probably only the convention, a convention implanted in us for centuries, that compels us to measure this factor, without which there could be no action, against the yardstick of rationality. This explains why we tend to think that these final events are somehow puppet-like or ridiculous, since we fail to notice that what is happening is that this additional spontaneous factor, or what we might even call this irrational element, forces its way to the surface. I do not believe that I am likely to stand accused of lending support to any irrationalist theory of the will, in the spirit, say, of Carl Schmitt,[8] or even of Max Weber, but I do believe that, if you think seriously about these matters, you should not let yourselves be put off by the traces of such an idea, and that you should try to the best of your ability to see these things just as they are, in all their complexity. This factor, which I have called the additional or the irrational factor, survives as if it were the indestructible phase in which the separation between inner and outer had not yet been consolidated. If I can express it again in the context of the philosophy of history, I would say that, for Hamlet to be able to put into practice the moral and political ideas he has formed, he must perforce regress; he must return to an earlier, archaic stage – the stage of immediate expression, that is to say, of hitting out, something we are all familiar with from our dreams, where it happens often enough that we only need to conceive a hearty dislike for someone for us to feel like killing him in our dreams. Perhaps you are not wicked enough for that, but I at any rate have frequently experienced such things, and always felt a little disappointed when I woke up. Hamlet, then, must in a sense have acted in accordance with some such archaic desires in order to obtain his revenge. Revenge, for its part, is likewise an archaic phenomenon that is not really compatible with a rational, bourgeois order of things.

What is happening here, the factor that I should like to show you as being integral to the constitution of what we call will and freedom, is the factor that we refer to in pre-scientific discourse as spontaneous action, or, psychologically perhaps, as impulse – even though psychologists use the phrase 'impulsive characters' to describe people whose entire behaviour is conditioned exclusively by this aspect of their psyche. This impulse is both somatic and mental at the same time, and in all probability these two aspects cannot be separated out entirely. This is because, as I have already told you, when we act on impulse, we regress to a phase in which the separation between outer and inner is not as clear-cut, not as definitive as it is today. We might say that, setting aside its rational, modern, bourgeois, unified qualities, the will contains archaic features, to the point where we may legitimately ask whether something like the will is still possible today in a society that has become rationalized through and through. In the *Dialectic of Enlightenment*, Horkheimer and I wrote at one point, in connection with the problems of the culture industry, that, in the framework of total planning characteristic of the culture industry, human beings regress to the reactions of amphibians.[9] We might say that, once this archaic aspect of the will has been entirely ousted by planning and rationality, it paradoxically provokes a regressive reaction on the part of human beings. It means that they are no longer capable of will, impulse or spontaneity, but that they increasingly behave like guinea pigs about to be subjected to vivisection. It is my belief that in our society there are countless symptoms of the most terrible kind that amount to the sort of regression I have in mind – from the concentration camps that deprive people of their will-power down to certain methods of treating mental illnesses, so-called shock treatment. In a radically administered world, that is to say, in a world which, as I hope I have described it to you in the first part of these lectures, really had fallen under the thumb of the universal, undialectically and exclusively, the will would lose all its power. It would be supplanted by human reflex actions, in other words, by that dreadful realm that was first established by Pavlov's experiments. I have told you that the impulse of which I have been speaking is the same as the will and that its existence is the strongest and most immediate proof that there is such a thing as freedom; it is neither blind nature nor suppressed nature. It is quite possible that this impulse was originally a kind of reflex, too. In that case, it was only through the participation of consciousness in actions that were originally blind and reflexive in nature that this additional factor that I regard as a constitutive element of the will came into being. I can imagine that many of you who have not been trained or are disinclined to think dialectically will want to object at this point. You will want to tell me that I am appealing to an element that is supposed to be absolutely crucial for the constitution of freedom; and at the same time, if I trace the genesis, the origins, of this element back to its ultimate roots, I find myself back at something that has been determined by blind nature. It is my belief that this objection, which I have raised on your behalf, brings us to a point that is of crucial importance for philosophical thought as such.

It seems to me that what one has to learn in order to gain access to dialectics – I am not speaking here of the educational background and the technical knowledge required – is this: you need to free yourselves completely and utterly from the idea that everything that has ever existed is able to preserve itself in a form identical with what it once was. It is possible, and may even be the decisive factor that enabled human beings to emerge; it is possible, I say, for something age-old to survive and nevertheless to become radically different from what it originally was. In order to illustrate this, I usually refer to an example from[10] the world of aesthetics. The same music that has achieved such heights in Viennese classicism arose from the society of the absolutist courts and their need for entertainment; if the members of the aristocracy had had no need to amuse themselves, to kill time, such music would not have come into being. The innermost essence of this music is to compress temporal extension to a single point so that a lengthy elaboration sounds as if it had lasted no more than a moment. What I say is that, but for society's heteronomous need, a need quite external to art, a need that took the form of asserting: just make sure that we don't get bored – we should probably never have progressed to the style of the quartets of Haydn and Mozart and, ultimately, Beethoven's last quartets. Incidentally, these quartets will be the subject of a lecture tomorrow in the Music Department given by my young friend Rudolf Stephan.[11] If you look at works of this kind you will see that despite their origins, and despite the fact that *something* of the experience of time characteristic of the divertissement is preserved in them, they no longer have anything in common with the heteronomous phenomena that you will find in lesser products, such as the *Gebrauchsmusik* of Viennese classicism. Of course, it is very risky applying such arguments in such a speculative context, particularly where the subject matter is so well known, however plausible they may have seemed in historical terms.

But I should like to say that something that begins as a reflex often tends to make itself autonomous – and this is probably connected with the withdrawal of the subject from the world and the corresponding strengthening of the ego. This has the consequence that the reflection of the modern subject in its new-found strength falls upon what seems at first sight to be the ego-alien element of impulsive action; and that this action likewise turns into an impulse that is more powerful, and different in a certain sense than what the subject had intended vis-à-vis the object, but is nevertheless determined by the subject's desire for autonomy. We might even say – to put it crudely – that the reflex reaction ends up in the service of the ego-principle. Genetically speaking, this is not actually as outlandish as it may seem because the ego itself consists of libidinous energy that has split off and turned to the testing out of reality. In other words, the ego is not absolutely alien to this additional factor, this impulse, that I have been talking about.

With this impulsiveness, freedom extends into the realm of experience. If we behave spontaneously we are no more simply blind nature than we are suppressed nature. We feel that we are ourselves. But at the same time we feel we have been released from the spiritual prison of mere consciousness and this impulse enables us to enter, to take a leap – call it what you will – into the realm of objects that is normally barred to us by our own rationality. It is extremely hard for us to find the right expressions with which to describe these very profound matters without instantly reifying them. The irresistibility of impulses that we observe in ourselves, or at any rate that I observe in myself, and that I am sure you will perhaps also notice once you have trained yourselves to observe yourselves, is perhaps connected with the fact that in yielding to impulse we find that what I have called the Hamlet syndrome has for a moment been overcome. The sense of being divided, of being between inner and outer, is overcome as in a flash. Thus we believe that as long as we obey our impulses we shall find ourselves once again in the realm of objects from which we had withdrawn by an absolute necessity, albeit perhaps only in appearance. Thus the phantasm of freedom may be said to be something like a reconciliation of spirit, the union of reason and nature as it survives in this impulse. If I have represented the will or the acts of the will in a peculiarly dualistic way that will appear to many of you as over-mechanical and schematic – and I am well aware of the misunderstandings that can arise from an overly mechanical way of speaking – the fault lies with the way in which the utterances of freedom are tied to a reality full of contradictions. Moreover, these utterances themselves bear the stamp of those contradictions as I have described these two aspects. For – and with this comment I should like to bring this lecture to a close – you must not forget that both the elements that are needed if freedom is to make its appearance, in other words both reason and impulse, are mutually interdependent. Thus practice, including political practice, calls for theoretical consciousness at its most advanced, and, on the other hand, it needs the corporeal element, the very thing that cannot be fully identified with reason.

LECTURE 26

18 February 1965

KANT'S THEORY OF FREE WILL

I told you last time – and that was the final point in my last lecture as far as I can now reconstruct what I said then – that what is needed for a willed act or for practice in general is the coincidence of two antagonistic elements that do not become completely fused. On the one hand, there is intellect, reason, about which I would say that, if you take the notion of practice very seriously, it contains or presupposes the idea of the unrestricted, highly progressive theoretical consciousness. On the other hand, there is what I have labelled the additional factor, the bodily impulse that cannot be reduced to reason. I should like now to flesh out this idea with a few illustrations of what I mean. I believe that you can best obtain an idea of what I have in mind if you imagine the situation in which a man simply cannot stand by and watch any longer an incident of the kind I told you about in connection with Peter Altenberg in the context of my discussion of the idea of progress.[1] Altenberg described a man who is so hopelessly hysterical (as he put it ironically)[2] that he simply cannot bear to watch a coachman maltreating a horse, and so he intervenes and grabs his arm, or perhaps clouts him. I would say that where this kind of reaction is completely absent, where there is no indignation about the lack of freedom, there can be no room for ideas of freedom and humanity. Perhaps the gravest objection to Kantian moral theory is that it has no room for motives of this kind. In this context, when I returned from emigration I had an encounter that made an indelible impression on me and that I should not like to withhold from you. In the first few months after my return I met some of the very few survivors of the bomb plot of 20 July 1944 against Hitler, among them Herr von Schlabrendorff,[3] with whom I had a lengthy conversation. I asked him: How was it possible for you and your friends to go ahead with this plot, knowing that you faced not just death – something that might fit with a so-called heroic attitude – but things that were inconceivably more horrific than death? I told him that I could not imagine people who were able to muster the strength to look all that in the face and to go ahead in spite of it. Herr von Schlabrendorff replied, without much hesitation: 'The fact is I just couldn't put up with things the way they were any longer. And I didn't spend much time brooding about the possible consequences. I just followed the idea that anything would be better than for things to go on as they were.' I would say that this is the true primal phenomenon of moral behaviour. It occurs when the element of impulse joins forces with the element of consciousness to bring about a spontaneous act.

In Kant, in contrast, the situation is very different. The Kantian system abounds in assertions about the radical distinction between theory and practice, and the whole modern debate about the problem of theory and practice goes back to this distinction in Kant's philosophy. Nevertheless, it is a very remarkable fact that, all this notwithstanding, Kant remains under the spell of theoretical thought, even in the *Critique of Practical Reason*. All the descriptions that he gives, all the explanations of morality, are themselves theoretical explanations. His own 'practical reason' contains all sorts of ideas and the only thing that is missing is a statement about how to turn them into practice, and about what distinguishes them from purely theoretical ideas. For the distinction he himself draws is that the object of the moral, namely action, is something that flows purely from reason; it is something brought into being by the subject, whereas all other forms of knowledge refer to pre-existing subject matter. But, obviously, this distinction is purely epistemological, and it remains inside the entire dichotomy Kant sets up between form and content, a dichotomy that has nothing to say about the factor that actually determines the transition to practice. I have told you that the problem of freedom is historical in nature and it is not uninteresting to note that Kant has at least perceived the historical origins of our *reflecting* on freedom – even though within the framework of his system he always has to treat freedom itself as a constant, as transcendental, as something that transcends time. There is a passage in the *Groundwork of the Metaphysic of Morals* that speaks of a kind of Copernican turn in ethics and represents this turn as what might be thought of as a significant event in the history of ideas. He states, in chapter

2 of the *Groundwork*, that 'their authors [i.e., of previous efforts to ground morality] saw man as tied to laws by his duty, but it never occurred to them that he is subject only to *laws which are made by himself* and yet are universal, and that he is bound only to act in conformity with a will which is his own but has as nature's purpose for it the function of making universal law.'[4] By 'nature's purpose', of course, he does not mean the purpose of nature with its mechanical laws of causality, but something more like 'the nature of mankind', 'the conception of mankind'; this is one of the key passages demonstrating the changing meaning of the term 'nature' in Kant, and I commend it to you *en passant* for your own study of Kant. Incidentally, I should take the opportunity of telling you that it cannot be the task of a course of lectures like this one to reproduce the contents of books. Lectures as a form of instruction date back to a time when written books were not generally available and they have for a very long time preserved this archaic tradition of simply reporting the contents of books. Nowadays, when books are widely available such a procedure would be utterly pointless. Instead, it is assumed that students can read. I believe it is not a waste of time to say this, and I do so explicitly because of problems that have arisen in connection with the new law governing universities. Moreover, it is assumed not only that students can read, but that they do read in fact. What lectures can and should provide is reflections on such reading material, reflections that are driven by theory, but are not mere reproduction. I assume, therefore – I believe I have said this already, but it will bear repetition – that you really should read, and, indeed, study the basic works of Kant on moral philosophy relevant to these lectures. If you have not yet done so, you must do so in the vacation. Those of you who have not yet done the reading will only understand a whole series of things I have said when you have caught up with it. And I should like to say that this holds good for lectures in general. Philosophy is not a subject like law, for instance, where the lecturer tries to impart a body of knowledge that students then have to reproduce. Philosophy consists, as Kant would say, largely in philosophizing – and we must not regress to a position anterior to this Kantian definition.[5] Moreover, in the examinations you cannot expect only to be asked about things I have talked about here, but you can of course (and in the first instance) be examined on things that provide the materials for the reflections that I have been offering you here. All of this is basically too obvious to need saying, but I have every reason to remind you of it. And if I ever forget to give you proper references to what I regard as absolutely indispensable reading matter, I would be grateful if you could bring this to my attention so that it doesn't

get overlooked, something that can very easily happen to someone like myself who more or less lives in these things.

The passage that I have read out to you shows that according to Kant theoretical reflection about the universal validity and the autonomy of the moral law really comes at a later stage. However, and here is a very remarkable fact for you to ponder: the fact that theory emerges only at a late stage – and, as is well known, he equates it with his own discovery – does not lead him to conclude that if in all seriousness the categorical imperative is to be regarded as the yardstick of all right action, and that without it we cannot act morally, then it follows that all action that does not flow from this consciousness is in fact heteronomous, a form of action that is not moral at all, strictly speaking. Kant does indeed deny explicitly that this is the case, but only by appealing to natural law, to the more or less vague assurance that, even if people are not fully conscious of the moral law, it is somehow inherent in mankind as a kind of natural code and mankind needs only to discover it. Of course, this leads to a split in the concept of reason such that the objective reason of the moral law that is supposed to exist in every human being is said to be distinct from subjective thinking about the moral law. This split leads inevitably to a duplication of the concept of reason that is simply incompatible with the decisive theme of Kant's theory of reason, namely the *unity* of reason. Thus Kant's notion here is that it was not until quite a late stage that people became aware of morality as a purely autonomous state that was both universal and also specifically tied to the individual – and these are its two salient characteristics: it must be my *own* consciousness, but in so far as it is *my* consciousness it must necessarily be the *universal* consciousness. But if we agree with Kant on this point, it follows that if *reflection* about freedom is historical in nature, then freedom *itself* must be a historical category too. This truth is in fact implicit in the Kantian system and it was by no means overlooked or neglected. Nevertheless, although Kant arrives at this conclusion with regard to the species, he entirely fails to mention it as far as it affects the individual. The fact is that there are whole epochs in which concepts such as freedom – and hence the will – are completely absent. Kant is forced into all sorts of contortions to demonstrate the presence of moral consciousness everywhere, even in radical evil, just as he had argued for its presence in the minds of evil-doers and scoundrels in the passages I told you about earlier.[6] Had he not done so he would have been compelled to admit that these periods and stages of human development that lacked a so-called sense of morality did not deserve to be called human. For an adherent of Rousseau – which, as you know, is what Kant was – this would have been intolerable. Nevertheless, at this point where he needs to demonstrate that the consciousness of freedom and autonomy actually exist, he comes into an insoluble conflict with the facts because this claim cannot be made good in this way. I need only to remind you of the prevalence of blood vengeance in primitive societies for you to see the folly of believing in the empirical reality of the moral law as the expression of a universal law. For us to maintain that even headhunters have acted in accordance with the moral law, because that law is purely formal and without content, would surely be self-contradictory, since a universal principle according to which one man should cut off another's head to the best of his ability can hardly be deemed rational. It is an anachronism to talk of freedom before the individual has come into existence through a process of self-reflection – and when we speak of individuals here, we do not mean individual beings in a purely biological sense. What we mean are individual human beings who are capable of reflection and are constituted as individuals in a spiritual sense.

The inference to be drawn from this relates paradoxically to the inner composition of the concept of freedom. For if in fact freedom and the concept of freedom fall within the scope of historical consciousness, and if they are constituted by history and are, as I have suggested, historically ephemeral, then both the idea of freedom and freedom itself must be dependent upon the world, on the state of affairs in the world, even though by definition they are supposed to be independent of them and to have separated themselves off. It might be said that in a very real sense freedom now slips into the realm of determination, in other words, that the idea of freedom and the realization of freedom really are connected with the basic categories of bourgeois society in which so-called natural forms of dependence have disappeared in favour of the rational principle of equality and the equivalence of units of work in the course of exchange. Freedom can only be understood through the further development of this contradiction: namely, as the determinate negation of any given concrete expression of unfreedom, not, however, as a constant of the sort envisaged by Kant in his definition of freedom. We encounter the covert interlocking of freedom and unfreedom in Kant in a passage in the *Groundwork of the Metaphysic of Morals* that I would like to read to you in this connection: 'Now I assert', he says, and he says it with great emphasis, almost as if he were banging the table with his fist, 'Now I assert that every being who cannot act except *under the Idea of freedom* is by this alone – from a practical point of view – really free; that is to say, for him' – for every being like him – 'all

the laws inseparably bound up with freedom are valid just as much
as if his will could be pronounced free in itself on grounds valid for
theoretical philosophy.'[7] You can see, then, from this quotation that
this element of the dependent nature of freedom, this element of
unfreedom, casts the shadow of relativity over the concept of freedom
and by the same token over Kant's absolutist ethic. This is one of the
few passages where I would say that Kant in fact behaves in tune
with what his later psychologizing interpreters such as Hans
Vaihinger[8] say about him: the idea of freedom and freedom itself are
transformed into a fiction and as such, as an 'As if', they necessarily
lose the absolute validity they ought to have. It then becomes something of a necessity that, because I cannot escape from the notion of
freedom, I cannot act otherwise than 'under the Idea of freedom' –
regardless of whether or not freedom is a reality. In effect, Kant is
saying: because I cannot act otherwise than under the idea of freedom,
otherwise than under this idea, which might well turn out to be an
illusion, this means that in practical terms every being is genuinely
free. Whereas the truth is that we might infer from this quite simply,
with just as much rigour and with even greater certainty, that if I
possess only the consciousness of my freedom without being assured
that this freedom really exists in itself, as would surely be necessary,
then I am self-deceived in believing that my own actions are free
actions. The doctrine of freedom thus turns out to be a necessary
fiction, we might even add: in utilitarian terms, in pragmatic terms.
This is because, were it not for this supposition which, according to
Kant, remains theoretically unproven, I would be unable to act at all;
indeed I would be unable to live at all. At the very point where it
would have been essential to demonstrate the objective nature of the
concept of freedom, and to make good its largest possible claims, to
'salvage'[9] them, as Kant puts it, at the point where an extreme objec-
tivism would have been called for, we find him relapsing into a primitive subjectivism. Elsewhere Kant's philosophy set its face against
such subjectivism by maintaining that objectivity was itself constituted by the subject. You can see how deeply the antinomies that we
are struggling with reach down into the Kantian theory, and how
they are recorded there. It is a mark of Kant's greatness that these
things always emerge clearly in his writings, but it goes without
saying that he does not reflect on them as such in any detail in the
Critique of Practical Reason or in the simpler *Groundwork on the
Metaphysic of Morals*.

Kant is discussing a creature that is supposed to be unable to act
except in obedience to this idea; he is discussing actual human beings
who, according to the *Critique of Pure Reason*, are subject to the

laws of causality. He wishes to overcome the impasse, the *non liquet*, with which the Third Antinomy of the *Critique of Pure Reason* had ended, namely its conclusion that the thesis of absolute determination and the thesis of infinite freedom are equally plausible. He desires to overcome this *non liquet* and to achieve a positive outcome for the sake of practical reason, namely, by demonstrating that freedom is a *given*. He does not succeed, however. Despite this, he is compelled to maintain this theoretical *non liquet* because even in practical reason his conclusions must be reached within the realm of theory. This is connected with the primacy of theory in his thought to which, against his will, even practical reason is subject. This explains why this *non liquet* keeps making its appearance. He thus finds himself constantly being forced into these rather sophistical arguments: whatever the position of the subject, it could not act otherwise; we are compelled to bow to the 'As if'. It is evident that it is precisely this attempt – and this is Kant's actual attempt to salvage his argument – to shake off the impasse of the Third Antinomy that forces him into mediations again and again, despite his blunt dualism. That is to say, he finds himself forced to establish a link between the idea of freedom and actual human subjects who, according to him, are supposed to be free to act. As I have already suggested, it is this manoeuvre that makes the idea of freedom appear curiously paradoxical: human beings cannot act otherwise than under the idea of freedom, their subjective consciousness is chained to it. This means that freedom has its basis in unfreedom. Put in another way, the very thing that is defined in Kant's theory of freedom as rational action presupposes that rational reflection has been broken off: in other words, a form of behaviour in which I abandon rational analysis and rational questioning, but simply float without questioning within a horizon 'as if I were free'. And at the very point where I imagine myself to be free, I find myself dependent upon my so-called nature, my constitution, the fact that I am like this and not otherwise – this is something we have discussed at length, namely how the human subject knows that he is free – and in this sense freedom is chained to causality. This, if you like, is the point at which the emphatic conception of nature as human nature, the concept of nature that is at work in natural law, comes together after all with the idea of nature as a mechanism of cause and effect, nature as something constituted, a *constitutum*, the so-called *natura naturata*. In other words, this is the point at which the power and the spell of the Kantian *natura naturata* extends its sway to include the Kantian *natura naturans*, the free and spontaneous human being.[10] The idea [of *natura naturans*] is grounded in the empirical mind that is very prone to self-deception, as we can see

from countless acts of introspection; freedom is at the mercy of the
contingencies of time and space.

This is a point at which we can pause and reflect on the extent to
which the progress of the individual sciences has impinged upon
philosophy. In Kant it is still the case that he continues to place his
trust in the bourne of introspection: I need only immerse myself in
the hidden depths of my own mind, and need only observe whatever
is stirring and whatever is going on and whatever is achieved there
and I shall be able to discover the universe and its laws within myself.
Kant was ignorant of a truth that had been recognized relatively early
on by the great psychologists, the moralists, people such as La Rochefoucauld, long before Kant. This was that even my knowledge of
myself is just as imperfect, just as much at the mercy of the *idola fori*,
the 'idols of the marketplace',[11] as my conventional views of the
external world. I believe that one needs only observe oneself becoming involved in some dispute or other with other people, and see how
one behaves in a naïve, uncontrolled way, to realize that the motives
we give ourselves for our actions are always a lot nobler than they
are in fact. I am often struck by this and by the way in which everyone, absolutely every human being, believes that he is in the right.
Infinite intellectual and moral strength is needed to set limits to this
tendency and to refrain from claiming the moral high ground in even
the pettiest details of daily life. Now, in its formal structure this self-
justification fits very well with Kant's theory of the moral law. The
moral law is so similar to this and his idea of freedom seems to be
so completely modelled on this procedure that we have to admit that
there is a real source of self-deception here. We might well conjecture
that one of the sources, and not the least important one, of the idea
of the absolute nature of the good or of the moral law to which
Kantian philosophy aspires is the belief people have in their own
goodness, not just in their relations with others, but also in themselves. This belief is the product of the mechanisms of rationalization
and self-justification, as well as narcissism, but its most profound
source lies in people's desire to ward off reproaches and criticism. We
should say that the task of morality should really be to destroy this
illusion instead of borrowing one's own categories from it, as is the
case with Kant. The great moralists such as La Rochefoucauld and
La Bruyère and Chamfort are frequently made the butt of criticism,
and dismissed as rhapsodic, essayistic and fragmentary. But in this
sense they are far more radical in a moral sense than the great sys-
tematizer of morality, who would undoubtedly have looked down on
them with contempt. The way in which causality and freedom inter-
lock in Kant reveals the cloven hoof in his philosophy in the fact that

almost all the so-called mediating concepts that are meant to bridge the *chorismos*, the gulf, separating the pure, intelligible sphere from that of empirical existence, are repressive in character. Whenever the moral law is supposed to reveal itself in the minds and actions of empirical human beings, *in* their empirical consciousness, it takes on the aura of coercion. You can easily see this by looking at his terminology, that is, the figures of speech Kant uses whenever he sets out to explain the impact of the intelligible subject upon the empirical one. He speaks constantly of law, coercion, respect, duty and suchlike. Through the will, Kant says – here we have the Kantian definition of the will. I hope that I shall find time to give you a different definition of the will in the course of these lectures, which now are unfortunately drawing to an end far too soon – Kant's idea is that through the will reason will be able to procure reality for itself. This is the point at which all of Kant's statements converge, and reason turns out to amount to the idea of pure laws.

I can't read you all the examples that I wanted to give you because there is not enough time, but I should like to read one brief passage from chapter 2 of the *Groundwork of the Metaphysic of Morals*, where Kant states that 'The will is conceived as a power of determining oneself to action *in accordance with the idea of certain laws.*'[12] This conception of law is derived from reason, which is designated by Kant as thinking in terms of necessity and universality, that is, as thinking according to rules. This conception of law entails restrictions on freedom, since it turns freedom into something that might be termed unfree because of the need to obey the laws. It is precisely the same motif that freedom is actually nothing but the consciousness of the law that dominates the whole of German idealism and recurs in the vulgar-Marxist thesis that at bottom freedom means acting and forcing onself to do according to one's consciousness what objective determining factors are supposed to have made necessary. Reason creates reality for itself independently of the material: this – as I explained at the beginning of this lecture – and not its *opposition* to the concept of law is what defines Kant's conception of freedom. Thus freedom is to be found exclusively in the way in which a rationality that is regarded as conforming to laws relates to the sphere of objects. Thus freedom consists in the fact that I am not bound to any given material in order to exercise the functions of my reason, but that I can simply follow them in a pure fashion. But since according to Kant reason is nothing but the ability to think in accordance with laws, freedom is necessarily reduced to obedience to lawfulness. Kant finds nothing to object to in the idea that reason is determined, that it is determined by the concept of law and that it must abide by laws. He goes even further in this respect since his conception of reason consists in this identity of action with the conformity to law. The paradox that freedom is nothing but a conscious lawfulness lies at the heart of Kant's grounding of his ethics. It follows that, if abstract subjectivity falls away, that is, if this purely legislative rationality ceases to be imagined as the absolute *constituens* or regulative – both are essential for Kant – this can only detract from the theory of freedom. And given what I have told you about the relation of Kant's theory of freedom to his conception of law, it is no accident that at one point in the *Groundwork* he opts for the paradoxical statement that freedom is a kind of causality. He opens chapter 3 with the emphatic statement that '*Will* is a kind of causality belonging to living beings so far as they are rational. *Freedom* would then be the property this causality has of being able to work independently of *determination* by alien causes.'[13] Thus freedom does not mean that I do not act in accordance with laws, that I am not subject to laws; it means that these laws are to be identical with the laws governing my own rationality. However, since in Kant all the laws that actually exist are the laws of my own reason, it follows that, in the light of the definition of freedom I have just read out to you, the theory of freedom is profoundly restricted and even revoked by Kant himself. This is because, astonishingly, the laws of consciousness in Kant are thought not to impair freedom, but actually to create the conditions for its emergence. The oxymoron of 'causality born of freedom' is based on the equation of will and reason regarded as conformity with law. It is the supreme expression of rationalism, of what might be called the rationalist wing in the army of Frederick the Great which Kantian philosophy draws up on parade.

LECTURE 27

23 February 1965

WILL AND REASON

Ladies and gentlemen, since I face a hopeless task in dealing with all the material I had intended to present to you, I believe that my best course will be simply to proceed as if nothing were amiss and to break off next Thursday at the point I happen to have reached. Any other solution, any attempt to 'round off' these lectures, would be artificial and of no benefit to you. I hope, therefore, that their fragmentary nature, something that seems almost inherent in their form, will not come as too much of a disappointment to you.

I shall perhaps repeat what I brought to your attention last time. This was that, despite the opposition between theoretical and practical reason of which Kant makes so much, reason *qua* reason remains the same, separate from objectivity of every kind. That is to say, this Kantian concept of reason remains purely instrumental, and even the concept of practical reason lacks all trace of what I have called the additional factor. If we think of the will as a unity in tension between reason and this other factor, then we might speak of it as the voluntaristic element in a narrower sense. Now in Kant – and I believe this will give you an idea why reason has the same meaning in both theory and practice in Kant, and why the concept of reason should play this peculiar, even ambivalent, role in his thought – in Kant reason is the refuge of ontology. By this I mean the following: formerly an order was supposed to exist in Being itself, and was looked for there; this was an *objective* order, however you might wish to interpret the word 'objective'. This objective order was then dissolved by nominalism, but elements of it were transposed into the very organ which nominalism has used to effect that dissolution, namely, reason itself which nominalism came to regard as Being in itself. On the other hand, however, in its Kantian formulation, reason is nothing but the quintessence of the subjective capacity for thought or subjective thought as such. This is the source of the curious ambivalence in the concept of reason as it is employed by Kant. On the one hand, reason is pure subjectivity. That is to say, it is purified of everything non-mental, everything that is not itself subjective. On the other hand, it is the prototype of every conceivable objectivity, that is, it is Being-in-itself, the thing in which the possibility of an order of contingent being is concentrated. This is summed up in Kant's famous definition:[1] objectivity is simply what can be known according to the rules of reason. Thus the entire Kantian project of salvaging the idea of objective truth that had been undermined by nominalism[2] was founded on this ambiguity. Note that this project was based not on a leap outside subjectivity, but was enacted *in* subjectivity, or at least passed *through* it.

The ambiguity in Kant's concept of reason, which I have touched on without being able to explain its implications fully, is extended to his concept of the will. This will come as no surprise to you now that I have made it clear that his notion of will is basically nothing but reason in the sense that reason is supposed to be capable of creating its own objects, namely, actions. As spontaneity, the will is supposed to be the innermost principle of subjectivity, the thing that cannot be objectified, as we see in his conception of theoretical reason, whose central idea is the idea of spontaneity or, as he calls it, the original apperception. However, since it is both stable and identical with itself, it becomes objectified and is converted into what goes by the name of '*character*' in the developed form of Kant's moral philosophy, where it plays a crucial role. In other words, it becomes a hypothetical being within the empirical world or, at any rate, a being that is credited with the possibility of impinging on the empirical, something that would be inconceivable in the absence of an affinity to that world. And this makes it commensurable with the empirical world. Because the will gives itself a shape in existence, this *ontological* objectivity we find in Kant, an objectivity of pure efficacy, itself achieves a sort of existence, if you like a second-degree existence, a derivative existence. This purely ontological aspect of the will, of the will as something that exists in itself, independently of all conditions, then reverts in Kant, without his drawing attention to it explicitly, into something ontic, a piece of existence in itself – something that is expressed in his use of the term 'character'. It is only because of this ontic dimension that we can say that the will *creates* its own objects in the object-world, namely, actions. Were this not the case, were the will really nothing more than pure possibility and not also something existing in the world, this would imply the existence of such a Platonic abyss between the will as an idea and the world to which it stands opposed that we would be unable to conceive of real actions proceeding from the will into the world. Such an idea would be exposed to the same criticism as Aristotle's criticism of Plato's doctrine of ideas,[3] and it is worth noting that this aspect of Kant's philosophy is in fact very close to Plato.

We may perhaps home in on this criticism of Kant's doctrine of the unity of reason by saying that it presupposes the abstract separation of reason from its referent, from what it relates to and what it continues to be determined by. In the same way, every synthesis – and reason is after all the capacity for synthesis – does more than create order and structure in things that are external to it and contingent. It becomes truth only by expressing as a synthesis the substantial content of the underlying objects. This is one of the hardest things to grasp about philosophical or speculative logic, because the fact is that these two elements cannot be separated. There can be no synthesis, no judgement, unless what is being joined together in fact belongs together. In other words, it does not belong together simply because it is joined together (if I may put it in this way). The difficulty is the curious one that every attempt to resolve it in one direction or the other, without including its opposite, is necessarily doomed. Incidentally, this contradiction at the heart of synthesis seems to me to contain the innermost philosophical justification of what we understand by dialectics. Kant does not proceed in the spirit of this duality, this insistence that there can be no synthesis in the absence of the things synthesized, but instead he splits the form of knowledge from its content. This was the objection that Hegel forcefully advanced by way of criticism. He was the first to do so, although the same objections had been implicit in Maimon and Fichte. However, this criticism applies also to Kant's doctrine of the will because his theory of the will and hence of freedom is structured in the same way as his doctrine of reason.[4] This definition of the will, this doctrine of the will, is falsified by the absolute separation of the will from its material – in other words, of the will from what it is supposed to set in motion. Instead of giving you a long-winded explanation of this I would prefer to show you what is meant with a very simple and, as I believe, very persuasive illustration. It is well known that in one of its versions the categorical imperative states that we should never treat human beings merely as means, but always also as ends – whatever we are to understand here by 'treat'.[5] If other human beings were simply

material with which to ignite the 'pure' action of the will (to use
Fichte's way of speaking), if, then, the will were not also determined
by the objects of its action, namely by other human beings – to whom
Kant makes explicit reference – then action strictly in accordance
with the categorical imperative would *at the same time* violate that
same imperative. That is to say, it would bring about the very thing
that the categorical imperative wishes to prevent. Human beings
would in fact be no more than a means; they would be a means
whereby the categorical imperative is to be fulfilled, instead of being
included within the scope of the categorical imperative as ends in
themselves. In consequence, the very mode of behaviour that Kant
recommends as the supreme expression of the principle of morality
turns into immorality pure and simple. For, in that case, human
beings would in fact become mere means for a second time, not
indeed the means to any inferior or secondary ends, but the means
by which the moral law could be fulfilled. This is a conclusion which,
monstrous though it may appear to you, was one actually drawn by
Fichte in his moral philosophy. We can put it another way: we can
say that in Kant's philosophy moral behaviour is supposed to be more
concrete than mere theoretical behaviour – this is because it is enacted
and takes shape in reality. In the event, it turns out to be even more
formal than theoretical action because in his philosophy theoretical
action is at least attached to some sort of material. This material may
be thought of as free of all qualities, as chaotic or amorphous, but it
still makes its presence felt in every possible way in the formulations
of theoretical reason, even if only as a marginal concept.

Here we have reached the point where modern critics – Scheler,
above all – have raised objections to Kant's moral philosophy. What
they disliked was its formalism. Before saying something briefly about
that formalism, I should like to make you aware that, in contrast to
Scheler's position – Scheler, incidentally, was my predecessor in this
post, many years ago[6] – things have changed in important and even
crucial respects. Kant is always castigated for his formalism, by which
is meant that substantive and concrete elements of the good or of
good actions are not only absent but are in fact taboo. However, the
point is that this fact in itself contains an element of content or substance. This formalization contains the entire history of rationalization of Western philosophy and Western society, including its
progressive aspects. It is my belief that, when people talk about the
problem of so-called formalism in ethics, they are all too easily
tempted to ignore this element. If I may formulate this more concretely, I would say that so-called Kantian formalism incorporates the
recognition of the bourgeois equality of all subjects, not just before

the law, the legal system, but also before the moral law. Anyone who
like me has had experience of what the world looks like when this
element of formal equality is removed – from the legal system, let us
say – in favour of specific substantive values that are asserted in an
a priori fashion, he will know from his own experience, or at the
very least from his own fear, just how much of humane value resides
in this concept of the formal. When distinctions all vanish in their
object, that is to say, when all human beings are reduced to the
abstract definition of 'human being', to the exclusion of their specific
characteristics, this provides people with a measure of protection and
justice. If I call this principle the bourgeois principle or a progressive
bourgeois principle, what I mean to say is simply that it spells the
abolition of feudal privileges at the hands of bourgeois society, privileges that extended even into logic, or at least into the logical foundations of moral philosophy. Thus the idea of equality before the law,
on the one side, and, on the other, the fascist distinction according
to specific, allegedly *a priori* differences that are supposed to exist
between people once and for all – this distinction is truly crucial.
Let me sum up the position more generally, more fundamentally, in
a thesis, or what would formerly have been called a theorem. Our
world, as you know, is organized according to the principle of
exchange, the principle of equality; it is a world governed by abstract
rules. In an unchanging abstract system every appeal to concrete distinctions always, necessarily, becomes an injustice to concrete human
beings. It could be shown that Scheler's material value-ethics already
signals the return of ideas based on privilege. And even though it
would be wrong to accuse Scheler of fascist leanings, Ernst Troeltsch
was not far off the mark in his book on historicism when he claimed
that the turn to the concrete and material in Scheler was a kind of
prelude to a general political reaction.[7] If you think that the concept
of the concrete has to bear the kind of metaphysical weight I assume
it does,[8] if you believe that utopia has what I would call the colour
of the concrete, it becomes all the more important to oppose the terrible, catastrophic misuse of the term, and to prevent it from being
hypostasized and from being used as a weapon with which to sabotage reason. On the other hand, however, and this has to be said if
we wish to be even-handed, the abstract nature of legal and moral
systems is no less unjust. They cut away everything specific to living
human beings and treat them as if they were merely impersonal
parties to contracts. For in our world every category conceived in
isolation inevitably leads to violence and injustice. Aristotle showed
he understood this in the *Nichomachean Ethics* when he supplemented the concepts of justice and righteousness with that of fairness,

equity.[9] And this involved an admirable attempt to incorporate the incommensurable natural distinctions between beings in the rational order without bursting the bounds of that order. This theory still survives in our ordinary phrase 'that's all right and proper' [*recht und billig*],[10] so deeply is this problem engraved in the spirit of the language, but whether this attempt at inclusion is possible or whether a far greater effort and a far more radical solution is called for is something I should like to leave for you to meditate on.

At any rate, Kantian ethics owes its semblance of objectivity exclusively to this formalism and hence to its utter subjectivism. By excluding every objective determinant, it becomes in its own view, according to its own self-understanding, pure being, Being-in-itself. But that in turn condemns it as pure being to the kind of irrationality that proclaims itself in the coercive principle of Kantian ethics, the coercive side of the categorical imperative about which I have talked repeatedly. And if I may try once again to clarify this I would say that, when you come down to it, to act in accordance with the moral law really always means: obey, fit in with the moral law without having complete insight. The attempt to obtain complete insight is associated by Kant himself with doubting its absolute validity and is accordingly defamed by his use of the term 'pseudo-rationality' [*Vernünfteln*][11] or sophistry or sophistical scepticism. But by the same token an element of truth is unmistakable in the objectification of the will of which I have spoken. This consists in the way in which the self achieves autonomy, in which the various stirrings, the divergent and frequently diffuse stirrings of the self, nevertheless retain a certain identity, and come to form what the language of our experience is accustomed to call our 'character'. Character is an intermediate term between nature (because it has its place in the constituted world as a synthesis of manifestations) and the *mundus intelligibilis* (because by virtue of that unity it can oppose the natural impulses of the isolated individual, or at any rate keep them under control). Since Kant's philosophy is constructed on the principle of non-contradiction this gives rise to the difficulty that its concepts become aporetical, that is to say, they must give rise to assertions that are mutually contradictory. Since these difficulties arise from the criteria of non-contradiction that Kant has made his own, he must bear the blame for them. However, they disappear as soon as we free ourselves from the idea that any concept of this sort, in this case the concept of character, must be all of a piece and free from contradictions. For in fact the very essence of such a concept requires it to contain contradiction, to be antithetical or full of tensions. Incidentally, this highly significant intermediate position of character between nature and the intelligible world has been explored in great depth, without any of the methods of dialectics, in a very important early essay by Walter Benjamin, 'Fate and Character', which I suggest that you should all read at some point. I believe that it is one of the most important recent contributions to the problem we are discussing here.[12]

The will, then, is always a diversion from the immediate goal of the instincts, it is sublimation. If we talk about the will in general terms, if we say, for example, that someone is strong-willed, then we are talking about his character, the harmonious unity of his actions according to a central principle that dominates him, an idea that is in fact not too far removed from Kant's own localized principle. The opposite of the will and the character would then be what has been dissolved – just as, to remind you of something you all know, the subtitle of Mozart's *Don Giovanni* is *Il dissoluto punito*, that is, 'The Rake Punished', in which the word 'rake' translates *'dissoluto'*, a dissolute man, one who dissolves in all directions, who is not subject to a sustained, harmonious rational principle. This leads us to the heart of the moral taboos on polygamy and libertinism – the use of infidelity as an example always points to the failure of the unifying discipline of the concept of the ego. Those of you who possess a copy of the *Dialectic of Enlightenment* – I know that it is not easily obtainable[13] – but those of you who have managed to get hold of one will find some very interesting things in the second excursus, the one dealing with the Marquis de Sade's *Juliette*, about this idea that a strict morality is a way of turning against a diffuse nature. They are very interesting because the wish to glorify the dominant, unifying principle over an instinctual and diffuse nature in the bourgeois age brings together thinkers whose ideas are otherwise incompatible. Indeed, on this point they are so very much in agreement that it would be easy to discover passages from one in the writings of another even though on other matters they would be willing to condemn one another to the flames of Hell. The progressive element in this Kantian doctrine can be compared to the progressive aspect of Protestantism: there is a decisive break with the medieval justification by works, and this takes place inwardly, in the moral world of the subject – and not just in the idea of a justification before God. Human beings are to be judged not by their individual acts, but, as the saying goes, by what they *are*. I may remind you of Schiller's saying with which you are probably more or less familiar: 'Common natures pay with what they *do*, noble ones with what they *are*.'[14] I would note that what is interesting about this quotation, particularly from the point of view of theory, is that Schiller, who was a Kantian, makes use of the concept of nature here, at a point where it is least expected, something that would surely have been anathema to Kant. This will be comprehensible only if you recollect that Schiller was very concerned to bridge the radical gulf, the Kantian *chorismos*, between spirit and nature that Kant had introduced, and in this respect he was very much in agreement with Goethe. Hans von Bülow, the disciple and friend of Richard Wagner, a man of a caustic turn of mind, joked about this Schillerian sentiment that common natures pay with what they do, while noble ones pay with what they are. He remarked that this must mean that it was the noble natures who avoided paying their debts. This joke points to the central issue – and there is no reason to believe that Bülow was conscious of its far-reaching philosophical implications – that the sedimented interiorization that is involved here constitutes an offence against the individual, living person. It also has the further consequence that, by establishing a polarity between a person's individual acts and his individual works, on the one hand, and his actual being, on the other, this anti-naturalistic moral philosophy goes into reverse and ends up in a kind of doctrine of nature that amounts to the assertion that if a person is noble, that is to say, noble by nature, everything is permissible to him, whereas 'lesser' human beings are not similarly entitled. This idea, incidentally, was not completely alien to Goethe. His Faust, after all, asserts that 'A good man, in his dark bewildered stress, / Well knows the path from which he should not stray.'[15] And having said that, he is promptly taken up into Heaven despite the fact that he has committed foul murder, as well as other horrific crimes, and that in old age he has tacitly colluded in the violent death of Philemon and Baucis, an elderly married couple, simply because he cannot bear the fact that their wretched little house blocks the view of his vast estate.[16] I do not know whether Kant scholars have ever taken a closer look at these matters.[17]

I should like to return briefly to the relationship between reason and will. From what I have said you will have understood that I understand this relationship to be one of discontinuity. I have explained this discontinuity from the vantage point of the will; but it might equally well be explained from the point of view of reason. In the shape of objectivity, of so-called logical reason, reason has its origin in the suppression of impulse and of impulses of the will. Reason has become what it is only because it has separated itself from that additional factor, from the element of impulse that is characteristic of the will, and this testifies to the fact of discontinuity. It is like the common figure of speech about 'wishful thinking'[18] which I have mentioned several times in the course of these lectures, a type of thinking in which the wish is father to the thought. This kind of wishful thinking has parted company with theoretical reason in the narrower sense, with pure thought as such. This voluntaristic element has vanished from logic in the Hegelian sense. What is crucial for logic is to be something in its own right. But this disappearance of origins, of the impulse behind thought in logic, conceals the fact that it is above all the logical form of organization that serves domination; that logical thought and the discipline that logic requires of human beings is itself dependent, conditioned by the power of the will. Reason only becomes available as an instrument for every conceivable desire through its objectification, through its being uncoupled from desire. The eradication of will from thought, from reason in its succinct sense, from theoretical thought, is the price reason must pay for its being put absolutely at our disposition for every conceivable purpose – in other words, for its being of practical use. The *relatedness* of logic, in other words, the element of will contained in the fact that logic is always concerned with something not itself and what it wants, or what something or other wants with it, survives in a highly etiolated state in the fact that logical propositions are all necessarily related to something or other. This compels me to modify and refine a number of theoretical statements that I have made in the past about 'logical absolutism and objectification', in my *Against Epistemology*.[19] But I find that time has run out and this will have to wait for next time.

LECTURE 28

25 February 1965

MORAL UNCERTAINTIES

Last time, we talked about how to differentiate the will from the definition of pure reason, not from the standpoint of the will, but from that of reason. Perhaps you will recall that I pointed out that the specificities of pure logic, which in general are those of reason, are also in reality the sedimented specificities of the will, which admittedly disappear in it. I mentioned then – and I would like to remind those of you who wish to go more deeply into this question – that I have found it necessary to make a major correction to what I wrote in the chapter on 'The Critique of Logical Absolutism' in *Against Epistemology*, since what I wrote there was too one-sided and could even be misunderstood as a relapse into a psychologistic approach to logic. Those of you who are familiar with the tenor of the book will know that this was not my intention, nor could it ever be. Nevertheless, I think it worth mentioning at this point. In *Against Epistemology*, I had placed great emphasis upon the genetic aspect in so-called formal logic, and hence ultimately upon its relation to existing reality, and brought out this aspect very strongly through what I hope were convincing analyses. But in the course of my argument I neglected the Hegelian element that constantly recurs in Hegel under the heading of 'disappearance'. In this instance, this refers to the idea that, despite its dependence on the genetic elements I have referred to, logic possesses an objective validity – and this is something Hegel really did understand very clearly. What this means is that these genetic elements, in other words, the elements related to particular aspects of being, 'disappear' in the context of the validity of logic.

Thus logic is both absolute and something that has developed, that has arisen – precisely by virtue of that objective process of reification that I had described in my book, a process that was not merely something negative, a forgetting, but one that also formed the constitution of an objective region (as Husserl's 'Logic' would call it). We might go so far here as to speculate whether the absolute separation of genesis and validity that I retained even while criticizing it is not itself a false distinction, a pseudos.[1] Perhaps we have accustomed ourselves under the influence above all of Husserl and Scheler to thinking of validity and genesis as absolutely distinct, as a *choris*, and in the process have fallen victim to a false consciousness; and perhaps, once we admit that these two elements are not mutually exclusive and irreconcilable, we shall be able to see how a mediation may be brought about between objective validity, objective ontological validity (if I may call it that) and an ontic state of having developed, a genesis. You may say – if I may continue for a moment with this speculative line of thought – that even though the system of logic is a realm free of contradiction, it nevertheless contains a profound contradiction by which it is in a sense enchanted and which cannot be resolved by recourse to logic itself. To put it in a nutshell, this contradiction is the fact that logic both is and is not a historical product. This will perhaps enable you to see that dialectics is not simply an additional factor to be superimposed on traditional logic, but something that penetrates to, and is encapsulated in, the innermost cells of pure logic itself.

We might say that Schopenhauer was a thoroughgoing idealist in the sense that reason itself is what he called the negation of the will to life or, at any rate, reason is *also* that. In other words, reason is a reification, albeit one in the service of the so-called will to life. There is a real conflict here. Its theme is the age-old, constantly recurring problem of killing yourself in order to survive, the problem of imitation, of making oneself resemble something, of mimesis, a problem that has taken on a peculiar force in our own phase of history. But the situation that I am describing is inverted for the idealist; it is turned upside down. Because without will there is no consciousness, the idealist view is that will is much the same thing as consciousness. Nevertheless, if I may repeat the decisive point, the will is to be found in thinking; it is its active component. If I am to reflect, I have to wish to do so; in order to reflect, I have to *want* to reflect. Otherwise, in the absence of this element of will, even the simplest act of thought is inconceivable. The purely contemplative, thinking, judging act, the intentional act of consciousness in the broadest sense, always contains this element of will, something that is only denied or conjured away by intellectualizing theories of knowledge after the fact. But, as an activity, consciousness is never pure, as the philosophers fondly believe, but is always actual behaviour; it is an ontic reality, or, to put it provocatively, it is always a material reality. Hence, just as I maintained earlier on in connection with the concept of logical reason, albeit very briefly, the concept of the will can only be grasped dialectically, namely, as the power of consciousness through which consciousness breaks out of its own bounds *and* out of what existed already, mere being. But we should likewise be wary of hypostasizing this more narrowly voluntaristic notion of will. After what I have said, it should no more be hypostasized than should the intellectual dimension. If the will were nothing but what I have called 'the additional factor', if it were no more than an impulse as the so-called decisionist theories teach, then the will would be at the disposition of every conceivable purpose, just as much as instrumental reason is according to the analysis with which you are familiar.[2] As long as the two aspects remain entirely separate from one another, they tend to converge by virtue of the fact that they become available in a quite arbitrary way – and precisely this random availability is incompatible with the idea of the will.

The memory of the irrational aspect of the will, incidentally, has always been the companion of idealism, for example in the statement by Fichte that I have referred to several times to the effect that morality is self-evident,[3] and that therefore thinking is not really necessary as guide to moral behaviour. Of course, if morality is self-evident, and if therefore the human subject is exempted from the need to make judgements about what he has to do, this obviously already implies that the will is irrational. This remains true regardless of the extent to which Kantian and Fichtean ethics may have thought of themselves as rational. However, the idea that the will or, more generally, morality is self-evident is one we cannot avoid criticizing. The self-evident nature of morality, the dispensation of morality from rational, critical reflection, belongs to the unenlightened residue of all the things that are self-evident because we simply accept them without reflecting on them critically – it is the refuge of repression. This truth extends into the heart of moral philosophy. The one, the identical, the immutable is supposed to be the good, according to Plato and especially all more recent moral philosophers. Whatever refuses to dissolve into this unity, this identity, this immutable condition is declared to be the legacy of nature and hence of evil. It can be said that just as the old nature gods were turned into the embodiments of evil by Christianity, and the popular outlook associated with it into demons and devils, a comparable process took place in the sublime sphere of metaphysics. By this I mean that, where nature was not completely tamed by the single, unifying principle, it was denigrated; the aspects of nature that were not mastered or shaped were equated without more ado with evil and the demonic. The things that are regarded by traditional bourgeois morality as evil are in reality the post-existence of older forces that had been partly, but not entirely, subjugated, and that subsequently returned. If we reflect on this for a moment, we will have to confess that this process of denigration is not entirely without justification because, when nature is repressed and then returns in that repressed shape, it assumes the destructive features that at least provide us with a powerful pretext for identifying them with the evil principle. If you read Freud's essay *Civilization and its Discontents*[4] with this in mind, you will see Freud as a late representative of Enlightenment who in this respect finds himself in complete agreement with the modern philosophical tradition of the West, but who nevertheless demonizes nature, that which returns, condemning it as destructive. At the same time, you will find a highly rational explanation of why nature actually is evil and demonic. An idea of the good that is meant to inform the will, but into which the concrete specificities and mediations of reason do not fully enter because they are supposed to be taken for granted, ends up simply submitting to the reified consciousness, ossified conditions, and whatever is socially approved. Hegel actually took this step when he equated a self-evident morality with the substance of society or the nation, that is, with whatever was found to be already established in a community. In line with this he condemned as mere caprice any critical scrutiny of such an established order.

By emancipating itself from the specificities of reason, will in itself, without any further specification, necessarily includes the domination of nature in its archaic, primitive form, namely, the rule of force, direct, naked force. It can be said that pure will is not merely the readiness to do good, it is also the readiness to do evil – an extreme reversal of the celebrated dictum on the opening page of Kant's *Groundwork of the Metaphysic of Morals*.[5] It is not by accident that the National Socialists called one of their frenzied party congresses the 'Triumph of the Will'[6] – without its being indicated in this case what this will was for or what it was supposed to achieve. And in general, it could be shown in great detail that fascist irrationalism almost always involves breaking off the process of reflection. So the message conveyed is something like, 'Live dangerously', as Nietzsche put it. This watchword may indeed contain a core of truth, for example, if what is wanted is that we should accept risks in order to bring about conditions that are more worthy of human beings. But

as soon as 'danger' or 'sacrifice' become ends in themselves, the
injunction becomes a thing of evil. This fetishization, this exaltation
into absolute norms or values, of ideas that only become meaningful
if they result from a process of reflection – ideas such as 'sacrifice' or
'Make yourselves free!', or the ideas of the 'Triumph of the Will' or
'Live dangerously' that I have just referred to – this fetishization is
the key, the signature of the modern form of irrationalism. What
distinguishes it is the fact that it is in a sense infected by reason while
denying its influence. However, if in fact and in contrast to the irrationalist undercurrent that casts its shadow over the entire history of
Western rationalism, a substantial, indubitable certainty with regard
to moral behaviour *does not exist*, then it follows that there is no
such thing as moral certainty or a self-evident morality, or direct
moral self-certainty. We might almost say that to suggest that we
could ever know beyond doubt and unproblematically what is good,
would be the beginning of all evil. You are all familiar with the statements in the New Testament attacking the Pharisees.[7] These criticisms
all make clear that the positive and unproblematic assumption of the
good, independently of that risk, independently of the extremely
serious and concrete possibility that even where you do Kant's bidding
and act in accordance with the 'pure' will – these criticisms mean that
you will have reached the point where you are likely to do bad and
even catastrophic things. And those passages in the New Testament
provide us with the most succinct expression of this. This fallibility
is an essential characteristic of all moral action, all acts that intend
the good, the good in an emphatic sense. The entire moral sphere has
its serious aspect, the dimension that raises it above the level of
Sunday sermons and cheap words of comfort, in the fact that, at the
very point where we feel certain that we are doing the right thing
and are acting in good faith, we often end up behaving quite wrongly.
This leads to the consequence that the most extreme mental efforts
are called for if we are ever to enter the sphere in which it may be
proper to speak of the good. However, the more society develops into
an overpowering, objectively conflict-ridden totality, the less will any
individual moral decision have claims to be judged authentic and
right. We could put this a different way – and I am not deterred from
doing so by the possible accusation that I am depriving you of something or that I am undermining your sense of moral certainty. The
fact is that I believe that this sense of certainty should be undermined
and that moral consciousness only begins at the point where that
certainty is not thought to be self-evident. Thus we are all ensnared
by the false totality, whatever we do; we are all afflicted by the false,
catastrophic totality. I once ventured to write that 'there can be no

good life within the bad one',[8] an idea I found later on in Nietzsche, though I can no longer recollect the passage.[9] This idea applies not just to happiness or to a good life in an aesthetic sense or something of the sort. It must be applied strictly to the idea of the good itself. You need only attempt to do something within the existing order of things, something you feel would be the decent thing to do, and you will soon find yourselves caught up in a dialectic without end, one in which the good you are trying to achieve has to be paid for with infinite quantities of the bad and the dubious, with injustice, unkindness and forgetting. But if we were then to conclude – as do some moral philosophers – that the most moral course of action would be simply to sit back and do nothing, we should be no better off. For that would be simply to leave the dubious totality in place, to allow it to wreak what damage it will – and thus to submit to it.

Kant's disapproval of psychology is grounded in his desire to salvage an ontological authority which I have referred to several times.[10] This disapproval also contains the authentic insight that the so-called moral categories of the individual are more than strictly individual. I believe that it is important to point this out now, towards the very end of these lectures, when I wish to concretize my thesis of the essentially conflict-ridden nature of the moral. I wish to make sure that I am not misunderstood here: on the one hand, our task must be to carry out the critique of the moral as the bad universal in its repression of the individual, and to pursue this in an uncompromising way. On the other hand, however, it is no less impossible to conceive of a moral system without a universal dimension with which to set bounds to the unreflecting being-for-self of the individual.

The concept of *mankind*, which, as you know, plays such a crucial role in Kant's moral philosophy, contains the idea of reason as a universally valid notion in the sense that it is applicable to all rational beings, that is, it applies to society as a whole. We might say, then, that universality in the moral realm points to the plurality of subjects and thus, in the final analysis, to society. In this respect Kant's moral philosophy converges surprisingly, even paradoxically, if you like, with its chosen adversary, namely, psychology. For psychology teaches that what Kant thinks of as the supreme moral authority, namely conscience, which in the language of psychology is the super-ego, is nothing but the internalized social norm. With this idea that the conscience, the super-ego, which is the decisive layer of individuality or of the monad, actually contains the whole of society, that it is the agent of society in each individual – with this idea, psychology breaks through its own monadological limits. The super-ego, the conscience, contains an undifferentiated amalgam consisting on the one hand of mere heteronomous coercion, and on the other of the idea of a human solidarity that transcends all individual interests. The norm that we have criticized as repressive always testifies to the aspects of society that point beyond particularity, even while particularity remains the principle of society. The only problem is that in the here and now this norm is incompatible with the justified and legitimate interests of the individual. This is the source of what is wrong with the concept of the super-ego. Thus conscience is inhabited by both right and wrong and the power of solidarity of which I have just spoken can grow only by working its way through its own repressive nature.

Perhaps I may be allowed at this point to read out to you a few sentences from a text on moral philosophy on which these lectures have in large measure been based. I do so simply because time is so short and because they sum up succinctly the ideas that I have been telling you about.[11] The question of right and wrong in matters of conscience cannot be answered definitively because right and wrong are part of conscience itself and cannot be separated by any abstract judgement. As I have just said, the spirit of solidarity is only able to develop on the back of the spirit of repression, which that of solidarity then annuls. The fact that the gulf between individual and society is so small, but equally that the two are never reconciled, is essential to moral philosophy. To this day the bad side of universality protests against the socially unfulfilled claims of the individual. That is the supra-individual element of truth in the critique of morality. But the individual, whom need has made guilty, and who has come to be his own be-all and end-all, falls victim to the delusion of an individualistic society and thus fails to know himself – a consequence which Hegel perceived, and perceived most acutely at the very moment when he was colluding in reactionary abuse. Society is in the wrong vis-à-vis the individual in its universal claims, but it is also in the right since the individual hypostasizes the social principle of pure, unreflecting self-preservation, the very principle embodying the bad universal. The late statement by Kant[12] that the freedom of each human being need be curtailed only in so far as it restricts someone else's freedom encodes a reconciled condition that rises above not just the bad universal, the coercive machinery of society, but also the obdurate individual who is a copy in miniature of that machinery. The question of freedom does not call for a simple Yes or No, but a theory that rises above society as well as above the individuals existing in it. Instead of applying sanctions to the internalized and entrenched authority of the super-ego, the task of theory should be to make transparent the dialectic of individual and species, a task to which I have devoted these observations on the philosophy of history. The unyielding harshness of the super-ego is no more than a reaction to the fact that such transparency is impossible as long as conditions full of conflict persist. The human subject could be liberated only where it had achieved reconciliation. This would place it above freedom which, as privilege, the inheritance of the feudal lord, primarily involved taking for oneself, and hence nobility.[13] As such, it is in league with its opposite, repression. The presence of aggression in freedom becomes visible whenever, in the midst of unfreedom, human beings practise the gestures of freedom. In a state of freedom, the individual would not be too concerned with preserving his old particularity – individuality is both the product of pressure and the focal point of resistance to it – but neither would that freedom be able to acquiesce in the current conception of collectivity. The fact that, in the countries that monopolize the name of socialism, collectivism is recommended and even prescribed in the shape of a subordination of the individual to the collective gives the lie to their socialism and consolidates the presence of conflict, antagonism. Infected by an irrational cult of community, the term 'alienation' has recently become fashionable in both East and West, thanks to the veneration of the young Marx at the expense of the old one, and thanks to the regression of objective dialectics to anthropology. This term 'alienation' takes an ambivalent view of a repressive society; it is as ambivalent as genuine suffering under the rule of alienation itself. The self is weakened by a socialized society that tirelessly drives people together and renders them both literally and figuratively incapable of solitude. This weakening of the self manifests itself in complaints about isolation and also in the truly unbearable coldness spread over all things human by the expanding exchange relation. The idea that a union of free human beings should find it necessary constantly to flock together belongs to the mental world of parades, marches, flag-waving and the ceremonial speeches of political leaders of whatever hue. Such methods are needed only as long as society seeks irrationally to cement relations between its members who have no choice but to belong. Collectivism and individualism join forces to bring about a false state of affairs. 'Tout cela sera balayé',[14] as André Gide has remarked, unless the cyclical return of the bad triumphs after all.

Well, ladies and gentlemen, despite all that, there is a genuine possibility of freedom even in a totality steeped in guilt. Again and again, human subjects feel intermittently that they are potentially free, even though unfree in reality. And in tune with our discussions up to now – you see that I am trying to keep my promise not to begin with definitions, but to end with them[15] – we may say that an action is free if it is related transparently to the freedom of society as a whole. By way of conclusion, and in a desperate attempt to save time, I should like to read out to you one or two more sentences from something I have written.[16] Human subjects are free, on the Kantian model, in so far as they are conscious of and identical with themselves; but then again, they are unfree in this identity in so far as it acts as a form of coercion to which they submit. Again: they are unfree as non-identical beings, as diffuse nature, and yet as such they are free, after all, because the impulses that overpower them – and that is what non-identity amounts to – rid them of the coercive character of identity. Personality is the caricature of freedom. The basis for the aporia is that truth beyond coercive identity would not be its absolute other, but would always pass through that coercive identity and be mediated by it.

Ladies and gentlemen, we have come to an end.[17] I am fully conscious, as I have already mentioned, of the fragmentary nature of what I have been saying, although I have at least made the attempt to pull the different threads together. The ideas I have tried to convey have not always been easy to grasp, but if you have followed me attentively I hope that you will have been able to understand some of the very difficult material that I have been attempting to communicate to you. It has surprised me and also given me great pleasure to see that you have persevered with this course and that so many of you have kept coming right to the end. I am very well aware that the questions that I have been exploring here are not capable of being readily converted into examination questions, and consequently that you have shown your interest with that disinterestedness that Kant praised so highly. I should like to express my sincere gratitude to you all for this. I wish you all a good vacation and hope that many of you will return next term, when I intend in a sense to offer a sort of continuation of this course by lecturing on a different aspect of my little *work in progress*.[18] I am thinking here of my discussion of the concept of *metaphysics*. I shall try both to tell you about the concept of metaphysics and the problems arising from it and also to link this up with the metaphysical theses that I have been pondering for some time now.[19]

Thank you all for having been such attentive listeners.

NOTES

Lecture 1   Progress or Regression

1   Four of the twenty-eight lectures given in the winter semester 1964/5 have no audiotape transcriptions, but only the notes made by Adorno as the basis of his lecture. No doubt the tape recorder failed to function in the case of the missing tapes – these were for lectures 1, 11, 13 and 20. At all events, the draft of the transcriptions (Theodor W. Adorno Archive, Vo 9735-10314) explicitly states that these lectures were 'missing'. While Adorno was still alive, the drafts of the first three missing lectures were augmented by the notes taken by Hilmar Tillack, who had attended Adorno's lectures over a number of years. The present volume prints both Adorno's own notes (Vo 10315ff.) and those of Tillack in full, whereas for lecture 20 only Adorno's own notes have survived. These have been supplemented by an extract from an early version of the chapter on freedom from *Negative Dialectics*, to which the notes refer.

2   Between 1964 and 1966 Adorno discussed in three successive lecture courses topics that would figure centrally in his book *Negative Dialectics*. That book, which appeared first in 1966, is the 'book on dialectics' to which he refers in the next sentence in his notes. The present lecture course addresses the questions concerning morality and the philosophy of history that would form the subject of the chapters on Kant and Hegel in *Negative Dialectics*. This was the 'special situation' to which he refers, and he does so because as a rule his lectures and his research interests ran on parallel lines without intersecting. He commented on the 'special' factors that led him to proceed differently in the case of *Negative Dialectics* at the beginning of the lectures on that very subject

in the winter semester 1965/6. What he had to say on this subject sheds
light on the climate in which he had to teach in the university:

> You are aware that the traditional definition of a university calls for the
> unity of teaching and research. You will also know how problematic this
> idea has become even though people still cling to the idea. My own work
> has suffered considerably in this situation, since the increase in both
> teaching and administrative duties that have fallen to me bit by bit makes
> it almost impossible for me to carry out my research obligations in term
> time – if indeed we can speak of research in connection with philosophy
> – as conscientiously as is called for objectively, and above all as would
> correspond to my own inclination and disposition. In such a situation,
> and under such pressures and compulsion, one tends to develop certain
> qualities that might best be described as peasant cunning. I am therefore
> attempting to do the situation justice by . . . taking much of the material
> for my lectures from the extensive and really quite burdensome [belas-
> teten] book I have been working on for the past six years and that will
> bear the title of *Negative Dialectics*. . . . I am fully aware that this proce-
> dure might well be objected to, in particular by those with a positivist
> cast of mind. Such critics might well argue that as an academic teacher I
> should present you only with secure knowledge that is genuinely cast-iron
> and watertight. I have no wish to make a virtue of necessity, but my own
> view is that such ideas do not quite fit philosophy. Philosophy consists of
> ideas in a permanent state of flux, and, as Hegel, the great progenitor of
> dialectics, has argued, in philosophy the process is as important as the
> result; process and result are . . . really the same thing. Moreover, I believe
> that what characterizes philosophical thought is its tentative, experimen-
> tal, inconclusive nature and it is this that distinguishes philosophy from
> the positive sciences. . . . In consequence, the arguments I shall present to
> you here will bear the marks of their experimental nature since they have
> not yet achieved the linguistic polish, the definitive shape that I would
> like to give them as far as it is in my power to do so. And I can . . . really
> only encourage you to think along with what I say and develop your own
> ideas rather than to imagine that I am providing you with established
> knowledge that you can take home with you in black and white. (Quoted
> from *NaS*, vol. 14, p. 296f. Cf. *Metaphysics*, p. 192f.)

As early as 1960/1 the three lecture courses of 1964 to 1966 had been
preceded by a course entitled 'Ontology and Dialectics', and it was this
that planted the seed from which the book that would later be called
Negative Dialectics would be born. It is not without significance that
all four lecture courses were given before the parallel passages in the
book had received their definitive shape. The lecture courses were all,
as Adorno liked to say, part of a 'work in progress', or, rather, each
marked a particular stage in the composition of the book.

3   Adorno treats Kant's theory of social conflict above all in lecture 6, see
    p. 49ff. above; Hegel's doctrine of progress in the consciousness of
    freedom is discussed in lecture 12, p. 105ff. above. The fact that in Kant
    the aporias of freedom are located not in the noumenal but in the phe-

nomenal realm, in other words, in the conflicts of bourgeois society is a line of thought Adorno developed in the section on 'Ontic and idealist aspects' in the chapter on freedom in *Negative Dialectics* (pp. 255–60). This chapter had first been entitled 'Determinism: Paraphrases of Kant' and its definitive title was 'Freedom: On the Metacritique of Practical Reason'. Its first two versions, that is to say, Adorno's first dictated version and the first typed version with his handwritten corrections, were produced between 3 December 1964 and 20 January 1965, in other words, they are practically contemporary with the present lecture course, which ran from 10 November 1964 to 25 February of the following year. Adorno's critique of Hegel's definition of history should be compared to the chapter 'World Spirit and Natural History' in *Negative Dialectics* (p. 300ff.), which originally bore the title 'Objective Spirit' and had been written immediately before the chapter on freedom; the first corrected version of this chapter was finished on 15 November 1964.

4   What Adorno meant by 'a spiral theory' was probably the theory of history contained in Arnold Toynbee's *A Study of History* (1934–61). In Toynbee's conception civilizations of the most various kinds rise and fall in a comparable cyclical movement. At the same time, however, particularly in the later volumes of his *magnum opus*, he takes a gradual upward development for granted that is essentially determined by religion. In this sense, Toynbee's view of history occupies an intermediate position between linear, progressive theories and cyclical ones. For his explicit critique of cyclical theories, see *Der Gang der Weltgeschichte: Aufstieg und Verfall der Kulturen*, trans. Jürgen von Kempski, Stuttgart, 1954, p. 248ff. No less a person than Goethe frequently invoked the image of a spiral when discussing the history of mankind, and it is Goethe on whom all subsequent cultural morphologies are based (see notes 5 and 6 below): 'The orbit pursued by mankind is specific enough and, notwithstanding the great stasis imposed by barbarism, it has already run this course more than once. Even if we wish to ascribe a spiral movement to this journey, mankind nevertheless finds itself again and again in regions it has already once inhabited. It is in this way that all true ideas and all errors are constantly repeated.' J. W. von Goethe, *Sämtliche Werke*, Jubiläums-Ausgabe, vol. 40: *Schriften zur Naturwissenschaft*, Part 2, ed. Max Morris, Stuttgart and Berlin, 1907, p. 120f.

5   For Adorno's view of Spengler's 'cyclical philosophy of history', see his essay 'Über Statik und Dynamik als soziologische Kategorien' (*GS*, vol. 8, p. 237). See also 'Spengler after the Decline', in *Prisms*, p. 51ff., 'Wird Spengler recht behalten? (*GS*, vol. 10.1, p. 140ff.), as well as the early review of *Der Mensch und die Technik*, in *GS*, vol. 20.1, p. 197ff.

6   Like Spengler, Toynbee and Frobenius (see note 19 below) are commonly regarded as the exponents of cultural morphology, a doctrine that maintains that cultures are subject to organic change, analogously

to the development of individuals from childhood through youth and adulthood to old age. According to Spengler, every culture ends up in a state of decadence; civilizations 'are a conclusion, the thing-become succeeding the thing-becoming, death following life, rigidity following expansion, intellectual age and the stone age, petrifying world city following Mother Earth and the spiritual childhood of Doric and Gothic. They are an *end*, irrevocable, yet by inward necessity reached again and again.' Oswald Spengler, *The Decline of the West*, trans. Charles Francis Atkinson, New York: Alfred A. Knopf, 1939 [1926], p. 31.

7   The dates in the text are those introduced by Adorno himself. He inserted them at the point he had reached in his perorations so as to indicate where he wished to take up the thread in the following hour.

8   The printer's copy of Tillack's notes can be found in the Theodor W. Adorno Archive, Vo 9735-9739.

9   Adorno used the English phrase.

10 Hobbes maintained 'that during the time men live without a common Power to keep them all in awe, they are in that condition which is called Warre; and such a warre, as is of every man against every man.' Hobbes, *Leviathan*, Harmondsworth: Penguin, 1977, p. 185. He developed this idea in chapter 13 of *Leviathan* in the context of the hypothetical nature of his idea of the social contract. Cf. Max Horkheimer, *Gesammelte Schriften*, vol. 2: *Philosophische Frühschriften 1922–1932*, Frankfurt am Main, 1987, p. 213ff., and also Adorno, *Negative Dialectics*, pp. 217 and 356.

11 Georg Mehlis (1878–1942) was a philosopher in Freiburg, a follower of Rickert and co-editor of the journal *Logos*; cf. his *Lehrbuch der Geschichtsphilosophie*, Berlin, 1915.

12 Ernst Bernheim (1850–1942) was a historian in Greifswald; cf. his *Lehrbuch der historischen Methode und der Geschichtsphilosophie*, 6th edn, Leipzig, 1908.

13 For Georg Simmel, see lecture 3, notes 3 and 4 below.

14 Bruno Liebrucks (1911–85) was a philosopher in Frankfurt; in his *magnum opus*, *Sprache und Bewußtsein* (8 vols, Frankfurt am Main, 1964–74), he devotes vol. 5 to a discussion of Hegel's *Phenomenology of Spirit*.

15 On Huxley's novel, which first appeared in London in 1922, see Adorno's essay 'Aldous Huxley and Utopia', in *Prisms*, p. 95ff.

16 Cf. *GS*, vol. 10.1, where Adorno cites this passage from Spengler: the great universal concepts, freedom, justice, humanity, progress . . . 'all these abstract ideals possess a power that scarcely extends beyond two centuries – the centuries of party politics. In the final analysis they are not refuted, but simply become a bore. Rousseau has long been one, and Marx will soon join him.' Oswald Spengler, *Der Untergang des Abendlandes*, vol. 2, Munich, 1922, p. 568. [This quotation is missing from the translation of the essay on Spengler in *Prisms*, p. 60. (Trans.)]

17 Riesman defines the other-directed personality as follows: 'The type of character I shall describe as other-directed seems to be emerging in very recent years in the upper middle class of our larger cities. . . . What is common to all the other-directed people is that their contemporaries are the source of direction for the individual – either those known to him or those with whom he is indirectly acquainted, through friends and through the mass media. This source is of course "internalized" in the sense that dependence on it for guidance in life is implanted early. The goals towards which the other-directed person strives shift with that guidance: it is only the process of striving itself and the process of paying close attention to the signals from others that remain unaltered throughout life. This mode of keeping in touch with others permits a close behavioural conformity, not through drill in behaviour itself, as in the tradition-directed character, but rather through an exceptional sensitivity to the actions and wishes of others.' David Riesman with Nathan Glazer and Reuel Denney, *The Lonely Crowd: A Study of the Changing American Character*, abridged edn with a new foreword, New Haven, CT, 1961, pp. 19 and 21f.

18 In his notes to the lecture course on 'An Introduction to the Philosophy of History' which he gave in the summer semester of 1957 – a preliminary draft of the current lectures, one which survives only in Adorno's own notes and the written-out shorthand record – Adorno bases his comments on *cyclical* theories of history on Georg Mehlis's *Lehrbuch der Geschichtsphilosophie*: 'Thesis: no Greek philosophy of history (349) despite Heraclitus's cyclical theory, which then recurs in the Stoics. (350) NB cyclical theory is an inauthentic philosophy of history. The cyclical is the mythical. To this extent history always implies freedom' (Vo 2306). The shorthand record of the 1957 lectures refers to Vico as an instance of a more recent cyclical theory: 'Vico retained the idea of the cyclical character of history; that is to say, he defended the view that mankind could and perhaps would relapse into barbarism. Spengler's conception of the cyclical nature of history, something that would show humanity its own worthlessness and the indifference of nature, has quite a different meaning. What underlies Vico's view is not a blind fatalism that actually excludes history, but its opposite: his horror of the Middle Ages that were experienced as dark and that had not yet acquired the transfiguring aura with which the Romantics endowed them. Vico's limitations were that the age he lived in did not yet possess the dynamism of a ceaselessly advancing society; that his view remained anthropological in the last analysis; that for all his talk of the historical nature of mankind, he still believed in the immutability of human nature and that he kept returning to a belief that a relapse into barbarism was a possibility. This can be explained by the fact that, although the concepts of the individual and his fate, history, mediated one another, he failed to work out their implications in a radical way' (Vo 2047f.).

19   Leo Frobenius (1873–1938) was an ethnologist and cultural historian. Together with Spengler and Kurt Breysig (1866–1940) he was a leading representative of cultural morphology. From 1932 he had a chair in Frankfurt am Main, where he established an institute for cultural morphology that since 1946 has been known as the Frobenius Institute; see e.g., his book, *Paideuma: Umrisse einer Kultur- und Seelenlehre*, 3rd edn, Frankfurt am Main, 1921.

20   A quotation from Goethe's poem 'Destiny' in 'First and Last Words: Orphic', *Goethe: Selected Verse*, trans. David Luke, Harmondsworth: Penguin, 1964, p. 302.

Lecture 2   Universal and Particular

1   This lecture is the first to have survived as the transcription from a tape recording. However, a few sentences appear to be missing at the very beginning. The transcript has only the phrase 'something about history as an academic discipline' (Vo 9740). The rest has been supplied by the editor.

2   See Leopold von Ranke, *Geschichten der romanischen und germanischen Völker von 1494–1514*, 2nd edn, Leipzig, 1874 (*Sämtliche Werke*, 3, Gesamtausgabe, vol. 33/4, p. VII: 'History has been given the task of judging the past, of instructing the contemporary world for the benefit of future generations; the present attempt does not presume to undertake such lofty tasks: it wishes merely to tell how it really happened.'

3   From the French word for event. Adorno is probably thinking of the Annales school of history, whose interdisciplinary approach contrasts with that of a *histoire événementielle*, a form of historiography that confines itself to the recording of events.

4   The Great Elector, i.e., Friedrich Wilhelm of Brandenburg (1620–88), laid the foundations for the rise of Prussia to the status of a major European power under his grandson, Frederick the Great [Trans.].

5   Cf. *Negative Dialectics*, p. 320: 'No universal history leads from savagery to humanitarianism, but there is one leading from the slingshot to the megaton bomb.'

6   Max Weber's concept of rationality was the subject of a study by Adorno's friend Hermann Grab, who had written a thesis on it in Frankfurt under the supervision of Gottfried Salomon-Delatour; see Hermann J. Grab, *Der Begriff des Rationalen in der Soziologie Max Webers: Ein Beitrag zu den Problemen der philosophischen Grundlegung der Sozialwissenschaft*, Karlsruhe, 1927 (Sozialwissenschaftliche Abhandlungen 3).

7   The first edition of *Dialektik der Aufklärung* appeared in Amsterdam in 1947. Horkheimer resisted a new edition for a long time and it was not until the year of Adorno's death that it appeared again, with the imprint Frankfurt, 1969.

8   To bolster his objections to the concept of examples, Adorno liked to
    appeal to Kant, as he does in *Negative Dialectics*. There was no lack
    of evidence in Kant for 'the aversion of speculative thinking from the
    so-called example as something inferior'. 'Such sharpening of the judge-
    ment is indeed the one great benefit of examples. Correctness and preci-
    sion of intellectual insight, on the other hand, they more usually
    somewhat impair. For only very seldom do they adequately fulfil the
    requirements of the rule (as *casus in terminis* [i.e., limiting cases]).
    Besides, they often weaken that effort which is required of the under-
    standing to comprehend properly the rules in their universality, in
    independence of the particular circumstances of experience, and so
    accustom us to use rules rather as formulas than as principles. Examples
    are thus the leading-strings of judgement; and those who are lacking in
    the natural talent can never dispense with them.' Immanuel Kant, *Cri-
    tique of Pure Reason*, trans. Kemp Smith, A 134/B 173, p. 178.
9   Adorno came across this theory of Spengler's in *Der Mensch und die
    Technik: Beitrag zu einer Philosophie des Lebens*, which appeared in
    1931 and which he reviewed in 1932: 'Consistently with his mythical
    outlook, Spengler speaks of "The crime and fall of Faustian man" and
    prophesies the imminent demise of Western technology, which he
    believes is doomed to oblivion because for the non-Faustian souls of
    the future "Faustian technology is no inner necessity", although accord-
    ing to Spengler himself, "within thirty years ... the Japanese will be
    technological experts of the first rank". The Westerners affected by this
    change will be left with no alternative but a heroic and tragic view of
    life' (*GS*, vol. 20.1, p. 198).
10 'The only Thought which Philosophy brings with it to the contempla-
    tion of History, is the simple conception of *Reason*; that Reason is the
    Sovereign of the World; that the history of the world, therefore, presents
    us with a rational process. This conviction and intuition is a hypothesis
    in the domain of history as such. In that of Philosophy it is no hypoth-
    esis. It is there proved by speculative cognition, that reason – and this
    term may here suffice us, without investigating the relation sustained
    by the Universe to God – is *Substance* as well as *Infinite Power*; it is
    the *Infinite Material* underlying all the natural and spiritual life which
    it originates, as also the *Infinite Form* – that which sets this Material
    in motion.' G. W. F. Hegel, *The Philosophy of History*, p. 9.
11 Adorno discusses the relation of Dilthey to Hegel in the 'Introduction
    to the Philosophy of History' of 1957: 'The fundamental assumption
    of this philosophy of history is the idea that history is the work of
    conscious human beings. In so far as it is based on spirit, on the mind
    of these people, it is objective, and the subject that knows history in a
    sense recognizes itself in history, or, alternatively, by recognizing itself
    in history, the subject is liberated from the limitations of its own posi-
    tion whatever that might be. It thus experiences the absolute relativity
    of every individual spiritual structure and becomes absolute in the

consciousness of this relativity. There is a strange combination here of Hegelian elements with a sceptical, positivist mood and a kind of *Lebensphilosophie* that rejoices in identification. His philosophy is like an amalgam of metaphysics and anti-metaphysics. This gives Dilthey's philosophy a kind of floating quality, difficult to pin down. The nerve of this entire epistemology of history, the *Critique of Historical Reason*, is that an objective knowledge of history is possible – even though there are no historical laws comparable to scientific laws – because history is essentially made of the same stuff, the same core as the knowing subject. It follows that the subject can understand it objectively because by understanding it he really understands himself' (Vo 2004).

12   Adorno discussed Hegel's concept of spirit in a number of passages in *Hegel: Three Studies*; see, especially, pp. 5 and 17 passim.

Lecture 3   Constitution Problems

1   This was Eduard Steuermann, the pianist and composer, who died in New York on 11 November 1964. Cf. Adorno's obituary 'Nach Steuermanns Tod' (*GS*, vol. 17, p. 311ff.) as well as the selection from their letters ('Die Komponisten Eduard Steuermann und Theodor W. Adorno: Aus ihrem Briefwechsel', in *Adorno-Noten: Mit Beiträgen von Theodor W. Adorno* [and others], ed. Rolf Tiedemann, Berlin, 1984, p. 40ff.

2   Joseph Arthur Count Gobineau (1816–82) was a French diplomat, orientalist and writer. He developed a doctrine of intellectual distinctions between different races, arguing that only the 'Aryan' race was capable of developing culture. In this respect he was an important intellectual forerunner of the Nazis. Cf. his *Essai sur l'inégalité des races humaines*, 4 vols, Paris, 1953–5.

3   Cf. Georg Simmel, *Die Probleme der Geschichtsphilosophie: Eine erkenntnistheoretische Studie*, Leipzig, 1892, 5th edn, 1923.

4   On Simmel's book, see also the lecture 'Über das Problem der individuellen Kausalität bei Simmel' that Adorno gave in New York in 1940 and that was published in the *Frankfurter Adorno Blätter* VIII, Munich, 2002.

5   First edition, Munich, 1919.

6   Marginal utility economics and marginal utility theory are terms used to describe an economic theory developed in the last third of the nineteenth century. This theory defined the exchange value of commodities with reference not to the quantity of labour required to produce them, but to the values or 'utility preferences' of the economic subjects. The 'marginal' utility refers to the overall decreasing benefit or utility of goods as their quantity increases, e.g., if a family of four has thirty pieces of bread, the addition of one further slice is of only marginal benefit.

7   'There's nothing better, on a holiday, / Than talk and noise of war, in Turkey, let's suppose, / Some place where armies come to blows. / One watches from one's window, sips one's glass, / While down the river all those fine ships pass. / And back home in the evening, we congratulate / Each other on our peaceful happy state.' J. W. von Goethe, *Faust, Part One*, trans. David Luke, Oxford and New York: Oxford University Press, 1987, p. 29, lines 860–7.

8   In *Negative Dialectics* Adorno discusses the empiricist critique of naïve realism, 'culminating in Hume's abolition of the thing', on p. 186f. [Trans.].

9   See Feuerbach to Hegel, 22 November 1828, in *Briefe von und an Hegel*, ed. Johannes Hoffmeister, vol. 3:*1823–31*, 3rd edn, Hamburg, 1969, p. 244ff.

10 Cf. *Negative Dialectics*, pp. 119 and 187; see also *Hegel: Three Studies*, p. 11, and 'Parataxis', *Notes to Literature*, vol. 2, p. 137.

11 Adorno uses the same quotation in the *Problems of Moral Philosophy*, p. 164, and also in *Negative Dialectics*, p. 318. Franz von Sickingen (1481–1523) was a marauding Knight of the Empire. In 1522, as a supporter of Martin Luther, he attacked the Archbishop of Trier, and in May 1523 he received a mortal wound during the siege of his own castle near Landstuhl by the Archbishop's troops. [He has the reputation of a Romantic, swashbuckling rebel and figures in a number of literary works, including Goethe's *Götz von Berlichingen* (which celebrates a similar folk hero) and a play by Ferdinand Lassalle, one of the founders of German socialism. (Trans.)]

Lecture 4   The Concept of Mediation

1   *Notes to Literature*, vol. 2, p. 3ff.

2   Cf. the section on 'Group Spirit and Dominion', in *Negative Dialectics*, pp. 307–9, for a statement of Adorno's conviction that the bad triumphs in committees because it is the more objective reality.

3   See *Introduction to the Sociology of Music*.

4   First published in Leipzig, 1900.

5   See Georg Simmel, *Soziologie: Untersuchungen über die Formen der Vergesellschaftung*, Leipzig, 1908.

6   Adorno is referring to the Cologne banker Kurt, Freiherr von Schroeder (1889–1966), in whose house Hitler and Papen met on 4 January 1933. Following that meeting Papen won President Hindenburg over to the idea of inviting Hitler to form a coalition government.

7   See Werner Mangold, *Gegenstand und Methode des Gruppendiskussionsverfahrens: Aus der Arbeit des Instituts für Sozialforschung*, Frankfurt am Main, 1960.

8   The source of this remark has not been discovered. It is conceivable that Adorno had in mind arguments that are at least echoed in his lectures

and that Engels presented in connection with Saint-Simon, even though these are not directly attributed to him; see *Socialism: Utopian and Scientific*, Karl Marx and Frederick Engels, *Selected Works*, vol. 2, pp. 109–13.

9   Cf. Friedrich Nietzsche, *Thus spoke Zarathustra*, trans. R. J. Hollingdale, Harmondsworth: Penguin, 1969, p. 226: 'O my brothers, am I then cruel? But I say: That which is falling should also be pushed! Everything of today – it is falling, it is decaying: who would support it? But I – *want* to push it too!'

10   See Max Horkheimer, 'Egoism and Freedom Movements', in Max Horkheimer, *Between Philosophy and Social Sciences*, trans. C. Frederick Hunter, Matthew S. Kramer and John Torpey, Cambridge, MA, and London: MIT Press, 1993, pp. 49–110.

11   Adorno used the English expression [Trans.].

12   See Gerhart Baumert, with the assistance of Edith Hunninger, *Deutsche Familien nach dem Kriege*, Darmstadt, 1954 (Gemeindestudie, Monographie 5). In his introduction to the study, Adorno wrote: 'This monograph is a contribution to sociological knowledge in the sense that it does not conceal the disintegration of traditional social institutions and attitudes, but allows them to emerge without any ideological superstructure. There can be no question of claiming that the current threat to the institution of the family has somehow been lifted in the long term by the solidarity displayed in the recent emergency. It should only be mentioned that the divorce figures have in fact gone down following their sharp rise, but still stand far above their prewar level. The same thing holds good for the numbers of "incomplete" families. What is striking is the increase in marriages between young men and older women. A socio-psychological interpretation of this finding could shed light on profound structural changes in society' (*GS*, vol. 20.2, p. 630).

13   See Werner Sombart, *Der moderne Kapitalismus: Historisch-systematische Darstellung des gesamteuropäischen Wirtschaftslebens von seinen Anfängen bis zur Gegenwart*, 3 vols, Berlin 1902–27; and also *Der Bourgeois: Zur Geistesgeschichte des modernen Wirtschaftsmenschen*, Munich, 1913.

14   The passages Adorno has in mind come from *The German Ideology*: 'When the reality is described, a self-sufficient philosophy loses its medium of existence. At the best its place can only be taken by a summing-up of the most general results, abstractions which are derived from the observation of the historical development of men. These abstractions in themselves, divorced from real history, have no value whatsoever. They can only serve to facilitate the arrangement of historical material, to indicate the sequence of its separate strata.' *The German Ideology*, Karl Marx and Frederick Engels, *Collected Works*, London: Lawrence & Wishart, 1976, vol. 5, p. 37. A textual variant is even more pointed: 'We know only a single science, the science of history. One can

NOTES TO PP. 38–41

look at history from two sides and divide it into the history of nature and the history of men. The two sides are, however, inseparable: the history of nature and the history of men are dependent on each other so long as men exist.' Ibid., p. 28. On the transition of philosophy to history anticipated by Marx but disavowed by history, a transition which forms the starting-point of *Negative Dialectics*, see Adorno's remarks in the lectures of 1957 on the philosophy of history: 'Hegel's concept of mediation, of becoming, when you extract it from its terminological shell, means nothing other than history. Marx expressed this in the extreme statement that philosophy passes over into history. Of course, to maintain that history as we have experienced it hitherto, actual history which has been a slaughterhouse of unending suffering, could be the site of truth calls for a greater degree of confidence than is possible at present. What is meant by Marx's statement is that the self-understanding of history, history raised to the level of self-knowledge, is identical with what philosophy traditionally claims to be; it is that in a higher sense historiography and philosophy merge into one' (Vo 1959f.).

15 'God governs the world, the actual working of his government – the carrying out of his plan – is the History of the World. This plan philosophy strives to comprehend; for only that which has been developed as the result of it, possesses *bona fide* reality. That which does not accord with it, is negative, worthless existence [*faule Existenz*].' (Hegel, *The Philosophy of History*, p. 36.)

Lecture 5   The Totality on the Road to Self-Realization

1 Adorno gave 'An Introduction to the Philosophy of History' in the summer semester of 1957. His handwritten notes for the course have survived (Theodor W. Adorno Archive Vo 2305–2338), as well as the fair copy of a shorthand record (Theodor W. Adorno Archive, Vo 1899–2069). Cf. on the 1957 lectures, p. 271 above, note 18 (lecture 1), p. 273, note 11 (lecture 2), pp. 276–7, note 14 (lecture 4), et al.

2 Theodor W. Adorno, *Hegel: Three Studies*, p. 1ff. and, especially, p. 123f.

3 See also note 14 above (lecture 4), pp. 276–7.

4 See 'Classicism, Romanticism, New Music', in *Sound Figures*, p. 106ff.

5 See, above all, Thesis VII of 'On the Concept of History', in which the question is raised 'with whom does historicism actually sympathize? The answer is inevitable: with the victor. All rulers are the heirs of prior conquerors. Hence, empathizing with the victor invariably benefits the current rulers. The historical materialist knows what this means. Whoever has emerged victorious participates to this day in the triumphal procession in which current rulers step over those who are lying

prostrate. According to traditional practice, the spoils are carried in the procession. They are called "cultural treasures".' Walter Benjamin, *Selected Writings*, ed. Michael Jennings, trans. Harry Zohn, Cambridge, MA, and London: Belknap Press, 2003, vol. 4, p. 391.

6 See the Introduction to the *Philosophy of History*, p. 26f. where Hegel writes: 'He is happy who finds his condition suited to his special character, will, and fancy, and so enjoys himself in that condition. The history of the World is not the theatre of happiness. Periods of happiness are blank pages in it, for they are periods of harmony – periods when the antithesis is in abeyance.' For a critique of Hegel's negative comments on happiness, see *Negative Dialectics*, p. 352f.

7 See especially the chapter on the Concept from part II of *The Science of Logic*, trans. A. V. Miller, London: George Allen & Unwin; New York: Humanities Press, 1969, p. 612: 'Determinateness in the form of universality is linked with the universal to form a simple determination; this determinate universal is the self-related determinateness; it is the determinate determinateness or absolute negativity posited *for itself*. But the self-related determinateness is *individuality*. Just as universality is immediately in and for itself already particularity, so too particularity is immediately in and for itself also *individuality*; this individuality is, in the first instance, to be regarded as the third moment of the Notion in so far as we hold on to its opposition to the two other moments, but it is also to be considered as the absolute return of the Notion into itself, and at the same time as the posited loss of itself.'

8 See the section entitled 'Virtue and the Course of the World', in *Hegel's Phenomenology of Spirit*, pp. 401–12.

9 Adorno probably has in mind the passage he quoted in a letter to Horkheimer in 1949. 'I found a passage from Turgenev's *Fathers and Sons* quoted in an essay that may be of interest to you. Bazarov declares "that he finds the idea of progress unbearable if it is based on the terrible torments of previous generations who did not suspect that they were in a sense the 'guinea pigs' of history so that one day, in the distant future, a new generation might be better off" ' (quoted in Max Horkheimer, *Gesammelte Schriften*, vol. 18, *Briefwechsel 1949–73*, ed. Gunzelin Schmid Noerr, p. 51f, note 4). However, the cited passage is not to be found in Turgenev's novel (see *Väter und Söhne*, ed. Klaus Dornacher, Berlin, 1985).

10 See the definition of justice in the 'Metaphysical Elements of the Theory of Right': 'Right is therefore the sum total of those conditions within which the will of one person can be reconciled with the will of another in accordance with a universal law of freedom.' Immanuel Kant, *The Metaphysics of Morals*, in Kant, *Political Writings*, p. 133. See also Adorno, *Problems of Moral Philosophy*, p. 122.

11 See above, note 15 (lecture 4), p. 277. Cf. also the introduction to *Negative Dialectics*: 'The matters of true philosophical interest at this point in history are those in which Hegel, agreeing with tradition,

declared his lack of interest. They are to be found in whatever lacks a concept, individuality and particularity – things which ever since Plato used to be dismissed as ephemeral and insignificant, and which Hegel labelled "worthless existence".' *Negative Dialectics*, p. 8.

12 This applies above all to the *Critique of Practical Reason*, in which Kant defines the categorical imperative, this 'basic law' of moral philosophy, as a 'fact of reason'. Cf. also Adorno's lectures on the *Problems of Moral Philosophy* of 1963, in which he writes that what the general thrust of Kant's moral philosophy 'amounts to is the reduction to the purely subjective principle of reason in order simultaneously to salvage the absolute, unimpeachable objectivity of the moral law. This makes it possible to say that the supreme principle of morality, namely the categorical imperative, is in fact nothing other than subjective reason as an absolutely objectively valid thing. The extreme opposite of this is the sceptical approach, which denies the existence of any such objectively valid principle. And this distinction between the sceptical method and scepticism as a philosophy is enough to enable you to see something of Kant's moral position. Unlike the Sceptics and the Sophists his concern with the subjects and human beings is not a strategy to enable him to dispute the universal necessity and the binding nature of moral laws, but precisely to reinstate them.' *Problems of Moral Philosophy*, p. 31.

13 Adorno explained this passage at greater length in his Hegel studies: His 'aversion to ornate and emphatic formulations is in harmony with this; he has unkind things to say about the "witty phrases" of the spirit alienated from itself, of mere culture. Germans had long reacted this way to Voltaire and Diderot. There lurks in Hegel the academic resentment of a linguistic self-reflection that would distance itself all too much from mediocre complicity.' *Hegel: Three Studies*, p. 118. The quotation about 'witty phrases' is to be found on p. 547 of the *Phenomenology*.

14 See the final chorus in Goethe's *Faust*, part 2, 'The Eternal Feminine / draws us on.'

15 See Schiller's poem 'Würde der Frauen' [The Worth of Women]: 'Ehret die Frauen, sie flechten und weben / Himmlische Rosen ins irdische Leben.' [All honour to women: they plait and weave / heavenly roses in life on earth.] *Werke und Briefe*, vol. 1, p. 185.

Lecture 6   Conflict and Survival

1 See p. 43 above.

2 According to bourgeois economists, the law of value is the 'law' which governs the exchange of goods of equal value in the capitalist system of production. Marx exposed the 'anarchy' of production associated with the fetishistic form of the capitalist economy. At the same time, he analysed the crises that beset that economy, enabling the law of value

to achieve fulfilment, a law that can only be termed such with a dose of irony. In the fetishism chapter of *Capital*, Marx states that, 'in the midst of all the accidental and fluctuating exchange-relations between the products, the labour-time socially necessary for their production forcibly asserts itself like an over-riding law of nature. The law of gravity thus asserts itself when a house falls about our ears.' Marx, *Capital*, vol. 1, p. 75. For the current state of the discussion, see Hans-Georg Backhaus, *Dialektik der Wertform: Untersuchungen zur marxschen Ökonomiekritik*, Freiburg im Breisgau, 1997. For his part, Adorno too believed that the law of value was the chief structural law governing society, even though it features in his writings mainly in metaphorical form; see, especially, *Negative Dialectics*, pp. 262, 300, 345n.; and also *The Jargon of Authenticity*, p. 85.

3   In the lecture lists for Frankfurt University in the summer semester 1933, Horkheimer and Adorno announced a joint course on the political philosophy of Thomas Hobbes. At that time Adorno was no longer permitted to carry out his duties as a *Dozent* and Horkheimer had already emigrated. In consequence, Hobbes is referred to only sporadically in Adorno's writings (see *Negative Dialectics*, pp. 217, 318, 321, *The Jargon of Authenticity*, p. 78, and also *GS*, vol. 8, pp. 36, 459).

4   See Frederick Engels, *Anti-Dühring: Herr Eugen Dühring's Revolution in Science*, London: Lawrence & Wishart, 1969; *The Origin of the Family, Private Property and the State*, in Karl Marx and Frederick Engels, *Selected Works*, vol. 2, p. 155ff.

5   See the preface to *A Contribution to the Critique of Political Economy*, Karl Marx and Frederick Engels, *Selected Works*, vol. 1, p. 327f.

6   This was the section entitled 'Fish in Water'; see *Minima Moralia*, p. 23f.

7   Cf. Engels's letter of 5 August 1890 to Conrad Schmidt: 'The materialist conception of history has a lot of dangerous friends nowadays, who use it as an excuse for *not* studying history. Just as Marx, commenting on the French "Marxists" of the late seventies used to say: "All I know is that I am not a Marxist".' Marx and Engels, *Selected Correspondence*, Moscow: Progress Publishers, 1975, p. 393.

8   In the winter semester of 1964/5, Hans-Magnus Enzensberger had given the guest lectures on poetics in Frankfurt University. His lectures were devoted to the topic: 'Do writers have a role to play?' They have not appeared in print.

9   Cf. Brecht's poem 'To Posterity': 'But you, when at last it comes to pass / That man can help his fellow man, / Do not judge us / Too harshly.' Bertolt Brecht, *Selected Poems*, trans. H. R. Hays, New York: Grove Press; London: Evergreen Books, 1959, p. 177.

10 For an account and critique of Stirner's philosophy, see the dissertation by Kurt Adolf Mautz (1911–2000), one of the earliest of Adorno's students. This was entitled *Die Philosophie Max Stirners im Gegensatz zum Hegelschen Idealismus*, and it could still be published in Berlin as

late as 1936. See also a book on Stirner that Hans G. Helms was able to present in the Institute for Social Research in the 1960s in Adorno's presence while it was still in preparation: Hans G. Helms, *Die Ideologie der anonymen Gesellschaft: Max Stirners 'Einziger' und der Fortschritt des demokratischen Selbstbewußtseins vom Vormärz bis zur Bundesrepublik*, Cologne, 1966.

11   This concept was introduced by Karl Mannheim. See *Ideology and Utopia*, London: Kegan Paul, Trench, Trubner & Co.; New York: Harcourt, Brace & Co., 1946, p. 53.

12   On this point see Adorno's 'Beitrag zur Ideologienlehre', *GS*, vol. 8, p. 457ff., especially p. 472f.

Lecture 7   Spirit and the Course of the World

1   This was originally a radio talk that was given in 1954. It can now be found in *Essays on Music*, ed. Richard Leppert, this essay trans. Robert Hullot-Kentor and Frederic Will, pp. 181–202.

2   This effect is not so visible in subsequent musical composition, not even in the so-called Darmstadt School, as in the theoretical research of Heinz-Klaus Metzger; cf. his *Musik wozu: Literatur zu Noten*, ed. Rainer Riehm, Frankfurt am Main, 1980, esp. pp. 61–128.

3   See p. 13ff., above.

4   See p. 45f., above.

5   'The attitude of thought to objectivity' is a Hegelian expression; see *Hegel: Three Studies*, p. 54.

6   On Durkheim's attempt 'to give a sociological explanation of space, time and a series of categories, and above all, the forms of logical classification', see Adorno's *Kant's 'Critique of Pure Reason'*, p. 168.

7   G. W. F. Hegel, *Elements of the Philosophy of Right*, p. 17. For an interpretation of this quotation, see also *Negative Dialectics*, p. 310.

8   These names must have been inserted by the editor since they are missing in the original transcript and so were presumably inaudible on the tape.

9   See, for example, the *Lectures on the History of Philosophy*, where he writes about Socrates: 'Infinite subjectivity, the freedom of self-awareness was born in Socrates. I must be absolutely present, at home with myself in all my thoughts. In our own day, this freedom is an infinite and absolute requirement.' Hegel, *Werke*, vol. 18, *Vorlesungen über die Geschichte der Philosophie* I, p. 442.

10 Hegel says of his own philosophy of history: 'Our mode of treating the subject is, in this aspect, a theodicy – a justification of the ways of God – which Leibniz attempted metaphysically, in his method, i.e., in indefinite abstract categories – so that the ill that is found in the World may be comprehended, and the thinking Spirit reconciled with the fact of the existence of evil. Indeed, nowhere is such a harmonizing view more

pressingly demanded than in Universal History; and it can be attained only by recognizing the *positive* existence, in which that negative element is a subordinate and vanquished nullity. On the one hand, the ultimate design of the World must be perceived; and on the other hand, the fact that this design has been actually realized in it, and that evil has not been able to assert a competing position.' Hegel, *The Philosophy of History*, p. 15f.

11 A *Reflexionsphilosoph* is one who thinks in the categories of the understanding, i.e., of scientific thought, and has not yet attained the higher reaches of speculative philosophy [Trans.].

12 'How do I find the secret again? / It has been stolen from me. / What has the world done to us! / I turn around, the lilac blooms again.' (Karl Kraus, *Schriften*, ed. Christian Wagenknecht, vol. 9: *Gedichte*, Frankfurt am Main, 1989, p. 289 ('Flieder'). Adorno often quoted this verse; see for example, *Negative Dialectics*, p. 297; *Prisms*, p. 152; *GS*, vol. 17, p. 326, or *GS*, vol. 18, p. 380.

13 See p. 56f., above.

Lecture 8   Psychology

1 The crucial passages are to be found in vol. 1 of *Capital*, viz. 'It is only because his money constantly functions as capital that the economic guise [*Charaktermaske*] of a capitalist attaches to a man' (Karl Marx, *Capital*, vol. 1, p. 566); and 'The practical agents of capitalistic production and their pettifogging ideologists are as unable to think of the means of production as separate from the social mask [*Charaktermaske*] they wear today, as a slave-owner to think of the worker himself as distinct from his character as a slave' (ibid., p. 608). Adorno regarded this concept as a central category of social theory: 'The task of a theory of society would be to advance from the immediate evidence [of antagonisms] to the knowledge of its basis in society: why human beings are still wedded to their roles. The Marxian concept of the character mask points to a solution since it not only anticipates that category, but has inferred it socially' (*GS*, vol. 8, p. 13).

2 There is a similar passage in *Negative Dialectics*: 'Hegel joins in the beer-hall wisdom that it is necessary to sow one's wild oats. This idea that coming to terms with the world is only natural is an aspect of the general notion of the world spirit as a spell' (*Negative Dialectics*, p. 348 – translation altered). Adorno's source for this quotation was Lukács's late essay *The Meaning of Contemporary Realism* (London: Merlin Press, 1963) and also Adorno's essay on Lukács, 'Reconciliation under duress' (*Aesthetics and Politics*, London: NLB, 1977, p. 176): 'Lukács quotes a cynical sentence by Hegel which sums up the social meaning of this process as it was seen in the traditional bourgeois novel of education [*Erziehungsroman*]: "For the end of such apprenticeship

consists in this: the subject sows his wild oats, educates himself with his wishes and opinions into harmony with subsisting relationships and their rationality, enters the concatenation of the world and works out for himself an appropriate attitude to it."' Even in the German edition no source was given for this quotation and hence nothing to indicate that it came not from the *Philosophy of History*, but from the *Aesthetics*, trans. T. M. Knox, Oxford: Clarendon Press, 1975, vol. 1, p. 593, slightly adapted.

3   The source of this remark is not known.

4   *Minima Moralia*, p. 109.

5   What is meant is not that Freud paid particular attention to avarice as a phenomenon. In fact, there are only occasional references to it; see, for example, 'Character and Anal Erotism' (1908), Standard Edition, vol. 9, p. 169; Penguin Freud Library, vol. 7, p. 205. Instead Adorno is focusing on the concept of mutilation as an aspect of the central complex of symptoms resulting from socially nonconformist behaviour, a subject to which the theory and practice of psychoanalysis are devoted.

6   Aristippus (c. 435 to after 366 BC) was a follower of Socrates and founder of the Cyrenaic school, which was named after Cyrene, his place of birth, a Greek colony in what today is Libya. For his life and teaching, see Diogenes Laertius II, 65–104; he is known in Germany above all from Christoph Martin Wieland's late, fragmentary novel *Aristippus and some of his Contemporaries* (first appeared in 1800–1; on this see Jan Philipp Reemtsma, *Das Buch vom Ich*, Zurich, 1993).

7   See Anna Freud, *Das Ich und die Abwehrmechanismen*, London, 1946, p. 125ff. Adorno has written about Anna Freud in his essay 'Zum Verhältnis von Soziologie und Psychologie', *GS*, vol. 8, p. 76.

8   The source of this idea has not been found, but see *GS*, vol. 9.2, p. 375: 'Incidentally, the term "concretism" derives from C. G. Jung and it was I who introduced it to social psychology. I would not wish to equate it automatically with the idea of the authoritarian personality.'

9   See, for example, *Critical Models*, pp. 74, 267 and 273.

Lecture 9   The Critique of Universal History

1   There is more by way of criticism of Dilthey in the shorthand record of the 'Introduction to the Philosophy of History' of 1957. Adorno maintains there 'that his [Dilthey's] philosophy no longer has the self-confidence to embark on speculative journeys. Instead, following the analogy of the natural sciences, something like a static conception of truth, a static object, is assumed. This static object is history in which man constantly rediscovers himself, but in a definitely unchanging way. It might be said that strictly speaking we cannot speak of a philosophy of history at all in the sense of a knowable, transparent movement of

subject and object. What we really see here is a kind of edifying observation of history in which we constantly rediscover ourselves, but we do not perceive anything like a definite historical figure who really amounts to anything or has any particular tendency. The substratum of history turns out to be merely the blind, aimless surge of life itself. Wherever there is life, there is something like insight into history, but the stubbornness of the object is entirely absent. There is something remarkably affirmative and over-reverential towards culture about Dilthey' (Vo 2004f.).

2 See, for example, the passage on Herder and Jacobi in *Faith and Knowledge*: 'Herder's way of doing philosophy is only a slight modification of this typical pattern. The Absolute cannot be tolerated in the form that it has for rational cognition, but only in a game with concepts of reflection, or in sporadic invocations which bring philosophy directly to an end, just as they seem to be about to begin it – even as Kant ends with the Idea as practical faith. Or else the rational can only be tolerated as beautiful feeling (*Empfindung*), as instinct, as individuality. But Herder's philosophizing has the advantage of being somewhat more objective. Jacobi calls Herder's philosophy Spinozistic froth, a preaching that confuses Reason and language alike. But the froth and the sermonizing arise precisely from Herder's putting a reflective concept in the place of rational thought. This veils the rational, just as the expression of feeling, subjectivity of instinct, etc. – which Jacobi puts in the place of rational thinking – does.' *Faith and Knowledge*, trans. Walter Cerf and H. S. Harris, Albany: State University of New York Press, 1977, p. 118.

3 Wendell L. Wilkie (1892–1944) was an American politician who stood as the Republican candidate against Franklin D. Roosevelt in the presidential elections of 1944, in which he was defeated. The title of his book, *One World* (New York, 1943), became a well-known political slogan.

4 See p. 29, above.

5 According to Adorno, Benjamin's intention, as described in his preface to *The Origin of German Tragic Drama*, 'was to rescue inductive reasoning. His maxim that the smallest cell of visualized reality outweighs the rest of the world is an early testimony to the self-confidence of the current state of experience; it is all the more authentic because it was formulated outside the domain of the so-called great philosophical issues which an altered form of dialectics calls on us to mistrust' (*Negative Dialectics*, p. 303; translation changed). In an earlier piece, his introduction to Benjamin's *Schriften* of 1955, he remarks: 'Paradoxically, Benjamin's speculative method converges with the empirical method. In his preface to his book on tragedy, Benjamin undertook a metaphysical rescue of nominalism; he does not draw conclusions from above to below, but rather, in an eccentric fashion, "inductively".' *Notes to Literature*, vol. 2, p. 222.

6 The Philosophicum is an examination in philosophy designed either for beginners or for mature students transferring to philosophy or wishing to obtain an extra qualification, often for teaching purposes [Trans.].

7 See *The Philosophy of History*: 'The History of the World is the discipline of the uncontrolled natural will, bringing it into obedience to a Universal principle and conferring subjective freedom. The East knew and to the present day knows only that *One* is free; the Greek and Roman world that *Some* are free; the German World knows that *All* are free. The first political form therefore which we observe in History, is *Despotism*, the second *Democracy* and *Aristocracy*, the third *Monarchy*.' *The Philosophy of History*, p. 104.

8 Attributed to Hegel by Walter Benjamin, *The Origin of German Tragic Drama*, p. 46, but no source in Hegel has been discovered.

9 See p. 3, above.

10 Immanuel Kant, *The Moral Law: Groundwork of the Metaphysic of Morals*, pp. 99–100; see also Adorno, *Problems of Moral Philosophy*, p. 122 and note 3.

11 Panaetius (c. 185–109 BC) was a disciple of Diogenes the Babylonian and Antipater of Tarsus. In 129 he succeeded Antipater as head of the Stoa, and he held that position until his death. Cicero made use of one of his writings in *De Officiis*. Posidonius (c. 135–50/51 BC) studied philosophy under Panaetius and then settled in Rhodes. 'In the history of ancient thought he can be compared to no one but Aristotle' (*The Oxford Classical Dictionary*, 1970, p. 868). He exercised a considerable influence on Lucretius, Cicero, Seneca, Plinius the Elder and Virgil [Trans.].

12 See Epicurus, Fragment 551 Us. On the fragment that is transmitted by Plutarch (On the principle of *Ladei biosas*, see 1.1128A), see also Eduard Zeller, *Die Philosophie der Griechen in ihrer geschichtlichen Entwicklung*, part 3, section 1: *Die nacharistotelische Philosophie*, part 1, Hildesheim and elsewhere, 1990, p. 473, as well as Friedrich Ueberweg, *Grundriß der Geschichte der Philosophie*, part 1: *Die Philosophie des Altertums*, ed. Karl Praechter, 14th edn, Darmstadt, 1957, p. 460.

13 Burckhardt discusses the individual in Hellenistic society in the last part of vol. 4 of his posthumously published *The Greeks and Greek Civilization*, more particularly in connection with the decline of the *polis* and the correlated retreat of people from public life to private. See, e.g., Jacob Burckhardt, *Gesammelte Werke*, vol. 8: *Griechische Kulturgeschichte*, 4 vols, ed. Jacob Oeri, Basel, 1957, p. 480ff. In *Minima Moralia* Adorno cites the relevant passage: 'It is not the least merit of Jacob Burckhardt's history of Greek civilization to have connected the drying-up of Hellenistic individuality not only with the objective decline of the *polis*, but precisely with the cult of the individual: "But following the deaths of Demosthenes and Phocion, the city is surprisingly depleted of political personalities, and not only of them: Epicurus, born as early as 342 of an Attic cleruch [colonial] family on Samos, is the last

Athenian of any kind to have world-historical importance." The situation in which the individual was vanishing was at the same time one of unbridled individualism, where "all was possible": "Above all, individuals are now worshipped instead of gods." That the setting-free of the individual by the undermining of the *polis* did not strengthen his resistance, but eliminated him and individuality itself, in the consummation of dictatorial states, provides a model of one of the central contradictions which drove society from the nineteenth century to Fascism.' *Minima Moralia*, p. 149. On Burckhardt's treatment of the theme, see also Karl Löwith, *Sämtliche Schriften*, vol. 7: *Jacob Burckhardt*, Stuttgart, 1984, p. 184ff.

14   The name of Descartes was added by the editor. The transcript contains only omission marks at this point. Needless to say, many other names suggest themselves.

15   On this point, see *Negative Dialectics*, 'And yet it is at the outset of the self-emancipating modern subject's self-reflection, in *Hamlet*, that we find the divergence of insight and action paradigmatically laid down. The more the subject turns into a being-for-itself, the greater the distance it places between itself and the unbroken accord with a given order, the less will its action and its consciousness be one.' *Negative Dialectics*, p. 228.

16   See Walter Benjamin, *Schriften*, ed. T. W. Adorno and Gretel Adorno with the assistance of Friedrich Podszus, Frankfurt am Main: Suhrkamp, 1955, vol. 1, p. 494ff. See also Walter Benjamin, *Selected Writings*, vol. 4: *1938–1940*, trans. Harry Zohn, p. 389ff.

Lecture 10   'Negative' Universal History

1   Adorno is mistaken here. In the *Letters*, i.e., the correspondence with Benjamin, the Theses are scarcely mentioned, and where they are referred to it is without any title whatever; see Benjamin, *Gesammelte Werke*, vol. 1, p. 122ff. On the question of the title, see Rolf Tiedemann, *Dialektik im Stillstand: Versuche zum Spätwerk Walter Benjamins*, Frankfurt am Main, 1983, p. 135, note 7. [In the English-language editions of Benjamin's writings, 'Theses on the Philosophy of History' is the title given in *Illuminations* (London: Jonathan Cape, 1970). In the *Selected Writings*, vol. 4, the essay appears with the title 'On the Concept of History'. Harry Zohn is credited with the translation of both versions, but the more recent one has been extensively revised. (Trans.)]

2   *Selected Writings*, vol. 4, p. 396.

3   In 1964, when Adorno gave these lectures, the *Eastern bloc countries*, including the GDR, had taken absolutely no notice of Benjamin at all, apart from a lone essay in *Sinn und Form* by Hans Heinz Holz in 1956. Adorno was probably thinking of a number of articles in West German newspapers and periodicals which already foreshadowed the attacks on

his and his pupils' editions and interpretations of Benjamin first in West
Germany, but subsequently in the GDR as well.

4   On this point, see the paragraph 'Persistence as Truth', in the introduction to *Against Epistemology*, p. 17f. This idea is not so much one
borrowed from Benjamin as a core idea of Adorno's own philosophy.
According to the shorthand record of the lectures on the 'Introduction
to the Philosophy of History' of the summer semester 1957, Adorno
also named other advocates of this idea:

> He reminded his listeners of Hegel's thesis that the truth is a process, that
> it contains a nucleus of time; that it is not truth *in* time, but time itself is
> a constituent element of truth. Nietzsche is one of the very few thinkers
> to have articulated what was at stake in the context of his own immediate
> experience rather than in that of speculative logic (*Twilight of the Idols*).
> In that book he maintains that one of the great preconceived ideas of the
> Christian and idealist tradition or the Judeo-Christian tradition is the
> claim that whatever has come into being is not true, since the only thing
> that can be true is what lies outside time. . . . The two great antipodes of
> Greek philosophy, Parmenides and Heraclitus, agreed that what was
> needed was to define truth in a manner that ensured that history was an
> integral part of it. This idea is contested by the traditional view. What is
> characteristic of this latter is the rigid opposition of validity and genesis.
> When Nietzsche disputed the claim that what had arisen historically
> cannot be true, he impugned that tradition. Later on, this distinction
> between validity and genesis became a universal maxim throughout
> phenomenology and it went from there into the existentialist philosophy
> of our own day. (Vo 1991, 1994f.)

The concept of the *nucleus of time* that Adorno constantly claims for
his own is one which he does indeed owe to Benjamin. Benjamin's use
of it can be found in one of the notes for the *Arcades Project*: 'Resolute
rejection of the concept of "timeless truth" is in order. Nevertheless,
truth is not – as Marxism would have it – a merely contingent function
of knowing, but is bound to a nucleus of time lying hidden within the
knower and the known alike.' Walter Benjamin, *The Arcades Project*,
p. 463.

5   Adorno also took from Benjamin this idea of history as a succession of
victories and defeats. See, especially, Thesis VII, 'On the Concept of
History', p. 391f.

6   This was the formula Adorno used in his account of Benjamin himself.
'Sorrow – not the state of being sad – was the defining characteristic of
his nature, in the form of a Jewish awareness of the permanence of
threat and catastrophe as much as in the antiquarian inclination that
cast a spell even on the contemporary and turned it into something long
past' (*Notes to Literature*, vol. 2, p. 231). At this point, however, it is
perhaps more likely that he had in mind a sentence from *Dialectic of
Enlightenment*: 'The repetition of nature which they [symbols] signify
always manifests itself in later times as the permanence of social compulsion, which the symbols represent. The dread objectified in a fixed

image becomes a sign of the consolidated power of the privileged'
(*Dialectic of Enlightenment*, p. 16). Adorno may also have been thinking of the talk he had given on Wagner not long before in which he
said of *Götterdämmerung*: 'The absolute, the redemption from myth,
albeit in the form of catastrophe, is only possible as a reprise. Myth is
catastrophe in permanence. Whatever abolishes it also implements it,
and death, the end of the bad infinity, is also an absolute regression'
(*GS*, vol. 16, p. 561).

7   Walter Benjamin, Thesis VII, 'On the Concept of History', p. 392.
8   'The analysis of the beginning would thus yield the notion of the union
    of being and nothing – or, in a more reflected form, the union of dif-
    ferentiatedness and non-differentiatedness, or the identity of identity
    and non-identity.' *Hegel's Science of Logic*, trans. A. V. Miller, London:
    George Allen & Unwin; New York: Humanities Press, 1976, p. 74.
    Adorno refers to this passage in the introduction to *Negative Dialectics*:
    'The foundation and result of Hegel's content-based philosophizing was
    the primacy of the subject or – in the famous phrase from the Introduc-
    tion to his *Logic* – the "identity of identity and non-identity". He held
    the determinate particular to be definable by the mind because its
    immanent definition was to be nothing but mind. Without this supposi-
    tion, according to Hegel, philosophy would be incapable of knowing
    anything substantial or essential. Unless the idealistically acquired
    concept of dialectics harbours experiences that, contrary to Hegel's
    emphasis, are independent of the apparatus of idealism, philosophy
    must inevitably do without substantive insight, confine itself to the
    methodology of science and virtually cross itself out' (*Negative Dialec-
    tics*, p. 7f.; translation altered).
9   'The angel would like to stay, awaken the dead, and make whole what
    has been smashed. But a storm is blowing from Paradise and has got
    caught in its wings; it is so strong that the angel can no longer close
    them. This storm drives him irresistibly into the future, to which his
    back is turned, while the pile of debris before him grows toward the
    sky. What we call progress is *this* storm.' Walter Benjamin, Thesis VII,
    'On the Concept of History', p. 392.
10 'Public opinion deserves to be *respected* as well as *despised* – despised
    for its concrete consciousness and expression, and respected for its
    essential basis, which appears in that concrete consciousness only in a
    more or less obscure manner.' G. W. F. Hegel, *Elements of the Philoso-
    phy of Right*, p. 355.
11 See Thesis XI, 'On the Concept of History', p. 393f.
12 See p. 27, above.
13 The idea that history up to now cannot escape the clutches of myth was
    of essential importance to Adorno's philosophy of history. See also Rolf
    Tiedemann, 'Gegenwärtige Vorwelt: Zu Adornos Begriff des Myth-
    ischen', in *Frankfurter Adorno Blätter* V, Munich, 1998, p. 9ff., and
    Frankfurter Adorno Blätter VIII, Munich, 2002.

14 See Fr. 1 of Anaximander of Miletus: 'The beginning and origin of existing things is the boundlessly indeterminate. But whereof existing things are become, therein they also pass away according to their guilt; for they render each other just punishment and penance according to the ordinance of time' (Hermann Diels and Walther Kranz, *Die Fragmente der Vorsokratiker*, 6th edn, vol. 1, p. 89; quoted here from *Metaphysics*, p. 166) [Trans.].

15 On the principle of exchange in the pre-Socratics, see also Theodor W. Adorno, *Das Problem des Idealismus*, notes for the lectures in the winter semester 1953/4, and 'Fragments of a Postscript', *Frankfurter Adorno Blätter* V, Munich, 1998, p. 110. Cf. also *Hegel: Three Studies*, p. 86; *Negative Dialectics*, p. 267; *GS*, vol. 8, p. 234; *GS*, vol. 13, p. 112; as well as the lectures on *Kant's 'Critique of Pure Reason'*, p. 219 and note, and *Metaphysics*, pp. 74–5.

16 Belgium granted independence to the Congo (now the Democratic Republic of Congo) in 1960. This was followed by the chaotic civil war to which Adorno refers here: 1961, the murder of Patrice Lumumba; 1963, intervention; 1964, precipitate withdrawal of UN troops; November 1964, Belgian paratroops intervene in the civil war on behalf of Moise Tshombe by flying into Stanleyville where white mercenaries were already active.

17 See Franz Neumann, *Behemoth: The Structure and Practice of National Socialism*, New York, 1944. Cf. also Adorno's text written to commemorate Neumann: 'The idea underlying *Behemoth* is of symbolic importance for everything he wrote. It is original in the highest degree in its blunt opposition to all superficial interpretations of a monolithic fascism. In harmony with the views of Otto Kirchheimer and Arkadij Gurland, Neumann demonstrates that the National Socialist state was pluralistic in reality, despite its show of total uniformity. Political will established itself by means of the unplanned competition of the most powerful social cliques. Neumann was perhaps the first to perceive that the slogan of integration, which had been one of the keystones of fascist ideology ever since Pareto, was really a cover for its opposite, namely the disintegration of society into divergent groups. The dictatorship brought all these groups together under one roof in a superficial and abstract way without their being able to find a spontaneous modus vivendi in ordinary social life. They therefore threaten to destabilize the very state they worship. We owe to him the insight that, while the Nazis boasted that they would put an end to destruction and that they would build things up, they prove to be highly destructive in their turn, not simply as regards everything human, and not simply in the foreign-policy consequences of their actions, but intrinsically destructive. In short, under fascism we find destroyed the very things that they claimed they had set out to save. At a time when their slogans about constructive and positive forces threaten to seduce new waves of recruits, Neumann's theory that the would-be monolithic state characteristic of

authoritarian governments is no more than a threadbare cloak for the underlying antagonistic forces is topical in the extreme. Society, incapable of reproducing itself any longer at will, breaks apart into diffuse barbarian factions, the very antithesis of the reconciled plurality that alone would represent a condition worthy of human beings. He has foreseen where the irrationalism that the National Socialists claim as their Weltanschauung would finally lead' (*GS*, vol. 20.2, p. 702).

18   Cf. Theodor Eschenburg, *Herrschaft der Verbände?*, Stuttgart, 1955. Adorno says of this book elsewhere: 'The greatest contribution to the understanding of non-parliamentary interest groups has been the book by Theodor Eschenburg, *Herrschaft der Verbände?* . . . It has not only led to a principled discussion of the subject but has also triggered a flood of literature informing us about the organization, structure, membership, and programmes of the more important interest groups, as well as the membership of their officials in the first and second Bundestag and in the public service. . . . Eschenburg demonstrates the influence of important associations on political decision-making. Up to now, however, there have been no empirical analyses of the internal workings of these associations, their tendencies to form oligarchies, to perpetuate themselves, or of the scope and methods they use in their efforts to bring influence to bear on the parties, the government and the civil service, in short, of their actual political power. The reasons for this deficiency are obvious: in Germany as in the world as a whole, sociologists are hampered in their search for primary material wherever they run up against sensitive social issues' (*GS*, vol. 8, p. 511).

19   See p. 68, above. In *Negative Dialectics*, Adorno elucidates the concept of the spell which we are under: 'The spell is the subjective form of the world spirit, the internal reinforcement of its primacy over the external process of life' (*Negative Dialectics*, p. 344).

20   The crisis of causality is a constant motif of Adorno's thinking. It is a theme to which – together with Horkheimer – he devoted his senior seminar over two semesters in 1958/9. Causality is given its most penetrating treatment in the chapter on freedom in *Negative Dialectics*, p. 265ff.; see also *Kant's 'Critique of Pure Reason'*, pp. 91 and 140f.; *Problems of Moral Philosophy*, p. 44f. and passim.

21   What Adorno objected to in Heidegger's interpretations of Hölderlin was that he 'neutralizes' his work '*into something in league with fate*', by 'eliminating Hölderlin's genuine relationship to reality, critical and utopian' (*Notes to Literature*, vol. 2, p. 115).

22   See p. 92f., above.

Lecture 11   The Nation and the Spirit of the People in Hegel

1   Adorno provided his definitive criticism of Hegel's national spirit in *Negative Dialectics*, p. 338ff.

2   Cf. the passage in §33 of the *Philosophy of Right*: 'But the ethical substance is likewise (c) the *state* as freedom, which is equally universal and objective in the free self-sufficiency of the particular will; this actual and organic spirit (α) of a people (β) actualizes and reveals itself through the relationship between the particular national spirits (γ) and in world history as the universal world spirit *whose right is supreme*' (G. W. F. Hegel, *Elements of the Philosophy of Right*, p. 62f.).

3   See §340 of the *Philosophy of Right*: 'The principles of the *spirits of nations* [*Volksgeister*] are in general of a limited nature because of that particularity in which they have their objective actuality and self-consciousness as *existent* individuals, and their deeds and destinies in their mutual relations are the manifest [*erscheinende*] dialectic of the finitude of these spirits. It is through this dialectic that the *universal* spirit, *the spirit of the world*, produces itself in its freedom from all limits, and it is this spirit which exercises its right – which is the highest right of all – over finite spirits in *world history* as the *world's court of judgement* [*Weltgericht*]' (ibid., p. 371). Earlier, probably in 1786, Friedrich Schiller had written his poem 'Resignation', which contained the lines: ' "I love my children with equal love!", explained the unseen genius. / "Two flowers", he cried, "Hark ye, oh children of man. / Two flowers bloom for the wise finder, / They are called *Hope* and Pleasure. / Whoever plucks the one / should not desire its sister. / Let him enjoy who cannot believe. This doctrine / will live as long as the world. Whoever can believe, let him do without. / The history of the world is the world's court of judgement." ' Friedrich Schiller, *Werke uud Briefe*, vol. 1, p. 170f.

4   Adorno probably has in mind a passage from the chapter on 'Ethical Action' in *The Phenomenology of Spirit*: 'While only household gods, in the former case, gave way before and were absorbed in the national spirit, here the living individual embodiments of the national spirit fall by their own individuality and disappear in one universal community, whose bare universality is soulless and dead, and whose living activity is found in the particular individual *qua* individual. The ethical form and embodiment of the life of spirit has passed away, and another mode appears in its place' (*The Phenomenology of Spirit*, p. 498).

5   Adorno used the English word.

6   On Vico, see note 10, p. 292, below.

7   This refers to a restaurant, 'Veltliner Keller', in Schlüsselgasse in Zurich (see p. 109, above), but it is not known to what event Adorno might be referring.

8   This is where Adorno's notes end. Insertion 12a does in fact continue, but the material in it was not used in this lecture, as is indicated by the date at the end.

9   *Faust, Part One*, trans. David Luke, Oxford and New York: Oxford University Press, 1987, p. 41, lines 1339f. 'I am the spirit of perpetual negation; / And rightly so, for all things that exist / Deserve to perish and would not be missed – / Much better it would be if nothing were

/ Brought into being.' Ibid., lines 1338–42. This quotation is one Adorno
had earlier associated with Hegel in 'The Experiential Content of Hegel's
Philosophy': 'The Goethean-Mephistophelian principle that everything
that comes into being deserves to perish means in Hegel that the
destruction of each individual thing is determined by individualization
itself, by particularity, the law of the whole: "The individual by itself
does not correspond to its concept. It is this limitation of its existence
which constitutes the finitude and ruin of the individual"' (*Hegel: Three
Studies*, p. 79). The quotation comes from Hegel, *Logic: Part One of
the Encyclopaedia of the Philosophical Sciences*, trans. William Wallace,
Oxford: Oxford University Press, 1975, p. 353.

10   The names of Vico, Hamann and Herder are not often invoked in
Adorno's writings. They represent a significant but dangerous constellation whose substance is summed up succinctly in his essay 'On the
Static and Dynamic as Sociological Categories': 'in its thinglike, objectified form, ratio embodies something anti-historical and static; there is
at least that much truth in the all too simplistic theory of the unhistori-
cal nature of the eighteenth-century Enlightenment. This anti-historical
element is no mere matter of the kind of intellectual history that attempts
to compensate for every supposed deficiency of the Lumières by pointing to historical events in a manner that was in fact familiar to the
Enlightenment ever since Vico and Montesquieu. It is rather the case
that rationality increasingly lost the power of memory that had once
been its own' (*GS*, vol. 8, p. 230). Vico versus Descartes, Hamann as
a corrective to Kant – these may be seen as chapters from the prehistory
of the *Dialectic of Enlightenment*.

   Adorno discusses Vico in his lectures on the 'Introduction to the
Philosophy of History' of 1957. Since he does so only here, we may be
permitted to quote more extensively from the shorthand record, even
though, as Adorno says himself, his ideas are heavily indebted to
Horkheimer's interpretation of Vico in 'The Beginnings of the Bourgeois
Philosophy of History':

> It is astonishing that the fundamental question addressed by Vico in his
> principal work is concerned with the purpose, the meaning of history,
> much as Hegel later on, in the introduction to *The Philosophy of History*,
> thinks that the question of the purpose of history is the crucial one. . . . The
> purpose into which Vico inquires is in his own view that of the role of
> providence, which holds sway throughout history. The teleology that
> governs the course of events is easily recognizable as the secularization
> of the idea of a divine plan of the kind developed with great vigour in
> Augustine's *City of God*. This complex of ideas is of great importance
> for Vico, who operates on the fine dividing line between Catholicism and
> Enlightenment as it was drawn in the eighteenth century. The productive
> aspect of his thought springs from the cross-pollination of these two
> intellectual currents. We may say that he owes his historical sense to this
> Catholic, Augustinian strand of thought which is otherwise absent from
> the Enlightenment. He owes a pivotal element of his fundamental reli-

gious outlook, the radical transcendence of his conception of redemption, to a degree of scepticism towards all internal historical processes. This locates him in stark opposition to any kind of primitive faith in progress and justifies us in placing him first in the dialectical approach to the philosophy of history. What shows him to have been a dialectician is the way in which he envisages the goal of divine providence working through the actions of human beings. It does so moreover in such a way that human beings remain unconscious of the historical dimension, the historical consequences and the historical direction of their own actions. This motif is one of the most crucial in thinking about the philosophy of history because it is the real element of mediation between the idea of a historical trend, the course of history, on the one hand, and individual human behaviour, on the other. If the course of history is displaced into the consciousness of man, we realize that people are actuated by passions and interests in a manner that prevents us from extrapolating a basic structuring of history in this way. If, however, we stick with the idea of a providence that comes to prevail objectively without human intervention, then we remain in the realms of dogma. The problem of the philosophy of history is to combine these two approaches, that of the largely unconscious action of human beings and the idea of a structured meaning or course of history. Vico was the first to assert that human beings are, as it were, blind towards the effect of their own actions, but that they obey the tug of history and that providence achieves its own purposes through them. Here we see in a precise form the idea that Hegel subsequently made so famous under the name of 'the cunning of reason'. According to this idea, objective spirit, the world spirit, comes to prevail by dint of the passions and needs of mankind, who as a totality move towards that end through their interactions with one another, without this becoming evident to the individuals concerned. A further factor that makes Vico important to us is his monolithic opposition to Cartesianism. This opposition was not like that of the Jansenists, Descartes' earlier critics, but was based on the insight, unique to Vico, that it was the task of the philosophy of history to perform what Descartes had expected from epistemology, logic or deductive metaphysics. Vico realized that Descartes' reduction of philosophy to metaphysics essentially diverted attention from what really mattered, namely the law-governed nature of human behaviour. He implicitly criticized Cartesianism by substituting the philosophy of history for epistemology and simultaneously by defending an objective theory of history. In this sense he himself still stands on the side of objective theories of history: that is to say, the idea of reflection on mind, the self-knowing subject, remains alien to him, and he progresses no further than the notion of providence. However, his philosophy of history is dialectical in shape. (Vo 2040ff.)

One of the few passages in Adorno's writings, if not the only one, in which he speaks approvingly of Hamann is likewise to be found in the stenographic record of the 'Introduction to the Philosophy of History' of 1957. Hamann was an eccentric philosopher whose principled critique of systems and abstractions, as well as his insistence upon locating the truth in the particular, has marked affinities with Adorno's own thinking. Nevertheless, from the outset Adorno defines his work as 'pre-critical': 'We find the pre-critical opposition to Kant's philosophy of consciousness developed in its purest form in Hamann. Hamann's mythological conception of language, his instrument of choice for combating the Kantian dualism of the senses and the understanding, and thus one of the basic principles of the analysis of consciousness, is taken over directly and uncritically from the doctrine of revelation. A further pre-critical way of thinking can be seen in Herder's meta-criticism of Kant, which took its inspiration from Hamann. The same may be said of Jacobi's theories of a feeling-based faith, which do not consider the problems of rational critique as a foundation of scientific knowledge in a way that would make necessary its treatment in the framework of a discussion of the philosophies of the unconscious as scientific philosophies, (GS, vol. 1, p. 92). Hamann is given equally short shrift in Minima Moralia: 'The thicket is no sacred grove. . . . Locke's platitudes are no justification for Hamann's obscurities' (Minima Moralia, p. 86). In the 'Introduction' of 1957 Adorno seems to want to qualify such judgements. It is all the more regrettable that these lectures do not represent a precise record of Adorno's actual words.

On the questions raised by Herder's irrationalist objections to Kant, his Metakritik zur Kritik der reinen Vernunft, its prehistory in Hamann and the curious alliances that were formed subsequently, see Jan Philipp Reemtsma, 'Wie würde ein Kürbis philosophieren?', in Reemtsma, Der Liebe Maskentanz: Aufsätze zum Werk Martin Wielands, Zurich, 1999, p. 203ff.

Lecture 12   The Principle of Nationality

1   See Sigmund Freud, Civilization and its Discontents, Pelican Freud Library, vol. 12, Harmondsworth: Penguin, 1985. In Negative Dialectics, Adorno significantly extends the Freudian theory: 'Freud's Civilization and its Discontents has a substance that was scarcely in the author's mind: it is not only in the psyche of the socialized that aggressiveness accumulates into an openly destructive drive. Instead, total socialization objectively hatches its opposite, and there is no telling yet whether it will be a disaster or a liberation' (Negative Dialectics, p. 346).

2   Cf. Grillparzer's epigram of 1849: 'The path of modern culture goes / From humanity / Through nationality / To bestiality.' Sämtliche Werke / Ausgewählte Briefe, Gespräche, Berichte, ed. Peter Frank and Karl Pörnbacher, vol. 1: Gedichte, Epigramme, Dramen I, 2nd edn, Munich: Hanser, 1969, p. 500.

3   For this quotation and its continuation in what follows, see the Addendum to §394 of the Encyclopaedia: 'The racial varieties delineated in

the addition to the previous paragraph are the essential ones – the differences of the universal natural spirit determined by the notion. Natural spirit does not remain in this its universal differentiation however. The naturality of spirit is unable to maintain itself as the pure copy of the determinations of the notion; it progresses into the further particularization of these universal differences, and so falls apart into the multiplicity of local or national spirits. The detailed characterization of these belongs partly to the natural history of man and partly to the philosophy of world history' (*Hegel's Philosophy of Subjective Spirit*, vol. 2: *Anthropology*, ed. and trans. M. J. Petry, Dordrecht and Boston: D. Reidel, 1978, p. 67).

4   Ibid.

5   See the passage in *Negative Dialectics*, p. 354, where he quotes from the preface to volume 1 of *Capital*: 'And even when a society has got upon the right track for the discovery of the natural laws of its movement – and it is the ultimate aim of this work to lay bare the economic laws of motion of modern society – it can neither clear by bold leaps, nor remove by legal enactments, the obstacles offered by the successive phases of its normal development. . . . I paint the capitalist and landlord in no sense *couleur de rose*. But here individuals are dealt with only in so far as they are the personifications of economic categories, embodiments of class relations and class interests. My standpoint, from which the evolution of the economic formation of society is viewed as a process of natural history, can less than any other make the individual responsible for relations whose creature he socially remains, however much he may subjectively raise himself above them.' [The translation here is taken not from *Negative Dialectics*, but from *Capital*, vol. 1, p. 10. (Trans.)]

6   See Hegel's letter to Niethammer dated 'Jena, Monday, 13 October 1806, the day Jena was occupied by the French and the Emperor Napoleon arrived in it: . . . The Emperor – this world soul – I saw riding through the city to a review of his troops; it is indeed a wonderful feeling to see such an individual who, here concentrated in a single point, sitting on a horse, reaches out over the world and dominates it.' G. W. F. Hegel, *Briefe von und an Hegel*, ed. Johannes Hoffmeister, vol. I: *1785–1812*, Hamburg, 1952, p. 119f.

7   These eulogies are to be found in §§324–39, in the section on The State: 'War is that condition in which the vanity of temporal things and temporal goods – which tends at other times to be merely a pious phrase – takes on a serious significance, and it is accordingly the moment in which the ideality of *the particular attains its right* and becomes actuality. The higher significance of war is that, through its agency (as I have put it on another occasion), "the ethical health of nations is preserved in their indifference towards the permanence of finite determinacies, just as the movement of the winds preserves the sea from that stagnation which a lasting calm would produce – a stagnation which a lasting,

not to say perpetual, peace would produce among nations"' (*Elements of the Philosophy of Right*, p. 361).

8   The 'web or context of guilt' [*Schuldzusammenhang*] and 'web or context of delusion' [*Verblendungszusammenhang*] are concepts frequently used by Adorno in his theory of society. Their meaning is sketched in his *Metaphysics*, for example, in the course of a critique of the Stoics: 'I cannot undertake a criticism of Stoicism here. There is undoubtedly much which impels us toward the Stoic standpoint today, as appears very clearly in some motifs of Heidegger, especially in his early work. But I would say that even this standpoint, although it emphatically embraces the idea of the freedom of the individual, nevertheless has a moment of narrow-mindedness in the sense that it renders absolute the entrapment of human beings by the totality, and thus sees no other possibility than to submit. The possibility of seeing through this situation as a context of guilt [*Schuldzusammenhang*] concealed through blinding [*Verblendungszusammenhang*], and thus of breaking through it, did not occur to that entire philosophy. Stoicism did, it is true, conceive for the first time the idea of the all-encompassing context of guilt, but it did not discern the moment of necessary illusion in that context – and that, I would say, is the small advantage that we, with our social and philosophical knowledge, enjoy over the Stoic position' (*Metaphysics*, p. 112).

9   See, for example, the introduction to *The Philosophy of History*:

> The first glance at History convinces us that the actions of men proceed from their needs, their passions, their characters and talents; and impresses us with the belief that such needs, passions and interests are the sole springs of action – the efficient agents in this scene of activity. Among these may, perhaps, be found aims of a liberal or universal kind – benevolence it may be, or noble patriotism; but such virtues and general views are but insignificant as compared with the World and its doings. We may perhaps see the Ideal of Reason actualized in those who adopt such aims, and within the sphere of their influence; but they amount to only a trifling proportion of the mass of the human race; and the extent of that influence is limited accordingly. Passions, private aims, and the satisfaction of selfish desires, are on the other hand, most effective springs of action. Their power lies in the fact that they respect none of the limitations which justice and morality would impose on them; and that these natural impulses have a more direct influence over man than the artificial and tedious discipline that tends to order and self-restraint, law and morality. When we look at this display of passions, and the consequences of their violence; the Unreason which is associated not only with them, but even (rather we might say *especially*) with *good* designs and righteous aims; when we see the evil, the vice, the ruin that has befallen the most flourishing kingdoms which the mind of man ever created; we can scarcely avoid being filled with sorrow at this universal taint of corruption: and, since this decay is not the work of mere Nature, but of the Human Will – a moral embitterment – a revolt of the Good Spirit (if it have a place within us) may well be the result of our reflections. Without rhetorical exaggera-

tion, a simple truthful combination of the miseries that have overwhelmed the noblest of nations and polities, and the finest examplars of private virtue – forms a picture of most fearful aspect, and excites emotions of the profoundest and most hopeless sadness, counterbalanced by no consolatory result. We endure in beholding it a mental torture, allowing no defence or escape but the consideration that what has happened could not be otherwise; and that it is a fatality which no intervention could alter. And at last we draw back from the intolerable disgust with which these sorrowful reflections threaten us, into the more agreeable environment of our individual life – the Present formed by our private aims and interests. In short, we retreat into the selfishness that stands on the quiet shore, and thence enjoys in safety the distant spectacle of 'wrecks confusedly hurled'. But even regarding History as the slaughter-bench at which the happiness of peoples, the wisdom of states and the virtue of individuals have been victimized – the question involuntarily arises – to what principle, to what final aim these enormous sacrifices have been offered. (*The Philosophy of History*, pp. 20f.)

For Schopenhauer's 'cutting words on the horrors of the course of history', see Chapter 46, 'On the Vanity and Suffering of Life', of *The World as Will and Representation*: 'The truth is that we ought to be wretched and are so. The chief source of the most serious evils affecting man is man himself; *homo homini lupus* [Man is a wolf for man]. He who keeps this fact clearly in view beholds the world as a hell, surpassing that of Dante by the fact that one man must be the devil of another. For this purpose, of course, one is more fitted than another, indeed an archfiend is more fitted than all the rest, and appears in the form of a conqueror; he sets several hundred thousand men facing one another, and exclaims to them: "To suffer and die is your destiny; now shoot one another with musket and cannon!" and they do so. In general, however, the conduct of men towards one another is characterized as a rule by injustice, extreme unfairness, hardness and even cruelty; an opposite course of action appears only by way of exception.' Arthur Schopenhauer, *The World as Will and Representation*, trans. E. F. J. Payne, New York: Dover Publications, 1966, vol. 2, p. 578.

Lecture 13   The History of Nature (I)

1   The figures here and subsequently refer to the pagination of the typescript of the version then existing of *Weltgeist und Naturgeschichte* ['World Spirit and Natural History'], i.e., the intermediate version of 5 November 1964, which Adorno later reworked twice, in June and July 1965 (cf. Theodor W. Adorno Archive Ts 15305-15415); Adorno then based the lectures on this intermediate version, reading out from it on

occasion. The page referred to here, p. 64, corresponds to *Negative Dialectics*, p. 354; what he has in mind here is the sentence: 'The objectivity of historical life is that of natural history.'

2   The reading of this sentence is very uncertain.

3   Adorno is referring to the quotation from Marx in *Negative Dialectics*, p. 354, note 47. See also Lecture 12, note 5, above.

4   See the quotation from Marx in *Negative Dialectics*, p. 354f., note 49: 'The law of capitalist accumulation, metamorphosed by economists into a pretended law of Nature, in reality merely states that the very nature of accumulation excludes every diminution in the degree of exploitation of labour, and every rise in the price of labour, which could seriously imperil the continual reproduction, on an ever-enlarging scale, of the capitalistic relation. It cannot be otherwise in a mode of production in which the labourer exists to satisfy the needs of self-expansion of existing values, instead of, on the contrary, material wealth existing to satisfy the needs of development on the part of the labourer' (quoted here not from *Negative Dialectics*, but from the translation in Karl Marx, *Capital*, vol. 1, p. 620). See also pp. 117–18, above.

5   See the quotation from Marx in *Negative Dialectics*, p. 355, note 50: 'As much, then, as the whole of this movement appears as a social process, and as much as the individual moments of this movement arise from the conscious will and particular purposes of individuals, so much does the totality of the process appear as an objective interrelation, which arises spontaneously from nature; arising it is true, from the mutual influence of conscious individuals on one another, but neither located in their consciousness, nor subsumed under them as a whole' (quoted here not from *Negative Dialectics* but from the translation in Karl Marx, *Grundrisse*, trans. Martin Nicolaus, Harmondsworth: Penguin, 1973, p. 196f.).

6   See the quotation from Hegel in *Negative Dialectics*, p. 357, note 52; see also note 14 below.

7   See *Negative Dialectics*, p. 357. ['Looking into the abyss, Hegel perceived the world-historic derring-do as a second nature; but what he glorified in it, in villainous complicity, was the first nature.' (Trans.)]

8   See *Negative Dialectics*, p. 357, note 53. ['The basis of right is the *realm of spirit* in general and its precise location and point of departure is the *will*; the will is *free*, so that freedom constitutes its substance and destiny [*Bestimmung*] and the system of right is the realm of actualized freedom, the world of spirit produced from within itself as a second nature.' *Philosophy of Right*, §4, p. 35. (Trans.)]

9   Adorno evidently did not get further than p. 70.

10 In his dissertation *Der Begriff der Natur in der Lehre von Marx*, Frankfurt, 1962, which he completed under the supervision of Horkheimer and Adorno; cf. also *GS*, vol. 20.2, p. 654f.

11 Karl Marx, *Capital*, vol. 1, p. 620.

12 Karl Marx, *Grundrisse*, p. 196f.

13 See chapter 1, section 4, 'The Fetishism of Commodities and the Secret thereof', *Capital*, vol. 1, p. 71ff. [Trans.].

14 'Whatever is by nature contingent is subject to contingencies, and this fate is therefore a necessity – just as in all such cases, philosophy and the concept overcome the point of view of mere contingency and recognize it as a *semblance* whose essence is necessity. It is *necessary* that the finite – such as property and life – should be *posited* as contingent because contingency is the concept of the finite. . . . this necessity assumes the shape of a natural power, and everything finite is mortal and transient.' Hegel, *Elements of the Philosophy of Right* §324, p. 361. Cf. also *Negative Dialectics*, p. 357; and note 6, above.

Lecture 14   The History of Nature (II)

1 It is the editor's recollection that in lecture 14, and probably for lecture 13 too, Adorno had the typescript of the section on 'World History and Natural History' from *Negative Dialectics* with him and that he read passages from this. Sometimes the text he read out differed from that of the typescript, but the principal change was that he constantly interrupted himself in order to explain further what he was reading aloud. Lecture 14 deals essentially with the same subject matter as the concluding section of 'World Spirit and Natural History'; see *Negative Dialectics*, p. 354ff. The text of the typescript differs in minor respects from that of the printed version.

2 On this point, see *Negative Dialectics*, p. 357, which contains the relevant quotation from *Elements of the Philosophy of Right*. See also lecture 13, note 8, p. 298, above.

3 See Georg Lukács, *The Theory of the Novel*, trans. Anna Bostock, London: Merlin Press, 1971.

4 'A considerable part of the leading German intelligentsia, including Adorno, have taken up residence in the "Grand Hotel Abyss" which I described in connection with my critique of Schopenhauer as "a beautiful hotel, equipped with every comfort, on the edge of an abyss, of nothingness, of absurdity. And the daily contemplation of the abyss between excellent meals or artistic entertainments, can only heighten the enjoyment of the subtle comforts offered"' (ibid., p. 22).

5 Bernhard Grzimek (1909–87). In a letter to Grzimek dated 23 April 1965, Adorno wrote: 'Would it not be wonderful if Frankfurt Zoo could acquire a pair of wombats? I have fond memories of these friendly and cuddly animals from my childhood and would love to be able to see them again. . . . And may I also remind you of the existence of the babirusa, or the horned hog as I suppose it is called in English, which was also one of my favourite animals during my childhood; a delightfully bizarre little pachyderm. I hope it hasn't become extinct in the Malaysian archipelago? And lastly, what is the situation with the dwarf

hippos that they used to have in Berlin? But I do not wish to bother you with too many questions.'

6 Karl Marx and Frederick Engels, *Collected Works*, London: Lawrence & Wishart, 1976, vol. 5, p. 28.

7 From the very outset Adorno's thinking contains an insistent critique of the fundamental ontological concept of historicity. See, for example, his inaugural lecture 'The Actuality of Philosophy' of 1931, in which he is concerned to 'redefine in principle the relations between ontology and history, without resorting to the trick of ontologizing history as a totality in the shape of mere "historicity" in which every specific tension between interpretation and object is lost, leaving behind no more than a disguised historicism' (*GS*, vol. 1, p. 337). [This essay, 'The Actuality of Philosophy', is translated in full in *The Adorno Reader*, Oxford: Blackwell, 2000, p. 23ff., here p. 33 in a different translation. (Trans.)] The same critique is to be found in the lectures on the philosophy of history of 1957, where we find the following statement in the shorthand notes: 'Needless to say, in the philosophy of history we are not directly concerned with history itself, but with reflections on history. However, by reflecting on history and by introducing an element of conceptual mediation in our dealings with the so-called facts of history, we do not concern ourselves with the concept of history in the abstract, but do all the more justice to the process of reflecting on history, the more we immerse ourselves in the historical facts. But what we find being done in the name of historicity is either historicism or else an existential and ontological treatment of history. This concept of historicity appears to radicalize history to the point where it converts it into a state of existence itself, into something that is connected with the temporal nature of existence as such. This exaggeration effectively leads to the abolition of the concept of history. This way of looking at history ends up by converting history itself, change in time, into a constant. It perpetuates a prejudice of academic philosophy, by assuming that anything that is constant must possess the key with which to understand whatever problem we are confronted with. In this way, the conceptual detritus, whatever is left, the most abstract abstraction, is proffered as the surrogate for whatever we are inquiring into with our questions about the meaning or non-meaning of actual, concrete history' (Vo 1912f.).

8 Adorno is referring to the lecture 'The Idea of Natural History' ('Die Idee der Naturgeschichte', *GS*, vol. 1, p. 345ff.), which appeared posthumously.

9 Ibid., p. 354f.

10 Adorno probably has in mind, though not very precisely, some particular assertions by Helmut Kuhn, who had reviewed Adorno's book *Kierkegaard: Construction of the Aesthetic* back in 1934. 'To take Kierkegaard seriously as a philosopher means positively: responding to his philosophical intentions. This responsive reconstruction of his thought cannot be synonymous with a critical relation to a pre-existing

philosophical system of coordinates. And the book under consideration is far from succumbing to such a mistake. Its flaw lies rather in the opposite direction in that its energetic and intelligent flow of ideas fails to come together in a set of coherent concepts. Instead, it disintegrates into a number of expressive, polished, often strikingly illuminating, but also vague and fragile formulations.' Helmut Kuhn (reviewer), 'Theodor Wiesengrund-Adorno, *Kierkegaard: Konstruktion des Ästhetischen*, Tübingen, 1933', in *Zeitschrift fürÄsthetik und allgemeineKunstwissenschaft* 28 (1934), p. 104.

11   *The Jargon of Authenticity*, p. 79ff.

12   *The Origin of German Tragic Drama*, p. 179.

13   Ibid., p. 177.

14   See p. 134, above.

15   This was the message that appeared in a human hand on the wall of the royal palace in front of Belshazzar, and according to the Vulgate was interpreted as follows: '*Mane* numeravit Deus regnum tuum et complevit illud / *thecel* adpensus es in statera et inventus es minus habens / *fares* divisum est regnum tuum et datum est Medis et Persis.' The translation of the Revised Version is as follows: 'MENE; God hath numbered thy kingdom and brought it to an end. TEKEL; thou art weighed in the balances and art found wanting. PERES; thy kingdom is divided and given to the Medes and Persians' (Daniel 5: 25–8).

16   *The Origin of German Tragic Drama*, p. 177.

17   Adorno's critique of Simmel's pseudo-concretism can be found in the essay 'The Handle, the Pot and Early Experience', *Notes to Literature*, vol. 2, p. 213ff.

18   Adorno had earlier given an apologia for Alexandrianism in 'On the Final Scene of *Faust*', in *Notes to Literature*, vol. 1, p. 111.

19   He is obviously thinking of Proust's *A la recherche du temps perdu*.

20   See Enrico Castelli, *Die versiegte Zeit: Einführung in eine Phänomenologie unserer Zeit*, trans. Toni Kienlechner, Frankfurt am Main, 1951.

21   Adorno's own critique of the metaphysics of time with particular reference to Bergson and Hegel can be found in the section on the 'Detemporalization of Time', in *Negative Dialectics*, p. 331ff.

Lecture 15   On Interpretation: the Concept of Progress (I)

1   The proposition that the middle and later Schelling 'made extensive reference to the concept of allegory' is scarcely sustainable. In all probability, Adorno believed that Schelling's 'interpretative' or, better, 'narrative' approach to religion and myths of the gods in his late lectures on 'The Philosophy of Mythology' and 'Philosophical Revelation' had affinities with what he himself called *allegory*, following his reading of Benjamin's book on tragic drama. For his views on Schelling's later

philosophy, cf. *Metaphysics*, pp. 138 and 166 (note 4).

2   See p. 125, above.

3   The reference to Hölderlin has not been found.

4   The term 'the unhappy consciousness' derives from *The Phenomenology of Spirit*, where it refers to a 'new shape' of consciousness following on from Stoicism and Scepticism: 'This new attitude consequently is one which is *aware* of being the double consciousness of self as self-liberating, unalterable, self-identical, and as utterly self-confounding, self-perverting; and this new attitude is the consciousness of this contradiction in the self' (*The Phenomenology of Spirit*, p. 250). It has been shown that the concepts Hegel used to characterize the unhappy consciousness have their roots in the gnostic tradition. (Cf. F. Fulda, the article on 'Consciousness, unhappy', in *Historisches Wörterbuch der Philosophie*, vol. 1, Basel and Stuttgart, 1971, col. 905.) By using the term 'unhappy consciousness' to describe the kind of thinking that passively refrains from criticism and rests content, at home with itself, as 'unhappy consciousness', Adorno takes sides with the idea of philosophy as critique and against gnostic ideas in any form (see lecture 22, note 10, below). In *Negative Dialectics*, Hegel's inconsistency is explained by an 'urge to incapacitate the critical element that becomes entwined with the individual mind. Particularizing this, he came to feel the contradiction between the concept and the particular. The individual consciousness is almost always the unhappy one, and with good reason' (*Negative Dialectics*, p. 45). Thus, on the one hand, the unhappy consciousness was a critical concept for Adorno, while, on the other, he can say that it is the theatre of those experiences from which something like mind is generated: 'The unhappy consciousness is not a delusion arising from the mind's vanity but something inherent in the mind, the one authentic dignity it has received in its separation from the body' (ibid., p. 203, translation altered).

5   A reference to the verse from Karl Kraus quoted in lecture 7, note 12.

6   See his essay 'Parataxis', in *Notes to Literature*, vol. 2, p. 111f.

7   Friedrich Beissner was the editor of the standard edition of Hölderlin's works (the Große Stuttgarter Ausgabe, 1951–). The text of the poem in Richard Sieburth's translation reads: 'The forest sinks off / And like buds, the leaves / Hang inward, to which / The valley floor below / Flowers up, far from mute, / For Ulrich passed through / These parts, a great destiny / often broods over his footprint, / Ready, among the remains.' Quoted in *Notes to Literature*, vol. 2, p. 111n., from Friedrich Hölderlin, *Hymns and Fragments*, trans. Richard Sieburth, Princeton, NJ: Princeton University Press, 1984, p. 49.

8   Adorno formulates this idea more precisely in the 'Parataxis' essay: 'While the information Beissner adduces about elements of the content dissolves the appearance of confusion that previously surrounded these lines, the work itself continues to have, in terms of its expression, a disturbed character. It will be understood only by someone who not

only ascertains the pragmatic content, the content which has its locus outside the poem and which is manifested in its language, but also continues to feel the shock of the unexpected name Ulrich, someone who will be troubled by the "nicht gar unmündig" [far from mute], which acquires a meaning only in the context of a conception of natural history, and similarly by the construction "Ein groß Schicksal, / bereit an übrigem Orte" [a great destiny ready, among the remains]' (*Notes to Literature*, vol. 2, p. 111).

9   On this point, see, for example, *Aesthetic Theory*, pp. 197 and 334 and note, as well as *NaS*, I , vol.1, p. 243, and *Metaphysics*, p. 125. [Adorno frequently quotes this passage from §28 of the *Critique of Judgement*: 'Nature considered in an aesthetic judgement as might that has no dominion over us, is *dynamically sublime*. If nature is to be judged by us as dynamically sublime, it must be represented as a source of fear (though the converse, that every object that is a source of fear is, in our aesthetic judgement sublime, does not hold). . . . But we may look upon an object as fearful, and yet not be afraid of it, if, that is, our estimate takes the form of our simply picturing to ourselves the case of our wishing to offer some resistance to it, and recognizing that all such resistance would be quite futile. . . . Bold, overhanging, and, as it were, threatening rocks, thunderclouds piled up the vault of heaven, borne along with flashes and peals, volcanoes in all their violence of destruction, hurricanes leaving desolation in their track, the boundless ocean rising with rebellious force, the high waterfall of some mighty river, and the like, make our power of resistance of trifling moment in comparison with their might. But, provided our own position is secure, their aspect is all the more attractive for its fearfulness; and we readily call these objects sublime.' *Critique of Judgement*, trans. James Creed Meredith, Oxford: Clarendon Press, 1973, p. 109f. (Trans.)] The text of the lecture is highly defective on this page and the following one; it is full of omission marks and contains also this comment in the margin by the copyist: 'In what follows the tape contains two texts, one running backwards; hence the many gaps in the text; very hard to understand!'

10   To cite Thomas Hobbes. See the Epistle Dedicatory of the *Philosophical Rudiments concerning Government and Society*, London: John Bohn, 1841, p. ii, where Hobbes writes: 'To speak impartially, both sayings are very true: *that man to man is a kind of God; and that man to man is an arrant wolf*. The first is true, if we compare citizens among themselves; and the second, if we compare cities. In the one there is some analogy of similitude with the Deity; to wit, justice and charity, the twin sisters of peace. But in the other, good men must defend themselves by taking to them for a sanctuary the two daughters of war, deceit and violence: that is, in plain terms, a mere brutal rapacity.'

11   The concept of the realm of freedom first appears in Kant's chief work on religion (cf. Kant, *Religion within the Boundaries of Mere Reason, in Religion and Rational Theology*, trans. Allen W. Wood and George

di Giovanni, Cambridge: Cambridge University Press, 1996, p. 120), and then in different variations in Fichte, Hegel, Hölderlin and Schleiermacher, ending up with Marx (*Capital*, vol. 3, in Karl Marx and Frederick Engels, *Collected Works*, vol. 37, p. 828) in the version that was authoritative as far as Adorno was concerned. (There Marx contrasts the 'realm of necessity' with 'the true realm of freedom'.) See *Negative Dialectics*, p. 355, and also here pp. 3, 5 and 115, above.

12 Just as Adorno's account of natural history differed from the corresponding sections of *Negative Dialectics*, so too here: his discussion of progress provides a variation on the essay with the same title that he delivered as a lecture in 1962 at the Seventh Congress of German Philosophy. (See 'Progress', in *Critical Models*, pp. 143–60.) Ideas of central importance for his thought are summed up more succinctly here than almost everywhere else:

> By dissolving the apparent rigidities of the concept of progress, Adorno offers a challenge to reality which was what created these rigidities in the first place, both in progress and in opposition to it. As the idea of something other that does not yet exist, that transcends history and yet would wish to be redeemed *in* it, progress must not be ontologized or declared the preserve of any absolute. This results in the condemnation as untrue of theories of decay, and of attempts to reduce history to endless repetition of the same thing: *there is nothing good, or even a trace of goodness, without progress*. The concept possesses an underlying social substrate, but is not simply identifiable with society. It cannot be inferred from any philosophy and at the same time it is indispensable for philosophical work, unless it is to degenerate into its opposite as a mere tool of reason. Blind accumulation, a process of de-mythologization that has run wild, levelling out all individuality and thus mirroring totalitarian society – these are the objective marks of a failure of progress, the *perennial danger of regression*. (Rolf Tiedemann, 'Review of Helmut Kuhn and Franz Wiedmann (eds), *Die Philosophie und die Frage nach dem Fortschritt*, Munich, 1964', in *Das Argument: Berliner Hefte für Probleme der Gesellschaft*, 45, December 1967, p. 428f.)

Even though it is easy to understand why Adorno originally intended the essay on 'Progress' to form part of *Negative Dialectics*, it is no less easy to see why he finally decided to omit it.

13 See Ludwig Marcuse, 'Unsere hehren Wendriners: In der Nachfolge Tucholskys: Adornos Anmerkungen "Zur deutschen Ideologie"' (a review of *Jargon der Eigentlichkeit*), in *Die Welt*, 24 December 1964, supplement: *Die Welt der Literatur*, no. 21, p. 8.

14 Habeas corpus, literally 'thou shalt have the body [in court]', were the first words of the formula for arrest warrants in medieval Britain. Its authority was restricted by Parliament in 1679 in the so-called Habeas Corpus Act, which laid down rules for court procedure in arrests. The right of habeas corpus is designed to protect the individual's 'body' against arbitrary actions on the part of the state.

15 The phrase can be found in a number of letters, see e.g., the letter of 24 July 1889 to Friedrich von Preen, *Briefe*, ed. Max Burckhardt, Basel and Stuttgart, 1980, vol. 9, p. 203 [Trans.].
16 Possibly Karl Mannheim (1893–1947).

Lecture 16 On Interpretation: the Concept of Progress (II)

1 This is not meant literally, since the concept of synthesis occurs only once (see p. 136, above). On the point of substance, his criticism of the conflation of a number of meanings within a single concept, the identification of the non-identical, see, e.g., p. 97f.)
2 With this sentence Adorno takes up ideas already formulated in his essay 'Progress' [available separately in Henry Pickford's excellent translation in *Critical Models*, p. 144ff. That essay had originally been given as a lecture in 1962 and was then published in 1964. The rest of this lecture and part of the following one is a version of that essay adapted more for student consumption. (Trans.)]
3 Adorno's monograph on Wagner ends with a reference to 'the age-old protest of music' with its promise of 'a life without fear' (*In Search of Wagner*, p. 156). On the subject of fear in Adorno, cf. also his 'portrayal' of fear, namely, his '*Singspiel* after Mark Twain', *The Treasure of Indian Joe* (ed. Rolf Tiedemann, Frankfurt am Main, 1979, p. 57): 'We can't get away / from this old house ... / And if we run away in fear / We're still stuck here / We're full of fear / we can't get clear', and especially the passage from *Negative Dialectics* cited in lecture 17, note 4, below.
4 See Immanuel Kant, *Political Writings*, p. 43.
5 Ibid., p. 45f.
6 Walter Benjamin, *Selected Writings*, vol. 4, p. 394 (Thesis XIII).
7 A reference to one of the central theses of the *Dialectic of Enlightenment*.
8 Walter Benjamin, *Selected Writings*, vol. 4, p. 389f. (Thesis II).
9 Ibid., p. 396 (Thesis XVII).
10 Kafka's actual comment was 'To have faith in progress is not to believe that progress has already taken place. That would be no faith.' Quoted in Walter Benjamin, *Selected Writings*, vol. 2, p. 808 (translation modified).
11 He who has the great good fortune

> To be a friend to a friend,
> He who has won a dear wife,
> Let him mix his rejoicing with ours!
> Yes – and whoever has but one soul
> Somewhere in the world to call his own!
> And he who cannot, let him steal away,

Weeping, out of this company.
Friedrich von Schiller, *To Joy* [*An die Freude*], *Werke und Briefe*, vol. 1, p. 248.

12   Cf. also Adorno, *Beethoven*, p. 32f.
13   Adorno mistakenly attributed the idea of the universal state to the *middle* Stoa, at least in the draft (cf. Vo 9892 and also in the essay on 'Progress', *Critical Models*, p. 146). In fact, Zeno of Citium and Chrysippus, both early Stoics, defended a pronounced cosmopolitanism, whereas Panaetius, of the middle Stoa, appears to have favoured the individual state. For the political theory of the Stoics, see A. A. Long and D. N. Sedley, *The Hellenistic Philosophers*, Cambridge: Cambridge University Press, 1987, p. 429ff.
14   Adorno gave his interpretation of St Augustine as the prototype of an objectively intended philosophy of history in the *Introduction to the Philosophy of History* of 1957: 'Before Kant the philosophy of history had an objective orientation in the sense that it represented designs that were supposed to show how the universal plan was conceived and the meaning of the individual periods within it. The objectivity of these theories was christological in essence. They are based on the belief that the figure of Christ constituted a caesura in history, pointing to an incursion of the transcendental that cannot be reduced to human categories, or consciousness. The prototype of all these philosophies of history is St Augustine's *Civitas dei*, which represents the first great design for a thoroughly articulated system of the philosophy of history. It conceives the course of history as a struggle between the kingdoms of heaven and earth that will be resolved by the appearance of Christ and will end with the full realization of the kingdom of heaven and the annihilation of the merely terrestrial kingdom. Historical periodization is provided by the figure of Christ and the relation of different phases to him and the idea of his second coming. This philosophy of history remained the more or less constant model for all philosophies of history for centuries. The greatest and most independent recapitulation of it took place in the age of Louis XIV at the hands of the French preacher Jacques Bossuet' (Vo 2001f.).
15   Siegfried Marck (1889–1957), a student of Ernst Cassirer's, was professor of philosophy in Breslau in 1930. He emigrated in 1933 to Switzerland and then, in 1939, went via France to the USA, where he taught in Chicago. Adorno may have had in mind Horkheimer's polemical attack on Marck which bore the title 'The Philosophy of Absolute Concentration', in which we can read: 'Marck rejects "revolutionary opportunism". "An autonomous philosophy of history and anthropology will oppose both Christian and Marxist ideas on this subject with the critical dialectic of an immanent-transcendental standpoint."' Horkheimer countered such views in his article of 1938, with the statement: 'In the immanent social conditions of monopoly capitalism, the immanent-transcendental treatment of freedom cannot be sustained; it

is too transcendental for them.' Max Horkheimer, *Gesammelte Schriften*, ed. Alfred Schmidt, Frankfurt am Main, 1988, vol. 4: *Schriften 1936–1944*, pp. 299 and 305.

16 Cf. this sentence from *The Jargon of Authenticity*: 'Heidegger's defensive tactic of retreating into eternity takes place on the "pure and disgusting heights" of which Hegel spoke in his polemic against Reinhold' (*The Jargon of Authenticity*, p. 75f.). The quotation from Hegel is to be found in G. W. F. Hegel, *Werke*, ed. H. Glockner (Stuttgart, 1958), vol. 1: *Differenz des Fichteschen und Schellingschen Systems*, p. 43.

17 One of the *Zahme Xenien*; see J. W. von Goethe, *Selected Verse*, trans. David Luke, Harmondsworth: Penguin, 1964, p. 280.

18 See p. 144, above.

Lecture 17 On Interpretation: the Concept of Progress (III)

1 The plays by Ibsen to which Adorno is referring are *Rosmersholm*, *A Doll's House* (whose heroine is Nora), *Hedda Gabler* and *The Master Builder* [Trans.].

2 See Peter Altenberg, *Auswahl aus seinen Büchern von Karl Kraus*, Vienna, 1932; cf. also Adorno's discussion of this with the title 'Physiological Romanticism', in *Notes to Literature*, vol. 2, p. 280ff.

3 Altenberg, ibid., p. 122f.

4 Cf. *Negative Dialectics*, p. 362ff. Likewise with reference to Auschwitz, although without mentioning the name (ibid., p. 346f.): 'What some like to call *angst* and to ennoble as an existential fundamental is claustrophobia in the world: in the closed system. It perpetuates the spell as coldness between men, without which the calamity could not recur. Anyone who is not cold, who does not freeze himself as in the vulgar figure of speech the murderer makes his victims "freeze", must feel condemned. Along with *angst* and the cause of it, this coldness too might pass. In the universal coldness, *angst* is the necessary form of the curse laid upon those who suffer from it' (translation modified).

5 Altenberg, ibid., p. 135f.

6 Hegel treats the question of the individuality of the artist in the work of art in *The Phenomenology of Spirit*, among other places. See the chapter on 'Religion in the Form of Art', section 1, 'The Abstract Work of Art', p. 715. For Hegel's attitude to the concept of individuality, cf. Adorno's essay 'Aspects of Hegel's Philosophy', in *Hegel: Three Studies*, p. 47ff.

7 Cf. also 'The Truth about Hedda Gabler', one of the most extraordinary pieces in *Minima Moralia*, p. 93f.

8 Kant makes use of the concept of radical evil in *Religion within the Boundaries of Mere Reason* in order to ascribe to mankind 'a natural propensity to evil, and since it must nevertheless always come about through one's own fault, we can further even call it a *radical*, innate

evil in human nature (not any the less brought upon us by ourselves).'
Cf. Kant, *Religion and Rational Theology*, Cambridge: Cambridge
University Press, 1996, p. 80. Apart from in the essay on 'Progress',
Adorno also uses the term in *Negative Dialectics*: 'If a man looks upon
thinghood as radical evil, if he wishes to dynamize all that exists into
pure actuality, he tends to be hostile to otherness, to the alien thing
that, not for nothing, has lent its name to alienation. He tends to that
non-identity which would be the deliverance not of consciousness alone,
but of a reconciled mankind' (see also ibid., pp. 23, 218f., 346; and
GS, vol. 6, p. 529). Even earlier, in the essay on Hegel entitled 'The
Experiential Content of Hegel's Philosophy' (1958), he wrote, 'In a total
society, totality becomes radical evil' (*Hegel: Three Studies*, p. 62).

9 For Adorno's view of Condorcet, see his discussion in the *Introduction
to the Philosophy of History* of 1957: 'Condorcet's *Esquisse* is a relatively late example of this objectivist philosophy of history which has
not reflected much upon the knowing subject. Condorcet's explicit position is that of an anthropology and radical enlightenment, but in it the
features of a secularized Augustinianism are still visible: purification
and absolute perfectibility are now found in the *lumen naturale* that
previously were sought in divine revelation. His division of history into
clearly contrasting phases is likewise derived from Augustine's numerically ordered doctrine of historical phases' (Vo 2002). Cf. likewise the
translation of Condorcet's *Esquisse d'un tableau historique des progrès
de l'esprit humain* undertaken at Adorno's suggestion by Wilhelm Alff
and Hermann Schweppenhäuser: *Condorcet: Entwurf einer historischen
Darstellung der Fortschritte des menschlichen Geistes*, ed. Wilhelm Alff,
Frankfurt am Main, 1963.

10 Adorno probably has in mind Thesis II of 'On the Concept of History',
where Benjamin states: 'The idea of happiness is indissolubly bound up
with the idea of redemption. The same applies to the idea of the past,
which is the concern of history. The past carries with it a secret index
by which it is referred to redemption' (*Selected Writings*, vol. 4: *1938–
1940*, p. 389f.). Thesis XI makes mention of 'the progress in mastering nature' and the corresponding 'retrogression of society' (ibid.,
p. 393).

11 The reference has not been traced. Adorno may be referring to a remark
of Karl Heinz Haag's in the course of Adorno's philosophy seminar,
where he was a regular participant.

12 A reference to 'Ist die Soziologie eine Wissenschaft von Menschen? Ein
Streitgespräch zwischen Theodor W. Adorno und Arnold Gehlen'. This
was recorded by Südwestfunk on 15 January 1965 and first broadcast
by the Sender Freies Berlin on 2 February 1965. It has appeared in print
in Friedmann Grenz, *Adornos Philosophie in Grundbegriffen: Auf-
lösung einiger Deutungsprobleme*, Frankfurt am Main, 1974, p. 225ff.,
especially p. 242ff.

13 A reference to the 'wheel of Ixion', which Schopenhauer uses as a meta-
    phor in book 3 of volume I of *The World as Will and Idea*, §38: 'Thus
    the subject of willing is constantly lying on the revolving wheel of Ixion,
    is always drawing water in the sieve of the Danaids, and is the eternally
    thirsting Tantalus.' Not until we have overcome the will can 'we cele-
    brate' as an aesthetic intuition 'the Sabbath of the penal servitude of
    willing; the wheel of Ixion stands still.' *The World as Will and Repre-
    sentation*, trans. E. F. J. Payne, New York: Dover Publications, 1969,
    vol. 1, p. 196. In Greek mythology, Ixion, the Lapith king, was punished
    by Zeus by being bound to a wheel of fire. The most important account
    of this is to be found in Pindar's *Pythian Odes*, ii, 33–89, as well as
    in Karl Kerényi, *Die Mythologie der Griechen*, Darmstadt, 1965,
    p. 156ff.
14 Adorno is thinking here of the essay 'Die Rückschritte der Poesie' by
    Carl Gustav Jochmann, which appeared in the latter's anonymously
    published book *Über die Sprache* of 1828 and which Benjamin, or more
    accurately Werner Kraft, rediscovered in the 1930s (cf. Walter Benja-
    min, 'The Regression of Poetry', *Selected Writings*, vol. 4: *1938–1940*,
    p. 356ff.). In particular, his attention may well have been drawn to the
    statement that Jochmann 'recognizes that the progress of humanity is
    intimately bound up with the regression of several virtues, above all
    poetic art' (ibid., p. 363).
15 Cf. the statements about 'the epoch of social revolution' in the Preface
    to *The Critique of Political Economy*: 'With the change of the economic
    foundation the entire immense superstructure is rapidly transformed.
    In considering such transformations a distinction should always be
    made between the material transformation of the economic conditions
    of production, which can be determined with the precision of natural
    science, and the legal, political, religious, aesthetic or philosophic – in
    short, ideological forms in which men become conscious of this conflict
    and fight it out.' Karl Marx and Frederick Engels, *Selected Works*, vol.
    1, p. 329. Whereas Marx himself scarcely went beyond the assertion
    that 'the mode of production of material life conditions the social,
    political and intellectual life process in general' (ibid.), it was Adorno
    who constantly stressed that 'ideologies may be transformed more
    slowly than the supporting economic structures' (*GS*, vol. 8, p. 31) or
    'The discrepancies that arise from the fact that the superstructure is
    transformed more slowly than the base have become intensified into a
    regression of consciousness' (ibid., p. 110).
16 Cf. the first lines of Ovid's *Metamorphoses*: 'Before there was any earth
    or sea, before the canopy of heaven stretched overhead, Nature pre-
    sented the same aspect the world over, that to which men have given
    the name of Chaos. This was nothing but a shapeless uncoordinated
    mass.' Ovid, *Metamorphoses*, trans. Mary M. Innes, Harmondsworth:
    Penguin, 1955, p. 29.

Lecture 18   On Interpretation:
the Concept of Progress (IV)

1   This has not been traced. Cf., however, Adorno's own remarks in the *Aesthetic Theory*: 'The ideological character of such efforts, however, is no dispensation from reflection on the relation of art to progress. As Hegel and Marx knew, in art the concept of progress is more refracted than in the history of the technical forces of production. To its very core, art is enmeshed in the historical movement of growing antagonisms. In art there is as much and as little progress as in society. Hegel's aesthetics suffers not least of all because – like his system as a whole – it oscillates between thinking in invariants and unrestrained dialectical thinking, and although it grasped, as no previous system had, the historical element of art as "the development of truth", it nevertheless conserved the canon of antiquity. Instead of drawing dialectics into aesthetic progress, Hegel brought this progress to a halt; for him it was art and not its prototypical forms that was transient' (*Aesthetic Theory*, p. 208).

2   For Adorno's view of Carnap, see, for example, the introduction to *The Positivist Dispute in German Sociology*: 'Carnap, one of the most radical positivists, once characterized as a stroke of good luck the fact that the laws of logic and of pure mathematics apply to reality. A mode of thought, whose entire pathos lies in its claims to enlightenment, refers, at this central point to an irrational – mythical – concept, such as that of the stroke of luck, simply in order to avoid an insight that the supposed lucky circumstance is not really one at all, but rather the product of the ideal of objectivity based on the domination of nature or, as Habermas puts it, the "pragmatistic" ideal of objectivity' (p. 22).

3   This phrase was in English in the original [Trans.].

4   Part 1 of *Thus Spoke Zarathustra* was published in the summer of 1883. Probably in response to the promptings of his mother and sister, Nietzsche made efforts to return to university teaching. On 16 August 1883 he wrote from Sils Maria as follows about a plan to achieve this: 'Whenever I am not ill (or half-mad, as is also sometimes the case), I am busying myself with ideas about a lecture I should like to give at the university in Leipzig in the autumn. "The Greeks as judges of human nature" is the subject. I have already taken the first steps to enable me to give lectures at the university there – initially for four semesters, on an account of "Greek culture". I have already sketched out an outline' (Nietzsche, *Sämtliche Briefe*, Kritische Studienausgabe, eds Giorgio Colli and Mazzino Montinari, vol. 6: *January 1880–December 1884*, Munich, 1986, p. 430). Ten days later follows the report of his failure: 'But the idea has already been set aside: Heinze, the current rector of the University has told me very frankly that my application to Leipzig (and probably to every German university) would *come to nothing*; the

Faculty would not dare to put my name forward to the ministry – because of my attitude towards *Christianity* and *ideas about God*. Bravo! This explanation restored my courage' (ibid., p. 435).

5 From here on Adorno reverts to the text of his essay on 'Progress'. He begins by repeating, more or less verbatim, what he had already said at the end of lecture 17, p. 163.

6 On this question, see also the section on 'Progress and the Domination of the Material', in *Aesthetic Theory*, p. 210ff.

7 See, especially, the chapter entitled 'Opera' in *Introduction to the Sociology of Music*, p. 71ff.

8 Adorno is referring to the senior philosophy seminars that took place on Thursdays between 6 and 8 p.m., following his lectures which he gave on Tuesdays and Thursdays from 4 to 5. The seminars were held jointly with Horkheimer.

9 This reference has not been traced. Cf., however, the second of Nietzsche's *Untimely Meditations*, 'On the Uses and Disadvantages of History for Life', which contains this passage: 'A time [will come] when one will regard not the masses, but individuals, who form a kind of bridge across the turbulent stream of becoming. These individuals do not carry forward any kind of process but live contemporaneously with one another; thanks to history, which permits such a collaboration, they live as that republic of genius of which Schopenhauer once spoke; one giant calls to another across the desert intervals of time and, undisturbed by the excited chattering dwarfs who creep about beneath them, the exalted spirit-dialogue goes on.' Friedrich Nietzsche, *Untimely Meditations*, ed. Daniel Breazeale, trans. R. J. Hollingdale, Cambridge: Cambridge University Press, 1997, p. 111.

10 Adorno refers to a consciousness that is 'oblivious of Being' in *Negative Dialectics*, in connection with Heidegger's *Platons Lehre von der Wahrheit: Mit einem Brief über den 'Humanismus'*, 2nd edn, Berne, 1954, p. 84 (cf. *Negative Dialectics*, p. 88).

11 See the section on 'Absolute Freedom and Terror', in *The Phenomenology of Spirit*, p. 604: 'Universal freedom can ... produce neither a positive achievement nor a deed; there is left for it only *negative action*; it is merely the rage and *fury* of destruction.' [Hegel is thinking here of the conditions obtaining in France during the Reign of Terror in 1793–4. (Trans.)]

12 According to Brewer, *The Dictionary of Phrase and Fable*, New York: Avenel Books, 1978, p. 1167, the Sphinx's riddle was: 'What goes on four feet, on two feet, and three / But the more feet it goes on the weaker it be?' She plunged to her death from Mount Phicium when Oedipus guessed the answer [Trans.].

13 Karl Friedrich Hieronymus, Baron von Münchhausen (1720–97), achieved fame through his tall stories. These appeared first in 1781 with the title *Vade Mecum für lustige Leute*. In 1785 the book was published in English as *Baron Münchhausen's Narrative of his Marvellous Travels*

and Campaigns in Russia. This had been translated by Rudolf Erich
Raspe, who also added anecdotes of his own. The second edition of
this book appeared in a translation into German by Gottfried August
Bürger with the title *Wunderbare Reisen zu Wasser und zu Lande,
Feldzüge und lustige Abenteuer des Freyherrn von Münchhausen*. Published in Göttingen in 1786, it was this version that gave the collection
its definitive form. It included for the first time the story about how the
Baron escaped from a swamp by pulling himself and his horse out by
his own hair. 'Another time, I wanted to cross a swamp which at first
did not seem to be as wide as it turned out to be when I was in mid-
leap. Hovering in mid-air, I turned around to where I had set out from
in order to take a bigger run up to it. Nevertheless, my second jump
was likewise too short and I fell up to my neck in mud a short way
from the further shore. I should certainly have lost my life had I not
seized my own pigtail and managed by the strength of my own arms
to pull myself out, together with my horse which I held tightly clasped
between my legs.' Gottfried August Bürger, *Sämtliche Werke*, ed. Günter
und Hiltrud Häntzschel, Munich, 1987, p. 523.

14 Obviously a dig at Heidegger, but he also has the French version of
existentialism in mind.

15 Aesop (c. 550 BC) did not write the fables familiarized by his name, but
only collected them. In fable 258, 'The Wild Ass and the Lion', and
fable 260, 'The Ass, the Fox and the Lion', the shamelessly unfair share
that the stronger of the two animals takes at the expense of the weak
partner is referred to as 'the lion's share'.

16 'For, *that man may be freed from the bonds of revenge*; that is the bridge
to my highest hope and a rainbow after protracted storms.' *Thus Spoke
Zarathustra*, trans. R. J. Hollingdale, Harmondsworth: Penguin, 1969,
p. 123.

17 Adorno took over from Benjamin the concepts of dialectic at a standstill
and dialectical images but, typically, adapted them for his own purposes. Very early on, in his inaugural lecture of 1931 (cf. 'The Actuality
of Philosophy', in Brian O'Connor (ed.), *The Adorno Reader*, p. 23ff.),
he argued programmatically that the task of the historian is to decipher
enigmatic figures and to decode in the form of writing the dialectical
nature of the images in which existence manifests itself to the physiog-
nomical gaze. For Benjamin's use of the concept, cf. Rolf Tiedemann,
Dialektik im Stillstand, Frankfurt am Main, 1983, p. 32ff.; for Adorno's
usage, see Tiedemann, 'Begriff Bild Name: Über Adornos Utopie der
Erkenntnis', in *Frankfurter Adorno Blätter* II, Munich, 1993, p. 92ff.

18 [The Gotha Programme was the compromise programme that was
adopted in 1875 at the founding congress of what was to become the
Social Democratic Party of Germany (SPD). (Trans.)] For Adorno's view
of Marx's *Critique of the Gotha Programme*, see his 'Aspects of Hegel's
Philosophy':

Marx's *Critique of the Gotha Programme* describes a state of affairs hidden deep within Hegel's philosophy, and does so all the more precisely in that it was not intended as a polemic against Hegel. In his discussion of the familiar saying 'labour is the source of all wealth and all culture', Marx counters,

Labour is not the source of all wealth. Nature is just as much the source of use values (and it is surely of such that material wealth consists!) as labour, which itself is only the manifestation of a force of nature, human labour power. The above phrase is to be found in all children's primers and is correct in so far as it is implied that labour is performed with the appurtenant subjects and instruments. But a socialist programme cannot allow such bourgeois phrases to pass over in silence the conditions that alone give them meaning. And in so far as man from the beginning behaves towards nature, the primary source of all instruments and subjects of labour, as an owner, treats her as belonging to him, his labour becomes the source of use values, therefore also of wealth. The bourgeois have very good grounds for falsely ascribing supernatural creative power to labour; since precisely from the fact that labour depends on nature it follows that the man who possesses no other property than his labour power must, in all conditions of society and culture, be the slave of other men who have made themselves the owners of the material conditions of labour. (*Hegel: Three Studies*, p. 23f.)

Cf. also: 'In his famous letter to Kugelmann, Marx warned against the imminent relapse into barbarism which must have been foreseeable even at that time.' See 'Marginalia in Theory and Practice', in *Critical Models*, p. 267 (translation changed). In actual fact no such statement is to be discovered in any of the letters Marx wrote to Kugelmann. Adorno may have been thinking of the formula 'Socialism or Barbarism' that Rosa Luxemburg mistakenly attributed to Marx (cf. Helmut Fleischer, *Marxismus und Geschichte*, Frankfurt am Main, 1971, p. 124).

19   See p. 84, above.
20   Adorno is mistaken here. Marx did not in fact make efforts to avoid the word 'progress'. On the contrary, it occurs frequently, albeit not in the preface to the *Contribution to a Critique of Political Economy*.
21   Cf. Theodor W. Adorno, 'Progress', in *Critical Models*, p. 143ff., and also in *Can One Live After Auschwitz?*, Stanford, CA: Stanford University Press, 2003, p. 126ff.
22   See Theodor W. Adorno, 'Über Statik und Dynamik als soziologische Kategorien', in Max Horkheimer and Theodor W. Adorno, *Sociologica II: Reden und Vorträge*, Frankfurt am Main, 1962, p. 223ff. (Frankfurter Beiträge zur Soziologie, 10); now in *GS*, vol. 8, p. 217ff.
23   In English in the original [Trans.].
24   The final sentence of the *Dialectic of Enlightenment*, which, incidentally, comes from the pen of Horkheimer, states: 'Like the genera within the series of fauna, the intellectual gradations within the human species, indeed, the blind spots within the same individual, mark the points

where hope has come to a halt and in their ossification bear witness
to what holds all living things in thrall' (*Dialectic of Enlightenment*,
p. 214).

25 The Congress of Freedom of the Nazi Party took place in Nuremberg
from 10 to 16 September 1935. At this congress the so-called Nuremberg laws were unanimously approved by the Reichstag, which had
been transferred from Berlin to Nuremberg expressly for this purpose.
These laws effectively deprived Jewish citizens of their legal rights.

26 Dmitri Z. Manuilsky (1883–1959) started out as a supporter of Trotsky
and then became chief prosecuting counsel against the left opposition
in 1929–34. After that he was secretary to the Comintern and during
World War II he acted as Ukrainian foreign minister. After the war he
became a delegate to the United Nations. He was suspected of spying
for Stalin and Zhdanov. It is not known what Adorno had in mind
with his *famous programmatic statements*. On this issue, see Herbert
Marcuse: 'With the "socialization" of privacy, the locus of freedom is
shifted from the individual as a private person to the individual as a
member of society. Society as a whole, represented by the Soviet state,
defines not only the value of freedom, but also its scope, in other words,
freedom becomes an instrument for political objectives.' *Soviet Marxism:
A Critical Analysis*, London: Routledge & Kegan Paul, 1958, p. 213.

Lecture 19   Transition to Moral Philosophy

1 The following discussions are concerned with the so-called Third
Antinomy of the Transcendental Dialectic, cf. the *Critique of Pure
Reason*, trans. and ed. Guyer and Wood, p. 484ff. [See also *Critique of
Pure Reason*, trans. Kemp Smith, p. 409ff. The present translation
follows Kemp Smith, who retains the term 'antinomy', which Guyer
and Wood have replaced with 'conflict'.] Adorno has also treated the
problems arising from Kant's doctrine of freedom in the *Lectures on
Moral Philosophy* of 1963, lectures 4 and 5, p. 33ff.

2 Adorno criticized Sartre's conception of freedom in his essay on com-
mitment in art: 'In Sartre the category of decision, originally Kierke-
gaardian, takes on the legacy of the Christian "He who is not for me
is against me," but without the concrete theological content. All that is
left of that is the abstract authority of the choice enjoined, without
regard to the fact that the very possibility of choice is dependent on
what is to be chosen. The prescribed form of the alternatives through
which Sartre wants to prove that freedom can be lost negates freedom.
Within a situation predetermined in reality, it fails and becomes empty
assertion. Herbert Marcuse provided the correct label for the philosophical idea that one can accept or reject torture inwardly: nonsense.
It is precisely this, however, that is supposed to leap out at us from
Sartre's dramatic situations. The reason they are so ill-suited to serve

as models for Sartre's own existentialism is that – and here we must credit Sartre's truthfulness – they contain within themselves the whole administered world that existentialism ignores: it is unfreedom that can be learned from them' (*Notes to Literature*, vol. 2, p. 79f.).

3   The typed text (Vo 9927) contains a marginal note by the copyist: 'from here on the tape is very low and inaudible!' And in fact there are numerous gaps in the typed text from here up to the end of lecture 19; the present text is based largely on the conjectures of the editor.

4   See p. 229, above; cf. Eckart Goebel, 'Das Hinzutretende: Ein Kommentar zu Seiten 226–230 der *Negativen Dialektik*', in *Frankfurter Adorno Blätter* IV, Munich, 1995, p. 109f., and also Rolf Tiedemann, Introduction: '"Not the First Philosophy, but a Last One": Notes on Adorno's Thought', in Theodor. W. Adorno, *Can One Live After Auschwitz?*, Stanford, CA: Stanford University Press, 2003, p. xivf.

5   Ernst Bloch had given a lecture entitled 'Positivism, Idealism, Materialism' at Frankfurt University on 18 January 1965, just a week before Adorno's lecture. It seems to have formed the basis of chapter 44 of his book *Das Materialismusproblem, seine Geschichte und Substanz*, Frankfurt am Main, 1972 (*Gesamtausgabe*, vol. 7), p. 438ff. In it he writes as follows about Hegel's dialectic: 'What Hegel calls the "thesis" (the as-yet immediate part of the first leg of the dialectic, that which is still abstract and universal, the in-itself aspect of a thing that is still undeveloped) refers to a sketchy terrain, a real model of a material thing, prior to its concrete shape and the development of its content. . . . Hegel is not tentatively finding his way here, it is the thing itself that is undeveloped; what is meant is not simply the heuristic stage at which something is assumed or estimated, a mental experiment, but an explorative estimate. Above the simple model of the positivists appears a series of tentative models, trial excerpts in the course of the world – *ante rem*, but *in re ipsa*' (ibid., p. 444f.). Bloch goes on to write about a humane materialism to which we should aspire, saying that in such a materialism 'an ultimate model concept would become visible that would have nothing more in common with the agnostic, fact-based model of positivism; its ultimate implications would be comprehensible only from a metaphysical position' (ibid., p. 448). An account of Bloch's lecture (cf. Helmut Scheffel, 'Verteidiger des Lichts: Ernst Bloch sprach in Frankfurt, in *Frankfurter Allgemeine Zeitung*, 20 January 1965) makes it seem probable that Bloch's further discussion of the origins in positivism of the model-concept that he favoured were abandoned in the printed version.

6   *Interventions* has appeared in English in the volume *Critical Models*, translated by Henry Pickford. The subtitle is 'Nine Critical Models' [Trans.].

7   In the winter semester 1964/5 Adorno conducted a senior sociology seminar on the 'Sociology of Laughter'. In the introductory notes for this seminar, he writes: 'The subject of the seminar will be observations

on laughter as a social and psychological situation, with the intention of crystallizing at least some elements of a social theory of laughter. . . . The method I have in mind is that you will systematically make observations about laughter and will present your findings, in other words, these observations, together with your interpretation, to the seminar; we shall follow this with discussion.' Theodor W. Adorno Archive, unpublished typescript.

8 Adorno further explained what he meant by a model in the preface to *Negative Dialectics*. Models 'are not examples; they do not simply elucidate general reflections. Guiding [us] into the substantive realm, they seek simultaneously to do justice to the topical intention of what has initially, of necessity, been generally treated – as opposed to the use of examples which Plato introduced and philosophy repeated ever since: as matters of indifference in themselves. The models are to make plain what negative dialectics is and to bring it into the realm of reality, in line with its own concept. At the same time – not unlike the so-called "exemplary method" – they serve the purpose of discussing key concepts of philosophical disciplines and centrally intervening in those disciplines' (*Negative Dialectics*, p. xx). On 'constellations', cf. also ibid., p. 162ff. The present editor has discussed Adorno's use of models and constellations in his essay 'Begriff Bild Name: Über Adornos Utopie der Erkenntnis', in *Frankfurter Adorno Blätter* II, Munich, 1993, p. 92ff.

9 Cf. John Locke, *An Essay Concerning Human Understanding*: 'In this then consists freedom, *viz*. In our being able to act, or not to act, according as we shall choose, or *will*.' Harmondsworth: Penguin, 1997, book II, chapter xxi, p. 231.

10 David Riesman, *The Lonely Crowd*, New Haven, CT, 1961. See lecture 1, note 17, above.

11 The term 'interiorization' is used sparingly in the *Dialectic of Enlightenment*, but it is perfectly true that the dialectics of interiorization is one of the decisive motifs of the book.

Lecture 20   What is Free Will?

1 Adorno may well have had in mind here the parallel Kant drew between the thing-in-itself and the intelligible character. See, on this point, Adorno's discussion of the intelligible character in *Negative Dialectics*, p. 287ff.

2 In the German Adorno had written 'ihn', which would have to refer back to 'will', doubtless through a slip of the pen; he probably intended 'sie', i.e., freedom.

3 The numerals in parentheses refer to the intermediate copy, dated 4 January 1965, of 'Determinism: Paraphrases of Kant' (Ts 14974ff.), which was the original title of the section 'Freedom: On the Metacri-

tique of Practical Reason' in *Negative Dialectics*. The pages of Adorno's lecture notes are numbered from here on through to the end (cf. Vo 10331–10346). He evidently began the lectures with a kind of free variation of the Kant chapter, based on the intermediate copy. Since neither the transcript of the tape of this lecture nor any subsequent fair copy for it has survived, the editor decided to replace these with the first part of the notes which Adorno actually used during the lecture.

4 A reference to the question discussed by the Scholastics of how many angels could find space on a ladder.

Lecture 21   Freedom and Bourgeois Society

1 Cf. '*Logic* too depends on presuppositions with which nothing in the real world corresponds.' Friedrich Nietzsche, *Human, All Too Human*, trans. R. J. Hollingdale, Cambridge: Cambridge University Press, 1996, p. 16.
2 The concept of 'shading' [*Abschattung*] comes from phenomenology. According to Husserl, it means that an objectively given thing manifests itself 'in constantly changing ways', in constantly changing 'shadings'. See Edmund Husserl, *Ideas Pertaining to a Pure Phenomenology and to a Phenomenological Philosophy*, book 1, trans. F. Kersten, The Hague, Boston and London: Martinus Nijhoff, 1982, §41, p. 88 [where the word is translated as 'adumbration' (Trans.)].
3 See p. 188, above.
4 According to Adorno, the 'primacy of the object' is essential, both epistemologically, as a way of determining the union of subject and object, and as an unmistakable pointer to his inalienable materialism. His theory of the 'primacy of the object' was expounded in *Negative Dialectics*, p. 183ff. And also in 'On Subject and Object', a postscript to *Negative Dialectics*: 'The primacy of the object means . . . that subject for its part is object in a qualitatively different, more radical sense than object, because object cannot be known except through consciousness, hence is also subject. What is known through consciousness must be a something; mediation applies to something mediated. But subject, the epitome of mediation, is the "How", and never, as contrasted to the object, the "What" that is postulated by every conceivable idea for a concept of subject. Potentially, though not actually, objectivity can be conceived without a subject; but not likewise object without subjectivity. No matter how subject is defined, the existent being cannot be conjured away from it. If subject is not something, and "something" designates an irreducibly objective element, then it is nothing at all; even as an *actus purus* it still needs to refer to something that acts. The primacy of the object is the *intentio obliqua* of the *intentio obliqua*, not

a warmed-up *intentio recta*; the corrective to the subjective reduction, not the denial of a subjective share' (*Critical Models*, p. 249f.).

5   This is represented optically in the *Critique of Pure Reason*, where the left-hand side of the page contains the Thesis [of the Third Antinomy]: 'Causality in accordance with the laws of nature is not the only one from which all the appearances of the world can be derived. It is also necessary to assume another causality through freedom in order to explain them.' The Antithesis is printed on the 'right-hand side' of the page: 'There is no freedom, but everything in the world happens solely in accordance with the laws of nature.' *Critique of Pure Reason*, trans. and ed. Guyer and Wood, p. 484f.

6   See Karl Jaspers, *Die geistige Situation der Zeit*, 5th edn, Berlin, 1960, p. 154f.: 'Psychology became common knowledge in our own day in a form characteristic of our own age in the shape of *Freud's psycho-analysis*. . . . By claiming to be an empiricist, he hopes to be able to justify saying what amounts to the same thing endlessly, year in, year out. The self-reflection of the honest man . . . is distorted here into the exposure of sexual desires and the typical experiences of childhood; it represents the concealment of genuine, dangerous self-reflection through a simple rediscovery of well-known types in a supposed necessity which makes an absolute of the lower aspects of human existence.'

7   For Max Weber, the disenchantment of the world, in contrast to 'magic stereotyping', signifies the opposite pole of the legitimation of social action. Basically, he uses the concept synonymously with rationaliza-tion. Adorno frequently adopted this usage, modifying it significantly, as for example in these sentences on sociological theory: 'Theory seeks to give a name to what secretly holds the machinery together. The ardent desire of thought, which had once found the meaninglessness of mere existence unbearable, has become secularized in the impulse to disenchantment. This yearning seeks to raise the stone under which the monster lies brooding. In such knowledge alone meaning has been pre-served for us. Sociological research into facts resists this impulse. Dis-enchantment, of the kind Max Weber accepted, is in the eyes of such fact-finders no more than a special case of sorcery; and reflection upon powers that rule unseen and would have to be changed, a mere waste of time on the road to reforming what is manifest' (*GS*, vol. 8, p. 196f.). For a slightly different translation, see also 'Sociology and Empirical Research', in *The Adorno Reader*, p. 176, and also *The Positivist Dispute in German Sociology*, p. 68f.

8   Probably alluding to *Escape from Freedom* by Erich Fromm (New York, 1941). This book appeared in German translation with the title *Die Furcht vor der Freiheit* [i.e., The Fear of Freedom] (Zurich, 1945).

9   Immanuel Kant, *Critique of Pure Reason*, trans. and ed. Guyer and Wood, p. 485f.

10 Adorno may possibly have been thinking of Hobbes's theory in the *Elementa Philosophiae*, according to which human beings lapse into a

state of non-personality when absolute power passes to the monarch: 'As in *aristocracy*, so also a *monarchy* is derived from the power of the people, transferring its right, that is, its authority on one man. Here also we must understand, that some *one* man, either by name or some other token, is propounded to be taken notice of above all the rest; and that by a plurality of voices the whole right of the people is conveyed on him; insomuch as whatsoever the people could do before he were elected, the same in every respect may he by right now do, being elected. Which being done, the people is no longer *one* person, but a rude multitude, as being only one before by virtue of the supreme command, whereof they have now made a conveyance from themselves on this one man.' *Philosophical Rudiments concerning Government and Society*, London: John Bohn, 1841, p. 100.

11 See section 3 of the antinomy chapter, which is entitled 'On the interest of reason in these conflicts' (*Critique of Pure Reason*, p. 496, and elsewhere).

12 This has not been traced.

13 The name is missing in the transcript, probably because the copyist could not understand what was said on the tape. The preliminary version of the chapter on freedom in *Negative Dialectics*, referred to in lecture 20, note 3, above, contains the following statement: 'In its heroic period the Freudian school, in agreement on this point with the other Kant, the Kant of the Enlightenment, called for the ruthless criticism of the super-ego as truly heteronomous and alien to the ego. Psychoanalysis perceived the super-ego as the blind, unconscious internalization of social coercion. In his *Contributions to Psychoanalysis*, Sandor Ferenczi, writing with a caution that may be explained as a fear of social consequences, asserted that 'a real character analysis must do away, temporarily, at least, with every idea of the super-ego, including the analyst's own. After all, the patient has to be freed from all emotional ties that go beyond reason and his own libidinous tendencies. Nothing but this sort of dismantling of the super-ego can bring about a radical cure. Successes that consist only in the substitution of one super-ego for another still have to be classified as successes of transference; they certainly fail to satisfy the ultimate purpose of therapy, which is to do away with the transference.' Sandor Ferenczi, *Bausteine zur Psychoanalyse*, Berne, 1939, vol. III, p. 394f. Cf. also *Negative Dialectics*, p. 272.

Lecture 22   Freedom in Unfreedom

1 Friedrich Stoltze (1816–91) wrote poems in Frankfurt dialect. This one tells the story of 'Gedallje', a parasite who had grown fat sponging on his acquaintances. When his friend Nathan invites him to come to lunch 'if he can', he arrives promptly, only to discover that the door is locked.

Gedallje reminds Nathan that he had said to him, 'If you can, come to lunch'. Nathan replies, 'So can you? Well, then! – You can't.' (The name Gedallje or Gedalyah, incidentally, is of biblical origin and is associated with fasting. See Jeremiah 40-1 and Zechariah 7:5; 8:19.) Friedrich Stoltze, *Die schönsten Dichtungen in Frankfurter Mundart*, Frankfurt am Main, n.d., p. 79f.

2 Kant's discussion of the paralogisms of pure reason can be found in the *Critique of Pure Reason*, trans. and ed. Guyer and Wood, A341/B399, p. 411ff.

3 Adorno is referring to the term *Folterknecht*, torturer, which implies that the torturers are really servants or slaves (the word *Knecht* can mean either) [Trans.].

4 On the concept of radical evil, see lecture 17, note 8, above.

5 [Wilhelm Boger and Oswald Kaduk were officials in Auschwitz. They were among those put on trial in Frankfurt in 1964–5 for their part in the atrocities committed in the camp. They were both found guilty of murder and became notorious during the trial for their callous cynicism and the brutality of their actions. Boger was sentenced to life imprisonment and died in custody in 1971. Kaduk was sentenced to twenty-five years and was released in 1988, after which he lived in a nursing home (Trans.).] Cf. Adorno's lecture 'Education after Auschwitz': 'Walter Benjamin asked me once in Paris during his emigration, when I was still returning to Germany sporadically, whether there were really enough torturers there to carry out the orders of the Nazis. There were enough. Nevertheless, the question has its profound legitimacy. Benjamin sensed that the people who *do* it, as opposed to the bureaucratic desktop murderers and ideologues, operate contrary to their own immediate interests, are murderers of themselves while they murder others. I fear that the measures of even such an elaborate education will hardly hinder the renewed growth of desktop murderers. But that there are people who do it down below, indeed as servants, through which they perpetuate their own servitude and degrade themselves, that there are more Bogers and Kaduks: against this, however, education and enlightenment can still manage a little something' (*Critical Models*, p. 203f.).

6 Martin Niemöller (1892–1984) was a Lutheran theologian. Before that he had served as a U-boat commander in World War I and was awarded one of Germany's highest honours, the Pour le Mérite. He was a member of the Confessional Church and a critic of National Socialism, for which he was imprisoned in a concentration camp from 1937 to 1945. In 1945, at the first Conference of Church Leaders after World War II, he asserted that the Church had a share of the guilt for the Nazi dictatorship and thus initiated the so-called Stuttgart Confession of Guilt of the Lutheran Church in Germany.

7 Cf. Heidegger's *Being and Time*, Oxford: Blackwell, 1995, section I, chapter 6, 'Care as the Being of Dasein', p. 225f.; Adorno's critique is

to be found above all in *The Jargon of Authenticity*, p. 112 and p. 118ff.

8 This reminds us above all of *Beyond Good and Evil*, Nietzsche's book of 1880, with its subtitle 'Prelude to a Philosophy of the Future'.

9 Cf. Otto Erich Bollnow, *Neue Geborgenheit*, Stuttgart, 1956; for Adorno's view of Bollnow, see also *The Jargon of Authenticity*, p. 20ff.

10 According to the lectures on the philosophy of history of 1957, the 'rift between society and the individual' constituted the 'true historical consciousness as such'.

> Only where the *telos* of history, the measure or meaning, is not wholly absorbed into that which is, but confronts it as something other at which history is aimed, for which it is structured, is it possible to achieve an authentic historical consciousness. It is precisely the doctrines character-ized by a radical transcendence that have proved successful in constituting something like a historical consciousness. They have done so by defining the tension between existence and the idea, that which ought to exist, in a clear-cut way. Historical consciousness is not a simple, developmental consciousness in the sense of providing a steady progression from one step to the next. It arises wherever the consciousness of opposed entities or powers is present, entities that exist in a state of tension which medi-ates between them. The mediation of historical consciousness between time and eternity is antithetical and dialectical; it passes through extremes from the outset. What is meant by this can be seen clearly in the Book of Amos. In Amos the actual historical content, namely, the promise of a chiliastic, eschatological state, is produced by the consciousness of divine judgement. (Vo 1934)

The fact that Adorno speaks of 'the gnostic, antinomian implications of dialectical thought' does not entitle us to pin the label of 'gnostic' on *Negative Dialectics*, as sometimes occurs (cf., for example, Micha Brumlik, *Der Gnostiker: Der Traum von der Selbsterlösung des Menschen*, Frankfurt am Main, 1992, pp. 21, 381 and 384ff.), or to transplant excerpts from Adorno's writings into an anthology subtitled 'Lese- und Arbeitsbuch der Gnosis von der Spätantike bis zur Gegenwart' (cf. Peter Sloterdijk and Thomas H. Macho (eds), *Weltrevo-lution der Seele*, Zurich, 1991, passim). As early as his inaugural lecture Adorno had written about his own methodology of a thinking in models. He pointed out that these models attempted to revive the ancient con-ception of an *ars inveniendi*: 'Any other conception of models would be gnostic and indefensible' ('The Actuality of Philosophy', in Brian O'Connor (ed.), *The Adorno Reader*, p. 37). On Adorno's interest in gnostic, antinomian ideas, see also *Metaphysics*, p. 150, note 4.

11 The Greek city-state was the kind of society that Hegel described as 'substantial' (Trans.).

12 Adorno refers here, as he often does, to Lukács's *Theory of the Novel*, in which Lukács talks about the 'happy times when the starry sky is

the map of all possible paths', happy times which provide a foil against which the 'forms of great epics' are defined by means of which 'nature is bereft . . . of its meaningful symbolism' (*The Theory of the Novel*, pp. 29 and 63). See also *GS*, vol. 1, p. 355f.; *Negative Dialectics*, p. 191; *Aesthetic Theory*, p. 158; *Notes to Literature*, vol. 1, p. 216.

Lecture 23   Antinomies of Freedom

1 Adorno has in mind here part 5 of the *Discours de la méthode*, in which Descartes summarizes the argument of his unpublished treatise *Le Monde*, in which he describes 'how many different automata or moving machines can be devised by human ingenuity, by using only very few pieces in comparison with the larger number of bones, muscles, nerves, arteries, veins and all the other parts in the body of every animal. . . . I specifically paused to show that, if there were such machines with the organs and shape of a monkey or of some other non-rational animal, we would have no way of discovering that they are not the same as these animals.' René Descartes, *Discourse on Method*, trans. Desmond M. Clarke, London: Penguin, 1999, p. 40.
2 Immanuel Kant, *The Moral Law: Groundwork of the Metaphysic of Morals*, p. 115.
3 See Theodor W. Adorno, 'Aberglaube aus zweiter Hand', in Max Horkheimer and Theodor W. Adorno, *Sociologica* II, p. 142ff.; see also the English original *The Stars Down to Earth: The Los Angeles Times Astrology Column: A Study in Secondary Superstition*, London and New York: Routledge, 1994, p. 46ff.
4 Adorno's own English phrase [Trans.].
5 Adorno used the English phrase [Trans.].
6 Adorno used the English word [Trans.].
7 See p. 205f., above.
8 Adorno had been interested in a *prehistory of subjectivity* as early as the Odysseus chapter in *Dialectic of Enlightenment*; see especially p. 42f. Cf. also Theodor W. Adorno, 'Geschichtsphilosophischer Exkurs zur Odyssee' (an early version of 'Odysseus or Myth and Enlightenment'), in *Frankfurter Adorno Blätter* V, Munich, 1998, pp. 55 and 85 passim.
9 See Kant, *Critique of Pure Reason*: 'This schematism of our understanding with regard to appearances and their mere form is a hidden art in the depths of the human soul, whose true operations we can divine from nature and lay unveiled before our eyes only with difficulty' (trans. and ed. Guyer and Wood, A 141, B 180f., p. 273).
10 Ibid., p. 228 (A 99f.).
11 See the *Phenomenology of Spirit*, p. 219, where Hegel writes: 'With self-consciousness, then, we have now passed into the native land

of truth.' See also T. W. Adorno, *Kant's 'Critique of Pure Reason'*, p. 121.

Lecture 24   Rationality and the Additional Factor

1   See p. 191ff., above.
2   Luther's *De servo arbitrio* [The Bondage of the Will] of 1525 is a polemic against Erasmus's pamphlet *Diatribe de libero arbitrio*, which appeared in the previous year. For his part, Melanchthon had helped to underpin Luther's determinism, in particular his teaching about original sin and predestination, and only in his later writings did he attempt, to Luther's horror, to achieve a reconciliation with the philosophy of Aristotle who, in contrast to Plato, ascribed free will to human beings.
3   The general thesis of phenomenology is that all reality exists only by virtue of 'being given a meaning'. Husserl defends this against the criticism that he is promoting the nonsense of 'subjective idealism'. 'This nonsense only arises when one philosophizes and, while seeking ultimate intelligence about the meaning [*Sinn*] of the world, never even notices that the world itself has its whole being as a certain "meaning" which presupposes absolute consciousness as the field where meaning is bestowed; and when, at the same time, one fails to notice that this field, this *sphere of being of absolute origins, is accessible to observing [schauenden] inquiry* yielding an infinite wealth of knowledge . . . with the highest scientific dignity.' Edmund Husserl, *Ideas Pertaining to a Pure Phenomenology and to a Phenomenological Philosophy*, trans. F. Kersten, The Hague, Boston and London: Martinus Nijhoff, 1982, p. 13f. (translation slightly changed).
4   According to Schopenhauer, this story was mistakenly attributed by Bayle to the French philosopher Jean Buridan (c. 1300–1358), but in fact it comes from Dante: '*Intra due cibi, distanti e moventi / D'un modo, prima si morrìa di fame, / Che liber'uomo l'un recasse ai denti.*' ['Between two foods at equal distance and equally tempting a free man would die of hunger before he brought either to his lips.' *Paradiso*, canto 4, trans. John Sinclair, London, Oxford and New York: Oxford University Press, 1971, p. 61.] For the philosophical use and interpretation of this illustration, see also Leibniz, *Essais de Théodicée*, part I, §49 (*Philosophische Schriften*, vol. II:1, ed. Herbert Herring, Darmstadt, 1985, p. 278ff.), and Schelling's *Philosophische Untersuchungen über das Wesen der menschlichen Freiheit* of 1809 (*Werke*, ed. Manfred Schröter, vol. 4, Munich, 1974, p. 274f), as well as the parallel passage in *Negative Dialectics*, p. 223f.
5   It is not known what experiment Adorno is referring to here.
6   *Critique of Practical Reason*, p. 27f.

7   With the Law for the Protection of German Blood and German Honour
    of 15 September 1935, one of the notorious Nuremberg Laws, sexual
    intercourse between Jews and 'citizens of German or kindred blood',
    so-called Aryans, was forbidden on the penalty of imprisonment or hard
    labour. In the following period it was not infrequently punishable by
    death. According to Carl Schmitt (see also lecture 25, note 8, p. 325f.,
    below) this spelt 'the introduction of a new philosophical principle into
    the legal system of a European nation': 'Here a legal system based on
    the idea of race encounters the laws of other nations that in an equally
    principled way either fail to acknowledge racial distinctions, or even
    repudiate them.' Carl Schmitt, 'Die nationalsozialistische Gesetzgebung
    und der Vorbehalt des "ordre public" im Internationalen Privatrecht',
    in *Zeitschrift der Akademie für Deutsches Recht* 3 (1936), p. 205.
8   Adorno used the English idiom [Trans.].
9   Aphorism 5 of part I of *Beyond Good and Evil*: 'The tartuffery, as stiff
    as it is virtuous of old Kant as he lures us along the dialectical bypaths
    which lead, more correctly mislead, to his "categorical imperative" –
    this spectacle makes us smile, we who are fastidious and find no little
    amusement in observing the subtle tricks of old moralists and moral-
    preachers.' *Beyond Good and Evil*, trans. R. J. Hollingdale, Harmonds-
    worth: Penguin, 1990, p. 36.
10 *Critique of Practical Reason*, p. 34.
11 Hermann Sudermann (1857–1928) is almost forgotten nowadays. As a
    novelist and dramatist he was at first as famous as Gerhart Hauptmann
    as a literary representative of the naturalist movement. Adorno wrote
    about him in the *Aesthetic Theory*: 'The spiritedly unanimous rejection
    of Sudermann may be because his box office successes let out of the
    bag what the most talented naturalists hid: the manipulated, fictive
    aspect of every gesture that lays claim to being beyond fiction when,
    instead, fiction envelops every word spoken on stage, however it re-
    sists and defends itself. These products, *a priori* cultural goods, are
    easily coaxed into becoming a naïve and affirmative image of culture'
    (*Aesthetic Theory*, p. 249).
12 Cf. Hermann Schweppenhäuser, 'Der Begriff des intelligiblen Charak-
    ters', in Schweppenhäuser, *Tractanda: Beiträge zur kritischen Theorie
    der Kultur und Gesellschaft*, Frankfurt am Main, 1972, p. 9ff.
13 See Kant, *Critique of Pure Reason*, trans. and ed. Guyer and Wood, A
    341ff., B 399ff., p. 411ff.; see also Adorno's *Kant's 'Critique of Pure
    Reason'*, lecture 18, p. 190ff.
14 See p. 183, above.

Lecture 25   Consciousness and Impulse

1   From a poem by Ludwig Hölty (1748–66), 'The Old Countryman to
    his Son'.

2 See p. 218f., above.
3 It is no accident that this formulation echoes another statement of Adorno's, one in which, in the context of a discussion of Thomas Mann, he refers to another cliché common among literary historians: 'Not that I would think I could put a stop to the interminable string of dissertations . . . on what is discussed in seminars under the rubric of "the problem of death"' ('Towards a Portrait of Thomas Mann', in *Notes to Literature*, vol. 2, p. 13).
4 'Thus conscience does make cowards of us all; / And thus the native hue of resolution / Is sicklied o'er with the pale cast of thought, / And enterprises of great pitch and moment / With this regard their currents turn awry, / And lose the name of action' (*Hamlet*, Act III, Scene 1). [Adorno's choice of words reveals that it is the text of the Schlegel–Tieck translation into German that reverberates in his ears (Trans.).]
5 *Influxus physicus*, physical influence, is the name Descartes gave to 'the force with which the souls of men or angels move bodies'. *Die Prinzipien der Philosophie*, German trans. by Artur Buchenau, 7th edn, Hamburg, 1955, p. 52. Cf. also T. W. Adorno, *Kant's 'Critique of Pure Reason'*, p. 115 and note 15 and p. 257ff.
6 See p. 208f., above. Otto Erich Bollnow, an existentialist philosopher and disciple of Heidegger, published a book with the title *Die neue Geborgenheit* (The New Protectedness) in 1956 [Trans.].
7 Not traced. Adorno may have been thinking of the passage in the preface to *The Phenomenology of Spirit* where Hegel describes the contradictory evolution of philosophical systems: '[The ordinary mind] does not conceive of the diversity of philosophical systems as the progressive evolution of the truth; rather it sees only contradiction in that variety. The bud disappears when the blossom breaks through, and we might say that the former is refuted by the latter; in the same way, when the fruit comes, the blossom may be explained to be a false form of the plant's existence, for the fruit appears as its true nature in place of the blossom' (*The Phenomenology of Spirit*, p. 68) [Trans.].
8 Adorno's rare comments on Carl Schmitt (see *Minima Moralia*, p. 132, and the lectures on *Negative Dialectics*, NaS IV, vol. 16) would on their own scarcely call for a footnote. However, Schmitt's remarkable resurrection in post-unification Germany has been quite often accompanied by attacks on Adorno and his hostility towards Adolf Hitler's court lawyer. Schmitt was a constitutional lawyer and a lifelong anti-Semite. The fact that his name was omitted from the edition of Walter Benjamin's *Schriften und Briefe* of which Adorno was co-editor has time and again been hypocritically inflated into a scandal. In this respect, Schmitt himself set a precedent for this sort of treatment (see Carl Schmitt's correspondence with one of his students, ed. Armin Möhler, Berlin, 1995, pp. 218 and 409). See, for example, Jacob Taubes (in *Die politische Theologie des Paulus*, ed. Jan and Aleida Assmann, Munich, 1993, p. 133), who invents legends of the very worst sort. Scarcely less

grotesque is the performance of Jacques Derrida, who homes in on a solitary letter of Benjamin's in which the latter, who had been ignored by the world of academe, approaches 'Dear Professor Schmitt' – who, however, does not find him worthy of a reply. Derrida elevates this in one place to an 'exchange of letters' and then to a 'correspondence' (cf. *Gesetzeskraft: Der 'mystische Grund der Autorität'*, trans. Alexander García Düttmann, Frankfurt am Main, 1991, pp. 67 and 97; cf. also Joachim Schickel, *Gespräche mit Carl Schmitt: Eine Biographie*, Berlin, 1993, p. 77 passim, or Paul Noack, *Carl Schmitt: Eine Biographie*, Berlin, 1993, p. 112f). The fact is that Adorno was not interested in Schmitt and knew very little about him. No doubt, having been driven out of Germany himself, he can have had little desire to issue a denazification certificate to Schmitt, who was known for his friend/foe way of thinking. But he might well have been able to claim that he had managed to delay Schmitt's rehabilitation (which had long since been engineered by Schmitt's supporters) by preventing dubious speculation about 'points of contact and common ways of thinking' (cf. Susanne Heil, *'Gefährliche Beziehungen': Walter Benjamin und Carl Schmitt*, Stuttgart and Weimar, 1996, p. 199ff.) from establishing affinities between Schmitt and the philosopher of the Paris arcades who had been driven to his death by people who shared Schmitt's views and opinions.

9   Cf. 'The more complex and sensitive the social, economic and scientific mechanism, to the operation of which the system of production has long since attuned the body, the more impoverished are the experiences of which the body is capable. The elimination of qualities, their conversion into functions, is transferred by rationalized modes of work to the human capacity for experience, which tends to revert to that of amphibians' (*Dialectic of Enlightenment*, p. 28).

10 See, for example, the introduction to *Against Epistemology*: 'All music was once in the service of shortening the *longueurs* of the high-born. But the Late Quartets [of Beethoven] are no *Tafelmusik*' (*Against Epistemology*, p. 39).

11 Cf. Rudolf Stephan, 'Zu Beethovens letzten Quartetten', in Stephan, *Vom musikalischen Denken: Gesammelte Vorträge*, ed. Rainer Damm and Andreas Traub, Mainz, 1985, p. 42ff.

Lecture 26   Kant's Theory of Free Will

1   See p. 154f., above.
2   Altenberg's actual words are that the man is 'irritable and decadent', a 'decadent man of the future with weak nerves' (Peter Altenberg, *Auswahl aus seinen Büchern von Karl Kraus*, see lecture 17, note 2, p. 307).
3   Fabian von Schlabrendorff (1907–80) was a lawyer who served as a judge on the Federal Constitutional Court between 1967 and 1975.

From 1941 he had been an aide-de-camp in *Heeresgruppe Mitte*. He was arrested in August 1944 as an accomplice in the plot of 20 July, but was acquitted in March 1945. [While under interrogation he was tortured by the Gestapo but did not reveal the identities of his fellow conspirators. It has also been reported that his file was on the desk of the notorious Nazi judge Roland Freisler, awaiting attention, when the courtroom suffered a direct hit during an American daylight bombing raid, destroying the building and killing Freisler. (Trans.)] See also *Problems of Moral Philosophy*, p. 8 and note on p. 185.

4   *The Moral Law: Groundwork of the Metaphysic of Morals*, p. 94. Cf. also *Negative Dialectics*, p. 218 (Alternative translation [Trans.]).

5   Cf. Kant: 'Among all rational sciences (*a priori*), therefore, only mathematics can be learned, never philosophy (except historically); rather as far as reason is concerned, we can at best only learn to philosophize.' *Critique of Pure Reason*, trans. Guyer and Wood, A 838/ B 866, p. 694.

6   See p. 223f., above.

7   *Groundwork of the Metaphysic of Morals*, p. 108; cf. also *Negative Dialectics*, p. 231. [The latter gives an alternative translation. (Trans.)]

8   Cf. Hans Vaihinger, *The Philosophy of 'As if': A System of the Theoretical, Practical and Religious Fictions of Mankind*, trans. C. K. Ogden, London: Kegan Paul, 1924. Cf. also Adorno's judgement of Vaihinger in his lectures on *Kant's 'Critique of Pure Reason'*, p. 111f.

9   For the concept of 'salvaging', see lecture 28, note 10, p. 331, below.

10 The distinction between *natura naturans* and *natura naturata* goes back a long way, via Scholasticism and Neo-Platonism, to Arabian interpretations of Aristotle. As far as modern philosophy is concerned, Spinoza's use of the terms in his *Ethics* has been of crucial importance:

> Before I proceed further, I wish to explain here – or rather to advise the reader – what we must understand by *Natura naturans* and *Natura naturata*. For from the preceding I think it is already established that by *Natura naturans* [creative nature] we must understand what is in itself and is conceived through itself, *or* such attributes of substance as express an eternal and infinite essence, that is . . . by God, in so far as he is considered as a free cause. But by *Natura naturata* [created nature] I understand whatever follows from the necessity of God's nature, *or* from any of God's attributes, that is, all the modes of God's attributes in so far as they are considered as things which are in God, and can neither be nor be conceived without God. (*Ethics*, ed. and trans. Edwin Curley, Harmondsworth: Penguin, 1996, p. 20f.)

Spinoza's distinction, as opposed to his terminology, has exercised a profound influence on large tracts of German literature since Lessing, and also played a great part in German idealism. To speak of Kant's use of the *natura naturans/naturata* distinction is misleading since Kant made no use of these terms. But since the distinction they represent does occur in Kant's distinction between form and content, Adorno's figurative use of the terms may well seem justified.

11 The concept derives from Francis Bacon's *Novum Organon* of 1620, his teaching about the 'idols' in which at the dawn of modernity the Enlightenment set out to take up the struggle on behalf of reason and against prejudice, the false idols. Bacon distinguished four kinds of idols, the third of which he called the prejudices of the marketplace or society: 'Now words, being commonly framed and applied according to the capacity of the vulgar, follow those lines of division which are most obvious to the vulgar understanding. And whenever an understanding of greater acuteness or a more diligent observation would alter those lines to suit the true divisions of nature, words stand in the way and resist the change.' Francis Bacon, *The New Organon*, in *The Works of Francis Bacon*, London: Longman & Co., 1858, vol. 4, p. 61.

12 *The Moral Law: Groundwork of the Metaphysic of Morals*, p. 90.

13 Ibid., p. 107.

Lecture 27   Will and Reason

1 This reference has not been identified.

2 In the draft (Vo 10000) this read: 'that had been nominalistically undermined by objectivity'.

3 For Aristotle's criticism of Plato, see *Metaphysics*, p. 17f.

4 'Doctrine of reason' is an editorial conjecture; the draft has 'doctrine of the will' (cf. Vo 10001).

5 The German word Kant uses here is *gebrauchen*, literally, 'use'. Adorno cites the version given in the *Groundwork of the Metaphysic of Morals*: *'Act in such a way that you always treat humanity, whether in your own person or in the person of any other, never simply as a means, but always at the same time as an end'* (p. 91); see also *Negative Dialectics*, p. 257.

6 Max Scheler (1874-1928) was offered the chair in philosophy in Frankfurt am Main in succession to Hans Cornelius at the beginning of 1928. However, he died as early as 19 May of the same year. Adorno had briefly entertained the idea of studying with Scheler for his *Habilitation*, his second doctorate (cf. *Metaphysics*, p. 169f., note 12). In what follows Adorno is concerned with Scheler's major work on moral philosophy, cf. Max Scheler, *Gesammelte Werke*, vol. 2, *Der Formalismus in der Ethik und die materiale Wertethik: Neuer Versuch der Grundlegung eines ethischen Personalismus*, 6th edn, Berne and Munich, 1980 (trans. Manfred Frings and Roger L. Funk as *Formalism and Non-Formal Ethics of Values*, Evanston, IL: Northwestern University Press, 1973); cf. also *Kant's 'Critique of Pure Reason'*, pp. 44 and 246, note 11, and *Problems of Moral Philosophy*, pp. 2 and 16f.

7   See Ernst Troeltsch, *Der Historismus und seine Probleme*, book 1: *Das logische Problem der Geschichtsphilosophie*, Tübingen, 1922 (*Gesammelte Schriften*, vol. 3), p. 603ff. In his copy of this book Adorno had sidelined Troeltsch's claim that Scheler's theory 'achieves its highpoint in the synthesis of Nietzsche's theory of the superman with medieval Catholicism and patriarchy', and had added the word 'Good!' in the margin (ibid., p. 615).

8   The term 'concreteness' was first used by Hegel and his adversary Kierkegaard. In the preface to the 'Great Logic' the key elements are adumbrated: 'The system of logic is the realm of shadows, the world of simple essentialities freed from all sensuous concreteness.' *Hegel's Science of Logic*, trans. A. V. Miller, London: George Allen & Union, 1976, p. 58. Concreteness, whether as a term or a thing, then became the battle cry of phenomenology from Husserl on, but above all in Scheler and Heidegger. Adorno repeatedly criticized their alleged abandonment of abstract thought in favour of material philosophizing, dismissing it as specious and illusory. 'The illusion of concretization was what fascinated the school. The spiritual should be intuitable and immediately certain. Concepts are supposed to be sensuously tinted' (*Against Epistemology*, p. 36, translation modified). From the very outset we find Adorno opposing phenomenological 'pseudo-concreteness' with true concreteness. As early as his inaugural lecture of 1931 he made his position clear: 'The intrusion of the irreducible [into philosophy], however, takes concrete historical form and this explains why history calls a halt to the attempts of philosophy to go back to its ultimate premises. The productivity of thought can only prove its worth dialectically by testing itself against the historically concrete. The two things meet and communicate in [intellectual] models' (*GS*, vol. 1, p. 343; for a different translation, see 'The Actuality of Philosophy', *The Adorno Reader*, p. 38; see also lecture 19, note 8, above). Adorno's own concept of the concrete, its 'metaphysical weight', comes from Benjamin and likewise adopts his approach wholesale: 'Benjamin's micrological gaze, the unmistakable colour of his kind of concretion, represents an orientation to the historical in a sense opposed to the *philosophia perennis*. His philosophical interest is not directed to the ahistorical at all, but rather to what is determined by time and irreversible' (*Notes to Literature*, vol. 2, p. 226; see also p. 125f., above).

9   On this point, cf. also *Negative Dialectics*, p. 311, where Adorno writes that, 'to his eternal credit', Aristotle set up the doctrine of *epieicheiz*, of equity (translation altered). See also Adorno's lectures on *Metaphysics*, p. 31.

10   Literally, '*billig*' means 'fair' [Trans.].

11   Cf. also *Kant's 'Critique of Pure Reason'*, p. 72 and note 11, p. 250.

12   See Walter Benjamin, 'Fate and Character', in *Selected Writings*, vol. 1: *1913–1926*, p. 201ff.; for Adorno's interpretation of the essay, see *Notes to Literature*, vol. 2, p. 227f.

13 The first and, at the time, the only edition of *Dialectic of Enlightenment* had appeared in 1947 and had long since been out of print. A new edition did not appear until 1969, although pirated versions had been in circulation for some time before.
14 See Schiller's epigram, *Unterschied der Stände* [Class distinctions], *Werke und Briefe* vol. 1, p. 174.
15 J. W. von Goethe, *Faust, Part One*, trans. David Luke, Oxford and New York: Oxford University Press, 1987, p. 12, lines 328-9. It is not Faust himself, but 'The Lord' who is talking about Faust.
16 See J. W. von Goethe, *Faust, Zweiter Teil*, trans. Stuart Atkins, in Goethe, *The Collected Works*, vol. 2, Princeton: Princeton University Press, 1994, Act V, Palace, lines 11233-11281, p. 283.
17 Perhaps an error for 'Goethe scholars'.
18 Adorno used the English phrase [Trans.].
19 Cf. *Against Epistemology*, p. 3f.

Lecture 28   Moral Uncertainties

1 Adorno discusses the relations of genesis and validity in Husserl in *Against Epistemology*, p. 74ff.; he discusses it in its relevance to Kant in the introduction to *The Positivist Dispute*, p. 21ff., as well, of course, as *Kant's 'Critique of Pure Reason'*, p. 166ff.
2 Probably a reference to, among other things, Horkheimer's *Eclipse of Reason*, which appeared in German translation in 1967 with the title *Kritik der instrumentellen Vernunft*.
3 Fichte is frequently credited with the authorship of this dictum, which in reality is to be found in the novel *Auch Einer: Eine Reisebekanntschaft* by Friedrich Theodor Vischer (Leipzig: Insel-Verlag, 1879 [reprint 1919], p. 59). In actual fact Adorno had not mentioned it previously in the present course of lectures.
4 See lecture 12, note 1, p. 294, above.
5 'It is impossible to conceive anything at all in the world, or even out of it, which can be taken as good without qualification, except a *good will*' (*The Moral Law: Groundwork of the Metaphysic of Morals*, p. 59).
6 *Triumph of the Will* is the title of the film made in 1934 about the Nuremberg party congress of the National Socialist Party by Leni Riefenstahl, the actress, director and photographer.
7 The Pharisees – the term originally meant the 'separated' ones – were a sect in ancient Israel that had knowledge of the 'positive and unproblematic' knowledge about what God expected from men, and who insisted on literal adherence to the laws in their totality. Jesus interpreted the Pharisees' sense of superiority, not entirely fairly, as nothing but sanctimonious hypocrisy. See especially the Gospel according to St Matthew, but also John, both of which contain numerous passages

testifying to Jesus's attitude towards the Pharisees which underlies the modern use of the term in the sense of self-righteousness, sanctimoniousness and hypocrisy.

8 See *Minima Moralia*, p. 39. [Edmund Jephcott has translated this as 'Wrong life cannot be lived rightly.' (Trans.)]

9 A statement to this effect could not be found in Nietzsche.

10 Adorno's emphatic use of the term 'salvaging' [*Rettung* = saving, rescuing] once again places him in the succession to Benjamin, who was probably the first philosopher to elevate the term to conceptual dignity. In contrast, Kant only ever used the term incidentally, above all, in connection with the idea of freedom. An instance is in the *Critique of Practical Reason* where, with the existence of the practical faculty of reason, that of transcendental freedom is also established, 'taken indeed in that absolute sense in which speculative reason needed it, in its use of the concept of causality, in order to rescue itself from the antinomy into which it unavoidably falls when it wants to think the *unconditioned* in the series of causal connection' (*Critique of Practical Reason*, p. 3). With his formula of Kant's 'urge to rescue an ontological authority' (cf. also *Negative Dialectics*, p. 385), Adorno pinpoints the crowning moment of the abolition of metaphysical essences in Kant and the point at which he went into reverse: the apparently definitive limitation of knowledge to the world of 'phenomena' was matched, in his interpretation, by the resurrection of the intelligible sphere. Cf. also Rolf Tiedemann, 'Rettung II', in *Historisches Wörterbuch der Philosophie*, vol. 8, Basel, 1992, col. 938ff.

11 Adorno is referring to the intermediate draft text of 4 January 1965 mentioned in lecture 20, note 3, above, 'Determinism: Paraphrases of Kant' (Ts 14974ff., here Ts 15026ff.); the final version in *Negative Dialectics* can be found in the section 'Universal and Individual in Moral Philosophy', p. 282ff.

12 'Every action which by itself or its maxim enables the freedom of each individual's will to co-exist with the freedom of everyone else in accordance with a universal law is *right*.' *The Metaphysics of Morals*, in Kant, *Political Writings*, p. 133. See also the statement immediately preceding this one, cited in lecture 5, note 10, p. 278.

13 This involves an untranslatable pun on 'taking for oneself' [*Für-sich-Nehmen*] and 'noble or aristocratic' [*Vornehmen*] [Trans.].

14 'All that will be swept away' [Trans.].

15 See p. 190, above.

16 From here to the end of the paragraph; see Ts 15034 and also *Negative Dialectics*, p. 299.

17 Adorno's notes for this lecture course (cf. Vo 10344ff) show that he had hoped to make rather greater progress. The notes that he had prepared but was unable to use in the last hour are given here. (The numbers in parentheses refer to the page numbers of the version of the chapter on freedom in *Negative Dialectics* that he used in preparing the lecture.)

(57) The doctrine of the intelligible character: where Kant feels obliged to explain it further, he is forced to use it on an action in time; but this is to ridicule psychology.

Read the passage from the *Critique of Pure Reason*, p. 227f.

(58) Genesis wrongly attributed to early childhood.

Idiotic to credit small children whose intellect is still developing with fully mature powers of reasoning. Morality turns into an immoral, pedagogic judgement on the young.

Temporal priorities cannot be turned into *a priori* truths.

(59) What is *true* about indeterminacy + abstractness of the int[elligible] char[acter]: the prohibition on making images.

It [the intelligible character (Trans.)] is the possibility of the subject; it is what the subject *might* be, and so cannot be airbrushed out.

Nevertheless, its possibility, in the midst of the network of guilt, remains *genuine*.

Subjects experience themselves intermittently as potentially free, but unfree in reality. Every action is free that is transparently directed towards the realization of freedom.

(60) Crucial definitions, p. 60 of the MS, l.4, down to 'mediated'.

In Kant, intelligible character chiefly = personality, i.e., harmonious in itself, subject as unity.

(62) Integration *qua* mastery of inner nature becomes a *good*.

The dubious thing: he who is dominated turns out again and again to be good, unlike the compulsive person. Tom Jones, comic in the face of the conventions.

Last echo of this in Ionesco's 'Rhinoceros'.

In K[ant] intelligible character amounts to a strong ego; the question [is] whether in his view a *wicked* intelligible character is possible, whether wickedness is to be found only where integration *failed*. On this point, only people with a strong ego can be loyal.

(64) Inwardness = unifying – bourgeois, Protestant.

Int[elligible] char[acter] = irrationality of the election to grace.

More and more oppressive, keeps coming ever closer to blind fate.

The more, in the spirit of Enlightenment, the absolute nature [*Sosein*] of the subject is equated with its subjectivity, the more impenetrable the concept of the subject becomes. What formerly was an election to grace by divine will, can scarcely be thought of as a choice based on objective reason, which after all (65) would be forced to appeal to subjective reason.

An element of self-cancelling in Kantian ethics: autonomy if taken as a given is heteronomous.

(66) Totality of the human is indistinguishable from a pre-established chosenness.

What remains, noble + nasty, is not feudal for nothing, i.e., fused with the very same natural relations against which K[ant] protested.

The post-Kantian reconciliation of spirit + nature has its sinister aspect *as well*.

Freedom has gone awry in the society that is based on the concept of freedom.

In it freedom always = effrontery, i.e., the repression of others.

(67) Ranges   from   upper   bourgeois   arrogance   to   youthful criminality.

NB the guilt of *erotic* freedom towards women.

Lectures concluded 25 February 1965

18 '*Work*lein *in progress*' in the original [Trans.].

19 He is referring to the 'Meditations on Metaphysics' in *Negative Dialectics*, pp. 361–408; the first version was dictated and revised in the first half of May 1965. It was originally going to have the title 'On metaphysics'. Adorno further considered as a possibility: 'Is metaphysics possible after Auschwitz?' (cf. Ts 16017), a title echoing Kant's question in the introduction to the *Critique of Pure Reason*, before he finally settled on the one reminiscent of Descartes.

REFERENCES

Theodor W. Adorno

Wherever possible, reference has been made to existing English translations, as indicated below. Where no translation was available (or was available only in a relatively inaccessible publication) the source given, unless otherwise noted, is the *Gesammelte Schriften*, ed. Rolf Tiedemann, with the assistance of Gretel Adorno, Susan Buck-Morss and Klaus Schulte, Frankfurt am Main: Suhrkamp, 1970– (abbreviated as *GS*), together with the *Nachgelassene Schriften* (the Posthumous Writings, abbreviated as *NaS*), published by the Theodor W. Adorno Archive, Frankfurt am Main, 1993–. The abbreviation Ts refers to unpublished typescripts in the Archive, while Vo is used to designate typed transcriptions of the audiotapes and shorthand records of Adorno's lectures, as well as his own handwritten notes.

The audiotape transcriptions on which the present edition is based can be found in the Theodor W. Adorno Archive with the shelf-mark Vo 9735–10314; Adorno's manuscript notes for these lectures have the shelf-mark Vo 10315-10346.

The Adorno Reader, ed. Brian O'Connor, Oxford: Blackwell, 2000.
Aesthetic Theory, trans. Robert Hullot-Kentor, Minneapolis: University of Minnesota Press, 1997.
Against Epistemology: A Metacritique – Studies in Husserl and the Phenomenological Antinomies, trans. Willis Domingo, Oxford: Blackwell, 1982.
Beethoven: The Philosophy of Music, trans. Edmund Jephcott, Cambridge: Polity, 1998.

Critical Models: Interventions and Catchwords, trans. and with a preface by Henry W. Pickford, New York: Columbia University Press, 1998.

Essays on Music, ed. Richard Leppert, trans. Susan H. Gillespie, Berkeley, Los Angeles and London: University of California Press, 2002.

Hegel: Three Studies, trans. Shierry Weber Nicholsen, Cambridge, MA: MIT Press, 1993.

In Search of Wagner, trans. Rodney Livingstone, London: NLB, 1981.

Introduction to the Sociology of Music, trans. E. B. Ashton, New York: Seabury Press, 1976.

The Jargon of Authenticity, trans. Knut Tarnowski and Frederic Will, London and New York: Routledge, 1973.

Kant's 'Critique of Pure Reason' (1959), trans. Rodney Livingstone, Cambridge: Polity, 2001.

Kierkegaard: Construction of the Aesthetic, trans. Robert Hullot-Kentor, Minneapolis: University of Minnesota Press, 1989.

Metaphysics: Concept and Problems, trans. Edmund Jephcott, Cambridge: Polity, 2000.

Minima Moralia: Reflections from Damaged Life, trans. Edmund Jephcott, London: NLB, 1974.

Negative Dialectics, trans E. B. Ashton, London: Routledge, 1973.

Notes to Literature, trans. Shierry Weber Nicholsen, 2 vols, New York: Columbia University Press, 1991–2.

The Positivist Dispute in German Sociology (with others), trans. Glyn Adey and David Frisby, London: Heinemann, 1976.

Prisms, trans. Samuel Weber and Shierry Weber, Cambridge, MA: MIT Press, 1981.

Problems of Moral Philosophy (1963), trans. Rodney Livingstone, Cambridge: Polity, 2000.

Sound Figures, trans. Rodney Livingstone, Stanford, CA: Stanford University Press, 1999.

Max Horkheimer and Theodor W. Adorno, *Dialectic of Enlightenment*, ed. Gunzelin Schmid Noerr, trans. Edmund Jephcott, Stanford, CA: Stanford University Press, 2002.

Other sources

Benjamin, Walter, *The Arcades Project*, trans. Howard Eiland and Kevin McLaughlin, Cambridge, MA, and London: Belknap Press, 1999.

——, *Illuminations*, ed. Hannah Arendt, trans. Harry Zohn, London: Jonathan Cape, 1970.

——, *The Origin of German Tragic Drama*, trans. John Osborne, London: NLB, 1977.

——, *Selected Writings*, 4 vols, Cambridge, MA, and London: Belknap Press, 1996–2003.

Hegel, G. W. F., *Elements of the Philosophy of Right*, ed. Allen W. Wood, trans. H. B. Nisbet, Cambridge: Cambridge University Press, 1991.

——, *Hegel's Phenomenology of Spirit*, trans. A. V. Miller, Oxford: Oxford University Press, 1997.

——, *The Philosophy of History*, trans. J. Sibree, New York: Prometheus Books, 1991.

Kant, Immanuel, *Critique of Practical Reason*, trans. Mary Gregor, Cambridge: Cambridge University Press, 1997.

——, *Critique of Pure Reason*, trans, Norman Kemp Smith, Basingstoke and London: Macmillan, 1929.

——, *Critique of Pure Reason*, trans. and ed. Paul Guyer and Allen B. Wood, Cambridge: Cambridge University Press, 1997.

——, *The Moral Law: Groundwork of the Metaphysic of Morals*, trans. H. J. Paton, London and New York: Routledge, 1991.

——, *Political Writings*, ed. Hans Reiss, trans. H. B. Nisbet, 2nd edn, Cambridge: Cambridge University Press, 2002.

Lukács, Georg, *Theory of the Novel*, trans. Anna Bostock, London: Merlin Press, 1971.

Marx, Karl, *Capital*, vol. 1, trans. Samuel Moore and Edward Aveling, London: Lawrence & Wishart, 1967.

——, *Grundrisse*, trans. Martin Nicolaus, Harmondsworth: Penguin, 1973.

Marx, Karl, and Engels, Frederick, *Selected Works*, 2 vols, Moscow: Foreign Languages Publishing House, 1951, 1949.

Schiller, Friedrich von, *Werke und Briefe*, vol. 1: *Gedichte*, ed. Georg Kurscheidt, Frankfurt am Main: Deutcher Klassiker Verlag, 1992.

INDEX OF NAMES

INDEX OF SUBJECTS

Printed in Great Britain
by Amazon

68091151R00210